SCOTT STEMPSON

AMERICAN
SPORTS
History

THIRD EDITION

Kendall Hunt
publishing company

AMERICAN *Sports* HISTORY

Cover image © Shutterstock, Inc.

Kendall Hunt
publishing company

www.kendallhunt.com
Send all inquiries to:
4050 Westmark Drive
Dubuque, IA 52004-1840

Contents

Acknowledgments

The endeavor of writing a book is never accomplished alone even though there is only one name on the cover. Those that assisted me in this work are too many to mention them all here but I want to highlight a few. First of all, this book was written first and foremost for the student of sports history. More particularly, it was written for *my* students at the University of Nebraska. When I started teaching History 222 (History of Sports in America) in the fall of 2009 the thought of writing a textbook for it was nowhere near my radar screen. When I was approached by Jeff Huemoeller from Kendall Hunt Publishing in early 2011 about writing a textbook I hesitated at first but eventually agreed primarily because I wanted to provide my students with a text with which they would be comfortable and they would enjoy. It was for that reason that I looked to them for ideas and advice for the book. I want to thank the students from 2009–2011 who helped me with their ideas involving both content and organization. The class in the fall of 2012 was the first to be able to use the first edition (author's edition) of the book and they were extremely helpful in providing feedback that is included in this edition. I also wanted to thank Benjamin Rader who is a pioneer in this field and for whom I followed in teaching this course at UNL. Ben casts a long shadow in this arena and I appreciate his counsel and his research which provided me with much of the base for my teaching and this book.

Because this is my first foray into textbook writing the people at Kendall Hunt were extremely helpful to me throughout the process. Jeff Huemoeller has been a source of moral support from the beginning whether dealing with the book or our mutual love of running (although when I first met him he was nursing a running injury that he sustained while in Lincoln). Ryan Schrodt has also been extremely helpful to me as we've gone along. Both of these guys have shown a lot of patience with a first-timer like myself and I wanted them to know I appreciate it. The copy-editors at Kendall Hunt have made this book much more readable than it would have been otherwise and they have made me look much better through their efforts. My first editor (since I first learned to write) has always been my mother and this effort was no different. I want to publicly thank Tani Stempson for all the work she did on this book and also for always being my biggest supporter. Thanks Mom.

Last, but certainly not least, I wanted to thank the people closest to me—my wife Abby and my three children. Writing anything takes a large time commitment and with three kids under the age of seven finding that time is often difficult. Abby always was willing to take the kids when daddy needed to work and I want her to know how much I appreciate that. Next to my mother, she is my biggest supporter and she is also my best friend and I can't express in words how important she is to me and how much I love her. Time goes by so quickly and it's hard to believe our kids are as big as they are now but it won't be long before they are much bigger and we forget this moment in time so I wanted to remember exactly what they looked like during this busy time in our lives. It was

Image courtesy of the author

for that reason that I decided to have pictures taken of them in various sports outfits and have them throughout the book. My beautiful family can be seen in the picture above. Our oldest is John David (JD) who is 6; next is Henry who is 4 and finally our daughter Veronica is 16 months old in these photos. The boys are already developing a deep interest in sports (as you can probably tell from the pictures) and they usually can be found swinging a golf club or baseball bat or shooting baskets in the backyard. Much to their father's delight (and their mother's disdain) they are also developing an interest in watching sports (all sports involving the hometown Huskers as well as New York Yankees baseball, not the Royals—sorry Mommy and Papa John). I dedicate this book to my family.

Scott Stempson

Foreword

I cannot remember a time when sports did not play a role in my life. Sports are a major part of my life but they have also become a major part of American culture. On the first day of my sports history class I always show three clips from major sporting events involving the "Big 3" American sports (Baseball, Basketball and Football). The clips include Reggie Jackson hitting three home runs in one game during the 1977 World Series; Nebraska going for two points and the win against Miami in the 1984 Orange Bowl and Larry Bird stealing the in-bounds pass by Isaiah Thomas during the 1987 NBA playoffs to seal the win. I always ask the students what the three clips have in common and I usually receive answers like, "The plays had a direct impact on which team won the games and championships" or "They were moments that changed sports history" which are good answers and not incorrect. However, I tell them the answer I was looking for was that I remember exactly where I was when all of these events occurred. In other words, sporting events have become such a huge part of our culture that we can all remember certain athletic events in our own personal history that we were either involved in as a participant or watching as a fan. It hasn't always been that way, though. In fact there was time in our history where sports were not only looked down upon but actually outlawed. In the opening chapters of this book I explore that history and what was considered acceptable and not acceptable. In Puritan society, for example, even the word *sport* became synonymous with violent, unacceptable "bloodsports" which led to bad things like drinking or gambling as opposed to the words *games* or *recreations* which usually meant non-competitive activities which were needed for the betterment of society.

When looking at the history of sports it's important to try to define what *is* a sport? When I was in college I remember some friends and I having an argument about what really is the definition of a sport. Somebody offered that there has to be a ball involved. It's not surprising at a school like the University of North Dakota where I was an undergraduate at the time that somebody else said, "What about hockey?" Then there is the old question if car racing is a sport. One of my friends in the conversation said that there could not be a motor involved. "What about horse racing?" another questioned. There is a jockey involved so it's probably alright. Others said the competitors have to be "athletes" and break a sweat for it to be a sport. "That leaves out golf" a non-golfer said to needle us who played the game. "I'll grant you it's a skill," he said, "but not a sport." We continued the conversation during a game of sand volleyball when someone said, "is this a sport?" No, another offered—I think you have to wear shoes for it to be a sport. "What about swimming?" I think you get the point—the definition of what a sport is depends on each person's point of view. If you grew up playing a particular sport or enjoyed it watching it with your family then you would argue that it is a sport. If it's something you're not familiar with then you may not. I remember as a kid first being exposed to the sport of curling which is quite popular in the northern part of the country. I thought it was the strangest thing I had ever seen but there are dedicated curlers all across the country and in 1998 it actually became an official winter Olympic sport. In our many collegiate discussions we never arrived at a concrete definition of what it takes to qualify as a sport. I'm not sure anyone has ever come up with a complete definition. The American College Dictionary has 26 different definitions. The first definition is as follows: "A pastime pursued in the open air or having an athletic character, as hunting, fishing, racing, baseball, tennis, golf, bowling, wrestling, boxing, etc."[1] It's that "etc." that gets you in trouble—what is included in that "etc."? I personally like the third definition which states, "diversion, recreation, pleasant pastime."[2] In other words, something that takes your mind off your troubles and provides the participant with a good experience. To me, that's what sports is all about.

This book is by no means meant to be a comprehensive look at the history of *all* sports. I didn't have the room or frankly, the time. What I did try to do was look at the sports that I believe have most affected American culture and vice-versa over the years. Those include the "Big 3" team sports of baseball, basketball and football. I also look at the individual sports of golf, tennis, and boxing. The greatest sporting spectacle in the world over the past century has been the Olympics so I have included a chapter on that. Finally, one of the constants throughout sports history has been the influence of gambling on it so the final chapter looks at that influence. There are some topics that did not make it into this first edition and I do regret that I ran out of time and space. Many of my students requested that I include the sport of soccer, modern "extreme sports," and auto racing. Soccer has never been a hugely popular sport in the United States as it is been in Europe and elsewhere around the world but I admit that its popularity is growing in this country, especially with the younger generation, and I plan to include it in the future. With the extreme sports and auto racing we again have that argument of what do we consider to be a sport. What cannot be argued is the popularity of both of them and I hope to include them in upcoming editions. Another regret is the absence of a chapter on African-American sports history. I touch on it throughout the book but had originally planned on a distinct chapter in which I thoroughly examine the Jackie Robinson story, among others. Well, enough about what's *not* in the book—there's quite a bit *in* the book and I hope you enjoy it.

Notes

1. *The American College Dictionary* (Random House: New York, 1959), 1168.
2. Ibid.

CHAPTER
One

Origin of American Sports: Great Britain's "Festive Culture"

On March 24, 1603, Robert Carey carried an important message across the English country-side. Queen Elizabeth I, the longtime ruler of Great Britain, who brought her nation great wealth and power and whose reign has become known as England's "Golden Age," had died. Carey was bringing the news to Elizabeth's handpicked successor, King James of Scotland. The news did not come as a great shock to James, as Elizabeth's health had been declining for some time, and he knew the end was imminent. The greater surprise for James was that Carey had made the 400-mile trek from London to Edinburgh on horseback in less than 60 hours, including breaks to sleep. It was believed to be the fastest anyone had ever traversed that distance in the days before the rail-road. Carey may not have known it, but he had set a 17th-century precedent of trying to beat the reported time of the last person to make a particular trip—albeit usually shorter distances than Carey's famous ride.[1]

It is not surprising that the British would take any opportunity to set what they would consider to be sports records. The British culture is a sporting culture dating back to the Middle Ages and before. Monarchs would come and go, and anti-sports proclamations would constantly be made, and yet the people continued to play their games. Even after the English Civil War in the middle of the 17th century when an entire government was set up, without a monarch for over a decade, based largely on Puritan doctrines, one of which was completely antigames or any "idle amuse-ments," British sports would not die. It is always difficult to legislate morality in any society—espe-cially when it involves what citizens do in their spare time. When a large group of citizens wants to do something—in this case play games—they will do it, regardless of laws passed against it. It was during Queen Elizabeth's reign (1558–1603) that Britain made its first forays into the "new world" of North America. It would be her successor, James I (1603–1625), who would grant two charters to joint-stock companies (The Virginia Co. and Plymouth Co.) to make the first permanent British settlements there. Both would bring their ideas on games and sports to a new continent—one would try to emulate the British sporting ways, and the other would rebel against it in colonial America, which is discussed later in this chapter. Because of this relationship between Britain and her North American colonies—who would eventually break away and be granted their indepen-dence—it is important to examine the how and why of the British sporting ways.

It may be noted that the interaction between Britain and the United States over the years has resembled a parent–child relationship in many ways. This is certainly true in sports: There was a breaking away by the child, an emulation by the child, and eventually a rivalry between child and parent that would stretch well into the 20th century and perhaps is still with us today. Let us first look at the parent before we move on to the child.

Britain's "Festive Culture"

Encyclopedia Britannica notes that the first historical recorded athletic events were at the original Greek Olympic games around 800 B.C. The games lasted until Emperor Theodosius terminated them in 394 A.D. before the fall of Rome in the 5th century. For the next 14 centuries the historical record of sports is sketchy at best.[2] That does not mean, however, that games were not played. During the Middle Ages (commonly considered to begin with the fall of the Roman Empire in 476 through the 15th century), folk games were common throughout Great Britain. In what historians have dubbed Britain's **Festive Culture**, citizens would engage in various games to coincide with large gatherings of people either in celebration of religious or pagan holidays or simply celebrating everyday life. The Ecclesiastical, or church, calendar celebrated various important days in the life of Jesus as well as other important religious figures. These days afforded people a day off work and allowed them to gather together to have a feast, drink, and play games. Quite often, these religious celebrations were mixed with pagan customs, and it was sometimes difficult to distinguish the two. An example of this is **Shrovetide**, which is the Monday and Tuesday before Ash Wednesday. It inaugurates the season of Lent and is the final two days of "Carnival," an unofficial period beginning with Epiphany, and takes its name from the Latin *carnelevare*, or "taking away of the flesh," which is instituted by Catholics during Lent when no meat is consumed. Because this period was usually the first time people were able to recreate outside after a long winter of being cooped up, the games played tended to be more violent, as people let off the steam of the winter months. The Church tolerated most of these games as opposed to endorsing them. The winter months, however, were not without their celebrations—the Christmas season, Plough Monday, and Boxing Day (just after Christmas) were also very popular times to revel. Combining Sundays and all the other holidays on the ecclesiastical calendar, British citizens could nearly take off one day for every two days of work.

Painting of Carnival preceding the season of Lent. © Ali Meyer/CORBIS

The most popular of the British Festive Culture holidays was **May Day**. The annual rite of spring was also a rite of passage for British youth. The phallic maypole represented fertility of the soil and, critics would say, the fertility of the young people. On midnight of May 1, the youth of the village would go into the woods and cut down a tree that would be erected in the town and, after ribbons were tied to it, there would be dancing around the pole. The Puritans would do everything they could to stop this ritual because they believed it to be a form of "idolatry and loose morals." As one critic, Philip Stubbes, put it: "Of forty, three score, or a hundred maids going into the woods over night, there have been scarcely the third part of them returned home again undefiled."[3] Many games were associated with May Day, including more violent games like wrestling, but probably the most interesting game was the Pageant of Misrule, in which most all the males got together and elected a "Lord of Misrule." The "Lord" would always be a young bachelor, and he would mock married men, older men, the upper class, and even the monarch. The married would take the brunt of the mockery, as it was a time when a man had little say in who he would marry. His parents or the village would have the final approval in most marriages. A collection would be taken up for the pageant, and those who donated would be given badges. Those who did not would be, as quoted in Richard Holt's *Sport and the British*, "mocked and flouted at not a little."[4]

Football

The most popular of these violent games played throughout the British countryside was **football**. It was primarily known as a Shrove Tuesday tradition, but it would be played during other seasons as well. University towns developed their own teams and played regularly throughout the year, but in most locales it would remain an annual event. As historian Dennis Brailsford noted, a "necessary first step for the development of any folk sport" was its "exclusive association with a particular (annual) feast," and if the game was played more often than that, "the damage to life and property that it usually risked would have been more than bearable." The game was indeed very violent and often resulted in broken "heads and legs" and even "deaths were not unusual as the sides pushed, hacked and kicked their way through streets of shuttered shops, through streams and mud, waste land and fallow."[5] The game had different rules depending on the town where it was being played. In some places it appeared to have no rules at all, but in others, it had very complex regulations. In 1603, Richard Carew wrote a *Survey of Cornwall* in which he described the game as it was played in that town. The game was referred to as "hurling" and was comprised of 15, 20, or 30 players to a side. There was some resemblance to American football of today as there was "hurling to goales" by players and an opposition that "attempted to block his advance." There was even an offside rule (although a different version than its American counterpart): It stated that the player "may not throw it to any of his mates, standing nearer the goale than himself."[6] Any comparison to the American game ended there, and it seemed to be a closer cousin to the Australian rules version or rugby.

To be associated with the game of football was not good if one was an upstanding member of civilized society. The game even found its way into Shakespeare's plays. In *King Lear*, the character Kent derides Oswald by calling him a "base football player," which is an insult of the highest proportions.[7] Not surprisingly, because of the violence associated with the game, governments attempted to curtail its play or even outlaw the playing of it altogether. The earliest known attempt to ban the playing of the game came during the Middle Ages and was issued in London by King Edward II in 1314. The proclamation read, in part: "whereas there is great uproar in the City, through certain tumult arising from great footballs in the fields of the public, from which many evils perchance may arise—which may God forbid—we do command and forbid . . . upon pain of imprisonment, that such a game shall be practiced henceforth within the city." Leaders became worried that citizens were using their leisure time in wasteful pursuits like football as opposed to training themselves in the military arts, which would help in the ultimate defense of Britain if called upon. These beliefs could easily be seen in 1365 in a proclamation made by King Edward III one half century after his father's earlier pronouncement: ". . . every able bodied man . . . on feast days when he has leisure shall in his sports use bows and arrows or pellets and bolts . . . forbidding them under pain of imprisonment to meddle in the hurling of stones, loggats and quoits (forms of what would be known today as horseshoes), handball, football . . . or other vain games of no value."[8]

There were no fewer than 23 royal proclamations against football between the 14th and 17th centuries. The sheer number indicated how powerless the governments were at stopping an activity that the people loved and wanted to participate in. That did not mean that some individuals weren't prosecuted for violating the statutes. In 1576 there was an arrest of a number of individuals after as many as one hundred men "assembled themselves unlawfully and played a certain unlawful game called football." According to court records, that "unlawful game" was "likely to result in homicides and serious accident." A sober reminder of the truth of that statement could be found five years later in a coroner's inquisition. Two football players were accused of the death of a third: ". . . Roger Ludford ran towards the ball with the intention to kick it, whereupon Nicholas Martyn with the forepart of his right arm struck Roger Ludford a blow on the fore-part of the body under the breast, giving him a mortal blow and concussion of which he died within a quarter of an hour and that Nicholas and Richard in this manner feloniously slewe the said Roger."[9] None of this seemed to dampen the public's enthusiasm for the game.

Royal Sports

Royal resistance to football did not necessarily extend to other games. In fact, many of the British kings and queens not only condoned various sports but were also sometimes participants themselves. This included the legendary King Arthur and his Knights of the Round Table and their athletic and military exploits into the Middle Ages and both Richard the Lionheart (in 1199) and Richard III (in 1485) actually dying in battle. The death of the latter is commonly referred to as the end of the Middle Ages in England. The most popular athletic event in most royal circles was the **joust**. The joust was particularly enjoyed by Henry VIII, who participated in many himself, and in 1520 met King Francis I of France on what was called the "**tilt yard**." (The "tilt" was the dividing of the list, or the jousting field, which occurred after 1400 and led to a safer sport because there was less chance of participants crashing into one another.) It is not believed that Henry and Francis actually competed against each other during the tournament because it

Jousting on a tilt yard. Image © Vladimir Korostyshevskiy. 2013. Used under license from Shutterstock, Inc.

was not common practice in case of injury or death and the political upheaval it could cause between nations. Injuries were part of the joust, and Henry could not escape them. In fact, it was an injury in 1536 that not only ended his jousting career but also nearly killed him, and some have said this led to his becoming more and more tyrannical as the years went on. The combination of the head and leg injuries, it is said, changed his demeanor from "once sporty and generous," to one of "cruel, vicious and paranoid." He also began gaining weight—from a once athletic waistline of 32 inches he ballooned up to 52 inches by the end of his life. His subjects began talking about him in a new way, and the infamous turnover of his wives sped up.[10] Even though her father was often injured by it and other monarchs lost their lives as a result of it (including Henry II of France in

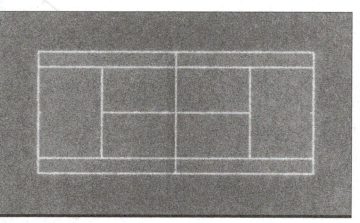

Grass tennis court. Image © zooropa, 2013. Used under license from Shutterstock, Inc.

1559), Elizabeth was an avid supporter and fan of the joust. Possibly as a result of the French king's death, she personally revised the old medieval rules of combat in 1562. Whenever she was involved in a festival for the remainder of her rule, there was a jousting tournament involved.

Before Henry VIII gained his infamous girth, he enjoyed many different sports, including **tennis**. It is believed tennis was imported to Britain from France after it gained popularity with the French royal family during the Middle Ages. It was so popular with the crown that it was known for a time as royal tennis. By the 14th century, tennis was well established in Britain and was mentioned in various writings, including the father of English literature, the poet Geoffrey Chaucer in 1370: "But canstow playen raket, to and fro, Netle in, dokke out. . . ."[11] Although most of that passage may be difficult to understand, there is no mistaking the word "raket" as the implement used to hit the ball "to and fro." No one is certain when the racket began to be used, but originally the palm of the hand was used (as in modern-day handball). The origin of the name of the sport itself is also uncertain. It is believed it comes from the French word *tenez,* which is what was called out by the server to warn his opponent that he is about to serve. The peculiar system of scoring (points starting with love and continuing with 15, 30, 40, and then game) can be traced back to early British wagering. It was customary to bet a crown per game. The crown was worth 60 pennies so if you divide a crown in fourths, you have 15, 30, 45 and game. Originally the third point was known as 45 but has since been abbreviated to 40 (two syllables as opposed to three). Even the term for no score, love, can be traced back to gambling, as it is derived from the old phrase, "For love or money."[12] It was the Italians who added the final scoring rule in 1555 when the provision was implemented that if the score reaches 45 (or 40) all, then it is considered a *due* or deuce, and a two-point lead is then needed to win.

Throughout the 15th century, the popularity of tennis grew in Britain—and not just for the royals. Many public courts were built, and King Edward IV in 1446 was petitioned by a local manufacturer of tennis balls to prohibit the import of tennis balls into the country. There is evidence that King Henry VIII was a decent tennis player, and the popularity of the sport grew during his reign in the early 16th century. As with many parts of British culture, the game of tennis flourished under Henry's daughter Elizabeth's reign in the late 16th century. Whether or not she played the game is unknown, but she did appear to have condoned the sport to be played by her subjects, as she licensed public courts in London, Cambridge, and Oxford. The caretakers of those courts were paid and sometimes played against patrons so they could be considered the earliest professionals in the sport. The popularity of the game began to decline in the 17th century. When James I took the throne after Elizabeth's death in 1603, he believed himself to be a great sportsman and athlete (although others dispute this). What is indisputable is James's belief in the importance of sports and games. He imbued this in his children when he gave them a list of sports that are "becoming a prince," which included "running, leaping, wrestling, fencing, dancing . . . tennis, bowls, and archery."[13] Although tennis may have waned for the general public during the remainder of the century, both James's son and grandson (Kings Charles I and II) took James's advice and enjoyed the game.

Book of Sports

James not only gave his sons a list of acceptable sports but he also provided one for the entire nation. In 1618, James issued his Declaration of Sports, or the **Book of Sports**, as it became known. The Puritan church was on the rise in Britain in the early 17th century and, along with "purifying" the Church of England of its Catholic tendencies, as their name suggests, they were also purifying the Sabbath—and that meant no work or recreation of any kind on Sundays. James argued against the Puritan vision of Sabbath observation. He believed that the prohibition of sports on Sunday "bred discontent, hindered the conversion of Catholics and deprived the commoner and meaner sort of people of their only opportunity for exercise."[14] In other words, if people could not play on Sundays, when could they? Six-day workweeks were the norm in England at the time. His declaration laid out the sports and games that were allowed, including a similar list that he compiled for his children, but he also added that the "Maytime festivities" were allowed as long as there was "no impediment or neglect of Divine Service."[15] The Book of Sports also included what games were not allowed, including blood sports like bull and bear baiting, football, and even forms of bowling when participated in by the "meaner sort of people."[16] The question remained who decided who the "meaner sort of people" were. There was also a warning that ends the declaration by ordering that "no offensive weapons be carried or used in said times of recreations."[17]

Charles I, who succeeded his father in 1625, felt compelled not only to reissue the Book of Sports in 1633 but also to order that the book be read from every pulpit in the country. Many clergymen refused, and many lost their jobs. It prompted others to develop clever ways of obeying the order. After reading the declaration, one minister said the people had heard the word of God and the word of man and now the "choice was theirs."[18] By reissuing the declaration, Charles was endorsing his father's beliefs about sports while also reacting to the tenor of the times. The Puritans were not only gaining numbers in the general public, but they were also now the majority in parliament. Indeed, in the very first debate made in the House of Commons during Charles's reign, the subject was not war, peace, or economic issues but Sunday sports. The first statute passed was "An act for punishing divers (sp) abuses committed on the Lord's day called Sunday."[19] Violators would be either fined three shillings, four pennies, or spend three days in the stocks. By 1629, Charles had enough of parliament and decided to dissolve it. He ruled without parliament for the next 11 years under "Divine Right," in which he claimed his power was given to him by God and therefore he did not need parliament's help.

Charles's father had granted a group of Puritans a charter to colonize in North America, and by the 1620s there was a thriving colony in Massachusetts Bay that would eventually be based on Puritan church rule. It was the increasingly despotic rule of Charles and the persecution of the Puritans during the 1630s that led to the "great migration" of over 21,000 people to New England between 1629 and 1642. The migration slowed in 1642 because many Puritans stayed to fight in the English Civil War, which erupted that year. Puritans backed the parliamentary forces led by **Oliver Cromwell**, who wanted to bring back the power of parliament, lessen the power of the king, and reform the Church of England. By 1649 the parliamentary forces were victorious, proclaimed Britain a republican commonwealth, and executed Charles I. There was no monarch in Great Britain throughout the 1650s, and the country was ostensibly ruled by parliament and Cromwell until his death in 1658. Although parliament again attempted to impose laws against sports on Sunday, there is evidence that Cromwell was more tolerant of sports than most Puritans, as he was an avid hunter and horseman. His death created a leader-

Oliver Cromwell. Image © Georgios Kollidas, 2013. Used under license from Shutterstock, Inc.

ship void that would end with the restoration of the monarchy with Charles II (Charles I's son and James I's grandson) in 1660. If anything, Charles II was even less tolerant of the Puritans than his father had been. This signaled the end of Puritan power in Great Britain and any hopes for tolerance toward them by the presiding government. One of the legacies of the Puritans in England is "English Sunday," which to this day bars most organized recreation on the Sabbath. There was also the export of the Puritan idea of Sunday observance to the "new world."

"Lawful Sport" in New England

The Puritans who migrated to the new world hoped to establish an example to the old world on what a successful community based on religious rule should look like—what founder and Massachusetts' first governor John Winthrop referred to as a "city on a hill." Winthrop was part of the first thousand immigrants during the "Great Migration" in the early 1630s who established Massachusetts Bay Colony. The colony was essentially a theocracy based on Puritan beliefs, and one of those beliefs was a strict observance of the Sabbath. Laws that were passed throughout the colony to enforce that observance were known as **Sabbatarian laws**. The laws not only banned recreation of virtually any kind but also proscribed activities that were deemed acceptable during the rest of the week such as sexual intercourse, unnecessary traveling, and "any type of frivolity."[20] The laws also provided for more severe penalties to be imposed should unacceptable activities occur on the Sabbath as opposed to any other day of the week. For example, if minor violations such as profanity or petty theft happened on the Sabbath, they could be elevated to major status. Some leaders even went as far as advocating the death penalty for Sabbath-breakers. The bottom line is that the Puritan leaders believed that from sundown Saturday to sundown Sunday every waking moment should be devoted to God and nothing else. Historian Bruce Daniels aptly described a typical Sabbath in colonial New England: "Family prayers, a three-hour service in both the morning and the afternoon, personal Bible study, acts of charity and public improvement, and evening meditations seemingly left little time for leisure. A good Christian spent the Sabbath re-creating his soul, not recreating his body."[21] Although some Sabbatarian laws were relaxed throughout the colonial period, restricting only "rowdy behavior, excessive drink, and hard work,"[22] a Newport, Rhode Island, town council order from 1739 shows how the laws continued over a century after New England was first colonized. The order instructed local constables (police) to "return the names of all tavern keepers and retailers whom you shall find selling strong drink . . . return the names of all persons whom you shall find drinking in taverns . . . sailing in boats, unnecessary riding, swimming, fishing, gunning, or using any other diversions or recreations . . . disperse all noisy and disorderly gatherings . . . (and) prevent all unnecessary walking in the streets and fields upon the said day, especially during the time of divine services."[23]

With these laws on the books, one might think that all sports and games were banned in Puritan New England. Although some sports were not welcome in Puritan society, others were not only allowed but encouraged. Games that were believed to foster drinking and gambling were expressly forbidden. Games that refreshed the mind, body, and spirit were allowed. These became known as **lawful recreation or sport**. To be lawful the recreation essentially had to satisfy two requirements: It could have no association with the British festive culture that the Puritans were rebelling against, and it had to refresh the participants so they could perform their worldly duties. Just having fun for fun's sake in idle amusement was not what the Puritans had in mind. Yes, they even took their sports seriously. If it did not have a higher purpose—they did not participate in it. Games one might find in a tavern like cards, dice, and shuffleboard were not allowed. Activities that were seen as healthy like foot races in warm weather and ice-skating in cold weather were deemed lawful. College students in the newly established Harvard College were encouraged by the faculty to participate in lawful recreation and, in 1655, specific time during the day was set aside for this purpose. In 1696, a tragedy occurred at Harvard in which two undergraduates broke through the ice while skating and were drowned. Harvard president Increase Mather's message to the grieving parents showed the importance of the distinction of recreation in the Puritan mind when he consoled them by saying "although death found them using recreations they were lawful recreations."[24]

It is important to note that the Puritans not only made a distinction between recreations that were lawful and unlawful, but also the word *recreation* itself would eventually be associated with allowable games, as the word *sport* became associated with activities that were banned. Hunting and fishing were allowable recreations because they would provide the community with food while ridding it of vermin and dangerous animals. The word *sport* began to be associated with violent ball games (like football) and blood sports like animal-baiting. Bruce Daniels believed the Puritans' opposition to what they defined as sport was based on at least seven reasons: "sport was frivolous and wasted time; sport did not refresh the body . . . but tired it instead; much of sporting activity was designed deliberately to inflict pain or injury; sporting contests usually led to gambling; more sport occurred on Sunday than on any other day, so, sport encouraged people to defile the Sabbath; sport was noisy and disrupted others, sometimes entire communities; and many sports had either pagan or 'Popish' origins."[25] Because of their definition of sport, it is easy to see why some have mistakenly believed that *all* sports, as we would define them, were banned from Puritan society. We know that not to be the case—in fact, not all ball games were completely off limits. Throughout the colonial period, especially in larger cities like Boston, games were brought over from England and modified to be played "in a more orderly manner"[26] to fit in with the Puritan culture. Two of these games would have a far-reaching effect on the future of not only sports in New England but in all of North America: One was referred to as the Boston game—it would eventually become American-style football; the other was known by many different names—the New England or Massachusetts game, and also town ball and round ball. We know the game today as baseball.

Another area where games, and what otherwise might be considered sport, were allowed was in military training. New England law required that all men between the ages of sixteen and sixty were required to meet a number of times a year to drill. Depending on the threat to the local villages, the men would meet six to eight times per year to train. Recreations that were common during military training were designed to either keep the men in shape or help prepare them for fighting. They would engage in martial arts, foot and horse races, jumping, and target shooting. The most popular competition they would engage in would be wrestling. It came the closest to combat without the possible injuries that came along with boxing or cudgel fighting (hitting each other with a stick). Wrestling also gained respectability when two of the most respected Puritan clergymen of the 17th century were also wrestlers. Two Connecticut ministers, John Trumball and Henry Smith, both were known for their "delight in sports of strength."[27] Training days would be whole town affairs—everyone would get up early and watch the training, and there would be a parade as well as a feast. In some towns, the training days resembled a county fair more than a military camp. At the turn of the 18th century, one of the most well-known social commentators, Sarah Kemble Knight, described the training days as "Olympiack games" and said that they were "by far the biggest diversion in rural towns."[28]

Almost everything done in New England Puritan society was an attempt to distance itself from Britain and its "Festive Culture." One way the Puritans hoped to curtail revelry was to do away with the opportunity to socialize—the most social days on the British calendar had been holidays. As many as 165 days per year were recognized by either the Catholic or Anglican Church as some sort of holiday—a term that had its origins from the old English word for holy day. Puritans had two main problems with holidays: First, the days would foster idleness, which the church should be against; and, second, they believed having a holy day recognized by the church would imply that all other days are less than holy. Puritans believed that "they for whom all days are holy can have no holiday."[29] Most Puritans took that belief to heart and observed no holy days (save the Sabbath). The holiday that was most despised was Christmas. There were many reasons Puritan New England refused to celebrate the most popular of Christian holidays for the entire colonial period. December 25, or "**Foolstide**" as it was locally called, was well known in Europe for its excessive behavior. Cotton Mather was reported to have said that "men dishonored the Lord Jesus Christ more in the twelve days of Christmas than in all the twelve months of the preceding year."[30] Puritans also disliked the holiday because they believed the date to be incorrect. They believed Christ was actually born in either September or October, and Christmas was only celebrated December 25 because that had been a Roman holiday that early Christians borrowed, and therefore "to celebrate Christmas was to honor a pagan custom."[31] When the Puritans came to power in England during the 1650s, they outlawed most holidays, including Christmas. New England followed suit and, in 1659, Massachusetts authorized a fine of five shillings to punish those who celebrated Christmas day by "abstinence from labor, feasting, or in any other way."[32] You know a sect is a serious group when they actually outlaw Christmas. What about that other company to which James I granted a charter to colonize the new world? What of the Virginia Company—were they as serious and austere a group?

Sports in the Southern Colonies

People colonized in different places, at different times, for different reasons. The Plymouth Company had been a push more than a pull—the Puritans leaving the persecution of Anglican England. The Virginia Company was more a flight of attraction to a land of adventure—pull more than push. Some came to escape debt and prison sentences, and some wanted to farm their own land or strike it rich. After the early lean years when Jamestown was first established in 1607, the colony had grown into a thriving settled area based on its first cash crop, tobacco, by the 1620s. When word spread back to Britain, Virginia seemed like the place to be, especially for those who wanted to own their own land, which was scarce in the old country. Whatever the reason for the colonists coming, religion was not at the center of their reasoning as it had been in Massachusetts. Once the Virginia Colony was established, the Anglican Church was the recognized religion, and that led to a different outlook on recreation and sports than in the North. There was much more tolerance of sports and games in the South. There was another difference in the South—a much more pronounced social stratification and class difference. English culture was based on the idea of **primogeniture**, or the firstborn son inheriting the family fortune. If you were not the firstborn, then your chances of owning property were slim, so many took a chance on the "new world." Many of those men copied the ways of their fathers by building large mansions in Virginia and other Southern colonies when they emerged. This group became known as the **landed gentry**, and they were the leaders of every aspect of Southern colonial culture. It would also be the gentry who would lead the cause in breaking away from Britain in the next century.

On the other end of the spectrum were those who arrived in the new world as indentured servants. These were usually poor white men from England who would provide most of the labor for the gentry in return for paid passage to North America. This system of servitude allowed the small group of landed gentry to amass a fortune while becoming the social elite of the colony. The problem with the system was that it was not permanent. As soon as the term of indenture was fulfilled (a matter of a few years, depending on the agreement), the workers were free to pursue their own independent lives. The impermanence of the system was one of the reasons Southern colonies turned to African slavery. Historian Edmund Morgan believes that the slave system that was at the heart of the reason the Revolution was begun by members of the Southern gentry. They believed, Morgan argues, that they had "solved" the problem "plaguing Republicanism for decades." Slavery "provided both a stable system for controlling the poor and an economic base elevating large numbers of whites to the status of free and independent yeomen."[33] This system provided more time for the gentry to participate in leisure activities. These activities also very often served to separate the classes and the races.

Because of the differences with Massachusetts highlighted earlier (religion and class), Virginia, and eventually other Southern colonies, was much more tolerant of sports than their counterparts in the North. Another reason for this tolerance was that Virginia was colonized less by families and more by single men. It was much easier to suppress rowdy behavior when the community was filled with women and children than in a community full of bachelors that resembled a "raucous mining camp," as early Virginia did.[34] Even after women joined the men and families were started, the sports and games continued because they were an accepted part of Virginia society from the beginning. The other thing that became acceptable in Southern society, which would have horrified the Puritans, was gambling. Gambling was viewed very differently by the emerging Virginia gentry. Not only was it acceptable, but it actually would reveal one's standing with God. If a person won, they were viewed favorably by the Almighty, and if they lost, the opposite was true. Nowhere could you find this idea more prevalent than at the colonial Virginia horse track. Horseracing emerged early on as a favorite of the upper and lower classes. Although it was supposed to be a sport in which only "gentlemen" competed, that did not preclude the lower classes from wagering on the event. In fact, that is how racing emerged as a spectator sport. As Jane Carson noted in her book, *Colonial Virginians at Play,* match racing began when "a proud owner's boast of his mount's performance was challenged by another horseman and they agreed to settle the argument in action." Then, when "each contestant backed his horse with his purse and spectators made side bets on the outcome of the race," it became a sport.[35] Those "side bets" were taken very seriously and viewed as contracts by Virginia law. One example of this is in 1690, when Robert Napier agreed to race Littlebury Eppes, who covered a side wager by William Soane. When Napier did not appear at the designated time for the race, Soane decided to sue Napier for the amount of the wager. A jury eventually found for Soane citing that the "wager was a legal contract" and awarded him the money, even though the race never occurred.[36] Rules were strict for racing—once a wager was made, it could not be withdrawn, and the only way a race would be canceled is if one of the horses died.

The races themselves were not for the faint of heart. By the middle of the 17th century, they were being held all over the colony, usually on Saturdays and holidays. The track was reduced from a mile (which was the custom back in England) to a straight quarter-mile track laid out in an abandoned field near a gathering place such as a church, courthouse, or a tavern. The large English thoroughbred that was brought to North America had been bred with some native horses descended from the Spanish horses brought to the continent by the Conquistadors in the previous century. The result was a much smaller horse with large hindquarters that excelled at sprinting shorter distances of a quarter mile or less. Because of this, they became known as **quarter horses**. When the official starter signaled the start of the race with either a gunshot or a trumpet blast, the horses took off at full speed. Unlike races of today, it was permissible for riders to either knock other riders off their mounts or drive the horses off the track. As the sport evolved, the straightaway track was replaced with an oval one that allowed spectators to see the whole race. Europeans who visited the colony were amazed at the speed of the horses. One English visitor in the 18th century wrote that the Virginia quarter horses raced with

Quarter horse. Image © Zuzule, 2013. Used under license from Shutterstock, Inc.

Horseracing. Image © Anastasiia Golovkova, 2013. Used under license from Shutterstock, Inc.

Preparing for a fox hunt. Image © Antonio Abrignani, 2013. Used under license from Shutterstock, Inc.

Cockfighting. Image © Alekcey, 2013. Used under license from Shutterstock, Inc.

"an astonishing velocity not to be excelled by any other horse in England, nor perhaps in the whole world."[37] The races were reserved for gentlemen, and if an individual entered a race who was perceived to be something other than a member of the gentry, there would be a price to pay. An often-cited case that illustrates this point is a 1674 race in which a common tailor, James Bullock, entered his mare against a horse owned by Dr. Matthew Slader, a gentleman. When Bullock's real identity was discovered, he was fined 100 pounds of tobacco for participating in a "sport only for gentlemen."[38] The fact Bullock's horse won the race was immaterial. The gentry was happy to take the commoners' gate fees or wagers, but participation in the races themselves were strictly forbidden.

Sports were often used as a vehicle to separate the sharp class distinctions of the South. Although hunting was participated in by all (often as a necessity to put food on the table), the fox hunt was reserved for the gentry. The necessary "tools of the trade," like fancy uniforms and hats and special hounds, were beyond the budget of the lower classes. The native gray fox proved to be difficult to catch and often led the hunters "through woodlands too dense for horseback riding." Because of this, the less elusive English red fox was imported to the colonies and often "carried along in a bag" and let loose in the hunt when the gray fox could not be caught.[39] Other activities reserved for the upper class included forms of what today we would call bowling (games they called *skittles, nine pins,* and *bowls*), a form of cricket, and billiards. As time went on, billiards would often be played by the lower classes as well, but the distinction was *where* it was played. In the large mansions built by the gentry, they would often include a large room used for dancing and billiards. So if one was playing the game in a private home, they were a member of the upper class—if they were playing it in a public house or tavern, they were a member of the lower class. Although the lower classes enjoyed the blood sports as they had in Britain's festive culture, those sports weren't limited to the lower classes exclusively. One example of this was cockfighting. According to Jane Carson, the popularity of this blood sport was just behind horseracing and hunting. One traveler described a match he watched and reported that the cockpit was "surrounded by many genteel people, promiscuously mingled with the vulgar and debased." He went on to describe the bloody scene that unfolded before his eyes: "they flew upon each other . . . the cruel and fatal gaffs being driven in to their bodies . . . frequently one, or both, were struck dead at the first blow, but they often fought after being repeatedly pierced, as long as they were able to crawl. . . ."[40] Another blood sport involving a bird that was a particular favorite among the common people of the South, and was more exclusive to them, was **ganderpulling**. This was usually staged on the Monday following Easter, which was a day of celebration in the Chesapeake Bay region, and it involved greasing the neck of a goose and hanging the animal by its feet from a rope stretched between two trees or tied to a tree limb. From horseback the contestants would gallop at full speed and attempt to pull the goose's head off. As a prize, the winner would take the goose home for supper.

Sports in the Middle Colonies and the Backcountry

David Hackett Fischer, in his epic work *Albion's Seed*, divided British colonization of North America into four distinct "folkways," two of which have been discussed already (New England and Virginia). The other two are what he described as the Middle Colonies and the Backcountry. The **Middle Colonies** are what is today New York, New Jersey, and Pennsylvania. The first English settlers in New York came in from New England and attempted to exert the Puritan ways over the colony, but because they were the minority (it was a Dutch settlement at the time), they were unable to gain control of the cultural ways. Once the Dutch were ousted by the British in 1664 and the Church of England became the official religion, the Puritans recognized they were not going to have the power they did in Massachusetts. The town of New Amsterdam's name was changed to New York, and it became a very cosmopolitan city, where many different sports were not only tolerated but encouraged. Just because control of the colony switched to the British did not mean the Dutch settlers all left. Those who stayed introduced many of their sports and games to the incoming settlers. They enjoyed various bowling games, boat races, and many ball games. One of those games the Dutch called **kolven**, which some authorities translate as "golf." The name apparently was anglicized by the next century, as an advertisement in 1766 would show when James Rivington put his "gouff clubs"[41] up for sale. It's not surprising that the first professionally designed golf course in America, Shinnecock Hills (see Chapter 8), was built in Southampton, Long Island, in the late 19th century.

As with New England, the Delaware Valley was settled primarily by a persecuted religious sect. They called themselves the Society of Friends. Others derisively referred to them as the Quakers for the shaking or "quaking" members exhibited when they received what was referred to as the "inner light" during a religious service. They were viewed as outcasts because their pacifist beliefs prevented them from joining the British military, and they refused to pay taxes to support the Church of England. A convert to the religious splinter group was William Penn, who wanted a place where his people could live and worship as they pleased. In 1681, as payback for a debt owed to Penn's father, King Charles II gave Penn the land that would eventually be known as Pennsylvania and Delaware. The laws Penn set up for the colony were very tolerant to all religions (there was no state religion) but quite intolerant of sports and banned a number of them. A sample of the forbidden activities included "all prizes, stage plays, cards, dice, May games, masques, revels, bull-baitings, cock-fightings, bear-baitings and the like."[42] As evidenced by the last three listed in this statute, blood sports were especially looked down on. They believed no person had the "right to make a pleasure of that which occasions pain and death to animal-creation." While killing "for the pot" was allowed, killing for fun was condemned.[43]

Puritan New England was a difficult place for sports, but Pennsylvania may have been tougher. As with New England's sabbatarian laws, Pennsylvania had what it termed **blue laws**. It is believed the name derived from the old English for feeling or looking "blue" or sad (which is what religious leaders hoped would be the look of their flock on the Sabbath), and they stipulated what activities were not allowed on Sunday. Penn divided the offenses into two categories: The more serious offenses for what he termed "rude and riotous sports" were punishable by 20 shillings or 10 days imprisonment at hard labor. The lesser offenses (playing cards, dice, or participating in lotteries) were subject to a fine of five shillings or five days imprisonment. Believing the statutes themselves may not be enough—especially for the young—Penn also established a Committee of Manners, Education, and Arts. The committee's purpose was to make sure that "all wicked and scandalous living might be prevented and that youth may be successively trained in virtue and useful knowledge and arts."[44] Also similar to New England's lawful sports, some sports and activities were allowed. They were termed "useful" or **needful recreation**." Swimming was allowed in summer and ice-skating in winter. Hunting and fishing were allowed if done so to put food on the table. Gardening was a popular leisure activity that would lead to a large number of Quakers in the horticultural industry. Children were especially encouraged to be physically fit. William Penn said that "children can't well be too hardy bred: for besides that it fits them to bear the roughest Providences, it is more masculine, active and healthy." George Fox, the founder of the Society of Friends, left 16 acres in Philadelphia on his death to be used "for a playground for the children of the town to play on."[45]

According to Fischer, the final "folkway" to be settled in the colonial period was known as the **backcountry**. This was the region beginning with Appalachia and eventually extending west to the Ohio and Mississippi River valleys and finally to the Ozark Mountains. This area was primarily settled by the northern British, Scots, and Scots-Irish. They came from an area that had been almost constantly at war for centuries. Border disputes and fights over land had cultivated a warrior ethic among the males of this region, and their colonization of the frontier regions of North America seemed to be a perfect fit for them. The folk games and sports they brought with them, not surprisingly, reflected this warrior ethic and border disputes. An example of a game that evidenced both was "Scots and English." The game was played by boys, who would pile their coats and hats behind them on either side of a "border" line. The object of the game was to cross that line and take the possessions of the opposite side and return without being captured. All the while they did this, they would scream the ancient warrior cries of their region that had been passed down to them.[46] This would seem to be an early incarnation of the game "capture the flag" that children would play years later. Another game reflecting the warrior ethic of the backcountry would be wrestling. It was usually pronounced "wrasslin" or "russlin" and there were two versions of it. The first was a more elaborate, regulated sport that would be staged in annual tournaments. Each contestant would face each other, lock their arms with their opponent, and tuck their chin into each other's right shoulder. There are two ways to lose the match: If any part of the contestant's body touched the ground (other than his feet) or if he lost his hold on his opponent, the match would be over. The other version of the sport was a much less regulated affair that usually began after consuming copious amounts of alcohol, which led to bragging and challenges. The fight was "a wild struggle with no holds barred that continued until one man gave up—or gave out."[47]

An even more violent and bloody "game" that also usually began with drinking and boasting was known as **rough and tumble**. It would normally start with a perceived slight to one's honor. Gentlemen participated in the duel, and members of the lower classes participated in the rough and tumble. There were absolutely no rules regulating the fights and, as a result, the participants were usually left bloodied and quite often maimed or even blinded. An Irish traveler named Thomas Ashe gave a graphic description of a rough and tumble fight between a West Virginian and a Kentuckian. The Virginian gained the upper hand in the battle and sunk "his sharpened fingernails into the Kentuckian's head." He "never lost his hold . . . fixing his claws in his hair and his thumbs on his eyes, (he) gave them a start from the sockets. The sufferer roared aloud but uttered no complaint." Even though his eyes were "gouged out, the struggle continued. The Virginian fastened his teeth on the Kentuckian's nose and bit it in two pieces. Then he tore off the Kentuckian's ears. At last, the Kentuckian, deprived of eyes, ears and nose, gave in." The winner, even though he was maimed and bleeding, was carried around the grounds to the "cheers of the crowd."[48] There were also less bloody and violent sports enjoyed by the backcountry, which included running and leaping contests. It was for his skill in these contests that a young Andrew Jackson first gained prominence. Jackson was the first famous American to hail from the backcountry, but it was the reputation of that region that he had to face his entire career. Even into the 19th century and into his presidency, Jackson had to overcome the image that he was a "frontier ruffian" that the violent games like "wrasslin" and "rough and tumble" helped foster.

Conclusion

In the British North American colonies of the 17th century, the games and sports of Britain's "festive culture" were looked on and emulated very differently, depending on which region one would visit. In Puritan New England and Quaker Pennsylvania, sports were seen as a waste of time—time being extremely important to both of those persecuted religions. Only sports that refreshed the individual for their "calling" in life and were disassociated with the "festive culture" were allowed. The Puritans tried to gain control of New York, but they were unable to do so and, as a result, a sporting life flourished in that colony. The same can be said for Virginia, which adopted the Church of England as its official religion, and the emerging landed gentry as well as the lower classes were therefore much more tolerant of sports and games. The gambling that developed as a result of the games was also accepted in Virginia society. Not only was it not seen as a waste of time or a mocking of God as the Puritans believed, but it would actually reveal to the individual his standing in the cosmos depending on the results of his wagering. Finally, the violent sports of the backcountry reflected where they came from (the violent borderlands of northern England) and where they settled (the often-violent frontier of the western regions of the colonies). As the colonial period moved into its second century, the various regions and their views on sports would develop differently, but there would also be similarities shared by all. As the 18th century wore on, these seemingly different people would put those differences aside, unite to defeat the greatest empire on earth, and form the first republic since Ancient Rome.

Notes

1. Richard Mandell, *Sport, A Cultural History* (New York: Columbia University Press, 1984), 140.
2. Eric Dunning and Elias Norbert, *Quest for Excitement; Sport and Leisure in the Civilizing Process* (Oxford, UK: Basil Blackwell Co., 1986), 130.
3. Benjamin Rader, *American Sports; From the Age of Folk Games to the Age of Televised Sports*, 6th ed. (Upper Saddle River, NJ: Pearson-Prentice Hall, 2009), 2–3.
4. Richard Holt, *Sport and the British; A Modern History* (Oxford: Clarendon Press, 1989), 14.
5. Dennis Brailsford, *Sport and Society; Elizabeth to Anne* (London: Routledge Kegan Paul, 1969), 53.
6. Richard Holt, *Sport and the British; A Modern History*, 13–14.
7. Brailsford, *Sport and Society*, 53.
8. Dunning and Norbert, *Quest for Excitement*, 175–76.
9. Ibid., 77–78.
10. Michael McCarthy, "The Jousting Accident that turned Henry VIII into a Tyrant," *The Independent*, 19 April 2009.
11. H. A. Harris, *Sport in Britain, It's Origins and Development* (Stanley Paul and Co.: London, 1975), 24.
12. Ibid., 28.
13. Brailsford, *Sport and Society*, 71.
14. Ibid., 102.
15. Ibid.
16. Ibid.
17. Ibid.
18. Ibid., 105.

CHAPTER *One*

19. Ibid., 104.
20. Bruce Daniels, *Puritans at Play; Leisure and Recreation in Colonial New England* (New York: St. Martin's Press, 1995), 75.
21. Ibid., 76.
22. Ibid., 79.
23. Ibid., 79–80.
24. David Hackett Fischer, *Albion's Seed; Four British Folkways in America* (New York/Oxford: Oxford University Press, 199), 147.
25. Daniels, *Puritans at Play*, 166.
26. Fischer, *Albion's Seed*, 149.
27. Daniels, *Puritans at Play*, 168.
28. Ibid., 98.
29. Ibid., 88–89.
30. Ibid., 89.
31. Ibid.
32. Ibid., 90.
33. Elliott Gorn and Warren Goldstein, *A Brief History of American Sports* (Chicago and Urbana: University of Illinois Press, 1993), 20.
34. Ibid., 19.
35. Jane Carson, *Colonial Virginians at Play* (Charlottesville: University Press of Virginia, 1965), 105.
36. Ibid., 107.
37. Ibid., 111.
38. Ibid., 109.
39. Ibid., 141.
40. Rhys Isaac, *The Transformation of Virginia* (Chapel Hill: University of North Carolina Press, 1982), 102.
41. Ibid., 8.
42. Fischer, *Albion's Seed*, 552.
43. Ibid., 553.
44. J. T. Jable, "Pennsylvania's Early Blue Laws: A Quaker Experiment in The Suppression of Sport and Amusements, 1682–1740," *Journal of Sport History* 1 (1974), 109.
45. Fischer, *Albion's Seed*, 554.
46. Ibid., 735.
47. Ibid., 736.
48. Ibid., 737.

CHAPTER

Two

The Colonies Develop Their Own Culture and Break from Britain

*T*he night before the big game there would be a large bonfire built and both spectators and participants would rally around it to promote the hometown team. The players had spent countless hours practicing to prepare for this momentous event—they ate a strict high-protein diet free of any form of grease and saturated fats. They abstained from alcohol for at least 48 hours and from sex for up to 30 days. There were hundreds of wagers made on the game, and bookmakers even roamed the sideline prior to and during the game. Moments before the players took the field they donned elaborate, colorful uniforms and were roused to near frenzied levels by an impassioned pep talk. When they arrived on the field of play, they were not only ready to play but also ready to tear the opposing team apart. Is this a description of a modern-day season-opening college football game? Although it could be, it is actually describing a game dating back to at least the early 18th century played by the Mississippi Choctaws known as *toli*. The previous chapter examined the sports and games of Britain's festive culture and the games brought to the North American continent by British colonists. This study would be remiss to not mention that sports and games (and people) were here when the colonists arrived.

Lacrosse stick. Image © Natalia Siverina, 2013. Used under license from Shutterstock, Inc.

Native Sports and Games

The game of **toli** was called stickball by Europeans who witnessed it, and it seemed to be an early version of lacrosse. It was an extremely physical and dangerous game that often resulted in serious injuries for not only participants but also spectators. There was not usually a uniform number of players per team, and they would range from a few dozen to a few hundred (often depending on the size of the villages involved). The object of the game was to move a small ball (*towa*) toward the opponent's goal using only their rackets (*kapoca*) to carry and throw the ball. Using one's hands was strictly forbidden. The winning team was determined when they scored a predetermined number of goals (usually 12). The game was popular with the original tribes of the American Southeast (Choctaw, Chickasaw, Creek, Cherokee, and Seminole), and some believe the game was diffused to that area from Mexico and the Southwest. Others attribute it to some of the Iroquois-speaking Cherokee of the Northeast who migrated to the Southeast. Whatever the origins, there was no question the game was very popular with native peoples by the turn of the 18th century. Although sometimes the game was played just "for the fun of it," it more often than not was taken very seriously by those involved. Matches were often scheduled by chiefs of villages "when other sources of conflict threatened to involve their respective towns in a war against each other."[1] This may explain why the participants took the games so seriously and why fights often accompanied the games—to many of the players, this *was* war.

The fights were not supposed to be part of the game, and the elders of the village would serve as mediators and would warn the participants that the game was "only a recreation and not something over which to fight."[2] That apparently did not stop the fights from occurring. Often the fights would be so serious that they would spark wars. Several intertribal wars during the 18th and 19th centuries were sparked by the game of toli. It was likely the high stakes that were wagered on the games that resulted in the serious way the game was taken. Virtually every worldly possession could and would be bet. The list included, but was not limited to: guns, knives, clothes, animals, cooking utensils, blankets, money, and whiskey. Women as well as men would take active parts in the wagering and sometimes would even *be* the wager. It was not uncommon when all else had been bet and lost that men would offer their wives and even children as stakes. One modern-day Choctaw seemed to state the obvious when he described a man who put up his family as having extra motivation and "something to play for." He also added, "I think he would have tried his best. If I had my wife and kids standing out there as my stakes, I would have played like hell."[3] Some villages lost everything; yet, in most cases, they showed incredible stoicism after the loss. After seeing a village lose "all their earthly possessions," one observer noted, "they bore their misfortune with becoming grace and philosophical indifference and appeared as gay and cheerful as if nothing had happened."[4] That "indifference" was not always evident. In one game a team was one goal away from winning when the opponent's "rainmaker" did just as his name suggests, and the resulting downpour washed out the game. Unfortunately, that was not the end of the story. The near-victorious team claimed they were the winners and attempted to recover the wagered items of the opposing team, who also claimed them, and a bloody riot ensued that lasted for hours.

The primary tool of the toli game was the racket, which somewhat resembled the modern-day lacrosse stick. It was carved from hickory and had a large loop at the end that resembled the eye of a needle. Across the hole was spread strands of leather that formed a net or pocket. The sticks were usually made in pairs so the pocket would interlock and allow the player to secure the ball and make it difficult for the player to drop it or for it to become dislodged by an opponent. The stick was extremely important to the player because the players were not allowed to touch the ball with their hands. The ball was also made of narrow strips of leather and was about the size of a golf ball. The two ends of the playing field were marked only by goalposts, and the distance between them varied largely from 100 feet to 5 miles. As for the sideline boundaries, there were none. This offered a chance for spectators to be truly involved in the game—sometimes *too* involved. A penalty could be assessed to any team in which their "fans" interfered with the game. Sometimes that interference proved costly to the spectators, as there were often serious injuries inflicted on anyone who got in the way of a speedy player either with the ball or pursuing it. It was the danger of the game not only to players but also to spectators that would lead to a decline in the popularity of the sport by the end of the 19th century and even lead some villages to ban the sport altogether. The game survived, however, and forms of it are still played by the Choctaw people today.

Although toli was an original game to the natives, other games were played that the Europeans no doubt would have recognized. Different native tribes played versions of wrestling, football, and even cudgeling (fighting with sticks played by the British). Although Indian games may have resembled those played in Europe, they were often played for different reasons. Festive culture games were usually played during religious holidays, but the games themselves did not necessarily involve religious ceremony. As Elliott Gorn and Warren Goldstein noted in their book, *A Brief His-*

tory of American Sports, the Indian games were "embedded in ritual," and the "athletic events kept them connected with their sacred beliefs, which gave meaning to the world and their place in it."[5] The games would accompany fertility ceremonies, burial rites, healing practices, and, as was discussed earlier, efforts to control the weather. The other difference was that participation in the British games was voluntary. Because of the inherent importance of the games and the fact that these ceremonies were crucial to the survival of the tribe, participation by able young men was mandatory. Every British folkway had some interaction with native peoples. From the beginning, there was an "Indian problem" in the colonies. The "problem" (from the colonists' standpoint) was that the Indians were here. Throughout the 17th century, there were armed conflicts in Virginia and New England. The Quakers of the Middle Colonies tended to treat the natives more humanely, as they were pacifists. The main thing the colonists wanted was Indian land and, with the exception of the Quakers, who in many cases paid for that land, it was generally acquired forcibly. By the dawn of the 18th century, there was not a British colony in North America that had not removed Indians, in one way or another, from its land.

Tavern Society and Games

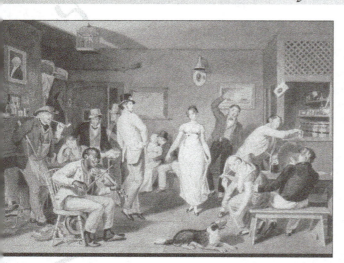

Revelers in a country tavern. © CORBIS

Another factor all the colonies shared in common was the prevalence and popularity of the **tavern**. Also called an "ordinary," "inn," and "public house" (later shortened to "pub"), it is where men went to seek shelter, company, and, probably more than anything else, drink. Taverns were centered around alcohol, and nowhere in the colonies was drinking alcohol itself thought to be a bad thing. This was, at least in part, due to health considerations. The impurity of the drinking water was a fear throughout the colonies, and that fear was dissipated when water was distilled into alcohol. Even in Puritan New England where one might think the harshest view on alcohol would be taken, it was accepted as common practice. Even those who came over on the *Mayflower* drank from kegs of beer when the pure drinking water ran out. There was so much drinking going on that the captain worried there would not be enough for the crew on the return trip. One of the first things Governor William Bradford himself wanted after landing at Plymouth Rock was "a small can of beer" because he did not feel well and believed the beer would help settle his stomach. Another settler wrote to his father back in England that one of the items he wanted was a "hogshead of malt unground for we drink nothing but water."[6] Part of the aversion to water may have actually come from the Bible and the often-quoted passage from the Apostle Paul's First Epistle to Timothy, when he said, "Drink no longer water, but use a little wine for thy stomach's sake and thine oft infirmities."[7] The key word of that passage was "little." As with nearly everything in Puritan life, moderation was key. In 1673 Increase Mather wrote a cautionary tract called "Wo to Drunkards" in which he said that "wine was from God but the drunkard is from the devil."[8] There was a line that had to be walked, and you were fine as long as you did not step over that line. Many did step over that line, however, as the amount of alcohol consumed by colonists staggers the imagination as we look back on it. Alcohol was consumed by people of all classes and ages—including children and even pregnant women. It was usually distilled at 45 percent alcohol or what is known as 90 proof. According to at least one study, by the early 18th century, the amount of hard alcohol (whiskey, rum, gin, and brandy) consumed annually in the colonies "approached four gallons a head."[9] This did not include the consumption of beer, wine, and hard cider (which was the most popular drink in the colonies).

There was a concentrated effort throughout the colonies to control public drunkenness beginning in the 17th and continuing into the 18th centuries. It apparently worked because Europeans and other foreign visitors would comment on the amazing amount of alcohol consumed but the relative lack of drunkenness witnessed. It could also be attributed to the fact that drinkers in the colonies were what in modern-day parlance would be known as having a "high tolerance level" or what was described at the time as being "seasoned."[10] One distinction between then and now might be the difference in definitions of "drunk." One definition subscribed to at the time illustrates the point, and it could be found in the following four-line poem: *"Not drunk is he who from the floor, Can rise again and still drink more, But drunk is he who prostrate lies, Without the power to drink or rise."*[11] With that definition in place, it is probably a good thing that there were no motorized vehicles at the time. Colonial legislatures passed laws throughout the colonies to address the problem with drunkenness. Most of the laws dealt with the excesses of drinking and not the act of drinking itself—that, as previously mentioned, was acceptable throughout the colonies. The only colony that contemplated outlawing the tavern altogether was Pennsylvania. In William Penn's Fundamental Constitution he said there should be "no Taverns, nor ale houses . . . nor Games as dice, Cards, Board Tables, Lotteries, Bowling greens, Horse races, Bear Baiting, bull Baiting, and such like Sports."[12] Eventually, even Penn recognized he was fighting a losing battle, and he allowed the taverns to exist but regulated them heavily. Two separate statutes were in place regarding punishable behavior: one for the patron and the other for the tavern keeper. Customers were not allowed to "swear, over drink, spread false news, or defame someone's character." The tavern keepers were required to "obtain a license, charge specific rates for food and beer, and be equipped with stable and a supply of hay for four horses."[13]

By the beginning of the 18th century, virtually every colony passed similar laws to Pennsylvania's, and it was difficult to distinguish New England from the Chesapeake (Virginia and Maryland). The difference was the enforcement of these statutes. In the South and the backcountry, they were practically ignored. In New England they were enforced with vigor. Massachusetts prosecuted the highest number of violators of both individual and tavern violations. Pennsylvania also had a high rate of prosecutions; however, they tended to concentrate more on policing the taverns themselves and overlooking individual public drunkenness. As the century progressed, prosecutions of these violations dropped across the board. Prosecutions tended to split along rural–urban lines. If the violation were to take place in an urban area, it was more likely to be pursued and prosecuted. They would also split along class and racial lines. If a tavern were to serve a lower class clientele, and especially if they served free blacks or Indians (which was expressly forbidden in statutes in every colony), the prosecution rate was much higher than if they served the "better sort."[14] By the eve of the Revolution, prosecutions in New England were down near the levels of the Chesapeake region.

William Penn feared the games that were associated with the tavern not necessarily for the games themselves but more for the gambling that they would invariably produce. Patrons of the taverns would wager on everything from board games to billiards to who would pass out first from their overindulgence. One drunk patron of a Maryland tavern named Roger Addams bet that "he could then Drink all the Wine left there in a Decanter. . . . He won the Wager; but Died a few Minutes later."[15] In some cases gambling was a requirement of the establishment. In an advertisement for a tavern in South Carolina, the *South Carolina Gazette* proclaimed that "the Billiard-tables will be continued as usual, the loser paying half a crown each game for the use of the table."[16] The mere mention of billiards in the advertisement showed the popularity of gaming in the taverns—so much so that it would be used as an enticement to draw people in. Another popular pastime in the taverns was card and dice games. Many different games were played, but the most popular seemed to be whist. Virginia took their card games seriously and even at some locations drew people in who had no intention of playing. One visitor from England noted after visiting several taverns that "even if tavern-goers wished only to drink and converse, they would find themselves involved in gambling."[17]

Larger spectator sports were also organized by and near taverns. Cockfights and horseraces were examples of these—though they were more prevalent in the South. Taverns provided a venue for those involved to toast their victories or drown their sorrows after a loss. Cockfights were such a part of life in Virginia that men would attend them for more reasons than just gambling—they would use the opportunity to conduct business or make a political deal with other men. Military training would also take place near taverns and, after the training was over, men would retire to that tavern. Often, the tavern was also the site of an impromptu spectator sport known as a fight between the patrons. Occasionally that fight could turn deadly. One example of this occurred in 1711 in a tavern in Massachusetts. The day had begun with militia training, and after moving into the tavern, Benjamin Davis and George Wortham had consumed a great amount of alcohol. Davis insulted Wortham's honor, and eventually a war of words began that escalated to Wortham raising his cane to Davis, who "struck at the cane with his sheathed sword, then drew the sword from its scabbard and cut the cane." Eventually both men stepped outside with swords drawn, and Davis "ran into Wortham's outstretched sword and died from his injuries."[18] Both of the men were very drunk at the time, as one witness pointed out that the "hard cider had been flowing for at least three hours."[19] This was the type of thing that the public drunkenness statutes were put in place to avoid. Another point that should be made about this incident is that the two men were of different social ranks. Davis was of a lower class than Wortham and was apparently frustrated by that. Taverns were often a place where the different social classes would mingle—especially when there were sports involved—but few forgot to which class they belonged. Eventually the taverns were replaced by hotels and saloons. The first hotels were built in the 1790s when the United States was just beginning. By the 19th century the taverns were a thing of the past, but the link between sports, games, alcohol, and gambling would not be broken and continues to the present day.

The Great Awakening

Benjamin Franklin. Image © Georgios Kollidas, 2013. Used under license from Shutterstock, Inc.

Taverns were not the only thing the colonies had in common by the mid-18th century. A new movement started in Europe known as the **Enlightenment** was an embrace of science and reason and a departure from religion and superstition. Some of that movement started to trickle into the colonies helped by a printer named **Benjamin Franklin**, who was the embodiment of Enlightenment thought. Franklin was not only a printer but also a scientist, inventor, and soon-to-be statesman, who would eventually be a strong advocate of American independence. Franklin's *Poor Richard's Almanac* would bring Enlightenment ideas and bits of wisdom to the colonists. The Enlightenment was good for sports and other entertainment. As the movement became more widespread, so did acceptance of various recreations. Franklin seemed to acknowledge this in 1743, when he wrote, "The first drudgery of settling new colonies is pretty well over, and there are many in every colony in circumstances which set them at ease to cultivate the finer arts and improve the common stock of knowledge."[20] Since the end of the 17th century there had been a relaxation of the strict Puritanism in New England and even a move toward the belief known as **Arminianism**. This was a change from absolute predestination (the saved were "predestined" to go to either heaven or hell even before they were born and nothing could change that), and it preached universal redemption and a savior that died for all mankind, not just the elect. The Enlightenment, and even more the reaction to it, changed that. Although the Enlightenment tended to be more of a movement among the upper class, the reaction to the Enlightenment in the colonies was much more widespread. Throughout American history whenever there has been a move toward science and technology, religious leaders have translated this into an attack on religion and God and mounted a counterattack. The first of these occurred in the 1730s, when a Puritan preacher named Jonathan Edwards began a movement known as "pietism" or, as it became more famously known, the **Great Awakening**. This was what today's society would call a "back to the bible" religious revival. Edwards represented a "New Divinity" and a "restatement of Calvinism"[21] that called for a closer relationship with God—a God that has absolute say over whether man is saved or not. The Great Awakening was not a good time for sports and games. Edwards called them "youthful frolicking" and thought they were "dreadful manifestations" and a waste of time.[22]

Although the Great Awakening began, not surprisingly, in New England (Edwards preached in Northampton, Massachusetts), it quickly spread throughout all the colonies. A big reason for this was a charismatic young contemporary of Edwards' named **George Whitefield**. Whitefield began preaching in England, but when the Anglican Church refused to allow him a pulpit, he went outside and began preaching his version of Calvinism in the open air to hundreds and eventually thousands who came to hear his emotionally charged sermons. Eventually he came to the colonies, met Edwards, and became a part of the Great Awakening. In 1739–40 he went on a tour of all 13 colonies preaching an "absolute submission of the self to a demanding and omnipotent God."[23] One of the qualities Whitefield was known for was a booming voice that could be heard for miles. When he spoke in Philadelphia, one of the citizens who attended the revival was Benjamin Franklin. Franklin heard that Whitefield had spoken to tens of thousands of people in England, but he thought that had to be an exaggeration. Being the scientist that he was, Franklin had to test his suspicion. He was very impressed with Whitefield's speaking voice and his intellectualism. While Whitefield was still talking, Franklin began to walk away from the revival. He measured how far he went before he could no longer hear the speaker distinctly, and he proved in his mind anyway that Whitefield *could* indeed be heard by over ten thousand people. Whitefield, as Edwards had, condemned the playing of games. He believed that every waking minute should be dedicated to God and that games divert one from that task. Although the Great Awakening seemed to be a reaction to the Enlightenment, its two leading crusaders, Edwards and Whitefield, paradoxically embraced many of the Enlightenment qualities, which is another reason they were different than previous preachers.

Even though the Great Awakening was present in all the colonies, it had different effects in different regions. In New England, George Whitefield had a large following, but he also had his detractors. Young followers of Whitefield and his ideas began to be known as "New Lights," and they had new ideas that many considered to be too radical. The more conservative, traditional Puritan (by this point known as "Congregationalists") and other Protestant members became known as "Old Lights." The New Lights believed in a much more emotional church service in which parishioners became involved in the ceremony. That included women for the first time, and the Old Lights could not stand that. The result was a split in most Protestant churches throughout New England and the middle colonies. Although this led to more strife in the colonies, there was at least one positive effect of the Great Awakening in the North: the establishment of various institutions of higher learning. The New Lights wanted colleges to train their preachers just as Harvard and Yale had trained the Old Lights. Colleges that would eventually be known as Brown, Dartmouth, Princeton, and Rutgers were founded by New Light churches. They would join Harvard and Yale to comprise what is known today as the Ivy League. Interestingly, it would be members of this league who would be some of the pioneers of college athletics in the next century.

CHAPTER *Two*

As far as its direct effect on sports and games, the Great Awakening was not a positive time for "idle recreation." In places like New England, where there had historically been a negative view taken of games, it was not such a radical lurch to have a dim view taken by the church. In the South, however, it made for a difficult choice for men of all social ranks. As was discussed in Chapter 1, the landed gentry of the South enjoyed their games as much as the lower classes. The Anglican Church either tolerated these games or looked the other way. But as that church began to lose its grip on Southern society during the Great Awakening of the 1730s and 40s, New Light churches took its place in many areas and had a very different view of recreation in general and games in particular. What did most men do as a result of this change? Although some may have bitten the bullet and given in to the preachers' pleadings for a "pure life" without idle moments, most of Southern society, it appears, chose to ignore the church. There is evidence that there was a bit of a downturn at midcentury in popular sports like horseracing, but by the eve of the American Revolution in the 1770s, the popularity had returned to pre-Great Awakening levels.

The cultural landscape looked fairly similar going into the Revolution in the South as it had a century before. In New England, it was much different. Although the Great Awakening had made its impact in midcentury, by the end of the century there were many examples of how much had changed since the founding of Massachusetts Bay Colony. Couples danced and kissed each other good night in public after a date, even on Saturday night when the Sabbath originally was observed to begin (sundown on Saturday). So, although the Sabbath was still important, it was shorter—beginning at sunrise on Sunday mornings. Sometimes dates would not end with just a kiss, as premarital sex became much more common. The much-maligned theater was more accepted in New England society on the eve of the Revolution. Puritans believed the theater embodied all the attributes that were evil in society: "idleness, sensuality, homosexuality, deception and civic disorder." Now those issues were not only accepted on the stage but also approaching respectability in many circles.[24] Even the way life was described in New England had changed, and it is quite telling. More often than not life in the early colonial period was described as a "pilgrimage or errand," and now it was being described as a "contest" or a "sport."[25] Yes, ballgames were being played in New England on the eve of the American Revolution. They could even be found in the village square for all to see.

One of the main problems with sports in the eyes of the early Puritans was its suspension of societal and moral rules. Games took place in their own physical space (a ball field or tennis court) with their own rules separate from society's rules and often at odds with them. Games allowed for violence, cutthroat competition, and deception (even outright lying) and in many cases "mocked the community and its moral standards."[26] What was more was that Puritan leaders believed the playing of games gave the participants a license to behave in such a manner because, after all, they were only playing. There was also the fear that the behavior would carry over into everyday life—and it often did. Probably the biggest objection Puritan New England had with sports and games was that the individual games had their own rituals that, at least momentarily, replaced the rituals of the church. Unlike the Choctaw game of toli that incorporated religious rituals of the community in the game, most games played in the colonies were strictly separated from any religious ceremony. Due to many reasons—not the least of which was the lessening of the grip the Puritan Church had over the colony (it had diluted into other various Protestant sects)—sports and games became much more acceptable in New England society by the eve of the American Revolution. The Great Awakening had not eliminated sports from the colonial scene—it would be the Revolution itself that would have more success in suppressing idle recreation.

Sports and Games during the American Revolution

"Games played with the ball and others of that nature, are too violent for the body and stamp no character on the mind," so wrote founding father Thomas Jefferson to his nephew advising him against the evils of idle recreation. Although Jefferson was a member of Virginia's landed gentry, he did not participate in the games of the elite—in fact, he blamed the gentry of England for the downfall of the young American "gentleman." Jefferson wrote that if the young American "goes to England he learns drinking, horse racing and boxing" and "he is led, by the strongest of human passions, into a spirit of human intrigue . . . or a passion for whores, destructive of his health, and in both cases learns to consider fidelity to the marriage bed as an ungentlemanly practice." Jefferson went so far as to believe that following in the footsteps of British culture would lead to the ruin of the American cause even before it had begun. He thought that the decadent monarchies of Europe were self-destructing and would cause a similar result in the colonies if they were to pursue the same decadence. When he penned the document that declared American independence from England, he was championing a cause that would become the fighting force of the American Revolution—that cause was **Republicanism**. This was the idea that the new nation that would emerge after the war would be very different than any European nation at the time—it would be a Republic that would give the power to its citizenry, not a hereditary monarchy. To accomplish this, that citizenry would have to be virtuous, abstain from luxury, and be frugal and hard-working. Idle recreation had no place in this society.

Thomas Jefferson. Image © Stocksnapper, 2013. Used under license from Shutterstock, Inc.

Jefferson was not the only one who believed this—many of the founding fathers echoed his sentiments. The first time all the colonies came together in one representative body was in 1774 as members of the First Continental Congress. The colonies were deciding on how to respond to their recent treatment at the hands of England. With all the issues swirling around the colonies, including the possibility of impending hostilities with mother country, the Congress actually took the time to debate the merits of certain entertainments. In a proclamation issued by the Congress, they advised the colonies to "discourage every Species of Extravagance and Dissipation, especially all horse racing, and all kinds of Gaming, Cock Fighting, Exhibitions of Shows, Plays, and other expensive Diversions and Entertainments . . ."[27] Historian Foster Dulles noted in his book, *America Learns to Play*, there must have been an extremely wide popularity of these "expensive diversions" to warrant a resolution such as this. Dulles also questioned the motives behind the resolution. Was it an "expression of popular discontent with an extravagant way of life which contrasted too sharply with the simple, frugal, hardworking life of the colonial yeomanry?" There was also the possibility the representatives from New England and their Puritan background were aiming this resolution at the "frivolity of the rich planters of the South."[28] Whatever the motives, the results of the order were real. The radical vigilante group known as the Sons of Liberty took it upon themselves to enforce the proclamation and banned, for example, all horseracing in the colonies. The horseracing industry took a severe hit during the Revolution and did not recover until well into the 19th century.

After the outbreak of hostilities in 1775, one of those "rich planters of the South" was put in command of the newly formed Continental Army. George Washington represented the landed gentry that had been schizophrenic about sports and games since the Great Awakening of the mid-century. Washington claimed he abhorred gambling, but he often participated in it and even recorded his wins and losses. In May of 1772, for example, he gambled 12 times. He won on four of

George Washington. Image © Victorian Traditions, 2013. Used under license from Shutterstock, Inc.

those occasions and lost on eight. The following month he gambled on six occasions and lost on five of them. From that point on his notations on gambling became more infrequent, perhaps because he realized he was losing more and gambled less frequently or possibly because he continued to lose and did not want to record it. He did record that he gambled at the First Continental Congress, "walking away with seven pounds."[29] Washington believed his men needed diversions during the war and allowed them to "play games of exercise for amusement." Some of the games played were bowling, wicket (a form of cricket), shinny (field hockey), base (a form of baseball), and football.[30] He did, however, ban all dice and card playing and any gambling in general. Although he instructed his subordinates to enforce this ban, it was probably the most disobeyed order in the war. When men get together to play games, there *will* be gambling, and to allow the first but ban the second was a failure from the outset. Whether Washington deep down really wanted that order enforced, given his proclivity to participate in both, is unclear, but it was not a charge that was brought against soldiers very often.

When the Revolutionary War began, and even as it continued, not everyone in the colonies was united in the effort against Great Britain. John Adams famously surmised that colonists were split into thirds. One-third were Patriots (in favor of the break with England) another third were Loyalists (loyal to the British crown), and the other third either were ambivalent about the whole thing or willing to back whichever cause benefited them at the time. The same can be said for the different regions in their feelings on sports and entertainment during the Revolution. Although some sanctioned recreation, most (at least officially) backed the Continental Congress's earlier proclamation, and some colonies even got into the act themselves. In March of 1779, the Pennsylvania Assembly enacted "An Act for the Suppression of Vice and Immorality." This act banned work and play on Sundays along with "cock-fighting, horse racing, shooting matches, and any form of gambling."[31] The South Carolina Assembly went so far as to not only ban gambling but to actually void all gambling debts. It made a provision for the recovery of "money or goods lost by playing cards, dice, bowls, tennis, betting, shuffleboard, billiards, skittles and ninepins."[32] An interesting conflict between the President of the Continental Congress Henry Laurens and one of his constituents in 1779 is quite illustrative of the two sides of the "idle amusements" question. Laurens was a conservative congressman from South Carolina who was urged by a liberal attorney named William Henry Drayton to celebrate the third anniversary of the Declaration of Independence with an "elaborate display of fireworks." Although Laurens described this as "a funny declamation," he was not amused when Drayton compared the celebration of America's Independence Day to that of the Olympic Games celebrating the birth of Ancient Greece. Laurens responded that "the Olympic games of Greece and other fooleries brought on the desolation of Greece." Drayton retorted that the games "were calculated for improving bodily strength, to make men athletic and robust." Although Laurens did not respond to Drayton directly on that, he did note in his diary a rhetorical question: "Is drinking Madeira Wine from 5 to 9 o'clock, then sallying out to gaze at fireworks, and afterwards returning to wine again, calculated to make men athletic and robust?"[33] Laurens would be amazed, and perhaps upset, to know that the Olympics and sports in general have not led to a "desolation" of the country and that the celebration of America's Independence Day over two centuries later continues to follow Drayton's "funny declamation" and include massive displays of fireworks from sea to shining sea.

Sports in the Early Republic and the Victorian 19th Century

Even though games and contests had been "officially" outlawed during the Revolution, that did not mean they disappeared from the American culture. Quite to the contrary, some regions never saw a drop-off in these amusements. One area in particular that always marched to its own drumbeat was the western Backcountry. Games of skill and chance were always a part of that culture, and no proclamation or law would change that. Those contests were often viewed as a rite of passage for the males in the Backcountry and a way to test their manhood. There was no more a prime example of that test than that of marksmanship with a rifle. As Foster Dulles wrote in his book, *America Learns to Play*, "pride in marksmanship made shooting matches of all kind even more popular than they had been in the colonies. They were an institution along the entire border at the close of the Revolution, and they followed the frontier westward."[34] Dulles noted that, unlike the colonial period, the custom of marksmanship contests had changed from live animal targets to targets posted on trees. Usually each entrant would supply his own target and 25 cents per shot. The bull's-eye would often have a nail in the center, and an impartial board of judges would determine the winner by who hit the most bull's-eyes or, even more amazingly, who drove their nail in the farthest. The winner would either take home a side of beef or, as one famous inhabitant of the Backcountry noted, an adult beverage. Davy Crockett later remembered that he "never bet anything beyond a quart of whisky upon a rifle shot—which I considered a legal bet, and a gentlemanly and rational amusement."[35]

A quart of "whisky" was also the prize in a more dangerous form of target-shooting. Although animals were rarely used by the early 19th century, sometimes a man was. In a contest called "shooting the tin cup," a cup was placed on the head of an individual, and the participants would, as the name implies, literally shoot the cup off the target's head at thirty paces. The game was not only dangerous to the target for obvious reasons, but sometimes it could be equally hazardous to the contestant. The legendary Mike Fink, Ohio keel-boat man, who was often the subject of tall tales, was a renowned champion of this game. As one might imagine, alcohol was not only the prize but also an active ingredient in this contest. Fink was supposed to have never missed his target until one occasion when "corned too heavy . . . he elevated too low"[36] and shot a long-time friend named Carpenter through the head. Another of Carpenter's friends supposedly picked up Carpenter's pistol and avenged his death by killing Fink. As with most stories about Fink, it is difficult to know what to believe. Another story has Fink and Carpenter quarrelling over a woman before the shooting took place. Perhaps Fink did not miss his intended target during his final contest.

Davy Crockett was not the only politician who hailed from the frontier and was involved in Backcountry contests. Andrew Jackson, who would become seventh president of the United States in 1829, was called "the most roaring, rollicking, game-cocking, horse-racing, card-playing, mischievous fellow, that ever lived in Salisbury (NC)."[37] It is telling to note that Jackson used this image in his rise to power in both the military and Tennessee politics, but once he began his quest for the White House, he hid from it, as he was trying to overcome the charge that he was a "border ruffian" from the frontier and not sophisticated enough for the highest office in the land. Another frontier-born politician who would rise to that office during the century was Abraham Lincoln. Lincoln was legendary in frontier Illinois for his weight-lifting and wrestling. He was well known for his strength and was said to have been able to pick

Davy Crockett. Image courtesy of Library of Congress

Abraham Lincoln the rail splitter. Image courtesy of Library of Congress

up a full barrel of whisky and drink from it. His friends in the town of New Salem would always pit him against any challengers in a wrestling match. He rarely disappointed them, but one time he was wrestling a local champion, and after a long battle he recognized that neither could defeat the other: "Jack, let's quit," Lincoln finally determined. "I can't throw you—you can't throw me."[38] It was that ability to recognize a no-win situation that would serve him well in his political career.

The opening of the frontier was a major component of the 19th century. The other big story was the industrialization and urbanization that led to the rise of the cities. At the beginning of the century, 1 person in 100 lived in urban areas—by 1860, that number had increased to 1 in 12. The overall population of the country also jumped dramatically during the same time period—from 5.3 million in 1800 to 33.4 million by 1860.[39] That rise can be credited not only to natural increase but also to a tremendous increase in immigration during the period. Most of those immigrants settled in the large cities, and it was in these cities, due in large part to the influence of those same immigrants, that modern sports were born.

The Rise of the American City and Its Effect on Sports

The rapid industrialization of the United States in the first half of the 19th century would lead to just as rapid an increase in urbanization. Early factories needed water for power, so they had to be located near rivers. The workforce was smaller, so they usually employed excess farm laborers. Because of that, large population centers were unnecessary. As the factories grew and the method of power changed to steam and eventually coal, rivers were no longer needed, but larger workforces were, so factories moved to the cities. Industrialization was thereby both a cause and effect of the increase in size and development of the American city. Old colonial cities grew bigger, and new cities emerged. By 1850, the nation's largest city, New York, boasted a population of over 500,000. Philadelphia's population reached 300,000, and six other cities topped the 100,000 mark. Steven Riess, in his book, *City Games*, divides the development of the American city into three periods. The first was 1820–1870, which he describes as the emergence of the "**walking city**," in which settled areas were no more than two miles from the center of town, and the pedestrian was the "principle method of locomotion."[40] Although it was during the colonial era where sports promotion in the urban centers began—primarily by publicans (owners of taverns)—Riess argues it was post-1820 in the walking cities when larger populations provided "a greater pool of potential spectators and athletes, which encouraged profit-minded entrepreneurs to establish sports businesses to cater to sportsmen."[41] There was also the reaction to the cities themselves that would lead to a rise in sports. The negative parts of urbanization—overcrowding, crime, disease—would give rise to what Riess calls a "**positive sports ideology**."[42] Good, clean sports could serve as an alternative to those undesirable elements of the city and serve to "promote morality, build character, enhance public health, and serve as a substitute for the lost world of small-town America and its values."[43]

The Resurgence of Horseracing

To describe horseracing as a "good, clean sport" is undoubtedly inaccurate, but there is no arguing that the sport made a major comeback in the early republic after being banned during the Revolution. As early as the 1790s, the sport was elevated beyond the popularity it had enjoyed before the Revolution. But it was the 1820s that saw it emerge as a major urban spectator sport. On May 27,

1823, at newly built Union Race Course in Jamaica, Long Island, an estimated 75,000 people packed around the mile-long track to see the fastest thoroughbred from the South, Sir Henry, race the northern champion, Eclipse. Another factor contributing to the rise of urban sports in the 19th century was the proliferation of communication and media. Newspaper advertising was seen as the prime reason for the incredible turnout for this race. It was the papers that dubbed it the "**Race of the Century**." The growing rift between North and South also played a key role in the popularity of the matchup. The incredible amount of $20,000 was put up as stakes by both sides, and it is estimated that $250,000 was wagered on the race. Those who put their money on Eclipse walked away happy that day, and many Northerners saw this victory as proof that the North was superior to the South in every way. One spectator described the event as more than just a race when he said, "In all the papers, and in every man's mouth, were the questions, 'Are you for North or the South?' 'The Free or the Slave States?' 'The Whites or the Blacks?'"[44]

One individual who definitely walked away happy that day was **John Cox Stevens**. Stevens was a wealthy heir to a steamboat fortune who wagered a small fortune on Eclipse, and if one is to believe an apocryphal story, he and his brother also "took their watches from their pockets and diamond breastpins from their bosoms, and bet them on the result."[45] Stevens won enough from the race that he bought both horses, Eclipse for $10,000 and Sir Henry for $3,000, and put them out to stud at his Hoboken, New Jersey, stables. By the 1820s, Stevens was widely known as the premier horseman of the North. Racing was making a major comeback in society, and this was due in part to the industry making attempts to "clean up its act." In an attempt to improve its image, "turf enthusiasts," as they were known (like Stevens), barred professional gamblers from attending races whenever they could. Some made the argument that racing thoroughbreds enabled the horses to perform other kinds of work—a very questionable argument indeed. These and other arguments must have worked because after the banning of racing by most states during and immediately following the Revolution, virtually all states allowed racing by the 1820s and even formed their own jockey clubs. Stevens served as either the president or vice-president of the New York Jockey Club for 22 consecutive years. What also made him a successful patron of racing was knowing when to get out of the game. He sold his stables just prior to the Panic of 1837. The ensuing economic recession practically killed the sport.

Stevens then turned to other kinds of racing. He renovated part of his family's estate in Hoboken into a park that became known as the **Elysian Fields**. The fields had many uses over the years including playing fields for both the St. George Cricket Club and New York Athletic Club. Always a fan of boat racing, in 1844 he started the New York Yacht Club and built a beautiful clubhouse on the Elysian Fields in which balls and dinners would be held. The New York Yacht Club was designed more than anything else to separate the upper crust of New York society from the lower classes. It also served to unite not just the American upper class but the upper class of Great Britain as well. In 1851, Stevens had a special boat built with the idea of challenging British yachts. It was called the *America*, and in its first race, it easily defeated 18 British boats it raced against. By 1857 a cup was presented to the New York Yacht Club that would be raced for between American and foreign yachts. It would eventually be known as the **America's Cup**, and the cup came to be dominated by American yachts until recently. Stevens could also be credited with the rise of another kind of race—human racing. In 1835 Stevens offered anyone a share in a purse of $1,000 if they could run 10 miles in under an hour. If only one runner did it, he would win not only the thousand

View of Hudson River from Elysian Fields in Hoboken, N.J. © CORBIS

Churchill Downs. Image © Joseph Hardy, 2013. Used under license from Shutterstock, Inc.

dollars but also an additional bonus of $300. At the same track that had hosted the "Race of the Century" 12 years earlier, Union Race Track, an estimated 20,000 fans showed up to what was billed "The Great Race." Nine contestants participated from all over the world, and at the halfway mark, five of them were on pace to finish in under an hour; but a local boy, Henry Stannard from Connecticut, was the only participant who finished in under an hour. He did it in exciting fashion by breaking the hour mark by only 12 seconds. The crowd of 35,000 was delighted that an American defeated the rest of the world's (presumably) fastest, and the *New York Times* reported that Stannard "had exhibited genuine Yankee agility and bottom."[46] The race kicked off a movement that became known as **pedestrianism**. Unfortunately for Americans, many of the ensuing races would be won by foreign-born athletes. Pedestrian racing would continue to be popular up to and following the Civil War. In the 1860s and '70s there were long-distance races known as "go-as-you-please" races in which contestants known as "peds" would cover as many miles as they could in a set time, usually on an indoor track. Because of his involvement in so many forms of popular racing, it can be said of John Cox Stevens that, at his death in 1857, he was the premier Antebellum (pre–Civil War) sports promoter in the country.

After the Civil War, horseracing would again rise from near death to reach heights it had never before seen. Due in large measure to Stevens's successor, Leonard W. Jerome, the sport would be rejuvenated and enjoy what many have referred to as its "golden era." Jerome was a Wall Street investor who had made his fortune selling short in the country's second major economic panic in 1857. Jerome was a flamboyant playboy who liked to throw some of New York's most lavish parties, attend the theater and opera, and engage in various love affairs. He was one of a group of new millionaires in the 1860s known as New York's "parvenu," who decided to revive the struggling race industry. In 1866, Jerome and two of his friends, William Travers and August Belmont, founded the American Jockey Club and purchased 200 acres in Westchester County to build the nation's finest race track, which they named Jerome Park. As was done in the Antebellum era to try to improve the image of racing, Jerome Park discouraged professional gamblers and also did not allow alcohol to be sold. Jerome also changed the old system of racing long, three- to four-mile races to a shorter, dash system. This put more of an emphasis on speed over stamina and allowed for more races to be held per day. Jerome Park set the standard, and others quickly followed. The decade of the 1870s saw other cities follow Jerome's lead and build racetracks, including Monmouth Park in New Jersey, Pimlico in Baltimore, and Churchill Downs in Louisville. Annual stakes races would also contribute to the popularity of racing, including the earliest of the current **Triple Crown** races, which was named for August Belmont. The Belmont Stakes would be run at Jerome Park from 1867 until 1890. The Preakness Stakes would begin at Pimlico in 1873 and the youngest of the three, The Kentucky Derby, would begin at Churchill Downs in 1875. Although the Jerome name would fade from racing, his most famous contribution to the world stage would probably be his grandson. It is rumored that Jerome's daughter met Sir Randolph Churchill at Jerome Park. Their marriage produced one of the great leaders of the 20th century, Winston Churchill.

Technology and Media

It is difficult to discuss the 19th century without mentioning the technological advances that would make it much easier to communicate with one another and also to move from one place to another. At the beginning of the century, if you wanted to attend a horse race, you essentially had two choices: walk or be transported by horse. By 1815 the steamboat was being used on rivers and lakes throughout the West. In some places the steamboats would not only carry passengers to sporting events such as racing and boxing matches, but they themselves would also sometimes be participants. Steamboat racing was a common and very dangerous practice. When the engines got overheated, they tended to explode, killing passengers as well as crew. By the middle of the century, the train was replacing the steamer as the primary means of transportation throughout Antebellum America. For the obvious reason of not needing a body of water to use, the train was nearly everywhere by the eve of the Civil War. After the war, the transcontinental railroad connected the entire nation from sea to shining sea. In 1830 it took nearly two weeks to travel from New York to Detroit. By the 1850s a train could carry passengers that same distance overnight. Without the railroad, it would have been impossible for sporting competition between cities to occur. The development of the National League of baseball in 1876 (see Chapter 3) would simply not have

Transcontinental railroad celebration. © Bettmann/CORBIS

worked with a team as far west as St. Louis being included without train transportation. Major League Baseball continued to use the train as its primary mode of transportation until the mid-20th century, when air travel and the expansion to the West Coast demanded a change. As early as 1842 an estimated 30,000 people boarded the Long Island Railroad, which took them to Union Race Track to witness a thoroughbred named Fashion run. The railroad also changed the way Americans viewed time. Prior to the railroad, time was measured in an imprecise way based on the position of the sun. Because train scheduling demanded much more precision, watchmaking became a much more mass-produced industry. Eventually, by the late 19th century, the schedules of the railroad would lead to the demarcation of the country into time zones.

Newspapers would be the primary way the country communicated on a mass level in the 19th century. In the 1830s there was a new way to send information almost instantly. Much as the development of the Internet has changed communication in the early 21st century, the telegraph changed communication in its day. Although the technology of sending messages with electronic pulses had been developed in Europe earlier in the century, it was Samuel Morse who patented his machine and his code alphabet signals in 1837 and sent the first message in the United States on January 8, 1838, along two miles of cable in New Jersey. This technology would have an immeasurable effect on all communication, but it would revolutionize how the outcomes of sporting events could be recorded. The telegraph would wire scores and stories to newspapers, which would be able to announce to their readers the scores as early as the following morning. The development of the telegraph, along with rising literacy rates and the emergence of a cheap process of printing in the 1830s, led to higher circulation numbers for these new dailies. Because these new papers only cost a penny, they were dubbed the "penny press," and they covered the seedy side of the news that the more respectable newspapers of the day ignored. Today they would be referred to as "scandal sheets" or "tabloids," as they would sensationalize stories about crime, gossip, and forms of entertainment. As they are in today's world, they were very popular at the time. Sports would tend to be covered more so in a publication like the *New York Herald,* which would qualify as a "penny press" paper, than in the *New York Times,* which was a more "respectable" publication. As the popularity of sports grew in the second half of the century, even the more respectable papers began to devote more coverage to sports. It was the tremendous competition between the various newspapers in New York City in the 1880s and 1890s that produced the first consistent sports pages. It was known as the era of "yellow journalism," when the respectable papers began to look more like the tabloid papers of the penny press, as the fight for readers did not always produce the most factual stories. It was not until well into the 20th century that most newspapers throughout the country began to run a separate sports page.

Second Great Awakening

In the early 19th century there was another religious revival movement similar to the Great Awakening of the previous century. This movement seemed to last longer—spanning much of the first half of the century. It is often referred to as the **Second Great Awakening**. Between 1800 and 1860 the number of evangelical Protestant churches grew twice as fast as the population. The leading evangelical denominations were the Methodists and Baptists, and their membership far surpassed the dominant colonial denominations, the Anglicans and Puritans (referred to as Episcopalians and Congregationalists after the Revolution). The Second Great Awakening was not only a longer-lasting movement than its predecessor, but it also seemed to have more depth and stridency. To show how the cultural landscape had shifted by the 19th century, the Puritans were considered a "moderate" denomination.[47] Whereas the Puritans had condoned drinking in moderation and some forms of lottery games, the 19th-century Evangelicals believed all gambling and drinking to be "utterly sinful."[48] As with the first Great Awakening, the second was not a good time for sports, but the later Evangelicals went even further. They not only condemned obvious sports the church always had problems with, like horseracing, cockfighting, and bear-baiting, but also seemingly innocent pastimes like boating, fishing, checkers, chess, croquet, and even storytelling. Whereas the first Great Awakening was more of a rural phenomenon, the second was both rural and urban. The Evangelicals not only controlled the pulpits of the nation but many of the public schools, magazines, and newspapers as well, so their influence was much more widespread in the 19th century. A Congregationalist magazine called *The New Englander* announced in 1851: "Remember that we were sent into the world, not for sport or amusement, but for labor; not to enjoy and please ourselves, but to serve and glorify God, and be useful to our fellow man. . . . The Christian fathers have a tradition that John the Baptist, when a boy—being requested by some other boys to join them in play—replied, 'I came into this world not for sport.'"[49]

Not everyone during this period was antisports. Dr. John Jeffries was a medical doctor turned theologian who told Christians in the 1830s that they needed to take greater care of their "mortal frame" through exercise and "wholesome games." Jeffries linked a healthy body with a healthy mind and believed them to be inseparable: "There must be peace and calmness in the soul, for the Spirit of God to dwell in the affections of the heart; and will more perfectly exist, with clearness of intellect and corporal strength."[50] Jeffries seemed to be a lone voice crying in the wilderness at the time, but he would be joined later in the century by others who believed Americans (especially males) were getting soft and falling behind the rest of the world in terms of physical strength. One American writer noted, "National pride was wounded when foreign critics referred to the underdeveloped physiques, wan complexions, and premature aging of Americans. Classicists and romanticists alike were inspired by the Greek Revolution; and ancient history was featured in the curriculum, which reminded the young of the gymnasiums of Athens and the vigor of Sparta."[51] To combat this image, a movement beginning in the 1850s known as **muscular Christianity** stressed a balance of physical and spiritual exercise. The leader of the American movement was Thomas Wentworth Higginson, who also brought up the classic Greek model of this balance: "Physical health," he said, was "a necessary component of all permanent success."[52]

Whereas the muscular Christianity movement would arrive decades later, for most of the 1830s there was a man in the White House who subscribed to its ideals. Andrew Jackson was a rough-and-tumble backcountry politician who not only condoned sports and games but was also an active participant in them for most of his life. He owned his own racing horses, took part in many wrestling and shooting matches during his youth, and even participated in several duels. He carried in his body at least one souvenir from one of the duels: a bullet was lodged too dangerously close to his heart to be removed. Jackson was no backwoods bumpkin, however—he was a master politician. He knew the tenor of the times, and it is curious to note that during his presidency his involvement in sports or gambling was either downplayed or stopped altogether. In fact, his campaign for the presidency in 1828 accused incumbent President John Quincy Adams of having brought a billiard table into the White House for the purpose of gambling games. Now coming from Jackson, a man who no doubt had participated in his share of billiard games for money, this must have seemed ironic. Because of the political traditions of the day, however, it was never a direct accusation from Jackson himself against Adams, only Jackson surrogates. It was these campaign workers who no doubt recognized how damaging the accusations would be at the height of the Second Great Awakening. Another reason that sports may have been downplayed during the Jackson administration is that Jackson himself inaugurated a brand new sport: politics. The election of 1828 marked the first election in which over half the states in the union allowed the average citizen to vote for president. The 1824 election was the first in which the popular vote was counted, and 356,000 votes were tabulated. In 1828 there were over 1.2 million due to more states counting the popular vote and also many states dropping property requirements for voting. Jackson represented the "everyman," and now the "everyman" was having his say and enjoying it. The 1828 election also marked the first time there were mass campaign rallies, slogans, and parades—prior to that, they weren't necessary because the only votes that counted were those amassed by the elite Electoral College. As John Lucas and Ronald Smith noted in their book, *Saga of American Sport*, politics in the 1830s was "a main source of interest and entertainment, a national sport."[53]

Andrew Jackson. Image © pandapaw, 2013. Used under license from Shutterstock, Inc.

Victorianism

The combination of men involved in politics, the Industrial Revolution, and the Second Great Awakening led to the perfect storm of a brand new phenomenon: a middle class. Although the middle class emerged early in the century, it was not until the ascension to the British throne of Queen Victoria in 1837 that it had a name: **Middle Class Victorianism**. This was the belief that there was a commonality between the middle classes of the rapidly industrializing Western world. They were linked by a common set of values, most notably, Evangelical Protestantism, hard work, and self-restraint in nearly all things. The period was named for the leader who presided over the country where the Industrial Revolution began. Queen Victoria would rule for the remainder of the century until her death in 1901, which was the longest reign in British history until Queen Elizabeth II broke her record in 2015, so the Victorian period (although its hold over American culture would weaken by the end of the century) was an extensive one. Because sports were seen as the antithesis of hard work and self-restraint, they were frowned on by the Victorians. Impulsive behavior was feared by the new middle class; sports fit into that category and were thereby condemned. The Americans were seemingly better Victorians than the British.

It was the impulsiveness of sports that Victorians worried would lead to drinking, gambling, and other behavior that would steer men away from the hard work and moral self-restraint that was the bedrock of society. It is important to note that it was really the men in society that were more susceptible to this temptation. During the Victorian period, there was a rigid division of the sexes into **separate spheres**. The male arena was known as the public sphere, and it included business and politics, and it was the duty of the female to provide a refuge for the male in the home—the private sphere. Women were the moral arbiters of the home by nurturing their children and keeping their husbands from succumbing to their impulsive tendencies. Although those impulsive tendencies included sports, that did not mean that there were no leisure activities engaged in by the middle class. The Victorians believed endeavors participated in that refreshed the mind and body for more serious activities were permissible as long as they were limited to the private sphere so the chances of the rowdy actions that they abhorred could be avoided. Things like reading newspapers and books and playing musical instruments or even some forms of exercise were deemed appropriate. These activities were known as **rational recreation**. Only sports that were seen as "noncompetitive" were allowed. Similar to the Puritans' "lawful sport," Victorians believed rational recreation could strengthen both their minds and bodies for more serious things like work.

Slowly, the Victorian view toward sports began to change as the century wore on. As the muscular Christianity movement gained momentum in the 1850s and the intensity of the Second Great Awakening began to abate after the Civil War, increasingly Victorians began to see athletics as a way to toughen up the boys. There was a belief as the century neared its end that Americans in general, and boys in particular, were becoming soft and even effeminate. Physical contests were beginning to be seen as a way to combat this problem as long as the contests were conducted under the umbrella of amateurism and the conditions under which they competed were very controlled. Even the violent sport of football began to be seen as a way for boys and even young men on college campuses to let out the primal aggressiveness that all males have in a way that will be beneficial to them and society. It would keep them out of trouble, and even some Victorians began to argue what many had argued for years, that sports could actually foster good values like personal responsibility, reliability, and character.

Victorian Counterculture

Some not only argued this for years but also wanted no part of the restrictiveness of Victorian culture. They kept on with their traditional ways and put a much higher value on their leisure time than their work time. This group is often referred to as the **oppositional** or **counterculture**. The industrial economy changed the workplace during the early 18th century. Early in American history it was artisans who fashioned consumer goods from scratch. When the product was finished, whether it was a piece of furniture or an article of clothing, the maker could take pride in the fact that they did it all themselves. The emerging factory would employ what would become known as the assembly line system in which each worker would fashion only a small part of the finished product, thereby lessening the pride taken in one's work. It also tended to be more tedious work, so the average worker would seek their sensual gratification and spontaneity elsewhere—usually with fellow workers after hours at a saloon or billiard hall. The working class made up a portion of Victorian counterculture, but another group that could be considered a member came from the other end of the spectrum. The upper class had always enjoyed their recreations, and the Victorian period was no exception. The landed gentry discussed earlier had always emulated their British counterparts, and although the American middle class seemed to have greater influence over the entire society than those in England, the upper classes were at least somewhat successful in preserving their traditions. Foxhunting and horseracing continued, but they also often joined the lower classes in some of their pastimes in what was often referred to as "slumming."[54]

Some of the these "slum" sports had been around for centuries and were earlier referred to as blood sports like bear- and bull-baiting, cockfighting, and ganderpulling, but there were other popular ones by midcentury. Prizefights, dogfights, and rat-baiting could be seen everywhere around the country. Usually it was the local saloonkeeper who would host such events (the saloon being the descendent of the earlier tavern), but eventually entire venues would be dedicated to the low sports. Probably the most famous of these by midcentury was Kit Burns' Sportsman Hall in New York City. The hall had a 400-seat amphitheater in which patrons could observe a fight between two men, two women (there is evidence of a small group of women being involved in the counterculture), or a pit full of rats trying to escape a dog who is trying to kill them. Because there was no escape for these rats, the dog would eventually kill all of them, and people would bet on how long it took him to achieve this. Although saloons and billiard halls were popular places for the counterculture to meet, another was **volunteer fire departments**. Nearly every town had one, and many had multiple companies, so there would be a competition to see who could put the fire out first. The men would get from these associations what they were not getting from their jobs— a sense of comradeship, pride, and self-esteem. Then, after the fire was safely subdued, they would often do what the Victorians worried about the most—drink and gamble. Making a wager was something else that gave members of the counterculture a sense of self-worth. It was not merely a chance to make some easy money, but it was a chance to prove your knowledge about something that you believed you were an expert on. Those chances had vanished in the workplace for most. The Victorians and especially evangelicals condemned gambling and believed it to be against God, but many counterculture members actually believed a successful bet could prove one's positive standing with the Almighty. A wager on a local boy could show solidarity with the hometown or, even more important in the mid-19th century, loyalty to your country of origin.

Horse-drawn fire engine. Image © YANGCHAO, 2013. Used under license from Shutterstock, Inc.

The steady influx of immigrants during the Victorian period added to the counterculture ranks. Most who arrived brought with them attitudes that the Victorian middle class would find counterproductive. They had a more laid-back approach to punctuality and work in general. They attempted to keep the holidays of the old country and also wanted the privilege of drinking alcohol on the job. When they were not allowed these things, they found solace in the enclaves of the counterculture. While there, they would notice the most of their comrades were not married. Bachelors made up the vast majority of the counterculture. In 1850 nearly 40 percent of men between 25 and 35 were unmarried, which is a much higher number than today. Once a man got married, he usually "graduated" into respectable Victorian society. That was not always the case, however. Irish immigrants were especially known for staying in the "bachelor subculture" even after they were no longer bachelors. Male Irish culture placed a high premium on its relationship with other males. They would be taught to drink, fight, and other important aspects of what it took to "be a man." That culture was difficult to leave even after acquiring a wife and family. Fighting was not only prized by the Irish but also by men in the South and West. Eighteenth-century philosopher Ralph Waldo Emerson pointed out that the Northerner asked what a man "can do" while the Southerner asked, "How does he fight?"[55] A good example of this was young Abraham Lincoln, who grew up on the edges of the American frontier and enjoyed, as a friend remembered from his single days, "out door recreations and sports and excelled at them." Apparently he engaged in "jumping, running, hopping, pitching quoits, swimming and shooting." Another friend summed up the time as when "a higher value is set upon physical than mental endowments."[56] By all accounts, Lincoln gave up the bachelor subculture when he married Mary Todd in 1842.

CHAPTER *Two*

Many of the counterculture began to break off into even more specific subcultures, and they were often devotees of specific sports and games. Calling themselves "fancies" for their fancying of the particular sport they liked, historians refer to them as **sporting fraternities**. They followed, promoted, and participated in their favorite sport such as horseracing or boxing and the associated gambling and drinking that went with them. As with other fraternities, there was a shared language, values, and "surrogate brotherhood."[57] They would also arrange **sporting spectacles**, which would feature their favorite sports and their most talented participants. The British were the first to do this, so the Americans followed the examples they set. For instance, the horseracing fraternity followed the English rules of Newmarket, prizefights would follow the rules established in London, and most wagering was based on the British method of betting. Most sports equipment used in the United States was made in England, and the early sports media was based in Great Britain. When there was talk of sports fraternities in the United States, it was almost always compared with those in England. It was comparable to a younger brother comparing his exploits to an older brother and always trying to live up to him. Eventually a fraternity would emerge that would take great pride in *not* being compared to British sports—early on, that fraternity would be referred to as baseball.

Conclusion

Throughout the 18th century there were attempts to curtail the growing popularity of sports, games, and other recreations. First there was the widespread religious revival of the Great Awakening in midcentury and then there was the American Revolution later in the century. Although both led to a slowdown or even stoppage of some sports, neither accomplished the end of "idle amusements" as its leaders would have hoped. Indeed, as early as the first decade of the new Republic in the 1790s, there was evidence that the popularity of sports and games and everything that went along with them were approaching and surpassing earlier levels of popularity and that would extend into the new century. It would be a new movement known as Victorianism that would emerge as the next threat to American sport in the mid-19th century. Although that movement would prove to be a strong adversary, athletics had gained enough momentum and become such a part of the culture that a United States without them seemed difficult to imagine.

Many factors conspired to end America's love affair with sports during the 19th century, but they were all ultimately unsuccessful. The Evangelical Protestants of the Second Great Awakening did their best to curtail or even abolish all sorts of entertainment and recreation, but they could not. The Victorians did their best to permeate all American culture and exert their values of hard work and self-restraint throughout society. These values had no room for the spontaneity and impulsiveness associated with sports. Many Americans were craving that spontaneity and impulsiveness. The century saw great changes in the economy, technology, and transportation. There was a massive movement to the cities from the country and from other countries. Instead of hurting the spread of sports throughout society they each, in their own way, served as a positive force for the emerging sports world. Nothing fostered this positive force more than the Victorian counterculture and its sporting fraternities. In most cases, these fraternities made no effort to be accepted in the wider Victorian culture. They were happy just to be an entity unto themselves, and if their sport became more popular, that was a bonus. There would be one fraternity that would be billed by its followers as the one truly American sport—they would actively court respectable Victorian society, though rarely be accepted by it. In the next chapter we examine the baseball fraternity.

Notes

1. Kendall Blanchard, *The Mississippi Choctaws at Play: The Serious Side of Leisure* (Urbana: University of Illinois Press, 1981), 28–29.
2. Ibid., 49.
3. Ibid., 39.
4. Ibid., 40.
5. Elliott Gorn and Warren Goldstein, *A Brief History of American Sports* (Urbana: University of Illinois Press, 1993), 5.
6. Bruce Daniels, *Puritans at Play* (New York: St. Martin's Press, 1995), 142.
7. Sharon Salinger, *Taverns and Drinking in Early America* (Baltimore: Johns Hopkins University Press, 2002), 3.
8. Ibid., 1.
9. Ibid., 2.
10. Ibid., 3.
11. Ibid., 86.
12. Ibid., 115.
13. Ibid., 115–116.
14. Ibid., 149.
15. Ibid., 73.
16. Ibid., 71.
17. Ibid., 72.
18. Ibid., 74–75.
19. Ibid., 75.
20. John Lucas and Ronald Smith, *Saga of American Sport* (Philadelphia: Lea and Febiger, 1978), 42.
21. Ibid., 40.
22. Ibid.
23. Benjamin Rader, *American Sports; From the Age of Folk Games to the Age of Televised Sports*, 6th ed. (Upper Saddle River, NJ: Pearson-Prentice Hall, 2009), 15.
24. Daniels, *Puritans at Play*, 218.
25. Ibid.
26. Ibid., 217.
27. Foster Dulles, *America Learns to Play; A History of Popular Recreation, 1607–1940* (Gloucester, MA: Appleton-Century-Crofts, 1963), 65.
28. Ibid., 65–66.
29. Ron Chernow, *Washington: A Life* (New York: Penguin Press, 2010), 134.
30. Rader, *American Sports*, 17.
31. Lucas and Smith, *Saga of American Sport*, 52.
32. Ibid.
33. Ibid., 53.
34. Foster Rhea Dulles, *America Learns to Play* (Gloucester, MA: D. Appleton Co., 1940), 71.
35. Ibid., 72.
36. Ibid.
37. Ibid., 75.
38. Ibid., 73.
39. Murray R. Nelson, *Encyclopedia of Sports in America* (Westport, CT: Greenwood Press, 2009), 14–15.
40. Steven A. Riess, *City Games; The Evolution of American Urban Society and the Rise of Sports* (Urbana: University of Illinois Press, 1989), 2.
41. Ibid.
42. Ibid., 3.
43. Ibid.
44. John Lucas and Ronald Smith, *Saga of American Sport* (Philadelphia: Lee and Febiger, 1978), 66.
45. Benjamin Rader, *American Sports; From the Age of Folk Games to the Age of Televised Sports*, 6th ed. (Upper Saddle River, NJ: Pearson-Prentice Hall, 2009), 38.
46. Lucas and Smith, *Saga of American Sport*, 84.

47. Rader, *American Sports*, 24.
48. Elliott Gorn and Warren Goldstein, *A Brief History of American Sports* (Urbana: University of Illinois Press, 2004), 59.
49. Ibid., 60.
50. Lucas and Smith, *Saga of American Sport*, 84.
51. Ibid., 85.
52. Rader, *American Sports*, 26.
53. Lucas and Smith, *Saga of American Sport*, 84.
54. Ibid., 27
55. Kenneth J. Winkle, *The Young Eagle; The Rise of Abraham Lincoln* (Dallas, TX: Taylor Trade Publishing, 2001), 65.
56. Ibid., 64.
57. Rader, *American Sports*, 33.

CHAPTER
Three

Base Ball

Albert G. Spalding.
George Grantham Bain
Collection (Library of
Congress).

It was the summer of 1839, and West Point Military Academy student Abner Doubleday was in Cooperstown, New York, laying out a diamond-shaped field in a cow pasture and formulating rules for a brand new game, which he developed and named "base ball." He invented the player's positions, put together the rules of the game and regulations for the playing field, and for the first time got them all down on paper. Doubleday was hailed as the "father" of the American pastime for a good portion of the 20th century. Major League Baseball's Hall of Fame was dedicated in Cooperstown in 1939, marking the century anniversary of Doubleday's "invention," and a field in Cooperstown that was named for him hosted the Hall of Fame Game every summer from 1940 to 2008. The problem is that no evidence supports that what was just described ever occurred.

At the turn of the 20th century, sporting goods magnate and former star pitcher for the Chicago White Stockings, **Albert G. Spalding** wanted to prove that baseball was truly an American sport. In 1888 he had sponsored an around-the-world tour promoting baseball as well as Spalding sporting goods. When the tour returned home the following year, a dinner was held in New York to honor the players. Former National League President **Abraham Mills** served as master of ceremonies before a star-studded crowd that included Theodore Roosevelt and Mark Twain. The dinner served not only as a testimonial for the players but also as a rally for the pro-American argument in baseball. Many believed that the game evolved from the British game of rounders. Those attending the dinner that night wanted nothing of that argument, as they broke out with chants of "No rounders! No rounders!" The argument continued into the new century, when British immigrant **Henry Chadwick** wrote an article in 1903 linking baseball not only to rounders but also to cricket. Spalding published an article disputing the claim and calling on Chadwick to appoint a committee to find the true origins of the game. Chadwick agreed, and a committee led by Mills was appointed in 1905. The **Mills Commission** ended up taking the testimony of one individual, Abner Graves, who recounted the story of Abner Doubleday. Graves had been a resident of Cooperstown in 1839, but he was only five years old, and his story was full of inconsistencies, not the least of which was the fact that Abner Doubleday had never once mentioned baseball. Graves's credibility was also questionable due to the fact he had murdered his wife and been committed to an institution for the criminally insane.

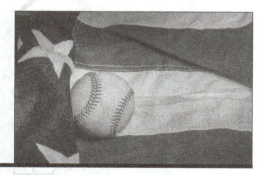

Baseball synonamous with America.
Image © Steve Collender, 2013. Used under license from
Shutterstock, Inc.

Doubleday was a military hero who had led the defense of Fort Sumter in the opening days of the Civil War and also distinguished himself at Gettysburg. After the Civil War he was involved in the Indian wars in the West and retired as a Lt. Colonel. Having an American war hero as the inventor of the American game was something that appealed to Spalding and his hand-picked commission (no one was allowed on the commission who believed in a British link to baseball), so the lone letter written by Graves was accepted as gospel, even though, as Mills noted later, no conclusive proof of the Doubleday story existed. Chadwick disputed the findings of the commission, but his argument seemed to fall on deaf ears, as the Doubleday myth was born and took hold. Even after the myth was exposed around the middle of the 20th century, that did not stop people from believing it. A line at the end of the movie, *The Man Who Shot Liberty Valance*, goes, "When the legend becomes fact, print the legend." In other words, when a myth is ingrained into a culture, it becomes difficult to dislodge it because most people don't want to. Even as late as 2010, the commissioner of baseball, Bud Selig, went on record as saying he believed that Doubleday invented the game. Americans love to have simple beginnings and endings, but in the case of baseball, the facts are much more complicated.

Abner Doubleday. Image courtesy of Library of Congress

Origins of the Game

In truth, the game of baseball evolved from many different origins. This is a fact that many Americans find distasteful because, as Tristram Potter Coffin acknowledged in his book, *The Old Ball Game*, "there is no excitement in evolution, and even less in the idea that America's national game is rooted in English antecedents."[1] There is no doubt of the direct line that can be drawn to both English games of rounders and cricket as Henry Chadwick had asserted. Albert Spalding, although opposing Chadwick on this point, respected Chadwick for his contribution to and knowledge of the game. In 1905 he asked Chadwick to put together a history of the sport, and although it was not finished (or possibly barely begun) on Chadwick's death in 1908, Spalding finished the book and published it under the title of *America's National Game* in 1911. Although he may have used much of Chadwick's research and writings, the book has Spalding's stamp all over it. The opening chapter is almost entirely a defense of his opinion that baseball was an American invention. He does offer a comparison of cricket and baseball (the use of bat and ball, innings, and other similarities), but he announces that where "Cricket is a gentile pastime . . . Base Ball is War!"[2] He then alludes to the just recently published Mills Commission report by "proving" his assertion that baseball is indeed a war because its "founder" was a major general in the American army (Abner Doubleday).[3] It is interesting to note that Spalding never once mentions the game rounders in his book, even though there are obvious similarities. Rounders was played on a diamond-shaped field with four "stones" or "posts" placed 12 to 20 yards apart. A "pecker" or "feeder" would toss the ball to a "striker" and upon hitting the ball would run to the posts in a clockwise fashion. "Outs" made would be made when a striker swung and missed three times, his ball was caught, or he was "struck by a thrown ball while trying to negotiate the bases."[4] The only difference between the rules of rounders and early baseball was that runners in baseball as early as 1839 ran the bases counterclockwise.

Perhaps Spalding refused to offer the comparison because whereas cricket was a game played by gentlemen (fostering a legitimate comparison in Spalding's eyes), rounders was merely a game played by British children. If baseball was going to evolve from any children's game, Spalding believed, it would be a game played by American children. Although he acknowledged that ball games had been played by children from time immemorial, Spalding mentioned in his work that Egyptian artists as long as four thousand years ago carved the images of people throwing and catching a ball. He mentioned the ancient Greeks, Chinese, and early Europeans playing ball—but it was strictly the early American game of "**barn ball**" that started it all. Spalding contended that a boy bouncing a ball to himself or playing catch with a friend were the natural first two steps of any ball game, but it was the "third stage" of the evolution that included a barn that would lead directly to baseball. A boy would bounce the ball off the barn, and his friend would try to strike it with an axe handle or some other stick. If the striker hit it the boy who threw the ball would try to field it and throw it at the striker before he ran and touched the barn and made it back to his spot before he was able to "count one." If he was hit before accomplishing this goal, the striker would then be out. Another way to record an out is if the striker missed the ball and the other boy caught it. The problem with the game was that a barn was not always available. The fourth stage of development included one more boy in place of the barn. Two bases were involved, and the feeder (pitcher) would throw the ball from one base to the catcher behind the other base with the striker (hitter) standing between them attempting to hit the pitched ball. All the rules of barn ball would apply, but instead of running to the barn and back, the hitter would run to the pitcher's base and back to his to score before he was thrown out. This game became known as "**one-old-cat.**" The derivation of the name is unknown, but it is possible it comes from a contraction of the words "one hole cata-pult," which was a game that sometimes used a catapult to sling the ball instead of a bat. When more people and bases were added, the game expanded to "two-, three-, and four-old cat." In all these games, only the hitter would earn a score, and the person with the most "tallies" or bases at the end of the game would be declared the victor. The more participants who played, the more cumbersome the game became, and eventually "four-old-cat" merged into something called "**town ball.**" Although every town developed its own rules for the game, some common features included the four-base square field, and instead of four pitchers to four different hitters, there would be one pitcher in the middle of the field throwing the ball to one hitter at a time, and participants divided into two teams. The teams tallied scores as a whole instead of individually. The old-cat games were played by children well into the 20th century and beyond when there were not enough participants to play a full game of baseball.

There are many examples of town ball and its variations being played throughout the colonial period and during the Revolution. The earliest known image of baseball in the media was an illus-tration showing three individuals dressed in colonial garb complete with tri-cornered hats standing by three posts printed in a children's publication called "A Little Pretty Handbook" titled "Base-Ball" from 1744.[5] Although it was printed in the London edition, it is unclear if the game was tak-ing place in the new or old world. Another variation of the game was known as stool ball. In this game, a batter stood before a target, usually an upturned stool, and his/her goal was to protect that target. If the pitched ball hit the legs of the stool, the batter was out. The legend goes that it was originally played by milkmaids after their job was done and to pass the time while they waited for the men to return from the fields. It is believed stool ball was more a forerunner for cricket than baseball. It was very popular with Dutch settlers in early New York. Harold Seymour believes the first ever recorded game of baseball may have taken place during the Revolutionary War. After the difficult winter at Valley Forge, American soldier George Ewing recorded in his diary that he par-ticipated in a game of "Base" on April 7, 1778. A Princeton student recorded in his diary in 1786 that he played a game called "Baste Ball."[6] If Albert Spalding wanted to prove baseball was *truly* an American game, perhaps he should have looked at native sports. Several Indian games played were with a ball and a stick, but the one that probably most resembled baseball was called "**shinny.**" One witness described a game seen in 1837, two years prior to Doubleday's supposed invention of the game of baseball. The witness recounted a "striker" using a hickory club to hit the ball with a "vigorous blow" to "an amazing height." When the ball came down, it was caught by another player, who would attempt to hit the striker, who had now dropped his club and was heading for a pile of stones "with a swiftness scarcely surpassed by the winds." If the runner reached the stones before being hit by the ball, he was "safe." If he was hit, he would "resign his club to the fortunate thrower of the ball against him, and take his place to catch." The object of the game was to maneuver safely to all the piles of stones assembled in a circular pattern. The games would go on for hours and in some cases days: "When the darkness of night had invaded the scene, and they could no longer discern the ball, they would drop asleep in the very spot where they had stood . . . and at the earliest gray of dawn, some arose, and immediately making the welkin ring with their shouts, thus awakened the others, and at it again they all went. . . until night again temporarily stopped the sport."[7]

The Base Ball Fraternity

As noted in the previous chapter, sporting fraternities began to emerge in the middle part of the century, and the most popular of all of them would be the baseball fraternity. The first of note was organized by New York bank clerk and volunteer firefighter **Alexander Cartwright** in 1845. Cartwright and his friends had been meeting informally as a social club and as a sidelight to play baseball near their meeting place at the corner of 27th Street and 4th Avenue in Manhattan. In 1845 he decided to make it more official and form the **Knickerbocker Base Ball Club** and secure permanent playing fields across the Hudson River at John Cox Stevens's Elysian Fields in Hoboken. The Knickerbockers seemed more interested in socializing than perfecting the craft of the game. To become a member, it was more important for one to be a gentleman than it was for one to be a good player. That was quite evident on June 19, 1846, when the Knickerbockers played in what is often billed as the first ever organized game at the Elysian Fields. A plaque remains there today commemorating the event and disputing the Abner Doubleday story. Unfortunately for the Knickerbockers, their opponents that day (The New York Base Ball Club) were more concerned with ability than the Knickerbockers were. At the time the rules stated that the first team to score 21 runs (or what they called "aces") won the game, regardless what inning it was, and the Knickerbockers were outscored that day 23–1 in four innings.

The 21-ace rule was not the only difference fans of the modern game would notice with the Knickerbocker rule book. The biggest difference was how the pitcher delivered the ball to the hitter. Instead of throwing as hard as he could to try and get it past the hitter, the pitcher would actually toss it underhand from a distance of 45 feet and get it as close to the plate as possible to try to give the hitter the best chance to hit the ball. It resembled more a modern-day slow-pitch softball delivery. Fielders (who wore no gloves at the time) would attempt to catch the ball in the air or on the first bounce, which were both considered outs. Although there were umpires, at first they were not involved in making decisions unless the captains could not agree on a call. The umpires wore top hats and tails and sat at a table along the first base line. After all, players were gentlemen, and they were expected to always be honest. Umpires became more and more involved as the game became more competitive later in the century. Initially in most town ball games, fielders were allowed to throw at the runners to try to hit or "soak" them for an out. Because of the obvious danger

An early baseball match at the Elysian Fields. Image courtesy of Library of Congress

posed to players by this rule, the Knickerbockers outlawed soaking (it was also referred to as "plugging") and adopted the rule of throwing to the base ahead of him or "tagging" him by touching him with the ball. This became one of the key differences between the Knickerbocker style, which became known as the New York game, and its chief rival, the New England or Massachusetts game.

Although there were some obvious differences from the modern game, there were also some core similarities, which remain part of the game today. It is believed that Cartwright laid out the bases 90 feet apart. When a batter swung and missed three times, he was deemed out, and three outs were allowed per team per inning. Each team had an equal chance at scoring (top and bottom of an inning). In town ball there were an indiscriminate number of players per team, but the Knickerbockers settled on nine players per side who batted in a set rotation (order). Each one of the players covered a position in the field, and at first there were four outfielders (again similar to softball). In 1849 it was decided to move one of the fielders to the infield and create the position of shortstop to have an equal number and space between the infielders (two on either side of the pitcher).

Membership in the Knickerbocker club was select, and those who were members were not only considered to be gentlemen, but also part of an emerging class of workers who were increasingly dissatisfied with their jobs in the industrial economy. Most of these workers were no longer appreciated for their craft so they were looking for a place where they could be. Frank Pidgeon, captain of another New York club, summed up the motivations of many of his fellow club members when he said, "We would forget business . . . go out into the green fields . . . and go at it with a perfect rush. At such times, we were boys again."[8] Only 40 men were allowed to be members of the Knickerbocker club at one time, and it would seem that the membership list did not change very often, as there were only "fifty-odd names on their roster from 1845 to 1860."[9] As with all clubs there were bylaws for the members, and if these laws were not adhered to, members could be expelled. One way to lose membership was to join another club—another way was to be blackballed. This was a particularly harsh way to sever ties with a member, as it allowed for a person to be removed from the roster on the basis of one or two votes for no more reason than personal dislike or prejudice against that member. Because it was a secret ballot, the offending member had no way of facing his accuser(s). He did, however, have the right to appeal within 30 days.

The discipline committee also had lesser penalties than expulsion to choose from for more minor offenses. Monetary fines were the most common of these penalties, just as they are today—the amounts were a bit different, though. For refusing to obey an order from his captain, a player would be fined 50 cents. For disputing an umpire's call, or "even expressing an opinion on a play before his verdict," the fine was 25 cents.[10] If it was determined a captain neglected his duty in any way, he would be fined the lofty sum of one dollar. It is believed the first-ever baseball fine was handed down to Knickerbocker J. W. Davis during that first game in 1846, when he was docked six cents for swearing. It is interesting to note how light the fine was for using "improper language," and although there were campaigns to "purify" the sport throughout the remainder of the century, it was a ruling by a judge in 1899 that seemed to give the baseball player the right to use whatever language he deemed necessary for the occasion. New York Giants Owner John T. Brush had launched a "purity campaign" in an attempt to rid the sport of language he found offensive. The case actually went to court, and it was determined that "a club was unjustified in suspending a player for using opprobrious language, because he was entitled to summon up stronger words than ordinarily used by the average citizen."[11] Thus, bad language was not only allowed in baseball but it actually had the endorsement of the courts (which seemingly has not changed over the last century of the game).

The Knickerbockers were the trailblazers when it came to the baseball fraternity, and although many clubs eventually followed them, it was not until 1852 when the Gothams formally organized that was there true outside competition. If the Knickerbockers had really wanted that competition to arrive, they certainly would have pressed for others to follow their lead, but they seemed perfectly content to play on an intramural basis for the six years that followed their embarrassing first game in 1846. As a matter of fact, the Knickerbockers did everything they could to stem the tide of the growth of the fraternity. The main concern of the pioneering club was that the ensuing clubs would not be of their social standing. They would be of a lower working class and not gentlemen like themselves. The first way they tried to control this was by controlling who they played and where. Three of the first four clubs on the scene by 1854 played at the Elysian Fields in Hoboken (Knickerbockers, Eagles, and Empires), and the Knickerbockers announced they would only play against those two teams. As the number of teams and venues grew, so did the number of games, and the control the Knickerbockers once had over the fraternity began to wane. In the summer of 1856, 53 games were scheduled between the 15 teams in the New York area. By the following season there were roughly two-dozen teams, and in 1858 there were as many as 50 teams operating in and around the city. What's more, junior teams were sprouting up as well. These teams served as "feeder" teams for the senior teams (much like current farm clubs do for major league teams). It is believed there were as many as 60 of these teams operating at the same time.[12] The year 1858 was also an important one in the evolution of the game because there was a challenge by the Brooklyn clubs to the New York clubs that they would defeat them in an all-star game. The challenge was accepted, and the Fashion Race Course was chosen because of its size (they expected large crowds and got them) and neutral location. The New York all-stars took two out of three games to win the series and bragging rights over Brooklyn. What was historic about the event was that the 1,500 spectators that attended to see the series were charged an admission price of 50 cents to cover the cost of preparing and maintaining the grounds for the games. This is believed to be the first time anyone was charged to watch a baseball game.

The preceding year was also important, as for the first time a convention was called to discuss the future of the game. In one of the last gasps of the dying pioneer club, the Knickerbockers called together representatives from 25 New York clubs, and in May of 1857, the convention was called to order. Not much was accomplished in that first convention, save for one important change to the rules. From that point on, the winner of games would not be the team to score 21 aces (runs), but the team that was leading after the completion of nine innings. It was also agreed a second convention would be held the following year. The second convention, although again called by the Knickerbockers, opened on March 10, 1858, with no representatives from that club present. Although the club would continue to play games over the next decade, they were never a serious player in the fraternity. The 1858 convention formed the **National Association of Base Ball Players**, which was the first organization of its kind that bound the players together. The convention also codified rules that would be used universally throughout New York and eventually the rest of the country. The biggest competitor to the New York game was the Massachusetts game, played by at least 10 teams in and around Boston by this time. The major differences in the rules played in Massachusetts included playing with a smaller ball, allowing the "soaking" of players, teams playing with 10 to 14 per side, and teams needing 100 runs to win. The beginning of the end of the Massachusetts game can probably be credited to Edward Saltzman, who had originally played for the New York Gothams, but when he moved to New England in 1857, he introduced the New York game to his workmates. When they formed a new club, the Tri-Mountains, they refused to play the traditional Massachusetts game, and eventually the other clubs followed their lead. The Massachusetts game was essentially dead by the early 1860s.

The New York game not only invaded New England by the late 1850s, but it also spread to points south and west. By the end of the 1850s, the game had spread south to the nation's capital, where the Potomac Club was formed in 1859, and shortly after that they had a rival, the Nationals, who were made up mainly of government clerks. The Nationals practiced and played their games on the backyard of the White House. Clubs were also formed in Detroit, Cleveland, and western territories such as Minnesota. Two former members of the Knickerbockers, brothers James and William Shepard, introduced the game to San Franciscans, who welcomed them because they came "direct from the center of the base ball universe."[13] The game probably could have taken hold much earlier in California because Knickerbocker founder Alexander Cartwright had left New York for the California Gold Rush in 1849, but he did not stay there long enough to establish much of anything. He ended up in the Hawaiian Islands by 1850, where he did introduce baseball to the natives and set up the first baseball field there. Cartwright became the fire chief of Honolulu and continued to encourage the growth of the game there until his death in 1892.

The New York game spawned a number of publications devoted to baseball; probably the most widely read sheet was the **New York Clipper**. The *Clipper* began publication in 1853 and covered not only baseball but other sports and entertainment as well. It should be given its due credit for helping the rise of the game in its formative years. The *Clipper* followed all the emerging New York clubs during the 1850s and reported the scores of the games and news from the teams. Some of the newspapers would also provide direct help in organizing clubs around the city. The more the game grew, the better it was for the newspaper business. In 1855, it was the *Clipper* and other baseball publications that began to refer to baseball as the "national game." The fraternity also referred to themselves in this way. Although regular daily newspapers rarely devoted much attention to baseball (or any sports) in the early years, it was the *New York Mercury* that, on December 5, 1856, first referred to it as the "national pastime."[14] This was a moniker that would stay with baseball for years, but it was hardly true at the time. For anything to be described as "national" during the decade that the country was falling apart was ludicrous. People wanted something to cling to that would not split them apart and, for many, baseball fit that bill. The 1860 election was the last before the outbreak of Civil War a few months later. Currier and Ives were famous lithographers at the time, and they printed an editorial cartoon describing the results of the election in baseball terms. There were four major candidates in the election, and they were all depicted holding bats, but only the winner, Abraham Lincoln, was standing on home plate. The cartoon was titled, "The National Game. Three 'Outs' and One 'Run.'" To show how the game had grown in such a short time, had the cartoon been used after the previous election, historian Jules Tygiel noted, "most Americans would have found this metaphor undecipherable."[15]

The Civil War and "Father Baseball"

The one part of the Abner Doubleday story that was true was that he was at Fort Sumter in Charleston Harbor on April 12, 1861, when it was fired on by Confederate troops. As a matter of fact, Captain Doubleday was second in command under Major Robert Anderson, and he aimed the cannon to return fire, so it can be correctly stated that he was part of the opening volley that started the war. The effect the four-year bloodbath would have on the fledgling game of baseball was probably the farthest thing from his mind because it has never been proven that Doubleday ever picked up a bat or threw a ball. Without a doubt, everything else took a backseat to the war from 1861 to 1865 but to say the war hurt the game would not be correct. In fact, the war could be credited with spreading the game and indeed making it more of a national game. Soldiers played the game throughout the war and taught it to those who did not know it. A remembrance from a soldier named Nicholas Young illustrates this point: "In my native town in New York State the modern game of Base Ball had not been introduced prior to the breaking out of the Civil War . . . (in 1863) a Base Ball team was organized in the Twenty-Seventh New York Regiment, so we turned our attention to Base Ball, and kept it up as we had the chance until the close of the war."[16] Young went on to become the president of the National League at the end of the century. Another future president of the National League, Abraham Mills, recalled participating in a baseball game on

Christmas Day 1862 during a ceasefire at Hilton Head, South Carolina. He estimated 40,000 soldiers attended the game that day. If that was the case, it would have been the largest crowd to ever witness a game to that point. The games were played by northern and southern soldiers alike, and rumors said that games were even played between Union and Confederate soldiers during ceasefires in the war. When the war began the National Association of Base Ball Players had 62 member teams, and nearly all were from New York and the surrounding area. In 1865 the number from New York dropped to 28, but the overall number of teams climbed to 91 representing 10 states. The following year saw an even larger increase to over 200 teams in 17 states and the District of Columbia. The Civil War, it would seem, not only restored the American Union but it also made baseball what it had claimed to be prior to the war—the national pastime.

What the war did hurt was the old baseball fraternity. No longer was the game played by gentlemen who cared more about companionship and social class than winning. It was becoming a much more competitive game postwar. It was not only getting away from the "gentlemanly" aspect of the game, but the idea of amateurism associated with baseball was also fading away. Some players by the late 1860s were actually being paid to play a boys' game. Along with this came the obligatory drinking and gambling element, which made Victorian society, who already had a natural distaste for baseball, look down their noses at it even more. A reporter for the *New York Clipper* understood that to truly reach a widespread Victorian audience, baseball would have to clean up its act and its image. Henry Chadwick launched a campaign to not only rid the game of its more unseemly elements but also to change rules to make it, in his words, more "manly" and "scientific." Chadwick believed the two biggest obstacles standing in the way of the success of ballplayers were "wine and women," and he proposed clubs have "prohibition planks" in players' contracts to keep them away from alcohol and brothels. Chadwick's brother Edwin was a reformer back in their native England, and he once joked, "While I have been trying to clean up London, my brother has been keeping up the family reputation by trying to clean up your sports."[17]

It is not surprising that Henry Chadwick was looking to make the game more "scientific" because, like most reformers of the day, he believed in the importance of science and statistical research. Whether one was involved in the Temperance movement (anti-alcohol), antislavery societies, or prison reform, all used statistical research to bolster their arguments. With the rise of the new market economy and more widespread education, more people were familiar with mathematics and numbers. Chadwick wanted to introduce statistics into the game and did so in a number of ways. The *New York Tribune* had published a detailed account of the scoring in the New York–Brooklyn All-Star series in 1858 (which Chadwick may have had a role in), but it was Chadwick himself who recorded the first published **box score** the following year. Box scores were not a novelty, as they had been used for the game of cricket, but Chadwick changed them by including runs and hits as opposed to cricket's runs and outs. He also included for the first time a line score which showed the scoring inning by inning. A 21st-century baseball fan would recognize that first box score, as it has not changed much in a century and a half. Chadwick also invented a scoring system adopted by baseball in 1864 that would use the shorthand system of one letter to represent "the movement to be described." Chadwick called this his "mnemonics plan" and the letter would be "prominent letter of the word . . . so far as remembering the word was concerned."[18] For example, the "k" in the word strike was the most prominent as was "f" in fly out so they were used in this system. Each position had a letter also, but eventually numbers replaced them, and the only remaining letters from the original system are the "k" for strikeout and "f" for fly out. So if a player flew out to right field, the scorer would simply write "F-9" to describe the put out.

Chadwick's greatest contribution to the game was an ingenious way to compare all hitters down through history: the **batting average**. This was the statistical way to show a hitter's prowess. To compute the average, one simply divided hits by the number of times at bat, and the resulting percentage was his batting average. Prior to this, the number of times a player scored was viewed as the important way to measure their value, but Chadwick rightly contended that put too much emphasis on the hitters behind you in the lineup and whether they batted you in or not. So the batting average became the accepted batting measurement and was adopted officially in 1865 and widely used by the late 1860s. This explains the "scientific" part of the Chadwick model, but what about the "manly" element? It was not what you may think—in fact, the two elements were actually almost synonymous in his mind. To be a true 19th-century man in Chadwick's eyes, one must think scientifically. Brute force, for example, was not manly to Chadwick. He was not a fan of the home run and railed against it his whole career. It flew in the face of scientific thought, control, and placement of the ball by a hitter. He called it "the easiest hit . . . which the veriest novice at bat can make," and besides it took away "all the attractive features of sharp in-fielding and active base running."[19] There was an original Knickerbocker rule that Chadwick thought was unmanly and fought hard to get abolished: the ability to get a batter out by catching the ball on the bounce. Chadwick thought this childish that a fielder could take a good hit away from a batter simply by nonchalantly reaching out and catching it after a high bounce. It took almost 20 years, but eventually the rule was changed in 1863 so that a ball must be caught on the fly to be recorded as an out. Another problem for Chadwick was how to categorize a base earned on balls. Many argued it should be considered a hit, but Chadwick thought it was more a case of error on the part of the pitcher than good discipline being shown by the batter. Chadwick won out, and the base on balls was not considered a hit. In 1887 baseball decided to experiment with counting it as a hit again, but when gaudy batting averages resulted, including a .492 average, the experiment ended, and baseball went back to Chadwick's way. It has remained the same ever since. Chadwick seemed to be right when it came to his ideas for the game, and he had such an influence on the game that he became known as "Father Baseball." He remained very much involved in the game for the remainder of the century and was editor of the *Spalding Guide to Baseball* when he died in 1908 at the age of 83.

The Beginning of Professional Baseball

Red Stockings stamp. Image ©
Charles Chen Art, 2013. Used under license
from Shutterstock, Inc.

Although many players were being paid in baseball during the 1860s, the first announced all-paid team was the **Cincinnati Red Stockings** in 1869. Young attorney Aaron B. Champion thought putting together a baseball team would be a good way to advertise his city and help local businesses. He made this argument to Cincinnati businessmen, who bought stock in the team at such a rate that Champion was able to lure the best players in the east to come to Cincinnati to play. Led by a former professional cricket player named **Harry Wright**, who would be the player–manager of the club, the Red Stockings amassed an incredible record of 57 wins, zero losses, and one tie in their inaugural season of 1869. Cincinnati businessmen were extremely pleased, as one exulted after the season: "Glory, they've advertised the city—advertised us, sir, and helped our business."[20] What they also advertised was how to put together a professional team, and cities all over the country began to follow their lead as the decade of the 1870s dawned. The first was Chicago, who organized in a very similar way to Cincinnati, even down to the name, the White Stockings. Unfortunately for the Red Stockings, their second season in 1870 proved to be their last. The Red Stockings went to Brooklyn to play the Atlantics in June of 1870, and the game proved to be memorable for two reasons. The two teams were tied at the end of nine innings and although the Atlantics packed up their gear and

**Harry Wright after his
playing days.** Image
courtesy of Library of Congress

were content with a draw, Harry Wright demanded the game continue. The captains agreed they would abide by "Father Baseball" Henry Chadwick's decision. Chadwick, who happened to be attending the game, announced the game would go on. Unfortunately for Wright and the Red Stockings, the first extra-inning game in baseball history was also historic because it was their first loss, as the Atlantics won 8–7 in 11 innings. After losing their first game (and five more for a final record of 67–6–1), attendance began to dwindle, and investors pulled out as they were realizing that the Red Stockings may have been good advertising, they were not profitable. To be fair, it was not just the Red Stockings; very few early professional baseball clubs made money. For his part, Harry Wright moved back east and took some of his Cincinnati comrades with him to Boston, where they were the foundation of a new club. Wright took not only some of the players but also the name, as they were now the Boston Red Stockings. There were enough teams by 1871 to form the first ever professional baseball organization, the **National Association of Professional Base Ball Players**. Adding the one word "professional" before "Base Ball" marked the symbolic death of the baseball fraternity and birth of the professional game. After losing the first championship to the Philadelphia Athletics in 1871, Wright and his Red Stockings dominated the next four seasons, winning the championship in each.

In 1875, the new president of the Chicago White Stockings, **William Hulbert**, decided to raid the Red Stockings' lineup and sign four of their best players, including star pitcher Albert Spalding, for the 1876 season. Spalding later remembered that after four straight pennants in Boston, "it was becoming monotonous," and attendance was beginning to decline because, as Spalding recalled hearing fans say, "there's no use going . . . Boston's sure to win."[21] Spalding was a shrewd enough student of the game to recognize that monopolization of winning by one team was not good for the overall health of the game. That did not mean that Boston fans were happy to see Chicago pick off four of their best players. When the "secret deal" was leaked to the press before the end of the 1875 season, Spalding and the others were forced to admit it, and they were savaged in the press and on the streets of Boston. Spalding remembered they were dubbed the "Big Four" and, much like one member of the "Big 3" of a different sport and time—LeBron James, who left the NBA's Cleveland Cavaliers to go to the Miami Heat in 2010—the locals "caricatured, ridiculed, and even accused (them) of treason."[22] The one difference between the two transactions was that James made his move between seasons—the "Big Four" had to finish out the 1875 season amid these taunts and accusations. It did not seem to diminish their play, as Boston once again won the championship in 1875. There were rumblings during the offseason that at the March 1876 meeting of the National Association, the "Big Four" and two players Hulbert also picked up from the Philadelphia Athletics would be expelled from the league. Hulbert decided to preempt this move by forming his own Association during the winter. He secured agreements of seven other clubs (Boston, Cincinnati, Hartford, Louisville, New York, Philadelphia, and St. Louis), and the **National League of Professional Base Ball Clubs** was born.

The National League's official title substituted the word *clubs* for *players*, and that was no accident. Hulbert, who had never played the game himself, forbade any teams from entering the association who were owned by the players. The other two restrictions of joining the league were a minimum population of 75,000 and approval of the existing teams. Hulbert also sought to rid the sport of its vices—particularly gambling and drinking. He appealed to the Victorians by banning the sale of alcohol at games as well as Sunday play. Ever since William Cammeyer had enclosed his baseball field in Brooklyn in 1862 with a fence and charged admission for those who wanted to watch, the practice of charging spectators at baseball games was commonplace. In what became known as the "enclosure movement," fields all over the country built similar fences to keep the nonpaying public out. Henry Chadwick went so far as to call Cammeyer's innovation the beginning of professional baseball. In 1876 Cammeyer was president of the Brooklyn Mutuals, who voted not only to enter the National League as a charter member but also to fix the rate of admission to games at 50 cents. Although Hulbert was not the first president of the National League (he thought that honor should go to someone from the east as an honor to where the game began—Morgan Bulkeley, president of the Hartford team was named), he did take over the presidency after the first season and held that position until his untimely death in 1882. Although his leadership was strong, it was often controversial. He had no problem kicking players out of the league for what he considered to be bad behavior. Sometimes he would do the same for entire teams, as he did with Cincinnati for selling beer at their games and playing on Sunday. Although he had his detractors, others lauded him for his abilities, including Albert Spalding, who eulogized him as "the man who saved the game."[23]

Although it may be debatable whether he saved the game, there is no doubt his actions taken against Cincinnati would have an immediate effect on it. Cincinnati joined with five other clubs in 1881 to form a rival league called the American Association. It was better known as the "**Beer and Whiskey League**," not only because they agreed to serve alcohol at their games but also because investors in four of the six clubs were also investors in breweries. The new league tried to appeal to lower classes by only charging 25 cents and allowing Sunday games. The American Association also encouraged National League players to jump their contracts and change leagues, which many did. By 1882, with Hulbert dead and the National League leaderless, they sued for peace and entered into an agreement with the new league. The leagues agreed to respect the contracts of the various teams and to play in a championship series at the conclusion of the season. The American Association would prove to be a worthy rival to the National League, and one team in particular, the St. Louis Brown Stockings (managed by Charles Comiskey, who would later own the Chicago White Stockings), won four consecutive American Association pennants from 1885 to 1888 and defeated the National League White Stockings in 1886 for the unofficial "World Championship."

The decade of the 1880s also witnessed the birth of the baseball star. The Chicago White Stockings boasted the first of these. Although Albert Spalding had retired from playing to manage the team by the 1880s, another player who had been brought over to Chicago by William Hulbert in 1876 was just reaching his zenith as a player during the early 1880s. **Adrian C. "Cap" Anson** played first base for Chicago and for 22 seasons he was one of the best hitters in the league. He only failed to achieve a batting average of .300 twice during his career and finished with a career average of .333 and 3,418 hits. His teammate during the early years of the decade emerged as an even more popular player—**Michael "King" Kelly**. Kelly may not have had the average that Anson did (career .308), but he was more colorful. He was known for a flamboyant style on and off the field. In one case Chicago White Stockings president Albert Spalding (who took over for Hul-

Cap Anson baseball card. Image courtesy of Library of Congress

King Kelly.
Image courtesy of Library of Congress

bert), who was trying to follow in his predecessor's footsteps by making sure his players were leading clean lives, hired Pinkerton detectives to follow his players. The detective reported to Spalding that Kelly was spotted in a bar drinking lemonade at 3 a.m. When Kelly heard this he scoffed, "It was straight whiskey; I never drank a lemonade at that hour in my life."[24]

By the end of the 1880s not all players who wanted to play could. Although black players had been allowed to play in some minor leagues and the American Association fielded teams with African American members, the National League enforced a "color ban" of both black players and black clubs from its inception in 1876. It is believed the last black player to play in the major leagues before Jackie Robinson in 1946 was **Moses Fleetwood Walker**, who played for Toledo in the American Association. In 1887 Cap Anson, who was no friend to the African American, refused to take the field unless George Stovey, a black pitcher for the American Association's Newark club, left the field. Newark agreed, and things went downhill from there. By the 1890s owners began to enforce an unofficial "**gentlemen's agreement**." Although never written into the bylaws, owners blocked the inclusion of African Americans from professional baseball for over a half century.

John Montgomery Ward was a very good player who would later be voted into the Hall of Fame for his exploits both as a pitcher and a hitter (he amassed over 2,000 hits in his career), but he became more famous for what he contributed to the game in 1885. While playing for the New York Gothams (later the Giants), he used his skills as an attorney to form the (at first) secretive **Brotherhood of Professional Base Ball Players**, the first ever sports labor union. Ward and other players were growing increasingly troubled by the actions of club owners. One of the issues was the "**reserve clause**," which allowed clubs to reserve the rights of players for their career. When the clause was first introduced in 1879, many players had no problem with it because it was a guarantee of a job for the next season, but it increasingly became unpopular with players because it gave them very little power in negotiating contracts. Owners could also sell players (or at least their contracts) to other teams without the consent of those players. The most famous of these sales came in 1887, when Albert Spalding sold King Kelly to Boston for the unprecedented price of $10,000. When owners began to discuss a salary cap in the late 1880s, Ward and the Brotherhood took drastic actions and formed their own league, the Players' League, in 1890. They took players from seven of the eight National League teams and set up rival teams in some of those same cities. National League leaders were shocked by this move, and Albert Spalding declared war on the Players, whom he referred to as "hot-headed anarchists."[25] He actually formed a "war committee," which he chaired. One of the tactics he tried was to lure some of the better players back to the National League with large sums of money. King Kelly was one of the players who had bolted, and Spalding reportedly offered him a "blank check" to come back. After thinking about it for a time, he refused saying, "I can't go back on the boys. And," he added, "neither would you." Spalding could not help but respect that, and he shook his hand "in congratulations of the great ball player on his loyalty."[26] Inevitably, it was not Spalding's war committee but decisions made by the Players' League that brought about its demise. They tried to appeal to Victorian culture by not playing on Sundays, selling alcohol, and charging 50 cents. They were competing for the same audience on the same days in the same towns, and it just did not work. The Players' League folded after one season and the following year, so did the American Association. The players reluctantly went back to the National League—the only game in town.

Conclusion

By the end of the 19th century baseball was beginning to look more and more like the modern game we know today. Players were using gloves in the field to protect their hands; pitchers were no longer pitching underhand, and the mound was moved back from 45 feet to 60 feet 6 inches; and base-stealing and the hit-and-run were being employed. Although the professional game was modernizing, it was also in deep trouble. Albert Spalding recognized early on that one team dominating a league was dangerous for the game—so too was one league dominating a sport. National League owners began cutting salaries because they knew they could. Players had little recourse—they had nowhere to go. To make matters worse, the best team of the closing decade of the century, the Baltimore Orioles, were not exactly poster boys for clean living. They were everything Henry Chadwick, William Hulbert, and Albert Spalding had been fighting against for a half century. They drank; they cursed; they spiked. They were one of the dirtiest teams in the history of professional baseball. Although they won, they did not endear polite society to the game. Yes, pro ball was in trouble, and someone or something needed to come along to save it.

Notes

1. Tristram Potter Coffin, *The Old Ball Game; Baseball in Folklore and Fiction* (New York: Herder and Herder, 1971), 6.
2. A. G. Spalding, *America's National Game* (Lincoln: University of Nebraska Press, 1992).
3. Ibid.
4. Harold Seymour, *Baseball* (New York: Oxford University Press, 1960), 5.
5. Ibid., 6.
6. Ibid.
7. Dean Sullivan, ed. *Early Innings; A Documentary History of Baseball, 1825–1908* (Lincoln: University of Nebraska Press, 1995), 4–5.
8. Benjamin Rader, *American Sports* (Upper Saddle River, NJ: Pearson Prentice Hall, 2009), 53.
9. Seymour, *Baseball*, 16.
10. Ibid., 17.
11. Ibid.
12. Ibid., 24.
13. Ibid., 26.
14. Jules Tygiel, *Past Time* (New York: Oxford University Press, 2000), 6.
15. Ibid., 4.
16. Spalding, *America's National Game*, 96.
17. Tygiel, *Past Time*, 19.
18. Ibid., 23.
19. Ibid., 29.
20. Rader, *American Sports*, 57.
21. Spalding, *America's National Game*, 200.
22. Ibid., 204.
23. Ibid., 214.
24. Rader, *American Sports*, 60.
25. Ibid., 61.
26. Spalding, *America's National Game*, 297.

CHAPTER

Four

The Rise of Collegiate and Youth Athletics

*T*he morning of August 3, 1852, dawned bright and sunny on the banks of the Winnipesaukee River in New Hampshire. Little did the roughly one thousand people who had gathered along those banks know it, but they were about to be witnesses to history. One of those witnesses was making history himself. Former Mexican War General Franklin Pierce, who had been the surprise nominee for president by the Democratic Party only two months before, was in attendance that day. Pierce had been the compromise candidate that emerged on the 49th ballot because he appeared to be inoffensive to both the North and the South in the rapidly growing split between the regions. Pierce would never have admitted that he was campaigning for president (the custom of the day precluded candidates from "running" for the highest office in the land—the candidate "stood" for office, and others "ran" or campaigned for him) but that he was merely enjoying the beautiful weather with a few friends and neighbors who had gathered to watch a boat race. Pierce, who hailed from Concord, which was just a few miles from this spot, was essentially in his backyard watching Harvard row against Yale. What Pierce and his "friends and neighbors" saw that day was Harvard defeat Yale in the country's first intercollegiate sporting event.

The whole event, which went well beyond the one race, was funded by a rising railroad magnate named James Elkins. Elkins provided an all-expense-paid eight-day vacation for the members of both teams, which followed the race. Elkins was not doing this because he loved the sport of rowing or had a particular rooting interest in either team—he knew this event would provide a boost for the local economy, including the local railroad, of which Elkins was the superintendent. He ran extra excursion trains to and from the event and figured he would more than pay for his investment. So even the first college sporting event in American history had its birth with a donor putting up a large sum of money. That is where the similarities to modern-day college athletics ended in this event. Both teams enjoyed themselves during the week they spent in each other's company, and there was none of the fierce competitiveness that one would expect from a college athletic contest held today. Three months after the race, Franklin Pierce was elected the 14th president of the United States. Unfortunately for Pierce, the future of American college athletics was much brighter than his presidency would prove to be.

British College Athletics

Before we look ahead, we must look back at the example set for American collegiate athletics by the British. Given the sporting history of Great Britain examined in the Chapter 1, it is not surprising that sporting activities were participated in by a wide variety of British citizens, including college students. The two most prestigious British colleges were, and are, Oxford and Cambridge. Oxford was founded in 1167 and Cambridge early in the next century. Ample evidence shows that students at both schools engaged in various sporting events throughout the centuries, but especially beginning in the 16th century. Examples of these activities include boating, cricket, horseracing, hunting, tennis, bowling, boxing, football, and swimming. The latter of these, it would appear, was especially popular with students and not so with university officials. So many students were swimming in the Thames River that in 1571 Cambridge University issued a ban on any student entering a pool or river in the county of Cambridge. It must not have been adhered to because 20 years later they had to reissue the ban. By the 19th century the ban had been lifted because eventually Cambridge built a "bathing pool" for its students to use, as it was reported one of its most famous graduates, George Byron (who would later be known as Lord Byron, the great British poet), would use it quite often. Byron entered Cambridge in 1805 and was said to have enjoyed "gambling, boxing, cricket, and swimming" and often he "was to be seen riding on his grey horse . . . out of town to bathe."[1]

Most sporting events in Britain prior to the 19th century were not well organized. It was the decade of the 1820s when one could say intercollegiate athletics were born. A quarter century before the Harvard–Yale rowing match inaugurated American intercollegiate sporting events, Oxford and Cambridge met not in the water but on the cricket field in London in 1827. Two years later they would meet on the Thames in the first of what would be many rowing matches. Rowing was a popular spectator sport from the beginning, as evidenced by the estimated 20,000 people who showed up for that first match in 1829. Ronald Smith, in his book, *Sports and Freedom*, surmised that the reason the crowd was so large was that "betting ran high" among the spectators on the outcome of the two-and-a-quarter-mile race. Although the race had a false start when the competitors' oars became locked with each other, when it started again, those who had bet on Oxford were rewarded with a two-length victory in a time of about 14 minutes. Thus began the annual race between the schools.

While still a colony of Great Britain, colleges in America participated in various sports during the 18th century. As early as the 1730s when there were only three colleges in the colonies—Harvard, Yale, and William and Mary—Harvard students were reported to have played early forms of both baseball and football. Freshmen were required to provide upperclassmen with "bats, balls and foot-balls."[2] The College of William and Mary in Williamsburg, Virginia, was attended by the sons of the planter elite, who had long been a sporting group. Although the students enjoyed the pastimes of their fathers (horseracing, fox hunting, cockfighting, and billiards), the faculty of William and Mary consisted primarily of ministers who had been trained at Oxford and were not as accepting of the activities. In fact, William and Mary banned students from having horses, racing them, or betting on them. They further added that no student should play or wager on table games or cockfighting unless the student wanted to be "under pain of ye like severe . . . punishment."[3] William and Mary was a forerunner of the many religious-based colleges to emerge in the colonies. Of the remaining six pre-Revolution colleges founded, four were based in the teachings of Protestant religious sects—with a distinct revivalist flavor formed in the Great Awakening of the 18th century. Those four were the College of New Jersey (Princeton), Dartmouth, the College of Rhode Island (Brown), and Queen's College (Rutgers). These schools (with the exception of Rutgers) would join Harvard and Yale in making up the majority of the first collegiate conference—the Ivy League.

Most of the leaders of these schools had no problem with physical activity of some kind but restricted organized sport. Various laws from the period leading up to the Revolutionary War are evidence of that. Yale University issued a document that read, "If any scholar shall play at Hand-Ball, or Foot-Ball, or Bowls in the College-yard, or throw any Thing against the College, by which Glass may be endangered . . . he shall be punished six pence." The president of Dartmouth warned against his students engaging in activities like playing with "balls," or "bowls." Shortly after the end of the Revolution when the idea of Republicanism was at its height, Princeton banned the playing of "shinny," which was a kind of field hockey because they felt it was "low and unbecoming gentlemen and scholars." Many campuses were closed, and if students were caught off campus without permission for recreation or anything else, they would find themselves in trouble. One student from King's College in New York caught swimming off campus was confined to his room for one week, where he was made to translate Latin for the entirety of his confinement. As Ronald Smith noted, "Cruel and unusual punishments were not uncommon in colonial America."[4]

As with so many things in Colonial America, the British influence was everywhere. Unlike other European universities, which were located in the larger cities, British colleges were set in more rural settings. American colleges, for the most part, would follow that tradition of being built in those settings. This was done intentionally to remove the temptations for the students that were believed to exist in the "wicked" cities. It was in these pastoral settings that students would grow both intellectually and spiritually in what would come to be called the "**collegiate way**." It was hoped by parents and administrators alike that students would expand their horizons but in a supervised fashion. Because the colleges were located so far away from students' homes, there was a need for housing and dormitories. Although college leaders hoped this would foster all the positive things they were hoping for the students, especially religious knowledge, what they neglected to plan for was (in their view) the negative things that would emerge from housing students all together (albeit supervised). One of those negative things was a reaction to the strict curriculum offered by the collegiate way. Sometimes this reaction would materialize as all-out rebellion by students—sometimes it would be something as seemingly harmless as a food riot. More often than not, the reaction would materialize as students participating in sports. It was a way to blow off steam and make the authorities crazy. Eventually, over the years, sports became more and more accepted by college leaders. By the 19th century, it would often be seen as a positive way to advertise the university and an integral part of the "collegiate way."

College Crew

The camaraderie that existed during that first collegiate rowing match between Harvard and Yale in 1852 would not be equaled during subsequent years. Lake Winnipesaukee officials invited the two schools back for a rematch the following year, but the race never materialized. Apparently, the profits for the railroad did not turn out to be as great as James Elkins had hoped. The two schools would not meet again until 1855, and it was evident that they were taking this match much more seriously than the first race. The venue for this race was on the Connecticut River near the town of Springfield, Massachusetts, and although the Springfield business community was pleased the have the race staged in their town, there seemed to be less commercialization of this race than the first. Yale participated in a more serious training regimen for the second race, but the result was the same. The Harvard crew was victorious, and the race also sparked other schools to begin to organize rowing teams. By 1858, Harvard and Yale decided to follow in the footsteps of British counterparts Oxford and Cambridge by inviting other schools to race with them in annual invitationals called regattas. The first of these regattas was supposed to have occurred in Springfield on the Connecticut River with Brown and Trinity College joining Harvard and Yale, but it was cancelled after Yale oarsman George Dunham tragically drowned six days before the event while training. The 1859 regatta was moved to Lake Quinsigamond near Worcester, Massachusetts, and for the first time received some major recognition in the press. The *New York Herald* devoted three columns of its front page to the regatta and noted that Yale was getting very serious in its preparation in hopes of finally defeating Harvard. The paper reported that they changed their diet and embarked on a physical fitness regime. Unfortunately for Yale, it did not work as they again lost to Harvard in front of an estimated 20,000 spectators.

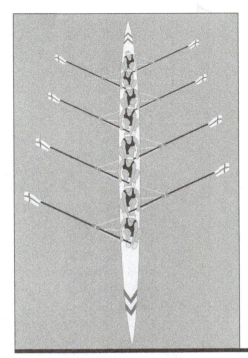

Above view of competitive crew boat.
Image © ben smith, 2013. Used under license from Shutterstock, Inc.

The regattas continued into the next decade as the country prepared to split apart during the Civil War. It was during the war that many colleges began to implement more "scientific" training methods as well as professional coaches. It is not surprising, given their history of losing to their archrival, that Yale was the first to hire a professional trainer. There had been a secession of races after 1861; but when Yale challenged Harvard to another race in the summer of 1864, William Wood, a New York gymnastics and physical education teacher, became the first trainer for an American college athletic team. Wood's regimen for the Yale team was a rigorous one. The Yale crew would rise at 6 a.m. and walk or run three to five miles before rowing four miles at racing speed both in the morning and afternoon. Wood was also an early proponent of weightlifting to build strength. The program worked, as Yale defeated Harvard that summer for the first time and by a comfortable 40-second margin. There were obviously more important things going on that summer on battlefields across the South, but for the Yale crew during that one moment on Lake Quinsigamond, there was nothing else in the world that topped what they had just accomplished. Yale retained Wood for the next year and again defeated Harvard in 1865. Although Harvard did not hire a professional trainer, they did have the advantage of having William Blaikie as their captain (he would be what today would be considered a coach, as he had already graduated). Blaikie had traveled to Oxford to learn their rowing techniques and returned to Harvard to teach them to his team. It was due to these improved training and rowing techniques that Harvard rattled off five consecutive victories over Yale.

It was also at least partially due to Blaikie that a race was set up between Harvard and Oxford in 1869. Rivalry between the United States and her once-mother country was evident in all areas of American culture but no more so than in the world of athletics. Britain, as has been discussed earlier, has a rich history of being a sporting nation and if the United States was going to be the best in whatever it endeavored to try, it would have to beat the best. In the world of college rowing that meant beating Oxford. The match was held on the Thames River, and estimates of the number of spectators there that day range from the incredible 750,000 to the almost unbelievable 1 million people. The **first-ever international collegiate sporting event** became much larger than just a contest between two tradition-rich colleges, but a metaphor describing the power of the two nations. For the first half of the race it appeared the "offspring" would have bragging rights over the "mother," as the Harvard crew led most of the way, but eventually Oxford drew even and won the race by about three lengths. The British offered the results of this race as proof of the supremacy of British culture. The rivalry that was borne out of years of colonial rule, two wars, and the recent American Civil War, in which the British offered the Confederacy some aid, was only stoked further by this race. Back home in America, the race also had an effect on the Harvard–Yale rivalry. Harvard sent its best rowers to Britain but did field a team to row against Yale in their annual race. After Yale lost to what was essentially Harvard's "B" team, one of the Yale oarsman actually put his oar through the bottom of his boat. Competition and that driving desire to win had indeed become much more important since that first race in 1852. After the combination of the 1869 loss and a collision during a "highly controversial contest" the following year, which also resulted in a Harvard victory, Yale decided to severe "all athletic relations" with Harvard after 1870.[5]

During the period that Harvard and Yale did not compete against each other, Harvard decided to "democratize" rowing and open up regattas to any school that wanted to enter. Had they known what would be the result by the middle of the 1870s, Harvard probably would have never organized the "Rowing Association of American Colleges." At its first meeting in April of 1871, there was no reason to believe that Harvard would not continue its dominance over the sport, no matter who the competition was. The members agreed to an open regatta in 1871 in which Harvard, Brown, and the Massachusetts Agricultural College would compete. Harvard crew members chastised the Aggies, calling them "farmers' boys" and asking them whether or not they had gotten the "hay-seed out of their eyes."[6] That was a mistake. Massachusetts Agricultural College, a land-grant college of only 150 students, defeated Harvard that day by 14 lengths and Brown by 20 lengths. This should have served as a frightening omen for Harvard, and it certainly gave hope to other small schools that they could not only compete with Harvard but maybe beat them as well. The following year, Yale joined the Association and lent more respectability to the event. Unfortunately for Yale, they finished last, and Harvard was again defeated—this time by Amherst. Now, the schools came out of the woodwork to race against Harvard and Yale. In 1873 11 teams crowded the starting line at the event. The race came down to the two old rivals and, as was often the case, there was controversy at the finish line. Harvard crossed what they thought was the finish line first, but they were off by a few yards, and Yale was declared the winner as the Harvard rowers quit stroking. After losses to Columbia and Cornell the next two years, Harvard and Yale decided that they would withdraw from the regatta and only race against each other. Although Yale had won one of the Regattas, Harvard had not, and many argued they should not pull out until they had won the event. Harvard agreed to race in one more regatta—the 1876 race would be their last. It would also turn out to be the last regatta staged—only six colleges participated, and Cornell won their second consecutive race. The announcement of both Yale and Harvard's pullout spelled the end of not only the annual regatta but also the popularity of the sport throughout the last quarter of the century.

Track and Field

Another popular sport on college campuses in the late 19th century was track and field. As with most other American sports, it had English origins. The earliest believed organized race in public schools occurred in the 1830s in Rugby, England. The race was called the "hound and hares," and the "hares" (usually two or three of Rugby's fastest runners) would be given a few minutes' head-start to scatter torn-up newspapers across a nine-mile countryside, which served as essentially a cross-country track. Roughly 40 "hounds" would run as fast as they could, attempting to pick up the "scent" of the newspapers and catch the hares before they reached whichever landmark had been chosen as the finish line. Author Thomas Hughes, who was from Rugby and participated in the races, described them in his immensely popular novel **Tom Brown's Schooldays**. The book had a major impact on the popularity of running as a sport both in Great Britain and the United States. In 1845, another English public school in Eton developed another form of cross-country race called the steeplechase. In this three-mile race, participants were required to negotiate various challenges such as plowed fields, jumps over water, and other obstacles. It wasn't until the 1850s that British colleges participated in track and field events. Oxford was the first to have a stee-plechase event and eventually added events ranging from the 100-yard dash to the two-mile cross-country run. When Cambridge began to formulate a track team in the early 1860s, it was not long before a challenge was mounted between the two great schools. Cambridge and Oxford agreed to an eight-event meet in March of 1864. It essentially ended in a draw when each university won four events. The winner of the mile run finished in four minutes, 56 seconds. Track grew in England over the remainder of the century but was never as popular as team sports such as crew and cricket.

When *Tom Brown's Schooldays* arrived in the United States in the late 1850s, it was as much a sensation here as it had been in England. As it had in England, it created a rise in the popularity of "hare and hound" races or as they were called in the United States, "**paper chases**."[7] Paper chases appeared sporadically on campuses throughout the 1860s, but it was not until the 1870s and '80s that they would be widespread and organized. Harvard held its first official paper chase in 1876. The race went far beyond the campus itself as there were reports of many "irritated property owners" around the town of Cambridge—it was probably at least partially to their "irritation" that the Harvard Athletic Association would not stage another race for three years.[8] By the 1880s, most campuses participated in some form of these races. Princeton formed its own Hare and Hounds Club in 1880. By the late 1880s, the name for these races had been changed from "Hare and Hounds" or "Paper Chases" to simply **Cross-Country**. In 1887 the National Cross-Country Association was formed, and it held its first intercollegiate championship in 1890 in which the University of Pennsylvania defeated Cornell. By this time the custom of spreading paper had been replaced by a premarked course for the participants to follow.

Cross-country. Image © patrimonio designs ltd. 2013. Used under license from Shutterstock, Inc.

Cross-country is not always considered to be a separate entity from other track and field events today, but in the 19th century it certainly was. No one knows for sure when the first track event took place on a college campus, but foot races were known to occur at various colleges stretching back to the 18th century. It was not until the mid-19th century, though, that they became organized events, and Princeton is commonly given credit for hosting the first of these races. Princeton held a track meet as early as 1859, but it did not begin to host annual events until a decade later. It is not surprising that Princeton would be at the forefront of this sport considering its background. Princeton was founded by the Presbyterian Church, which traces its lineage back to Scotland, and Scots were known for participation in track and field events. When Scots immigrated to the United States, they brought their traditions with them, including the establishment of **Caledonian Clubs** all across the country. The first of these was established in Boston in 1853. These clubs got their name from the Roman name for Scotland, which was Caledonia. In 1869, Princeton President and Scottish immigrant James McGosh hired fellow Scot George Goldie to be director of Princeton's new gymnasium. Goldie set up annual track

Track athlete. Image © benadamtov, 2013. Used under license from Shutterstock, Inc.

contests, which were called Caledonian Games. Scotland was not the only model for American collegiate track and field—as with all other American sports, England also played a role. Oxford–Cambridge held their first annual track meet in 1864, and after a Columbia University student named George Rives attended the 1868 meet, he was instrumental in persuading Columbia to form its own athletic association, which held its first meet in 1869. The meet was a combination of the British tradition and the Caledonian games that were gaining popularity in New York at the time.

One of the most influential personalities in the sport was a first-generation Scottish-American named **James Gordon Bennett**. Bennett's father had emigrated from Scotland and founded the

New York Herald newspaper in 1835. James Gordon Bennett Sr. built the paper into the world's most profitable one over the next 30 years. Control of the paper was turned over to the younger Bennett just after the Civil War in 1866. Bennett Jr. continued the profitability of the paper and even raised its profile in 1869 when he sponsored Henry Morton Stanley's search for David Livingstone, who had been missing in the jungles of Africa for years. In return for the sponsorship, Livingstone gave the *Herald* exclusive rights to cover the story. The world followed the search in the pages of Bennett's paper, and when Livingstone was eventually found by Stanley, it provided the happy ending that the public was hoping for, and his paper's profits and exposure skyrocketed. Bennett was also a sports promoter, and although his first sporting love was yachting (he joined the New York Yacht Club at 16 and at 25 won the world's first transatlantic yacht race), he also recognized the rising popularity of track. In 1873, he decided to add a track and field event to the popular intercollegiate rowing regatta that was discussed earlier. Bennett donated the winning trophy valued at $500 for the two-mile event. Only three contestants competed for the valuable prize (primarily because McGill University's entrant, Duncan Bowie, had won a number of recent Caledonian games and was seen as unbeatable). The contestants from Amherst and Cornell did not stand much of a chance, as Bowie won with a time of 11 minutes, 18.5 seconds. At the following year's regatta, Bennett again put up the winning trophies, but this time he had to donate five of them, as the meet was expanded to five events. Bennett called the event the New York Herald Olympic Games. The more Bennett and others offered valuable prizes, the more the popularity of the events expanded. One Harvard athlete described the Bennett trophies as the "decided incentive to athletic sports."[9]

These "decided incentives" were beginning to cause controversy in a Victorian America that thought amateur athletics should be played for the love of the sport and not for monetary prizes. In December of 1875, the presidents of Harvard and Yale invited 10 other colleges to join them in forming the **Intercollegiate Association of Amateur Athletes of America (IC4A)**. The hosting of track and field events would be the IC4A's responsibility and not outside interests like Bennett and his newspaper. The other thing they agreed on was the importance of making all the prizes of equal value. One of the big controversies had been that more athletes would compete in an event that had a higher-valued prize, so making the prizes equal would hopefully alleviate that problem. By the 1880s, that problem would disappear altogether as valuable prizes given to individuals would be banned as being against the amateur code. One of the other agreements that the IC4A made was to ban international competition for collegiate track and field. That rule was adhered to for almost two decades until Yale decided to challenge Oxford College to a meet that took place in London on July 16, 1894. Although Yale lost that first international collegiate match, they would win ensuing challenges against the best Britain had to offer. The sport also received a boost when the Olympic Games were revived in 1896, and the Greeks invited the world to participate in the first modern Olympics in Athens. British and American Victorians used this opportunity to point to the amateurism of the ancient Greeks as the pure form of sport. As we'll see in Chapter 9, Greek amateurism was actually a carefully calculated myth.

Baseball

Although different forms of baseball had been played on college campuses for decades and the game predated rowing as a college activity, the first organized intercollegiate baseball game did not occur until seven years after the Harvard–Yale crew meet. The 1850s were a decade in which the rules of the game were evolving and, as was discussed in Chapter 3, the debate was usually between the New England and New York versions of the sport. By the end of the decade, the New York game was becoming more widely accepted, but because the first college game took place in the heart of New England, Williamstown, Massachusetts, the old New England rules were used, including the practice of "soaking" baserunners to get them out as opposed to tagging them. When Amherst College came to play Williams in June of 1859, it was agreed that the first team to score 65 runs would be declared the victor. The other debated rule was whether to record outs only if a batted ball was caught on the fly or after one bounce. The players agreed that the more "mannish" way to play the game was to limit outs to balls caught without first bouncing.[10] So the college game was ahead of the National Association of Base Ball Players, which did not adopt the rule until 1863. Amherst was clearly the better team that day, as they dominated Williams by a final score of 73–32.

Baseball. Image © Danny E Hooks, 2013. Used under license from Shutterstock, Inc.

As with the Knickerbockers in New York, most colleges that adopted baseball treated it as a social club and were concerned more with the behavior of the participants than the outcomes of the contests. Harvard charged its members one dollar for initiation and charged fines if players missed games (10 cents) or meetings (3 cents). Princeton leveled fines if its members did not display "gentlemanly behavior." The fine for profane language was 10 cents; for disputing an umpire or captain the fine was 5 cents; and if they made an "audible expression on a doubtful play before the umpire made his decision" they would have to pay 3 cents.[11] Unlike the "professional" game, the Civil War slowed the progress of the college game—at least in the short term. Although most college-aged men were fighting in the war between 1861 and 1865, some did go to college and did play baseball. An example of a college that did play was Harvard. They organized their club in 1862, and by the end of the war they were the dominant program in all college baseball. They continued their dominance throughout the rest of the decade and into the next. In the summer of 1870 they went on a tour throughout the West taking on all challengers and winning 44 of the 54 contests they played. They even battled Harry Wright's Cincinnati Red Stockings to the end. An observer of the game noted, "The game was remarkably close, the Harvards outplaying their opponents at bat and in the field; but at a critical moment in the last inning, professional training showed its superiority over amateur excitability, and the Red Stockings won 20 to 17."[12]

During the decade of the 1870s, college teams continued to play against professional teams of both the first league (National Association of Professional Base Ball Players formed in 1871) and the National League, formed in 1876. There was little differentiation between the college teams and what were considered "professional." The best of the NAPBBP teams during its five-year existence was the Boston Red Stockings (it was a team led by Harry Wright, and its roster consisted of a great deal of former Cincinnati Red Stockings after the team disbanded in 1870). Harvard played the Red Stockings 20 times and won twice. Yale played nearly as many games against professionals as it did against other colleges. The differentiation between college and pro teams started at the end of the decade. In 1879 Harvard joined with Yale, Princeton, Amherst, Brown, and Dartmouth to form the **American College Base Ball Association**. One of the major issues the new association would have to deal with was: Who was a professional, who was an amateur, and who was eligible to play college ball? Unfortunately for the colleges, that issue was not solved for more than two decades. It was not until the establishment of the National Collegiate Athletic Association (NCAA) in the early 20th century that eligibility questions were seriously addressed. The schools had more problems deciding what games counted and who the mythical national champion was every year. By 1887 the "Big Three" of Harvard, Yale, and Princeton had decided that *only* games against one another counted toward the championship and games against other schools were "practice" or exhibition games. Not surprisingly, that led to a dissolution of the original association, and by the end of the decade, there were two separate college baseball leagues. By the 1890s college baseball had other problems. Although baseball had been the most popular team sport on college campuses since the Civil War, it was now being supplanted by a new sport—American football.

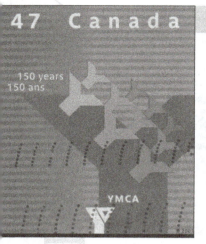

YMCA logo stamp. Image ©
rook76, 2013. Used under license from
Shutterstock, Inc.

Early Organized Youth Sports

College students were not the only youth becoming involved in athletics during the Victorian period—students in high schools and younger were also beginning to see sports as an activity they wanted to participate in. Even more important, adults began to buy into the idea of sports for youth as well. The Muscular Christianity Movement of the second half of the 19th century was at the heart of this thinking but a new movement would most vociferously be championed by Theodore Roosevelt, and its name would even be coined by Roosevelt himself—"**The Strenuous Life**." Roosevelt and others believed that the absence of war in the later stages of the century along with the new industrial economy led to a feminization of the males in society. To answer that, Roosevelt reasoned that young boys needed to participate in activities that would strengthen the body as well as the mind. Roosevelt had been a sickly child afflicted with asthma, and his father had encouraged him to make himself stronger, and he did. Now Theodore Roosevelt wanted the youth of America to follow in his footsteps. One of the first organizations that combined both of these ideas was the **Young Men's Christian Association (YMCA)**. The association was founded in England in 1851 and was first introduced to the United States just before the Civil War. In the early years of the organization, it focused its work on the Christian part of its name and offered more spiritual guidance to youth. After the war the YMCA began to broaden its programs to include more rigorous physical components. By the 1890s the YMCA began to attract not only youth but also younger male workers from the industrial economy who were no longer experiencing physical exercise in their work.

As the century came to a close, there was a more widespread belief that physical activity and sports was not only a good thing for the male youths, but it was also instrumental in building their character. One of the leading proponents of this idea was **Luther Halsey Gulick**. Much like Roosevelt, Gulick had turned to the idea of a strenuous life to compensate for problems in his youth. He had suffered from migraines, depression, and physical weakness and had witnessed his father suffer a nervous breakdown. He blamed his father's problems on his weak physical condition and vowed that it would not happen to him. He went into medicine and eventually became a spokesman for the muscular Christianity and strenuous life movements directed especially toward the youth. In 1887 he joined the YMCA's headquarters as an instructor in the physical department in Springfield, Massachusetts. It was an ideal position for Gulick, as he would be training other physical education instructors who would go out to various local YMCAs across the country. Gulick instilled in them the belief that physical training was as important as mental training for a well-balanced individual. It was Gulick who invented the famous emblem still used by the YMCA of the inverted triangle, which "symbolized the spirit supported by the mind and the body."[13]

In 1900, Gulick decided to leave the YMCA and become a high school principal in Brooklyn, but he never changed his beliefs on the importance of athletics for the youth of America. In 1903 he became the director of physical training for all the New York City schools, and he organized all the schools into the **Public Schools Athletic League (PSAL)** that same year. The league would organize competitions between the various schools and sponsor city championships in over a dozen sports. Baseball proved to be the most popular (not surprising, given its history in the city), and in 1907, 106 teams competed in front of over 15,000 fans at the Polo Grounds in Manhattan.[14] Other purposes were served by the league in particular and sports in general, and they were primarily aimed at the immigrant youth of the city. There was an emerging fear after the turn of the century that immigrant youth "exhibited a lack of understanding of American values and institutions," and sports was one way to "Americanize" them.[15] This belief alone showed the continuing emergence of the importance of sports in American culture as we move into the 20th century. Many believed

Playground. Image © Tinica, 2013. Used under license from Shutterstock, Inc.

athletics could serve another important purpose in American cities: a reduction in juvenile delinquency. So not only did it teach immigrant youth American ideals, but it also kept them busy after school doing something constructive as opposed to joining a gang or getting into trouble. Another avenue that was designed to foster the same results was the **Playground Movement**. This movement can be traced to 1903, when Chicago voters approved a $5 million bond issue for the construction of 10 parks. The idea that the more parks and playgrounds in the cities, the less youth would get into trouble. Prior to the 20th century most "playgrounds" were designed for younger kids, and the new movement was designed for the teenager. The numbers of playgrounds grew very quickly, and by the eve of World War I, cities with managed playgrounds jumped from 41 to 504. The key term in that sentence was "managed." Most adults believed these playgrounds needed to be supervised by adults, which led to not as many kids using the playgrounds as many had hoped for. After all, it is just not nearly as fun to play with your friends when your every move is being "supervised," is it?

Conclusion

The youth of America had always participated in sports and games—to a much greater extent than their adult counterparts. It was not until the second half of the 19th century, however, that these sports became organized—both in primary and secondary schools as well as college campuses. The idea of sports being a character builder for our youth is a relatively new idea, but it would be an idea that would continue to grow as we moved into the 20th century. Organized collegiate sports, as we observed, is also a fairly recent phenomenon. American colleges followed in the footsteps of their British counterparts but it only took a matter of a few years, not centuries, for this example to catch on here, as the British colleges, despite their much longer history, did not begin the tradition of intercollegiate athletics until the 19th century. Once begun on American campuses, the tradition spread quickly to different campuses and involved many sports. We observed three of those sports in this chapter (rowing, track and field, and baseball) and discussed that the most popular of those was baseball. For various reasons as the century came to a close, baseball's popularity began to decline. One of the reasons for this decline was the inclement weather that is prevalent during the school year in most northern climates in the country. That would usually mean teams would need to travel to warmer climates or they would not be able to play. The main reason for baseball's decline was the emergence of an increasingly more popular sport on campuses. That sport is detailed in the next chapter.

Notes

1. Ronald A. Smith, *Sports and Freedom, the Rise of Big-Time College Athletics* (Oxford and New York: Oxford University Press, 1988), 5.
2. Ibid.
3. Ibid., 9.
4. Ibid., 10.
5. Ibid., 37.
6. Ibid., 43.
7. Ibid., 101.
8. Ibid., 102.
9. Ibid., 106.
10. Ibid., 54.
11. Ibid., 53.
12. Benjamin Rader, *American Sports; From the Age of Folk Games to the Age of Televised Sports*, 6th ed. (Upper Saddle River, NJ: Pearson-Prentice Hall, 2009), 87.
13. Ibid., 106.
14. Ibid., 111.
15. Ibid.

CHAPTER
Five

Emergence of the King of Campus: Early College Football

*A*s the train rattled north from Princeton to New Brunswick in New Jersey on the morning of November 6, 1869, the Princeton students and student–athletes aboard could not have known the day's festivities that awaited them would be remembered as the starting point for what would become the most popular of all collegiate sports. The students were met at the train station by their counterparts from Rutgers College, who took them to eat and even to play billiards and other games before assembling at the Rutgers athletic fields at 3 p.m. The reason for the visit from the Princeton contingent would begin a short time later after the rules of the impending game could be agreed on. It was agreed that players could not "run with the ball or throw it" but the ball "could be batted with hands or fists." The field measured 360 feet by 225 feet that separated the two goals, which were "eight paces wide." The field needed to be large to hold the number of players—25 on each side. It was those players who would "bat or kick" the inflated rubber ball around the field until it went through the goal. The first team to score six goals would be the winner. The only way to distinguish the two teams (neither wore uniforms) was the red scarves worn around the heads of the Rutgers players. Although the Princeton players appeared to be "tall and muscular," the Rutgers team was more "small and light." Both teams battled to a 4–4 tie, but "small and light" eventually won the day as Rutgers scored the final two goals to win what would be the **first-ever intercollegiate football game**, 6–4.[1]

College Football in the 19th Century

This "football" game would be essentially what Americans today would call soccer. Although Rutgers won the first game, the rivalry between the two schools that began with that game would be very one-sided in favor of Princeton over the next century—in fact, Princeton would not lose to Rutgers for nearly 70 years. When the tide shifted back to Rutgers and they began a winning streak in the 1970s, Princeton took their soccer ball and went home. They ended the rivalry. The early meeting between the schools would set the stage for other schools to form teams throughout the 1870s, including Columbia, Yale, and Harvard. Harvard's game was decidedly different from the "**Association football**" (soccer) game and was much closer to rugby. In 1872, Harvard changed two rules from the original "Association" rules—one would allow fewer players per side and the other would allow any player to catch or pick up the ball. This was a dramatic change from the soccer style in which only the goalkeeper could touch the ball with his hands. An intriguing part of the new rule allowed for the player with the ball to run only if he was pursued by an opponent. The pursuer would "call out" when he stopped the chase, and if the runner with the ball did not stop, the "cry was taken up by the whole pack of opponents."[2] This was the gentlemen's way to police themselves, and apparently it worked well. The year 1872 was also an important year because it marked Yale's entrance into the college football world with their first game against Columbia, whom they beat. Yale would be the dominant school in that world for the first half-century of its existence. The first "Western" school to attempt to enter that world dominated by the Ivy League schools would be Michigan. In 1873, Cornell was challenged by Michigan to a game that would be played in Cleveland (the halfway point between the two schools). Cornell's president, Andrew White, refused to allow his team to answer the challenge. He was quoted as saying, "I will not permit 30 men to travel four hundred miles merely to agitate a bag of wind."[3] President White could not have known at the time that he was rejecting a challenge from a school that would one day have more wins than any other college football program.

The same year as the Michigan rejection, Yale called for a convention to be held in New York City to put together uniform rules for the game. Yale was joined by Princeton and Rutgers to codify the rulebook, which essentially adopted the same rules Yale had been playing by (soccer style). Although Harvard was invited to attend the convention, its representatives were noticeably absent. The captain of the Harvard Foot Ball Club, Henry Grant, refused Yale's invitation by announcing that "Harvard stands entirely distinct by herself in the game of football."[4] The problem for Harvard standing "distinct by herself" is that there was no intercollegiate competition for the school. It found a rival in McGill University from Montreal, who challenged Harvard to two games in the spring of 1874. The first would be a game played under Harvard's Boston game rules and the second would be strictly rugby rules normally played by McGill. The games were played on May 14 and 15 in front of about 500 spectators, including some Yale athletes who were curious about these different brands of football. The Canadian game seemed to strike a chord with not only the competitors on the Harvard side but also the students who watched. A student journalist summed up the feelings of the campus when he wrote: "The rugby game is in much better favor than the somewhat sleepy game played by our men."[5]

It was essentially the Canadian (or more accurately British) game of rugby that would be adopted by Harvard, and as much as they enjoyed the games and camaraderie with McGill (the teams had a banquet in Boston after the first matches and even traveled to Montreal in the fall of 1874 for a match), it was really their great rival Yale that they wanted to adopt the sport and with whom they wished to begin a series. Although Yale held onto their soccer-style game as long as they could and each school refused to bend to the other's ways for the next year, it was ironically the sport of crew (or rowing) that would change the future of college football. In the fall of 1875 Yale was trying to convince Harvard to withdraw from the annual regatta and only race each other due to recent losses to "inferior" colleges detailed in the previous chapter. In an effort to help influence Harvard's decision, Yale agreed to play a football match with Harvard using what it called "concessionary rules." They were essentially rugby rules, and although it was not the first all-American rugby match (Harvard had played Tufts University the previous spring), it was the first in a long-lasting rivalry between the two schools. Much like the Harvard–McGill match that was witnessed by Yale players, the Harvard–Yale match played on November 13 was witnessed by Princeton athletes. Princeton then decided to adopt the sport, and what would become the "Big 3" of the first half-century of college football was born. Even though Harvard won the game that day 4–0 (four touchdowns and four field goals—rules at the time called for field goals to be the only way to score, and they could only be attempted after a touchdown), they may have wished Yale had not adopted their rules, as they would dominate the next half-century of college football.

Walter Camp and Yale Domination

Walter Camp.
Image courtesy of
Library of Congress

Although not on the field for the first installment of what would eventually be referred to annually as "The Game," a Yale freshman would first take the field against Harvard the following fall and eventually would have more of an impact on the evolution of the sport than anyone else. **Walter Chauncey Camp** would be a great player for Yale and be elected team captain in 1878. It was his contribution to the game after his playing days that would eventually earn him the moniker of "Father of American Football." Camp was well known around New Haven even before enrolling at Yale because of his all-around athletic ability. He was a standout in rugby, baseball, track, crew, and tennis. After his undergraduate days at Yale ended in 1880, he stayed on attending Yale School of Medicine and continuing to play football (eligibility rules were much more lax at the time). After realizing he could not stand the sight of blood, he withdrew from school and decided a different career path was probably for the best. He got a job as an executive with a local clock manufacturing firm. His playing days behind him, he still stayed in touch with Yale football in many different capacities over the years. There are varying accounts on whether he was ever Yale's official coach, but there was no doubt about his influence on not only Yale's team but also on football in general. Part of the uncertainty as to his coaching status (he is sometimes listed as head coach from 1888–1892) is the different status assigned to coaches in the early days of football. The players were much more important and had more of an effect on the game than coaches (in the days before professional coaches were hired by schools).

It was while Camp was still playing in 1880 that he introduced the first revolutionary rule change to the game. In the game of rugby the ball is put into play in what is called a scrummage or "scrum" for short. The ball would be placed in the middle of a group of players who would attempt to kick the ball toward the opponents' goal (resulting in most of the injuries sustained in the game). When the ball popped out of this "scrum," the first player to pick it up would race toward the goal line until he was downed, at which time another scrum would ensue. The scrum did not make much sense to Camp, who proposed a change for the 1880 season. He wanted to differentiate between the offense and defense, so he initiated a rule change that would call for a line of "scrimmage" with the offense on one side of the line and the defense on the other side. Instead of the scrummage, the ball would be put into play when a player on the offense "snapped" the ball to another player who could then run with the ball until he was downed by an opposing player, which would result in a new line of scrimmage. Camp called the snapper the "center" and the player he snapped it to the "quarterback," and so two position names were born. A problem resulted from this rule change, however. Camp installed no provision for giving the ball up to one's opponent. The only way the opposing team could get possession of the ball is if the offense either kicked it to them or fumbled the ball. As long as a team did not do either of these two things, they could hold onto the ball even behind one's own goal line (which in today's game would be considered a safety) without any penalty being assessed. This glaring deficiency in the rule became painfully apparent in the 1880 championship game between Princeton and Yale. Princeton's captain told his players to neither kick nor lateral the ball to prevent fumbles, and the score ended 0–0; thus, Princeton retained its championship from the previous year. Even though he was part of this game, for some reason, Camp made no attempt to amend the rule until after the 1881 championship between the same two teams resulted in the same tactic and same outcome. Camp then decided to implement a "down and distance" system by which the team on offense must make five yards in three attempts (downs) or relinquish the ball to their opponents. The result was the field being divided by chalked lines every five yards and being forever after known as the "gridiron."

As Camp entered the industrial economy of the late 19th century after he left Yale, he began to transfer some of the same tactics used in that economy to football. He was particularly intrigued by

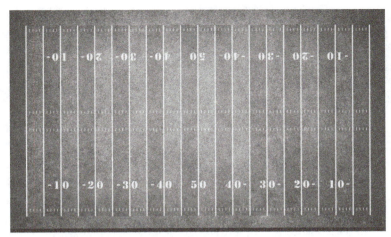

Football gridiron. Image © L.Watcharapol, 2013. Used under license from Shutterstock, Inc.

Harvard dropout Frederick Taylor's idea of "**scientific management**," which essentially looked at workers as cogs in a machine and treated them as such by timing how long they took to perform their tasks. Even though the results of scientific management were mixed (the treatment of people as machines by managers may have yielded some increased productivity, it also led to a more disgruntled workforce and the proliferation of unions), Camp believed the idea would translate well to the football field. Scientific management led to the de-emphasis of the individual and more of a concentration on the company (or team). This would also result in more designed plays, strategy, and signals that would require more organization and eventually the advent of the professional coach. Throughout the 1880s, Camp stayed in close contact with Yale's football team and was available for advice and strategy. Although his job prevented him from attending most of Yale's practices, his wife would often go to practice and take meticulous notes to report back to him. As the decade went on, Camp was to become the country's foremost authority on the game, writing articles and books on the sport. In 1889 he developed the first "All-American" college football team. He would personally select that team every year until his death in 1925. Yale's record with Camp somehow involved either as a player, advisor, or coach is unmatched in the history of the game. Between 1876 and 1909 Yale won over 95 percent of its games—only losing 14 times during that 34-year span. In the years 1890–93 Yale not only went undefeated, but they were not scored upon—outscoring their opponents 1,265–0. Camp and the other Yale players undoubtedly took particular pride in their domination of Harvard during that time period. On the other side, that domination was keenly felt by Harvard as one historian put it: "Harvard felt a certain loss of manhood by not winning a single football game with Yale in the eighties and only two in the nineties."[6]

According to many, that loss of "manhood" was a nationwide epidemic. By the late 19th century, the frontier was closed, and the country had not experienced a war for almost two generations. Those who favored the idea of "muscular Christianity" (see Chapter 3) had been advocating the need for exercise of the body as well as the mind. Now there was a group led by future president Theodore Roosevelt who believed the country as a whole was getting softer and was in need of some toughening up. Roosevelt and those who thought like him tended to also believe in a theory called "**Social Darwinism**." Followers of Charles Darwin espoused that the strongest species survive—believers in Social Darwinism talked about only the strongest nations and cultures surviving. To be the strongest nation, Roosevelt believed the United States needed a strong military (particularly navy) to exert power around the world. Roosevelt also believed that that the youth of America needed to be brought up in what he termed "the strenuous life." As a child, Roosevelt had been weak and sickly, and he had trained himself to become strong; he believed the nation could do the same thing. College men in particular were viewed at this time as wimpy, "egg-headed," and even effeminate. Football was emerging as one way to change that image. Even when describing his idea of the strenuous life, he used a football metaphor and urged his countrymen to not settle for "a lifetime of ease but for the lifetime of strenuous endeavor—hit the line hard; don't foul and don't shirk but hit the line hard."[7]

The problem was that by the 1890s football was getting extremely brutal. Football had always been a violent sport (even going back to the British Festive Culture that banned the sport numerous times) but a rule change in 1887 provided even more brutality. The Intercollegiate Football Association (IFA) led by Walter Camp passed a radical rule change that would allow for tackling below the waist for the first time. This would make it easier for stopping the open-field plays and would lead to more "mass-momentum" plays in which brute strength would become more important in gaining the needed five yards than speed and agility. As soon as the rule was implemented, coaches around the nation began to employ tactics to get around it. The most famous of the tactics was the "**flying wedge**" first used by Harvard. Essentially, this play provided for the five heaviest players to form a V-shaped wedge around the ball carrier and basically steamroll opponents. Almost every team employed some variation of the wedge. After the 1893 season, a blue-ribbon committee was established to look into the growing injuries and violence in the game. The committee, led by Walter Camp, was dominated by the "Big 3" and was very selective in its findings. Camp sent out over 1,000 questionnaires to coaches and former players regarding their experiences in the game, injuries, and how the game might be improved. The results were published in his book, *Football Facts and Figures,* and it came to the conclusion that football had had a "marked benefit" on them both "physically and mentally."[8] There is evidence that Camp left out a number of responses that did not meet the conclusions he was looking for. Left out of the report was the fact that 20 percent of former players reported permanent injuries. Included in the report was the response of former Yale standout Walter "Pudge" Heffelfinger, who commented that "during all the years I have played I have known no one personally who has been seriously injured."[9]

Camp's glowing report on the game was published in 1894, but other events of that year showed how problems in the game seemed to be spinning out of his control. After seeing the injury and hospitalization report of the previous season (24 players hospitalized; 82 sick days due to football), President Grover Cleveland cancelled the annual Army–Navy game. Other schools were seriously considering abolishing the sport. After a particularly brutal Harvard–Yale game in 1894, Harvard faculty voted to discontinue football (that would only last one season, however). Schools were beginning to pull out of the IFA at a rapid rate, and Camp knew something needed to change. Camp decided to outlaw the mass-momentum plays such as the flying wedge. The new rules called for no more than three players moving forward before the ball was put into play. In addition to the rules problems for Camp was the fact that college football was expanding westward, and Northeastern schools were losing their monopoly on the game and its rules. Camp was getting pressure from fellow Yale alum named Amos Alonzo Stagg. Stagg, who was athletic director and football coach at the University of Chicago, was in the process of forming the first conference in college football history. The Eastern schools had split on the rules, and Stagg wrote to Camp urging him to create a uniform set of rules or, he warned, the Western colleges "shall certainly get out a set ourselves."[10] When Camp refused, Stagg's answer was for the University of Chicago to join with six other schools (Illinois, Michigan, Minnesota, Northwestern, Purdue, and Wisconsin) to form the **Western Conference** in 1896. Upon the addition of Indiana and Iowa in 1899 and Ohio State in 1912, the conference would officially be known as the **Big 10**. At least partially as a response to the formation of the first intercollegiate football conference, the traditional Eastern schools banded together under the leadership of Walter Camp to form for the first time a rules committee led by alumni of the schools. Neither the formation of the various rules committees or the conferences did much to address the issue of the brutality of the game. As a new century dawned, those issues remained unresolved.

College Football: 1900–1945

The Yale–Harvard freshman football game of 1905 produced its share of injuries, as most of the contests of the time did. One particular injury sustained during that game should be noted. It was a plucky little defensive lineman who continuously was knocked down and kept getting back up to get knocked down again. He was knocked out of the game with a severely broken nose that would require reconstructive surgery. Many who witnessed the game noted that the Yale offensive line appeared to be targeting the player throughout the game. This was perhaps due to the fact he was the smallest player on the line (5′ 7″ tall and 150 pounds). Some believed he was made a target because of his name—Theodore Roosevelt, Jr. A few weeks before the injury, Ted's father had assembled representatives of the "Big 3" schools at the White House to discuss what could be done to lessen the brutality and the resulting injuries that were plaguing the game. President Theodore Roosevelt was a fan of the game, as previously noted, but he was becoming concerned with what he referred to as "mucker play," which was what he considered to be unsportsmanlike, unnecessary roughness in the game. The representatives of the meeting (the most famous being Walter Camp from Yale) agreed to increase the emphasis on the already existing rules and promised to clean up the game. That was

President Theodore Roosevelt.
Image © Olga Popova, 2013. Used under license from Shutterstock, Inc.

good enough for the president, and he instructed Camp to issue a press release detailing the conclusions of the meeting. Many lauded Roosevelt's efforts, including the *New York Times*, which praised the president for "taking up another question of vital interest to the American people. He started a campaign for reform in football."[11] Somehow, a rumor started that Roosevelt had threatened to abolish the sport in the United States if changes were not made. Although there was no evidence that this threat was ever made and it seems unlikely considering Roosevelt's fondness for the game, many believed it, and some thought it led directly to his son's injury by opponents, who were not happy that their sport was being targeted for possible extinction. The president did not believe this was the case (after all, these were future gentlemen), but First Lady Edith Roosevelt certainly believed it. Before Ted's final game that freshman year (he would not compete on the varsity because of his small stature), his father wrote him a letter telling him how proud he was of him that he continued to compete through the injuries and that he thought football had been good for him, but the founder of the "strenuous life" added at the end of the letter a note of fatherly worry when he said, "I sympathize with your mother in being glad that after next Saturday your playing will be through."[12] Theodore Roosevelt would never again be directly involved in the reform of football.

It did not take long for evidence to surface that reform was still needed and the Roosevelt meeting had produced no change. A particularly dirty play occurred in "The Game" between Harvard and Yale on November 25. Harvard player Francis Burr made a fair catch signal but was "struck . . . square in the face" by Yale player Jim Quill, breaking Burr's nose. Though blood was gushing from Burr's face, no penalty was called. Many Harvard partisans (including the president of the United States) cried foul because the official who should have made the call was Paul Dashiell, one of Camp's cronies and known as being partial to Yale, who said he detected "no intentional blow" to the player's face. Harvard president Charles Eliot wrote to Roosevelt saying that "Mr. Dashiell is one of the things that has to be reformed."[13] The same day this event occurred, a much more tragic event was taking place in New York City. In a game between Union College and New York University, Union player Harold Moore was struck in the head and died of a cerebral hemorrhage at Fordham Hospital. This one event, more than any meeting at the White House, led to serious reform in college football. NYU Chancellor Henry McCracken was not a fan of football and to have this happen on his watch was not something he wanted to take lying down. He contacted Charles Eliot and demanded that there be a conference to reform the rules of the game. The Harvard president refused because he had already come to the conclusion that the game was no longer salvageable—it needed to be abolished. He was not the only college administrator to feel that way, as the football programs at Columbia, Cal, and Stanford were all disbanded that winter. West Coast teams like Stanford and Cal temporarily replaced football with rugby. McCracken decided it was going to take a movement from outside the "Big 3" to make real changes.

College Football's Modern Age

The early years of the 20th century were known as the **Progressive Era**. It was a time of reform for virtually every aspect of American society. Although the leading progressive of the time, Theodore Roosevelt, could not get college football to reform through his White House meeting in October of 1905, it did lead to subsequent meetings in which it reformed itself and ushered in the "modern era" of college football. McCracken called for and convened a meeting of all the college presidents on NYU's football schedule that season. They decided that if any real reform of the rules was to be made it would have to come from somewhere other than the current committee dominated by Walter Camp and the "Big 3." On December 28, 1905, representatives from 62 colleges met and formed the **Intercollegiate Athletic Association (ICAA)**. The ICAA was made up of schools from all over the country except for the West Coast and the "Big Three." The primary duty of the ICAA in the early years was the formation of standardized rules followed by all participants. The ICAA rules committee did not replace the current rules committee because it really did not have the power to. In fact, the teams represented by the ICAA were really not the powerhouse schools of college football—those teams were represented on the current rules committee. What McCracken and other members of the ICAA hoped was to persuade the current committee to work with them in a power-sharing arrangement that would finally make drastic rules changes and reform the game to ultimately save it. Over a period of about five years, that is exactly what happened. It was during that period that the ICAA would change its name to the NCAA (National Collegiate Athletic Association) and would be the governing body of all intercollegiate sports for the next century and beyond.

One of the first things the ICAA wanted to get under control was the "pay for play" issues that had been an emerging problem in the game. The organization condemned "offering inducements to players to enter universities because of their athletic abilities." They also came out strongly against what they termed "proselytizing" players (today it is called recruiting).[14] There was a phenomenon known as "tramp" players who might play for one school one week and for that school's opponent the next week if there was a better offer. The development of conferences in the late 19th century was supposed to solve this problem, but it was still an issue by 1905. The main concern of the ICAA (and the old rules committee, for that matter) was the brutality of the game and the need for changes in the rules to combat that. On January 12, 1906, both rules committees met in New York City within a block of one another. Harvard coach Bill Reid (who suspected that his school was planning on abolishing football if radical changes were not made) decided to make his way over to the ICAA meeting and served as the intermediary between the two committees. Reid convinced the two committees to merge and come together to decide the future of their sport. Reid knew that no real changes would be made with Camp running the show, so a deal was made to replace Camp from any leadership role with the merged committee. The powerless "father of American football" looked on while the committee made three major changes to the game he essentially invented. Even though he did not have an official role on the committee (except as editor of the rule book), he was very involved in the refinement of the new rules. One of the major changes was actually an idea of his—it increased the number of yards needed to gain by an offense from 5 to 10. He had actually hoped this rule alone would be enough to open up the playbook and decrease the number of injuries occurring with the mass plays used to get the required yardage. A second rule change refined Camp's line of scrimmage by adding a "neutral zone," which was essentially the length of the football that neither team could encroach upon before the ball was put into play. Prior to the neutral zone, players lined up so close to each other that officials could not see the jostling, holding, and punching going on between teams. Now that it would be easier to spot and to make sure infractions were seen, a fourth official was added (the linesman). Camp insisted on a centralized board of referees that would ensure the officials were trained and impartial. Officials would also be instructed to enforce unnecessary roughness penalties after the high-profile problems during the 1905 season. The most revolutionary of the new rules was the one that Camp feared the most: legalization of the forward pass. Camp did not stand in the way of this rule change, but he did help impose restrictions on its use. He did not foresee the pass as a way to score touchdowns so the ball could not cross the goal line. If it did, it would result in a touchback for the opposing team. The ball *had* to be passed to a player who lined up on the end of the line, and the ball could not be passed within five yards either side of where the center snapped it. If it was determined the ball was passed inside that five yards, possession would go over to the defensive team. Likewise, if a pass was incomplete, the ball would be awarded to the opposition where it touched the ground. What was probably the oddest part of the forward pass restrictions (at least from a modern viewpoint) was that a ball that landed incomplete out of bounds was live and could be recovered by either team. This resulted in what rules maker and coach David Nelson described as players receiving "many a cinder burn when . . . scrambling for the ball on the running tracks surrounding the fields."[15]

Rules were implemented in the fall of 1906 and seemingly, at least for the short term, had a positive effect. Injuries and deaths were down dramatically in 1906 and 1907. The *New York Times* reported there were 11 deaths at all levels of football in 1906, down from 18 deaths in 1905. Serious injuries were down by 35 percent in 1906. Although many reformers pointed to the rules changes as the reason for this drop—what seemed to be overlooked was the number of casualties (three) at the collegiate level was exactly the same in 1906 as it had been the prior year. The deaths seemed less high profile, and a false sense of calm enveloped college football for the next three seasons. Although deaths in college football tripled in 1908 over the previous season (two to six), it was not noticeable enough to cause a stir; but the 1909 season would once again bring severe criticism to college football as the death toll rose. Eleven collegians lost their lives playing football that season, and deaths at all levels jumped to an all-time high of anywhere from 26 to 32 (figures vary). What is more disturbing is these deaths could be attributed to the rules changes of 1906, or more precisely, the loopholes in those rules. The rules of 1906 did not expressly outlaw the dangerous "mass plays" that were so prevalent with the Eastern schools and resulted in injuries and deaths. In fact, most of the deaths of 1909 occurred at Eastern schools that refused to open up their offenses and utilize the forward pass. Walter Camp's Yale team, for instance, went undefeated in 1909 and very rarely used the forward pass.

When the ICAA gathered in January of 1910, it knew it had to address this and other rules issues. One of the criticisms of the 1906 rules changes is that they had been rushed through—the ICAA was not going to take that chance in 1910. In meetings that spanned four months they introduced rules that would finally provide the death knell for the old style of football and bring it into its modern age. When the ICAA adjourned in May, it had finally outlawed the mass play by requiring seven players on the line of scrimmage (which they had done before, but this time they prohibited the interlocking of players and the pushing, pulling, or throwing players with the ball). That last point was actually a designed play by some teams to take smaller players and launch them over the line of scrimmage with the ball during short yardage situations—one could just imagine the injuries sustained from that play. The other cause of many injuries was the "flying" or "diving" tackle in which defensive players would launch themselves at the player with the ball. Players would now have to keep at least one foot on the ground when tackling an opponent. The forward pass was allowed to continue (on a close vote of 8–6) and its use liberalized. Passes could now cross the line of scrimmage at any point, and incomplete passes on first and second downs would not result in loss of possession but loss of down and the ball replaced at the original line of scrimmage (same as it is in today's game). The only limits on the pass were that it still could not be thrown across the goal line, and passes exceeding 20 yards were not allowed. The only member of the rules committee who did not sign off on the new set of rules was Walter Camp. He did not even attend most of the meetings in April or May when the changes of rules were being debated. He claimed he was too busy with his job as president of the New Haven Clock Company and his other various boards he served on. What was more likely the reason was his disenchantment with the rules changes and his lessening power within the college football community. As if sensing how these changes would affect his beloved Yale teams, he withdrew as advisor to the Yale football squads shortly after these rules were adopted, and the glory days of Yale football (and the Big 3, for that matter) began to wane, as 1909 marked Yale's last national championship, and the last time an Ivy League school would top the national standings would be Dartmouth in 1925. Eventually, Ivy League schools deemphasized football and were no longer part of the football elite by the 1930s.

Two years later, as a member of the newly named **National Collegiate Athletic Association** (the old rules committee and ICAA had combined to form one governing body forever after known as the **NCAA**) and no longer having ties to any school, Walter Camp not only did not hinder further changes to the rules but actively supported dropping the limits on the forward pass. The 20-yard maximum was eliminated, and passes could now be completed across the goal line for touchdowns. Because of this rule change, there would now need to be "end zones," which were deemed to be 10 yards deep. Camp proposed shortening the football fields from 110 yards to 100 to accommodate the new end zones so existing stadium dimensions would not have to be changed. Other changes Camp supported would lead to a more offensive-oriented game: The number of downs to make the necessary 10 yards was increased from three to four, and touchdowns would now be worth six points instead of five. The ball itself would be elongated to be more favorable to the passing game. Where in the past Camp had been very protective of the game he invented and not willing to change it, the "father of American football" can be credited with helping reinvent the game in 1912 and bringing it into the modern age. Although there would always be injuries and even deaths in football (many of them probably could have been prevented with mandatory use of helmets, which did not happen until 1939), never again after 1912 was there ever a serious call by anyone to abolish the sport—it only grew and became more popular.

The Army, Indians, and War

Although 1912 is considered the birth of the modern era of college football, a game took place that fall that hearkened back to the previous century. West Point Military Academy hosted a team from Carlisle, Pennsylvania, near the end of the season. Carlisle was an Indian school set up in 1879 as a vehicle for assimilating Indian children into American society by breaking them away from their traditional culture. The Carlisle Indians were led by one of the best young coaches in the country, Glenn "Pop" Warner, and the star of the team was running back Jim Thorpe, who had recently won gold medals for the pentathlon and decathlon in the 1912 Olympics in Stockholm. The press played up the historical relationship between the Indians and the military as the *New York Times* headlined: "Indians to Battle with Soldiers." Most experts did not give the smaller Carlisle team much of a chance against the bigger, more experienced Army cadets, but the innovative Warner had a plan. Part of that plan included motivation—as his quarterback Gus Welch remembered: "He reminded the boys that it was the fathers and grandfathers of these Army players who fought the Indians. That was enough."[16] Simple motivation was not enough to overcome the size differential of the teams so the other part of Warner's plan included new formations and a no-huddle offense to take advantage of Carlisle's speed. The plan worked, as the Indians shut down Army's star halfback Dwight Eisenhower and soundly defeated the Cadets 27–6. Although Eisenhower graduated to begin his remarkable military career prior to the next season, the 1913 Army team was again formidable. In October, the Cadets hosted a rising Midwestern power from South Bend, Indiana. The University of Notre Dame was led by quarterback Gus Dorias, who utilized the forward pass, especially to end Knute Rockne, to defeat Army 35–13. The combination of these two Army losses showed that the new rules that allowed more passing and speed could defeat the old tactics of power and brawn. It also proved to be very popular with the public—a touchdown could now be scored at any time from any place on the field. The old ways of grinding it out up the middle were gone.

Jom Thorpe in his Carlisle jersey. Image © Solodov Alexey, 2013. Used under license from Shutterstock, Inc.

In 1914 the first World War broke out in Europe, and although injuries and deaths still occurred in football (an estimated 500 died at all levels of the game between 1910 and 1950),[17] it seemed tame compared to what was going on in Europe as the death toll rose through 1915 and 1916, so there was little talk of any more reform in the game. In the spring of 1917, the United States joined the war, and most of the cadets who had played in those pivotal football games of 1912 and 1913 found themselves preparing for a much more serious battle as they headed across the Atlantic Ocean into the bloodiest war in human history—many of whom would not return. College football fields, for the most part, in the falls of 1917 and 1918 were quiet as many schools cancelled their programs due to lack of players and also to conserve fuel and energy for the war effort. This did not mean, however, that football was forgotten—in fact, it was used not only as a diversion for soldiers (one observer to a military training camp noticed no less than "forty-seven different football games" being played)[18] but also for training itself. Walter Camp was even brought in to help train soldiers. Camp had long been an advocate of exercise, and he incorporated that into the training of soldiers going to war. The games that were being played by soldiers were modeled after the "modern game" that had been adopted by the rules changes of 1910 and 1912, and when the soldiers begin returning home in 1918 and 1919, it was that game they wanted to play and watch. It was that game that would burst onto the scene in the 1920s as a more excitement-seeking public was craving a more exciting game.

The 1920s

By the dawn of the 1920s the Progressive Era was all but over, and the Victorian middle class had been replaced by a **new middle class** that was looking for stimulation from all aspects of American life. Sports became a source for that stimulation, and the modern game of college football was ideal for meeting that need. A prime example of the new game emerged with its first superstar— **Red Grange**. American heroes had always come from politics and the military, but beginning in this decade, with the emergence of movies and the popularity of athletics, Americans have since

Red Grange. Image ©
Neffali, 2013. Used under
license from Shutterstock, Inc.

Grantland Rice.
Image courtesy of
Library of Congress

primarily done their hero worship with athletes and entertainers. Harold "Red" Grange fit the mold of an American hero perfectly—he did not smoke or drink, he was a self-made, rugged individual who reacted to all his accomplishments with a humility that Americans appreciated. He also played the game of football in the style that the "new" middle class loved—he had an explosiveness and an ability to avoid tacklers and score at any given moment in a game. During his high school career in Wheaton, Illinois, Grange scored 75 touchdowns in four years, and because he worked delivering ice in the summer, which also built his strength, was given his first nickname of the "ice man." After being recruited by several Midwestern schools, he chose to attend his home state's University of Illinois, where he was given a new nickname by the most famous sportswriter in the country, **Grantland Rice**. Rice was known for his poetic writing and quotations like probably his most famous: "For when the One Great Scorer comes To mark against your name, He writes—not that you won or lost—But how you played the Game." Grange would later dispute that it was Rice who gave him his moniker—he claimed it was a Chicago sportswriter named Warren Brown. Whoever was responsible for the name, Grange was called the "**Galloping Ghost**" due to his ability to seemingly slip through would-be tacklers' hands. Grange showed that ability from his first game in 1923, when he amassed over 200 yards against Nebraska and led his team to an undefeated season, conference (now known as the Big 10), and national championship, as well as a place on Walter Camp's All-American team. It was a game against Michigan the following year that cemented his reputation and growing legend. Michigan coach Fielding Yost had proclaimed that his team would "stop Grange cold."[19] Grange proceeded to return the opening kickoff 95 yards for a touchdown and had touchdown runs of 67, 56, and 44 yards before the first quarter ended. He ran for a fifth touchdown in the second half and threw for another before ending the day with 402 yards rushing.

Throughout his senior year there was speculation on what Grange would do next—some thought he would turn professional, others said he would go to Hollywood and become a movie star; there was even talk of him running for Congress (even though he would have to wait at least three years to do that before he reached the minimum age of 25). The suspense ended immediately following the final game of the season after Illinois defeated Ohio State 14–9. Grange announced he had already signed a deal to play for George Halas's Chicago Bears of the fledgling National Football League. There was some criticism of Grange because being paid to play football was still looked down on by most in American society at the time. In fact, when asked about it, Fielding Yost commented that "he would be glad to see Grange do anything but play professional football."[20] There was also criticism that Grange would not finish his college career and get his degree—his own coach, Bob Zuppke was quoted as saying, "My only regret is that he will no more graduate from Illinois than will the Kaiser return to power in Germany."[21] Indeed, Grange did not even finish that semester as he joined the Bears for a Thanksgiving game the following week and a barnstorming tour throughout that winter. Grange had hired an agent named **Charles "Cash and Carry" Pyle** who had made a name for himself as a theater promoter and was now embarking on a career as a sports promoter. Pyle is often criticized as being money-hungry and of taking advantage of Grange, but Grange always defended Pyle and made no bones about the fact he made all his decisions based on his financial benefit: "I'm out to get the money," Grange said, "and I don't care who knows it."[22] Get the money he did, as he reportedly earned a quarter of a million dollars finishing out the Bears season and on the barnstorming tour with them that winter. Grange and the Bears played a grueling 24 games over an eight-week period filling stadiums to capacity all over the country. He also earned more money endorsing about every product imaginable. He and Pyle made so much money that they tried to buy one-third ownership of the Bears in 1926. When Halas refused, they attempted to add a second NFL team in New York. When the Giants blocked that, they decided to form their own team and a rival professional league called the American Football League. Grange played for and was part owner of the New York Yankees and although he helped fill the seats, the rest of the teams lost money, and the league folded after one season. Grange did convince the NFL to allow the Yankees to join the league as a permanent road team in 1927, but after a knee injury in the third game forced him to sit out the remainder of the season, the Yankees were forced to fold, and Grange and Pyle severed their professional relationship. Grange returned to the Bears, where he played out his career, finally retiring in 1935.

Grange was never the same player on the professional level as he had been in college. Many blamed that punishing tour he and Pyle embarked on in the winter of 1925–26. His body seemed to take a beating that winter from which it never really recovered. His career high watermark was that game against Michigan on October 18, 1924. That was also the day the University of Illinois was dedicating its new stadium. It would be christened Memorial Stadium in honor of the fallen from the First World War. Illinois was not unique in this, as campuses all over the country during the decade of the twenties built stadiums out of concrete and steel and often named them Memorial Stadium. From Columbus, Ohio, to Lincoln, Nebraska, and even out in Los Angeles, California, stadiums were being constructed at a record pace. These stadiums were much larger than in previous decades to accommodate the growing numbers of fans. During the decade, attendance at college football games doubled, and gate receipts tripled. In 1920 only one stadium in the country held more than 70,000 (ironically, it was the Yale Bowl, which had been built more on the reputation of its storied past than its unforeseen fading future), but in 1930 there were seven stadiums that held that number. If you could not get into one of these stadiums to watch your favorite team, you could use the new technology of the time to either hear the games on the radio or see highlights on the movie theater screens all over the country—this helped the legend of Red Grange and other great athletes of the 1920s because even though you may never have seen any of these players in person, millions listened to their exploits or saw them on the screen, and for the first time athletes developed a following that way.

Notre Dame

As the greatness of the "Big 3" and other Eastern elite schools faded during the 1920s, a school in the Midwest took their place. By the end of the decade, a small liberal arts school from South Bend, Indiana, emerged as the dominant program in college football, and its following would reach legendary status. The **University of Notre Dame** was established in 1844 by a French religious order known as the Congregation of the Holy Cross. It quickly became a haven for midwestern Catholics, and by the turn of the 20th century had a modest academic reputation, and its baseball team was more renowned than its football program. How did a small school like this gain such a reputation for football in the period of 20 years? The simple answer would be **Knute Rockne**. The 22-year-old Norwegian immigrant arrived in South Bend in 1910 feeling, as he put it, "the strangeness of being a lone Norse–Protestant invader of a Catholic stronghold."[23] He quickly established a reputation for himself as a track athlete and an end for the football team. It was his performance against Army in his senior year in 1913 noted earlier that helped establish the forward pass as a potent offensive weapon in the game. After he graduated, Rockne continued to perfect that weapon as assistant coach for the Notre Dame team and then when he took over as the school's head coach in 1918 at the young age of 30. Rockne was a perfect fit for the school and for the decade of the 1920s. He was a quick wit and was great at what would be known in modern parlance as "sound bites" in the press. The press helped the

Knute Rockne. Image © Neftali, 2013. Used under license from Shutterstock, Inc.

growing legend of Notre Dame from broadcasting games coast-to-coast on the new technology of radio to Grantland Rice naming the 1924–25 backfield the "Four Horsemen." After Notre Dame's victory against Army in 1924, Rice was at his hyperbolic best when he began his game report with the following poetic words: "*Outlined against a blue-gray October sky, the Four Horsemen rode again. In dramatic lore they are known as Famine, Pestilence, Destruction and Death. These are only aliases. Their real names are Stuhldreher, Miller, Crowley, and Layden. They formed the crest of the South Bend cyclone before which another fighting Army team was swept over the precipice. . . .*"[24] There was not much evidence that this backfield was particularly great, but they were on an undefeated team, and if Rice wrote it, it must be true.

Rockne's motivational skills were well known if not always based in complete truths. His most famous half-time pep talk occurred in 1928, when he gave his famous "Win one for the Gipper" speech. George Gipp had been an all-American star on Rockne's early squads. He contracted influenza, which killed him shortly after the 1920 season ended—a season that Gipp helped the "Catholics" (they would not be referred to as the "Fighting Irish" until sometime during the 1920s) go undefeated and become established as a national powerhouse. Rockne claimed Gipp had told him on his deathbed to someday relay to his team when things are not going their way to "go out there with all they've got and win just one for the Gipper." In the 1928 game against an undefeated and favored Army team, Notre Dame was tied 0–0 at the half when Rockne relayed the story. Notre Dame came out and defeated Army in the second half 12–6. Did Gipp really give that dying wish to Rockne? Although it was memorably recounted by Ronald Reagan playing Gipp in the 1940 movie, *Knute Rockne, All-American*, there is no evidence Gipp actually said those words to Rockne. In fact, one of Rockne's players, Jim Crowley, a member of the Four Horsemen, kept a long list of half-truths and outright lies Rockne would use to motivate his team. "They were all lies, blatant lies," Crowley remembered. "The Jesuits call it mental reservation, but he had it in abundance."[25] Whether or not his speeches were rooted in truth or not, there was no disputing his ability to be a motivator. There was also no disputing his innovations to the game. His offensive formations, including the box backfield formation and the "Notre Dame shift," were truly revolutionary and kept opposing defenses guessing as to what was coming next. He also was one of the first to recognize the importance of exercise in training and would even choreograph calisthenics much like a dancer would.

In the early days of college football, a coach was not used—usually the team captain acted as coach. As early as the late 19th century it became apparent that professional coaches would need to be hired by schools. By the 1920s those coaches were paid extremely well—often more than the highest-paid professor at the institution. Knute Rockne was at the top of this pay scale, and this was due, in no small part, to his ability to market himself. Rockne would often make it known to the Notre Dame administration that he was being sought after by other schools in a ploy to get a higher salary from Notre Dame to retain him. It was generally believed by the 1920s that a football coach was more important to his team and had more of an influence on the outcome of a game than coaches of any other sport, and this was certainly the case with Rockne. He also knew how to market his school. The old animosity against recruiting had not only vanished, but it was now a necessary part of a coach's job description—as long as the scholastic ability of that potential student was also being taken into consideration—and no one was better at it than Rockne. He actually had something else working in his favor—he had what were known as "subway alumni" in large cities like New York or "coal field alumni" in western Pennsylvania, eastern Ohio, and West Virginia.[26] These were people who may have never stepped foot on Notre Dame's campus or any other college campus, for that matter, but were Catholics who united behind Notre Dame during a decade that was not a particularly good one for their faith. There was a growing nativist movement that not only was anti-immigrant but also anti-Catholic because that was the most common religious affiliation of those immigrants. The Ku Klux Klan was rejuvenated during the decade, and it also would expand its hatred from Blacks to Jews and Catholics as well. Rockne, who had converted to Catholicism in 1923, would also use Catholic churches and organizations to help increase the school's following and add to his roster. Another way to increase the visibility of Notre Dame was to play as many different schools from as varying parts of the country as possible. Rockne was ready to take on all comers, but sometimes his schedule was limited by outside influences (like Eastern schools and the Big 10 schools refusing to play Notre Dame), and sometimes it was limited from the inside. An example of this was a growing rivalry with Nebraska that was ended in 1925 by Notre Dame. The two schools had played annually since 1915, and the record was even with five wins each. During the three years Notre Dame's backfield was comprised of the Four Horsemen, they only lost two games—both to Nebraska in Lincoln. After the 1925 game, the Notre Dame administration took Nebraska off the schedule due to poor treatment by Nebraska fans—largely believed to be of an anti-Catholic nature. Rockne acknowledged the treatment but was reluctant to end a series that was beginning to bring in big gate money to the school. Notre Dame replaced Nebraska with the University of Southern California, and the rivalry continues to this day. After the 1930 season, Rockne had amassed an incredible 105 wins, 12 defeats, and 5 ties in 13 seasons. Although recognized as one of the greatest coaches of all time, it's impossible to know how great he could have been because his career and life were tragically cut short when he was killed in a plane crash in March of 1931—he was only 43 years old.

Carnegie Report and the 1930s

There had been virtually no calls for reform in college football for nearly two decades until a report was released just before the end of the 1920s detailing the findings of a study looking into college football. The study was commissioned by the Carnegie Foundation in 1926, and when it released its findings in 1929, it was the first real indictment of the game and call for reform since 1912. The big issue now was the influence of money the game had brought into institutions of higher learning and the lessening importance put on academics. Although the report was very long and detailed, the findings were succinctly boiled down to the following sentence: "Apparently the ethical bearing of intercollegiate football contests and their scholastic aspects are of secondary importance to the winning of victories and financial success."[27] The chief executive of the Carnegie Foundation was Henry Pritchett, former president of MIT, who commissioned social scientist Howard Savage and a team of researchers to look into the programs of 130 colleges and universities. Neither Pritchett nor Savage was antifootball crusaders by any means, and although their findings were harsh, they were fair. The findings of the study pointed to recruiting based solely on athletic ability, not scholastic ability, which was bringing down the overall prestige of the institutions. There was a concern that time devoted to athletic endeavors left little for academics. Also, in a time before athletic scholarships, some colleges were essentially offering them without calling them that. The student–athlete would have their tuition and room and board paid for from funds that would be coded "student leadership" or "campus activities."[28] There would also be "jobs" that athletes would get paid for and rarely, if ever, have to show up for. Much of the funding came from wealthy alumni and boosters of the football program—this was a particular problem pointed to by the **Carnegie Report**. Boosters would often offer "loans" to athletes with no intention of ever having to be paid back. Secret accounts were even uncovered that were controlled by the head coaches or athletic directors to be used to pay the athletes directly. The reaction to the report was widespread shock and denial—many coaches claimed they had been duped by the investigators. The report was so pervasive and well researched that it was difficult to refute. What was the solution offered by the Carnegie Foundation? The game had grown too large to even contemplate its abolition, as had been the solution to many reformers in the early part of the century. Now more administrative control was called for. Presidents of universities would have to keep better tabs on their athletic departments. The problem with this solution was that most of the presidents were part of the problem. The report itself found that most presidents either had ignored the problem or wished to remain ignorant of it. Many of them simply did not want to challenge wealthy boosters willing to give large donations to their schools. Although a few presidents took the report to heart and actually tried to get some control back, most either paid lip service to it or ignored it completely. The report was big news for awhile, but events on Wall Street a few weeks later relegated it to the back pages of the newspaper. The stock market crash in October of 1929 plunged the nation into the worst economic depression in its history, and everyone had other things on their mind—including many of those wealthy boosters, many of whom who were no longer wealthy.

Although the Great Depression had a negative effect on all of American life, one area that was not touched as negatively was entertainment—people needed an escape. College football had become big entertainment by the 1930s. Although the early years of the decade hit colleges hard, and many dropped their football programs and attendance fell off, by 1937 college football attendance shot up to nearly 20 million annually—a figure that doubled the attendance of 1930.[29] Many of college football's enduring legacies began during this decade. While the oldest of the postseason bowl games began in 1902 in relationship to the Tournament of Roses in Pasadena, California, the **Rose Bowl** was started in an effort to reward two teams that had a good season with an extra game. During the Great Depression, boosters from hard-hit Southern cities decided to hold postseason bowl games in an effort to improve the economy of their communities. In 1933, Miami hosted the first Orange Bowl, and New Orleans staged the first Sugar Bowl in 1935. Two Texas cities got in on the act in 1936 and 1937 with El Paso's Sun Bowl and Dallas's Cotton Bowl, respectively. Although Walter Camp's All-American teams were still being chosen yearly, in 1936 New York's Downtown Athletic Club decided to award the **Heisman Trophy** (named for a former player and coach John Heisman, who had been athletic director of the club and had recently died) to the nation's outstanding individual player. Journalists had been naming national champions since before the turn of the century, but it was in 1936 that the weekly press poll was born. Alan Gould, sports editor of the Associated Press, invented the poll as a way to determine the nation's best teams. Each week he would poll 50 sportswriters and broadcasters and ask them to list their top 20 teams. Points were then given in decreasing order from 1 to 20, and the poll was determined based on that. College football appeared to be reaching incredible heights despite the economic times until just after the 1941 season ended. The Japanese attack on Pearl Harbor that thrust the United States into the Second World War had its obvious effects on the sport. Most colleges dropped their football programs due to lack of players. Those that kept their programs did so with a dramatic drop in skill level and ability of the participants. As a testimony to the enduring popularity of the sport, however, when the war ended in 1945, involvement and attendance shot back up to new heights.

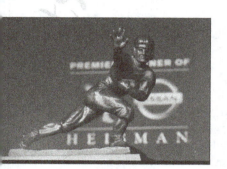

Heisman Trophy which was first awarded in 1936. Image © Debby Wong, 2013. Used under license from Shutterstock, Inc.

Conclusion

During its first three-quarters of a century, college football survived many attempts to abolish it and emerged as the king of all athletics on the college campus. The brutality of the game led many schools to drop the sport but rules changes and improvements in equipment led to a lessening of injuries and deaths and a more exciting style. The exciting style resulted in its ever-increasing popularity in the first decades of the 20th century. Even the Great Depression of the 1930s could not dampen the enthusiasm for the sport. Although World War II would diminish the numbers playing and the quality of the sport, college football would emerge from the war even stronger than it had been prior. The Carnegie Report of the early '30s showed that college football had changed the very nature of institutions of higher learning—it had put less emphasis on academics in many schools and more emphasis on winning football and making money. In the second half of the century college football would evolve into something that would make the Carnegie Report look very tame indeed.

Notes

1. Ronald Smith, *Sports and Freedom* (Oxford: Oxford University Press, 1988), 70–71.
2. Ibid., 73.
3. Ibid., 74.
4. Ibid.
5. Ibid., 75.
6. Benjamin Rader, *American Sports; From the Age of Folk Games to the Age of Televised Sports*, 6th ed. (Upper Saddle River, NJ: Pearson-Prentice Hall, 2009), 92.
7. Smith, *Sports and Freedom*, 97.
8. Ibid., 92.
9. Ibid., 93.
10. Ibid., 94.
11. John Watterson, *College Football* (Baltimore: Johns Hopkins University Press, 2000), 70.
12. Ibid., 69.
13. Ibid., 71.
14. Ibid., 78.
15. Ibid., 104.
16. Richard O. Davies, *Sports in American Life* (West Sussex, UK: Wiley-Blackwell, 2012), 58.
17. Ibid., 59.
18. Watterson, *College Football*, 139.
19. Davies, *Sports in American Life*, 123.
20. Watterson, *College Football*, 153.
21. Ibid., 154.
22. Ibid.
23. Edwin Pope, *Football's Greatest Coaches* (Atlanta: Tupper and Love, 1955), 195.
24. Davies, *Sports in American Life*, 127.
25. Ibid., 129.
26. Rader, *American Sports*, 187.
27. Davies, *Sports in American Life*, 130.
28. Ibid., 132.
29. Rader, *American Sports*, 184.

CHAPTER *Five*

CHAPTER

Six

CHAPTER Six

The Golden Age of Baseball

$\mathcal{I}$t was obvious from the start of the game that Cy Young had not brought his best "stuff" to the mound for the Boston Pilgrims that October day in 1903. He was hit hard and often by the Pittsburgh Pirates and gave up four runs in the first inning. The partisan Boston crowd of 16,000 sensed this was not going to be their day. The Pirates' pitcher Deacon Phillipe, fared much better, and Pittsburgh won 7–3. It was the first game of a series between two cities that were separated by less than 500 miles, but it was being touted as the "World Championship" series of baseball. Two years later the name of the series would be officially changed to the "World Series." Young was already a legend in his 14th major league season and well on his way to holding many major league records, including was the most wins by any pitcher (511). He would eventually have his name immortalized by the award bearing his name being presented annually to the best pitcher in the game. On this day, however, he was very mortal, and the Boston Globe even referred to the 36-year-old pitcher as "Uncle Cyrus," and also described him as getting "a bit fat."[1] Those words must have stung the old veteran, especially because he felt the responsibility of carrying not only the banner of the city of Boston but also a brand new baseball league—the American League. Although the official name of the Boston Club was the "Pilgrims," they were also referred to in the press as the "Americans," showing its representation of the new league. Young knew the importance of his league winning this first championship series in its first year of competition as a "major league" to prove it was on the level of the old National League. If he did not know it, the Boston owner surely did, as American League president Ban Johnson "ordered" him to win the series. Young was back to his old self in his next two starts, winning both of them and finishing with an earned run average of 1.85, and Boston won the nine-game series 5–3. Five years later, the Pilgrims would become the Red Sox, and they would win four more World Series Championships over the next 15 years.

The American League

Ban Johnson.
Image courtesy of
Library of Congress

Byron Bancroft Johnson was not a man to be trifled with. He was used to getting his way—as he did in the 1903 championship series after his "order" to the Boston owner was "obeyed." Ban Johnson was born in Norwalk, Ohio, in 1864, the son of a college professor. After attending college and playing collegiate baseball, Johnson spent some time playing semi-pro and studying law at Marietta College. Although he did not receive his law degree and he did not have the talent to play major league baseball, he did land a job as a sportswriter for the Cincinnati *Commercial-Gazette* in the late 1880s. He would eventually become the newspaper's sports editor and become friends with the manager of the Cincinnati Reds, Charles Comiskey. That friendship did not preclude Johnson from criticizing the Reds in print, and by 1893, Reds owner John T. Brush was fed up with Johnson and was looking for a way to get rid of him. After the 1893 season, he saw his opportunity, as he used his influence in the game to make Johnson president of a struggling minor league. The Western League was made up of eight Midwestern cities, and unfortunately for Johnson, one of those teams (Indianapolis) was owned by Brush; so leaving Cincinnati behind did not end the contentious relationship between the two. Fortunately for Johnson, his old friend Charles Comiskey soon gained ownership of the Western League's St. Paul club, and now he had a strong ally to counter his enemy in Indianapolis. Johnson proved to be a formidable businessman and leader of the league. Within two seasons, he had turned around the Western to where it was now making money, and it was being touted as the "strongest minor ever."[2] That was not enough for Johnson—he was not satisfied with his league remaining in the "minor" status and hoped to become a "major" league to rival the National League. He hoped to expand his league into the major cities of Chicago and Cleveland and hopefully even New York. As was pointed out in Chapter 3, the 1890s was a difficult time for organized professional baseball for two main reasons: the lack of competition for the National League and the league's brand of baseball that was considered dirty and its players too rowdy. Johnson promised an answer to both those problems by offering competition through an equally strong league and a better, purer form of the game. To accomplish this, Johnson ran the league with an iron fist and had autocratic control over everything that moved in the league.

By 1899, his firm control seemed to be paying dividends, and after just six seasons under Johnson's control, he decided it was time to begin making his move. After expanding into Cleveland and Chicago (the latter franchise was put under the control of Charles Comiskey), he decided to officially change the name of the Western League to the **American League**, thus giving the league a more nationwide flavor. The new century opened with a strong new league, and although not yet a major league, it was gaining a following and positive press coverage. The *Sporting News* noticed during the 1900 season that although the league may not have had the talent that the National League possessed, it was a financial success and its fans appreciated the cleaner version of baseball. According to the *News*, the American League lacked "the cowardly truckling, alien ownership, syndicatism . . . selfish jealousies, arrogance of club owners, mercenary spirit, and disregard of public demands" of the National League.[3] Johnson knew that to be a true major league, a name change would not be sufficient—he would have to have teams in the East as well as the West. He had four Eastern cities in mind—Washington, Baltimore, Philadelphia, and Boston. He thought the first two cities would be relatively easy to expand into because the National League had abandoned their franchises there. The latter two, however, would pose a greater obstacle because there was still a National League presence in those cities. In the National League winter meetings in December 1900, Johnson hoped to address the owners and inform them of his plans and possibly work out an agreement. The owners chose to ignore Johnson and adjourned before he had a hearing. That was a major mistake on their part. Johnson now felt absolutely no inclination toward civility to the established league whatsoever. Before the National League snub, he had considered a franchise in Buffalo, where there was no National League team, as opposed to Boston, where there was. After the December meeting, he went ahead with the Boston franchise. In February 1901, Johnson made his feelings public with a statement that ended with a challenge to those owners who had ignored him weeks before: "The National League has taken it for granted that no one had a right to expand without first getting its permission. We did not think this was necessary, and have expanded without even asking for permission. . . . If we had waited for the National League to do something for us, we would have remained a minor league forever. The American League will be the principal organization of the country within a very short time. Mark my prediction."[4]

Although Johnson honored the contracts of players in the National League, he did not honor its reserve clause. Beginning in the 1901 season, he openly recruited National League players with

CHAPTER Six

better salaries—on average a player could expect to be paid about $500 more per season in Johnson's American League. Whereas the National League owners could have avoided this had they met with Johnson and worked out a deal, now, because they ignored him, it was all-out war. Of the 180 players in the American League in 1902, 111 had played in the National League. That does not necessarily mean they were taken directly from a National League roster, but they had simply *once* played in the senior circuit. The *Spalding Guide* to baseball reported that 74 players jumped directly to the American League in the 1901 and 1902 seasons (thereby rendering the reserve clause meaningless in those seasons). Attendance rose in the American League from just under 1.7 million in 1901 to over 2.2 million in 1902, and that rise can be attributed at least in part to former National League fans following their favorite players to the new league because the National League saw a drop of almost a quarter-million in the same period (1.92 million to 1.68 million).[5] Six of the eight American League teams showed a profit in 1902, which was a good percentage for the time. Even the *Spalding Guide* had to admit that the American League "has more stars and can furnish a better article of baseball than the National League."[6]

Whether it was the loss of players, the dropoff in attendance, or the announcement that the American League was making plans to expand into New York (which it did do after dropping its Baltimore franchise), by the beginning of 1903 the National League owners were ready to sit down and talk with Johnson. In a hastily called emergency meeting in January 1903, the owners first proposed a consolidation of the two leagues, but Johnson flatly rejected that idea. He said the American League would remain intact with its eight teams (Boston, New York, Philadelphia, and Washington in the East; Chicago, Cleveland, Detroit, and St. Louis in the West), which would remain unchanged until the 1950s. The National League really had no choice and accepted the arrangement. The next source of controversy was territorial rights for teams and each league's rights to players. Cities that would have more than one team (Boston, Chicago, New York, Philadelphia, and St. Louis) were most worried about the arrangement, but eventually it was agreed those cities would have two teams, and there would be no consolidation. The team makeup of each league could not be changed without the consent of the majority of both league's owners. It was then agreed that each league would make a list of players that were awarded to each league (essentially the lists consisted of players who were on the respective league's rosters at the end of the 1902 season, which gave a distinct advantage to the American League because of all the former National League players who had jumped to the new league). Uniform contracts would be made between the leagues to keep salaries equal, and the reserve clause would be honored by both leagues. Finally, a three-man commission was formed to govern all disputes in the game. The commission would consist of the president of each league, and the third member would be chosen by the presidents and act as chairman. The arrangement would remain in place until 1920, when the idea of a baseball commissioner was introduced. When the final vote on the whole arrangement was made, there was only one dissenting vote—Ban Johnson's old nemesis from Cincinnati, John T. Brush, had become the owner of the National League's New York Giants. Due to the arrangement on players and the fact his Giants team would now face competition from an American League franchise in the same city, he voted against the new national agreement. Brush was not alone in his opposition to giving in to Johnson and the upstart American League. There was plenty of grumbling among the owners, but others recognized that it was a blessing in disguise for not only the National League but also for the national game. Albert Goodwill Spalding wrote a few years later that "in the evolution of Base Ball, it took many years for those in control of the game to learn the very simple lesson, known well to every man engaged in commerce, that 'competition is the life of trade.' It needed just such a man as (Ban) Johnson, and just such a league as he has established, to provoke the kind of public interest that now attaches to the game of Base Ball. It requires just such competition as is annually presented in the postseason contests to give zest to the sport.

So long as the National League was alone upon the field it occupied a position akin to that of the Old Knickerbockers."[7]

It was that postseason contest in 1903, agreed on at the January meeting, that not only added "zest" to the game, but also with the American League's victory ended any talk that there was not equity between the leagues. Johnson recognized the importance of a victory in that series, which is why he "ordered" Boston to defeat Pittsburgh, and he was extremely relieved when they accomplished it. The following year provided controversy in regard to the postseason championship. The Boston Pilgrims again won the American League pennant, but this time the National League crown was won by John Brush's New York Giants. Brush's player–manager was the pugnacious **John T. McGraw**. McGraw had been one of toughest and best players on the 1890s' most notoriously dirty National League team, the Baltimore Orioles. McGraw decided to jump to the American League in 1901 when it expanded to Baltimore; but his brand of ball and his combative personality did not mesh well with Johnson, and the relationship did not even last two seasons. Midway through the 1902 campaign, Johnson suspended McGraw indefinitely for arguing with umpires, and he went back to the National League when Brush hired him to play for and manage the team he had recently become the majority owner of—the New York Giants. McGraw never forgave Johnson for his suspension, and Brush was still harboring a grudge

John T. McGraw (middle). Image courtesy of Library of Congress

from Johnson's days as a sportswriter in Cincinnati a decade before, not to mention his American League invasion of New York. They both agreed the Giants would not play the Pilgrims for the championship in 1904. There was a myriad of negative press as a result, and when the Giants again won the pennant in 1905, Brush decided that for the good of the game, they would play the Philadelphia Athletics for what would be referred to for the first time as the "**World Series**." There may have also been money behind the decision; McGraw, who was always known as a "player's manager," wanted to make sure his players (and himself) would not miss out on the bonus they would receive by playing in the series. The Giants defeated the A's four games to one (the new agreement called for a seven-game playoff) to bring honor back to the National League. The series would be played every year (even during two World Wars) for nearly a century. The only year not to have a World Series was 1994, when a player's strike ended the season (and the postseason) prematurely.

In 1906, for the first time, teams from the same city were featured in the series when Charles Comiskey's Chicago White Sox defeated the cross-town National League champion Cubs. The Cubs would get their revenge the next two seasons by winning the World Series in both 1907 and 1908 over the Detroit Tigers. The 1908 Cubs deserve a closer look not only because, as Cubs fans certainly know, it was the franchise's last World Series victory, but also because of how they got to the series. Throughout the season they were battling John McGraw's Giants for the pennant. The two teams met at the Giants' home field, the Polo Grounds, on September 23. The game was tied in the bottom of the ninth, and the Giants had men on first and third with two outs. Shortstop Al Bridwell lined a single to centerfield, and the Giants scored what they thought was the winning run. The runner on first was 19-year-old rookie Fred Merkle, who was concerned for his own safety as the Giants fans began streaming onto the field, thinking the game was over. Merkle turned and headed for the dugout before touching second base, also thinking the game was over. Under baseball rules, however, because Merkle would have been a force-out at second, the winning run would not count if the Cubs would simply tag second base with the ball. The problem was in the chaos that ensued, the ball had been thrown into the stands, and a Giants fan was already on his way home with a

Fred Merkle. Image courtesy of Library of Congress

souvenir. It was reported that two Cubs players tackled the fan, relayed the ball back to the field to second baseman Johnny Evers, and he tagged second. Others claimed the ball Evers used was not the game ball but a different ball that the Cubs supplied to record the out. Umpire Henry O'Day, who had umpired a game in which there was a similar situation only a few weeks earlier and ruled that the runner should be out, called Merkle out and disallowed the winning run. National League President Harry Pulliam upheld the decision, declared the game a tie, and ruled that if the two teams had the same record at the end of the season, there would be a one-game playoff. Less than two weeks later that is exactly what happened, and on October 8 the Cubs defeated the Giants and won the pennant. The whole incident became known as the **Merkle Boner**, and although Merkle played for 14 seasons in the major leagues, he was always known for this play. It did not help when Cubs owner Charles Murphy was asked about the play and replied: "We can't supply brains to the New York Club's dumb players."[8] Giants manager John McGraw never blamed Merkle for the loss—he reserved his enmity for the decision by the league to call the game a tie, which thereby cost his team the pennant: "It is criminal to say that Merkle is stupid and to blame the loss of the pennant on him," McGraw said. "We were robbed of it and you can't very well say Merkle did that."[9] Years later, after seeing how the play affected Merkle, Al Bridwell, who had gotten the hit that started the whole series of events, said: "I wish I never would have gotten that hit. I wish I would have struck out instead. That would have saved Fred a lot of humiliation."[10] As sad of a story as Merkle's is, it pales in comparison to what happened to Harry Pulliam. The National League president continued to be berated by both Giants' fans as well and the management of the team. Manager John McGraw did not understand why the field was not cleared and the game continued into extra innings (O'Day claimed it was too dark to resume play). Things got so bad for Pulliam that he had a "nervous breakdown" in early 1909, and on July 28 of that year he committed suicide by shooting himself through the head.[11]

Ty Cobb

The team the Cubs defeated in 1908 in the World Series, the Detroit Tigers, had a young outfielder who was rapidly on his way to becoming the best hitter in the game and who is often mentioned in the conversation when the "greatest ballplayer of all time" argument is raised. **Tyrus Raymond Cobb** was born in rural Georgia on December 18, 1886, and was first called up to Detroit during the 1905 season and at the age of 18 was the youngest player in the major leagues at the time. Cobb had an odd hands-apart grip of the bat, which, along with incredible hand–eye coordination, allowed him to place the ball wherever he wanted. He would use that ability over a 24-year career to amass incredible batting records like winning batting championships in half of the seasons he played (12—including 9 in a row) and the highest lifetime batting average of all time (.367). He batted over .400 in three seasons and only hit below .300 once, which was his short rookie season in 1905, in which he only played in the final month. He played his entire career with a determination unequaled by most players at the time. Historian Harold Seymour wrote that Cobb "did not so much play baseball as wage it, for to him it was like a war. He was ruthless, even cruel, in his compulsion to be first."[12] That cruelty was evident on the base paths where opposing infielders' legs often got in the way of Cobb's spikes. His reputation for purposeful spiking was legendary, and it really gained ground after a controversy in 1909, when he severely spiked Philadelphia Athletics rookie Frank "Homerun" Baker in the forearm,

Ty Cobb. Image courtesy of Library of Congress

drawing blood. Cobb at the time denied that he had done it on purpose, but many years later seemed to contradict his earlier statements when he confessed that Baker was the only person in his career he intentionally spiked, and he did so because it was the only way he could get to the base. He was able to get to many bases over his career, as he stole 892 bases in his career—fourth most of all time.

Although there was no denying his greatness on the field, the fire that drove him as a player made him a difficult person to deal with off the field. Difficult would probably be a kind way to describe Cobb—some would say he was psychotic. He had few friends in the game, even on his own team. His treatment of anyone he deemed to be "wronging" him was particularly brutal. A famous example of this was a run-in he had with a butcher who had delivered spoiled fish to his wife. He pulled a gun on the butcher demanding that he apologize to his wife for this slight, and even though he did apologize, the butcher's assistant dared Cobb to put down the gun and fight him. After Cobb obliged the assistant and proceeded to beat him up, the police were called, and Cobb was arrested. He later pleaded guilty, paid a fine, and paid for the damages to the butcher shop. In another incident when Cobb was being robbed by three assailants, after driving them off, he gave chase to one of them and pistol-whipped the man nearly to death (some have claimed he did kill the man, but that was never proven). He reserved his most severe hubris to members of the black race. His racist attitudes were evident quite often, and they were not confined to black males. Although there were many cases in which he berated and even struck black men, there are at least two known incidents in which he struck black females. One of those incidents occurred in 1907 when a black woman came to the defense of her husband, who worked as a groundskeeper for the Tigers, after Cobb was chastising him for not "addressing him suitably." Cobb hit the wife and then fought with one of his teammates when the teammate found fault with Cobb hitting a woman. The worst case occurred when Cobb kicked a black hotel maid in the stomach and pushed her down the stairs when she objected to him calling her a "nigger."[13] Cobb's behavior is often linked to the mysterious death of his father, who was killed shortly before he was called up to the major leagues in 1905. He was shot by Cobb's own mother, who mistook him for a prowler climbing in their bedroom window. Cobb was quoted late in his life by biographer Al Stump as saying, "My father had his head blown off with a shotgun when I was 18 years old—by a member of my own family. I didn't get over that. I've never gotten over it."[14] Although there is no doubt this incredibly tragic event had a major influence on Cobb, historian Benjamin Rader has pointed out another factor contributing to his behavior. In what Rader terms as his "matters of honor," Cobb viewed everything through the prism of the Southern view of honor.[15] If there was a perceived slight to that honor, like the hazing of a rookie on a baseball team, Cobb would never forget it. This would explain why he had no friends on his team because he took the good-natured hazing very seriously and as an attack on his honor. Of course, by taking it that way, he invited even more hazing. Rader also pointed out that he was very defensive of his race and his class. He did not come from the old elite planter class of the South, and even though he was born 20 years after the Civil War ended, he was still fighting those battles.

Whatever one might think of Cobb's behavior on and off the field, there was little doubt of his ability and his contribution to the Tigers winning the American League pennants in back-to-back seasons in 1907 and 1908. He was also emerging as the league's best player. In the National League, the best player had been established for some time. **Johannes Peter (Honus) Wagner** has been the star shortstop for the Pittsburgh Pirates since he came over from the defunct Louisville Colonels after the 1899 season. It did not take him long to win his first of eight batting titles, which he did in 1900 when he batted .381. Although Cobb is often referred to as the greatest hitter of the era, Wagner is regarded as the best all-around player because of his ability to field his position. "He just ate up the ball with his big hands, like a scoop shovel," his

Honus Wagner. Image courtesy of Library of Congress

CHAPTER Six

Ty Cobb (Right) and Honus Wagner (Left). *Image courtesy of Library of Congress*

teammate Tommy Leach said of him, "and when he threw it to first base you'd see pebbles and dirt and everything else flying over there along with the ball . . . the greatest shortstop ever. The Greatest everything ever."[16] Cobb and Wagner could not have been more different—whether it was what they looked like, their temperament, or where they were from. Wagner was born to German immigrants in Pittsburgh on February 24, 1874. Although Cobb was tall (6' 1"), he was thin (175 pounds), Wagner was big (over 200 pounds), barrel-chested, and bow-legged. Very few people liked Cobb—very few disliked Wagner. After Cobb's Tigers won their third consecutive American League pennant in 1909, the two stars finally got the chance to face off in the World Series that year, when the Pirates won the National League. Although the series proved to be a good one—it was the first to go to a deciding seventh game—the matchup between the established veteran and the up-and-comer was not as close. Wagner outplayed Cobb in every facet of the game—he batted over 100 points higher (.333 to .231), batted in more runs (7 to 6), and stole more bases (6 to 2). A legend grew around one of the stolen base attempts in which Cobb was supposed to have challenged Wagner and called him a "Krauthead," and in response Wagner tagged him hard in the mouth, splitting his lip. This may have been a concoction of the press at the time because most witnesses say it did not happen. It seemed to go against Wagner's nature, and even Cobb denied it in his autobiography, saying they were on good terms. Although the series went to the seventh game, that game was not even close, as the Tigers were humiliated on their home field 8–0. It would be Wagner's only World Series title, and he would retire after the 1917 season. More sadly for Cobb, it was his third consecutive loss in the series, and it would be his last appearance in one, even though he would play for an astounding 19 more seasons, retiring after the 1928 season at the age of 41, having never won a championship. Cobb's incredible career statistics did not include the postseason where he only batted .262. Cobb and Wagner, the two greats of the "Dead Ball Era," would never meet on a baseball field again.

"Dead Ball Era"

Connie Mack. *Image courtesy of Library of Congress*

The year 1910 would mark the first World Series Championship for the Philadelphia Athletics. They would prove to be the dominant major league team in the early part of the next decade by repeating their championship in 1911, winning it again in 1913, and losing the 1914 World Series to the Boston Braves before breaking up the dynasty due to financial problems. There has rarely been such a dramatic fall so fast of a dynasty—the Athletics finished last in the American League for seven straight seasons (1915–1921), including what is often considered the worst team in American League history; the 1916 team certainly had the worst record of all time (36–117). Through the good and the bad, the leader of the Athletics was part-owner and manager Cornelius McGillicuddy, better known as **Connie Mack**. Mack was the embodiment of what Ban Johnson wanted his American League to be. He wore a suit in the dugout; did not smoke, drink, or curse; and never argued with umpires. He wanted players who were educated, refined, and smart. He would sometimes demand the same behavior from his players as he exhibited—for instance, sobriety before big games. The "Tall Tactician" (he was 6' 1" and 150 pounds) stood in stark contrast to the National League's most well-known manager, John McGraw. Although both were sons of Irish immigrants, that is where the similarity ends. Even their heritage can be considered a contrasting one—McGraw's family was from "regular Irish stock," whereas Mack's was more of the upper-class "lace curtain" variety.[17] McGraw was short (5' 7"), pudgy, and pugnacious. He would argue with umpires, managers, and players at the drop of a hat. Both managed during the time known as the **Dead Ball Era**. It was a time in which pitchers were dominant and offensive production was at an all-time low. The era is also referred to as the "National Commission" period due to the governing body of baseball from the time of the national agreement between the two leagues in 1903 and the establishment of a commissioner in 1920. The time is more widely known by the former name because of the belief that the offensive production dropped because of the makeup of the ball itself. The ball was believed to be more loosely wound than the current ball used, and only one ball was used per game. Although this was certainly a factor, more recent scholarship has added other factors to the argument.

In his book, *Baseball, A History of America's Game*, Benjamin Rader pointed to other factors, including rules changes, management style, and physical prowess of the pitchers. In 1893 the pitching rubber was moved back to 60' 6" from 50'. Although the change was not as dramatic as it might look on paper (the original 50' line was a release point, and the 60' 6" was the starting point, so the difference was closer to 5 feet than 10), it did lead to a rise in offensive output—the average runs scored per team in the 1894 season were just under 15. Pitchers adjusted throughout the remainder of the decade, and the offensive numbers declined gradually. Two additional rules changes at the beginning of the new century also helped the pitchers and led to a much more precipitous drop in offense. The first occurred in 1900, when baseball decided to enlarge home plate from a 12-inch square to a five-sided 17-inch-wide disk that added roughly 200 square inches to the strike zone. The second rule change, adopted in both leagues by 1903, was to count the first two foul balls as strikes. Prior to that, they would not count as anything, and a batter could foul off an endless number of pitches and not be any closer to striking out than he was when he came to the plate. Now he was only one strike away after his second foul. Pitchers were allowed to do about anything they wanted to the ball—from scuffing it to putting foreign substances on it. The same ball was used for almost the entire game, so by the later innings, the balls had darkened and become heavier and harder to hit—hence the name "dead ball." The most popular substance after 1904 was saliva. Many pitchers would lick their fingers before gripping the ball, and the added liquid caused the ball to move very erratically. This became known as the "spitball." Although it did allow some pitchers to improve their statistics, Rader downplayed the spitball as a major factor during the "age of the pitcher," largely due to the pitches not only being hard to hit but also hard to catch by the catchers, which led to an upswing in wild pitches and passed balls. He points to the fact that the dominant pitchers of the day were fast ball pitchers.

The pitchers were also bigger and stronger in this era than in previous times. When the mound was moved back in the 1890s, the pitchers had to adapt, and the strongest ones did. The pitchers began to be bigger following that, and by 1908 they averaged 1½ inches taller and 9 pounds heavier. A good example of this was Cy Young, whose career spanned this time period. He was 6' 2" and 210 pounds (even heavier later, as the *Boston Globe* pointed out at the beginning of this chapter). The two most dominant pitchers after the turn of the century were **Walter Johnson** and **Christy Mathewson**. Johnson was also a large man for his time (6' 1", 200 pounds) and after spending his early years in Kansas, he had moved to Idaho, where he spent his time doubling as a telephone company employee and a pitcher in the obscure Idaho State League. In the summer of 1907 19-year-old Johnson was spotted by a scout from the American League Washington Senators, who signed him to a contract, and he spent the next 20 years pitching for that club—and terrorizing his opponents. When Johnson made his major league debut on August 2, it was against Ty Cobb and the Detroit Tigers. Cobb at first was not impressed with the "rube out of the cornfields" with the easy, side-arm delivery until he stepped up to the plate and saw his first pitch up close: "Then something went past me that

Walter Johnson early in
his major league career.
Image courtesy of Library of Congress

made me flinch. The thing just hissed with danger. We couldn't touch him . . . every one of us knew we'd met the most powerful arm ever turned loose in a ball park."[18] For once, Cobb may have been overly gracious because he did get a hit off Johnson, and the Tigers would actually defeat Johnson that day 3–2. Cobb would go on to get more hits off Johnson than any other player and would have an excellent .366 average against him. He seemed to be the exception, as Johnson recorded 110 shutouts (a major league record that still stands), a career earned run average of 2.17 (12 lowest of all-time), and 417 wins, which is second only to Cy Young in all-time wins. Both Young and Johnson shared the fact that they pitched on some pretty bad teams, and when you pitch for a long time a pitcher is going to accumulate many losses. Young's 316 losses were the most in major league history, and Johnson's 279 was the fourth-highest total. Johnson's lack of support was largely due to the notorious frugality of the Senator's owner, Clark Griffith, who refused to pay large salaries to get the best players. Fortunately for Johnson, Griffith did piece together Washington's best team before Johnson retired, and the Senators won the American League pennants in 1924 and 1925, capturing their only World Series title in 1924.

Christy Mathewson, the "Christian Gentleman." Image courtesy of Library of Congress

Christy Mathewson first pitched for the New York Giants in 1900 and was the backbone of that pitching staff for 17 seasons. The six-foot two-inch 195-pound Mathewson won 20 or more games for 13 of those seasons and 30 or more for four of them. He won 373 games, which was third behind Young and Johnson and the most all-time for the National League. Unlike those two pitchers, the teams he played for were almost always in the pennant hunt, and as a result, his losses were much fewer—only 188. Mathewson was known as the "Christian Gentleman" and was a devout Christian, who refused to pitch on Sundays. Luckily for the Giants, only three teams in the American League did not have Sabbatarian Laws, which prohibited games on Sunday, so there were few games played on that day. Mathewson stood in stark contrast temperamentally to his manager, John McGraw. The combustible McGraw recognized the talent in the taciturn Mathewson early, however, and knew the important part he would play in his management style. McGraw was a master at what would become known as the **inside game**. In an era that put a premium on scoring runs, no one could scratch out a run like McGraw's Giants. The "inside game" (sometimes referred to as "small ball") was predicated on grinding out runs one base at a time. The hit-and-run, stealing bases, and the bunt, which all came into use in the 1890s were increasingly being used by McGraw and other managers after the turn of the century. The bunt would be used not only for sacrificing runners but also for base hits. An extreme example of this was St. Louis Cardinals manager Joe McCloskey having his players bunt 17 consecutive times. The tactic produced two runs that were needed to win the game.

The home run was a lost art during the days of the "inside game." Most of the time home runs occurred when an outfielder fell down and the runner could make it around the bases safely (inside-the-park home run). In 1908 the entire Chicago White Sox team hit three home runs all year, and in 1909 the National League leader for the season was John "Red" Murray, who hit seven for the Giants. Even the mechanics of the swing changed during this time period—hitters were instructed to shorten their swing, to punch the ball through the infield or just over their heads. As Benjamin Rader pointed out, "managers would fine or bench free swingers."[19] No one player exemplified the "inside game" like Ty Cobb. He viewed hitting as a science—more brain than brawn. He took pride in his ability to "hit 'em where they ain't," as "Wee" Willie Keeler so memorably phrased it. When the infield was in, Cobb would place it over their heads. When the infield was deep, he would lay down a bunt and beat it out to first. For the inside game to be effective, a manager had to have solid pitching because scratching out one or two runs won't matter if your pitcher gives up 10 runs. No one was better at using his pitching staff than John McGraw. He was also a pioneer in the use of the bullpen. In the early days of baseball, the starting pitcher was expected to finish the game. If his team was ahead, a manager rarely took out his starter. If the starter got tired, he would usually be replaced by another starter. The idea of the relief pitcher really started with McGraw. Due to his increased use of relievers, the number of starters who completed games went from 85 percent in 1901–1904 to 54 percent from 1913–1917.[20] Connie Mack did not fall in love with the bunt as much as other managers. It was his hope to have one or two "big" innings offensively and hope that would be enough to win the game. His Philadelphia Athletics did not have the spending power that McGraw's Giants did, so it was easier for McGraw to rely on a vast array of pitchers when you had so many good ones. The class of the staff was Mathewson, and he was relied on heavily by McGraw. His career ERA was a mere 2.13, and he recorded 79 shutouts in his career. Another amazing statistic was his ratio of strikeouts to walks—he struck out 2,502 while only walking 844.

Another factor in the lessening offense of the era was the construction of massive new ballparks. The older parks of the 19th century had been small, wooden structures that were not built very sturdily. They represented the transitory and impermanent nature of the game and quite often were extremely unsafe and susceptible to fire, or they simply collapsed. After the establishment of the two leagues and the increasing popularity of the game, parks began to be constructed that were made out of the more permanent concrete and steel. Their dimensions were also much larger. Between 1908 and 1923, 15 of these new parks were built. One of the earliest examples was Ebbets Field in Brooklyn for the National League Dodgers. The dimensions included the centerfield wall, which measured 477 feet from home plate. Although the left field wall was somewhat closer (419 feet) and right field was much closer (301 feet), very few players in the league at that time could hit the ball 477 feet, even if they were allowed to take a full swing. The short right field fence at Ebbets Field illustrates another point about the construction of these new parks. Owners were unable to clear out large tracts of land to build because there was no public funding or eminent domain at the time, so they had to buy smaller portions of land from numerous landowners in the area, and some simply would not sell. So park dimensions at the time were asymmetrical due to necessity of squeezing the field in where they could. Ebbets' right field fence was closer than they wanted because they were restricted by Bedford Avenue behind. When Fenway Park was built for the Boston Red Sox in 1912, to fit into the neighborhood (businesses behind left field refused to sell), a 37-foot wall was constructed in left field that would later be painted green and in later years became known as the "green monster." Today it is the most recognizable idiosyncrasy in the sport's oldest functioning ballpark. Most of these parks were built with larger field dimensions, but the space for spectators was where the corners were cut, and as a result seating capacity initially was not that large. As more and more people began to pack the stadiums, owners quickly realized that they could make more money by expanding the seating capacities. About the only way they could do that was to put seats beyond the outfield fences (initially seats would only be behind

The Green Monster at Fenway Park today. Image
© JASON TENCH, 2013. Used under license from Shutterstock, Inc.

home plate and down the baselines). To do that, they often were forced to bring the fences in, and consequently, it became easier to hit the ball out of the park. As the style of hitting changed in the 1920s, the age of the home run was born. The last of the 15 ballparks to be built during this era was for the New York Yankees in 1923. The other parks built before this one usually had a maximum capacity of 30,000, but this one doubled that with a capacity over 60,000. It was never referred to as a ballpark—it was the first to be called a stadium—Yankee Stadium.

As World War I raged in Europe starting in 1914, there was little effect in the United States or on baseball. The oceans, which had always insulated Americans from the ravages of European wars, kept them neutral once again. Even after the United States broke with tradition and officially entered the war in April of 1917 there appeared to be no effect on baseball. The 1917 season went on and there was no serious thought given to cancelling it. Knowing that it would devastate their rosters, baseball owners did not call on players to enlist. Seeming to sense the negative public image carrying on with baseball during wartime would have on the game, Ban Johnson required that the national anthem be played before every game (a tradition that continues today) and all teams participate in daily military training. Each team was assigned an army sergeant to train them. Before every American League game that season, fans witnessed the somewhat comical image of baseball players marching with a baseball bat in place of a rifle at right-shoulder arms. The *Spalding Guide* wrote that this drill "anticipated and nullified the charges of baseball's slackerism."[21] To be known as a "slacker" during World War I was to be viewed as avoiding military service. Although the 1917 season went off as if nothing had changed, 1918 was different. By early 1918 Americans were fighting and dying in the trenches of France, and all men between the ages of 21 and 35 were expected to register for the draft. In May Secretary of War Newton Baker issued a "work-or-fight" order, which required anyone who was not part of an "essential" wartime job to volunteer for military service. Two-hundred and twenty-seven players volunteered, and most of the rest found essential wartime jobs or did not serve because they were sole providers for their families. As the owners feared, the rosters were decimated, and players were temporarily replaced with players under the age of 21 or older players who came out of retirement. Not surprisingly, the quality of play suffered, and eventually the season was cut one month short. However, a World Series was held that year, and the Boston Red Sox defeated the Chicago Cubs in what would be the Red Sox' last championship of the 20th century. Two of the game's best did go overseas and enlisted in the newly formed Chemical Warfare Service, or "Gas and Flame Division," as it was commonly called, created to combat this new type of warfare. Christy Mathewson, who by this time was 38, retired from baseball, and certainly could have avoided service, and Ty Cobb, who at 32 was at the height of his career, were both exposed to the horrors of chemical warfare. Both survived, but Mathewson was never the same after his exposure. He eventually contracted tuberculosis and died at 45 in 1925, certainly a casualty of that war. Cobb returned to a game that was rapidly changing and, according to him, not for the better.

Age of the Home Run

Many reasons have been offered for the dramatic rise in offensive output that was ushered in with the decade of the 1920s. Whatever the reason, the "dead ball" era was officially over, and it died rather abruptly. If one looks at the numbers, they are staggering. The batting averages for both the American and National Leagues between 1901 and 1918 were .253 and .254, respectively. By 1921 they had jumped to .292 and .289. Runs per game average went from 7.9 and 7.8 during the same time periods to 10.2 and 9.2. The biggest change, however, was in the number of home runs hit. There was an average of 200 home runs hit per season in each league prior to 1919. By the mid-1920s, that number would triple to over 600 home runs per season.[22] Why did this happen? Historically various arguments have included smaller ballparks (mentioned earlier); the introduction in 1920 of a new kind of ball that jumped off the bat (sometimes called the "jackrabbit ball"); the outlawing of the spitball before the 1920 season; and finally, the use of more balls during the game. More recent scholarship, while acknowledging the contribution of each of these points, has also downplayed each of them for various reasons. Taking each of them individually: Although many ballparks were smaller beginning in the 1920s than they had been earlier, the smaller ballpark argument is a little wanting because the dimensions in the 1920s on average were still much larger than that of today's parks. The "jackrabbit ball" argument has been introduced by conspiracy theorists who say the owners changed the makeup of the ball to try to bring up sagging attendance after World War I and the Black Sox scandal of 1919 (the scandal is discussed fully in the last chapter of this book). The Bureau of Standards tested the ball in 1920 and found it to have no different qualities than previous baseballs used. Although the spitball was outlawed in 1920, what is not as widely known is that veteran pitchers who employed the spitball were allowed to continue to use it for the remainder of their careers. This "grandfather clause" of the rule would have produced very little change in the early part of the 1920s, as there would have been nearly as many spitballs thrown in the early years of the decade as had been thrown before. The introduction of more balls during games happened as a result of the first fatality in major league history in August 1920. Ray Chapman was hit in the head by a Carl Mays pitch, which crushed his skull and killed him. The argument was that because it was late in the game and the same ball had been used the entire game and because of all the foreign substances that had been added to the ball, it was difficult to see, and Chapman was unable to get out of the way. From that point on, when a ball became too dark to see in the view of the umpire, it was replaced by a fresh one. The problem with this argument is that it does not explain the fact that the offensive barrage had begun at least a full year before this change was implemented. To what, then, does modern scholarship attribute this dramatic rise in offensive output? Benjamin Rader and others essentially answer with two words: Babe Ruth.

Babe Ruth

It was not the mere fact of Ruth himself changing the game by swinging full-out every time at the plate but also that other players and managers began to copy the swing of Ruth and abandoned the inside game. Nothing signified the surrender of the old game more than the two most notable proponents of the old style, John McGraw and Connie Mack, recognizing the change and realizing they would need to adapt to be competitive. Both of these managers instructed their players to change their swings and built their teams in the 1920s more around power than finesse. Not everyone was willing to make that change. One of the biggest and most vocal critics of the new style was Ty Cobb. It went against everything he believed the game to be and worried him about the future of his sport: "The home run could wreck baseball," he warned. "It throws out a lot of the strategy and makes it fenceball."[23] Cobb believed it to be a passing fad and that eventually the game would go back to his scientific style of play. What Cobb had failed to realize was the shift in American culture. The Victorian period was

Ty Cobb (right) and Babe Ruth (center). Image courtesy of Library of Congress

long over, and there was now a "new" middle class that craved more excitement and liked the fact that one player could change the complexion of a game with one swing, as opposed to Cobb's strategy of the entire team scraping together runs, or as his biographer Al Stump aptly phrased it, "knitting together team offense."[24] The 1920s would become the "golden age" for not just baseball but other sports as well. Red Grange's explosive style in football and boxer Jack Dempsey's knockout punch appealed greatly to the public, and during a time known for its excesses, no one was more excessive than Ruth.

George Herman Ruth was born in 1895 to a Baltimore saloon keeper and his wife, who apparently had little time for their son. Because he was essentially left to his own devices, he became something of a juvenile delinquent, getting into scrapes with other kids and occasionally the law.

Young Babe Ruth in Boston showing his transition from pitching to hitting even before being sold to the Yankees.
Image courtesy of Library of Congress

Eventually, by the time he was seven, his parents wanted nothing more to do with him, and they placed him in St. Mary's reform school and orphanage. He spent the next 12 years there and discovered that the one thing he was truly good at was baseball. He came by it naturally—whether it was pitching or hitting. He was good enough to be signed to the minor league Baltimore Orioles in 1914 when he was 19. Before that season was over, he was sold to the Boston Red Sox, who signed him as a pitcher. He appeared in only five games that season and was then optioned to a minor league team in Providence for the remainder of the season. In 1915 he was named a starting pitcher for the Red Sox, helped the team win the pennant with 18 victories, and hit his first major league home run. The Red Sox won the World Series that year, although he did not pitch in the series. The following season he finished with five more wins from the year before, finishing with 23 and an ERA of 1.75. Both numbers led the American League, and this time he appeared in the World Series and won game two with a 14-inning shutout of Brooklyn. The Red Sox went on to win their second championship in as many years. In 1917 the Red Sox did not win the pennant, but Ruth won the most games of his career—24. The next season he made it known that he wanted to bat more than pitch, so he only appeared in 20 games as a pitcher (going 13–7) but played the rest of his games as an outfielder. He hit 11 home runs that year, which led the league. As the Red Sox defeated the Cubs that year, it was Ruth's last appearance in the World Series as a pitcher. He won games one and four and extended his World Series scoreless innings pitched to 29⅔ innings—a record that stood for over 40 years. The 1919 season turned out to be his last in a Red Sox uniform, and he only pitched in 17 games, but he broke the old major league record for home runs in a season when he hit 29. This also seemed to add to the argument that Ruth should be credited with the metamorphosis in the game because he set that record *before* all the other changes occurred in the 1920s.

After the 1919 season, he was sold to the New York Yankees, where he transformed from Ruth the player into Ruth the legend. For the next 15 seasons he was an everyday player (he pitched in five games as a Yankee, but they were largely seen as publicity stunts to get people to the stadium—interestingly, he did win all five of the games he pitched) and amassed incredible numbers. In his first season with the Yankees, he broke his old home run record by 25 when he hit 54. He also batted .376 that season and even raised his numbers further in 1921 when he hit 59 home runs and batted .378. His numbers helped his new team to win their first ever pennant that season. Every game of the 1921 World Series was played at the same location—the Polo Grounds. The Yankees sublet the ballpark from the Giants, and McGraw did not like to share the space. The Yankees took on the Giants, and John McGraw took particular pride in beating Ruth and his teammates that season and repeated the same feat the next year. McGraw instructed his pitchers to throw Ruth nothing but curveballs. He said they once again had the "big monkey's number." All they did was "pitch him low curves and slow stuff and he falls all over himself."[25] At the start of the 1923 season, the Yankees did not have to share space with the Giants anymore as massive Yankee Stadium had been built to hold all the people who wanted to see Ruth hit home runs—in fact, the stadium was christened, "The House that Ruth Built." On opening day against his old team, the Red Sox, Ruth christened the stadium in his own way with its first-ever home run. The 1923 season ended with the Yankees winning their third straight pennant, and across the field that October was a familiar sight—for the third consecutive year, their World Series opponent would be John McGraw's Giants. This time, the "big monkey" got his revenge as he dominated the series, batting .368, hitting three home runs, walking eight times, scoring eight times, and having an incredible

Babe Ruth and John McGraw.
Image courtesy of Library of Congress

slugging percentage of 1.000. The Yankees won their first-ever World Series title that season, and Ruth had now proven he was not only a great player during the season but that he could also perform in the clutch in the postseason as well, and his legend grew.

Yankee Stadium. Image © eddtoro, 2013. Used under license from Shutterstock, Inc.

His legend off the field grew as well. His appetites for pleasures of the flesh were well known throughout the league, even if not as well known to the public. The press had unwritten agreements to not publish stories such as his many trysts with women who would follow him from hotel to hotel throughout the season. Eventually, it became too much for his wife Helen, who left him, and they separated by 1926. Ruth also had incredible appetites for food (reportedly, he would eat up to 18 eggs for breakfast) and alcohol—even though for most of his career, it was illegal. He endorsed many products, and his agent (probably the first ever sports agent), Christy Walsh, got him deals that earned him an estimated $1 to $2 million off the field. Adding to what he made as a player, he was a multimillionaire, and Walsh astutely advised him to invest in untouchable annuities that were unaffected by the stock market crash in 1929, so he was able to retire comfortably. In 1930, he was holding out for a higher salary, and when he was told that he was asking for a higher salary than President Hoover in a time of economic depression, he supposedly answered, "What the hell has Hoover got to do with it? Besides, I had a better year than he did."[26] The press publicized positive things involving Ruth, including his many visits to sick children. On one of these visits he famously promised a dying child that he would hit a home run, and after he did, the child miraculously got well. Whether the story was true or apocryphal, there was no doubt children loved and idolized him. He seemed to connect with them, as he was really just a big kid himself. As umpire Billy Evans said: "Ruth has never grown up and probably never will. Success on the ball field has in no way changed him. Everybody likes him. You just can't help it."[27] They liked him enough to not only show up at Yankee Stadium (the Yankees' average yearly attendance went from 600,000 before his arrival to well over 1 million after) but also on the road, as attendance at parks that the Yankees visited also saw a jump in attendance. Win or lose, fans wanted to see him hit it out of the park. In 1927 the Yankees did not lose very often. In what is often called the greatest Yankee team of all-time and mentioned as one of the greatest all-time teams, the 1927 Yankees won an American League record 110 games that season. There was really no pennant race that season, as the Yankees had it wrapped up early and outdistanced the Philadelphia Athletics by 19 games. The race became Ruth against himself—could he surpass his home run record of 59 set in 1921? He ended up hitting his 60th on the final day of the season. He also batted .356 and batted in 164 runs as the Yankees swept the overmatched Pittsburgh Pirates in the World Series. Ruth was not the only slugger in the lineup, as that team was known as "Murderer's Row" for its incredible offensive numbers. Ruth later admitted the importance of those batting around him for his success, especially the young first baseman, Lou Gehrig, who batted after Ruth.

The year 1932 provided for one last legendary act for the Babe. He was appearing in what would be his last World Series against the Chicago Cubs. In game 3 he had already homered once, and he was taking some ribbing from the Cubs bench—by this point he was not the player he had been in the 20s, and his age and lifestyle was catching up to him. A film exists of the at-bat, and it can be plainly seen that he is carrying on a conversation with the bench as he takes the first two pitches for strikes. It can also be seen that he deposits the third pitch into right-center for one of the longest home runs ever hit in Wrigley Field (it was estimated at traveling close to 500 feet), and as he rounds the bases, he is really giving it to the Chicago bench. What is not seen in the film nor mentioned in the newspapers the next day was the legendary part. Ruth claimed he stepped out of the batter's box before the third pitch and pointed precisely where he was going to hit it. Very few admit to witnessing this, and the pitcher, Charlie Root, was quoted as saying: "Ruth did not point at the fence before he swung. If he had made a gesture like that, well, anybody that knows me knows that Ruth would have ended up on his ass."[28] It became known as the "called shot," and whether it truly happened or not, the legend around it grew like every other legend surrounding the man. It was his last home run, in fact last hit in a World Series, for Ruth—not a bad way to finish his postseason career. Unfortunately, his regular season career did not end as spectacularly. The Yankees failed to win the pennants in 1933 and 1934, and Ruth's production noticeably declined in those two seasons. He batted just over .300 in 1933 but dropped to .288 in 1934—respectable numbers for sure, but much below his career average of .342. His home run numbers also declined from 34 to 22 in those two seasons. He was voted on the first-ever all-star team in 1933 and hit a home run in that game, but film of him shows how overweight and out of shape he was. As he approached his 40th birthday and retirement, he really wanted to become a manager. His first choice was the Yankees, but Joe McCarthy was not going anywhere for awhile, so Yankees owner Jacob Rupert offered him the manager position for a minor league team; he refused. The National League Boston Braves offered Ruth a chance for part ownership and a future managerial position if he came over and played one more season. He jumped at the chance, but after only a few weeks, it became apparent that Ruth was not the player he was (he could not field the ball at all anymore, and three of the Braves' pitchers refused to take the mound if Ruth played), and it also became apparent the Braves had no intention of giving him any positions of power with the club—they had simply brought him over as a publicity stunt to fill the stands. He made up his mind in May that he was going to quit, but he had one last legendary feat to accomplish—he went into the May 25 matchup with the Pirates with his career home run total at 711. That day he hit the last three home runs of his career, including number 714, which was the first ever hit out of cavernous Forbes Field in Pittsburgh. It was measured at 600 feet. The pitcher that gave up that monstrous shot was Guy Bush, who described the day this way: "He was fat and old, but he still had that great swing . . . I can't remember anything about that first home run he hit off me that day . . . but I can't forget that last one. It's probably still going."[29] So is Ruth's legend. He may have ended his playing days that week, but every baseball player that came after him has had to live in his giant shadow. Numbers do not always do justice to a legend like Ruth, but they are amazing: From 1918 to 1934 he led the American League in home runs 12 times with an average of more than 40 a season. From 1926 to 1931 he averaged more than 50 home runs a season and hit one an average of every 11.7 times at bat. His single-season home run record of 60 stood until 1961 when fellow Yankee Roger Maris hit 61, and his 714 career record was not eclipsed until Henry Aaron passed him in 1974. Sometimes an individual player comes along that dominates his or her sport but very rarely does one player *change* a sport—and Ruth did that. There was virtually no player with which to compare him beforehand, and very few have come along since that can be mentioned in the same breath with him. Because of this lack of comparison, writer George Will described Ruth as "Mt. Everest in Kansas."[30]

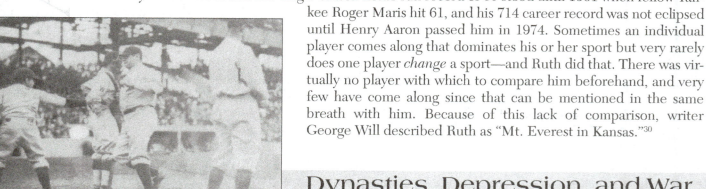

Babe Ruth crossing home plate. Image courtesy of Library of Congress

Dynasties, Depression, and War

The team that Ruth played most of his career for, the **New York Yankees**, is considered baseball royalty and the game's major dynasty. As of 2012 the team has won 40 American League pennants and 27 World Series titles—both records. The team's origins were pretty humble. The franchise actually began in Baltimore as the Orioles in 1901; but when Ban Johnson wanted to make his American League a major league, he knew he needed a team in the largest city, so he moved the club to New York and renamed them the Highlanders because of their park being on top of a hill—the highest point in Manhattan. They would have this name for the next 10 seasons. Although they never won an American League pennant in these years, they finished a close second three times (1904, 1906, and 1910). In 1911 the Polo Grounds, home of the Giants, burned down and needed to be rebuilt. During the rebuilding process, they played at the Highlanders' park, and when the new Polo Grounds opened in 1913, the Giants invited the other New York team to join them in the brand new park. Because the park was in a lower area of Manhattan, they could no longer justify the name Highlanders, so their name officially was changed to the Yankees. Two things contributed to the establishment of the Yankee dynasty: The first was when the franchise was sold to Colonel Jacob Rupert and Captain Tillinghast Huston for $1.25 million in 1915. Rupert was the heir to a brewery fortune and possessed enough money and the willingness to spend it to produce a winning product. The second factor was Boston Red Sox owner Harry Frazee's need for cash. There had been other multiple championship winning teams in the American League during this period, including the Philadelphia Athletics and the Boston Red Sox, but it is difficult to characterize them as dynasties because as soon as the championships

Jacob Rupert, Commissioner Kenesaw Mountain Landis, Tillinghast Huston, Harry Frazee and unidentified man.
Image courtesy of Library of Congress

were won, the teams were broken up and sold. Connie Mack did this twice in Philadelphia, and Frazee did this in Boston beginning in 1920. He famously sold Ruth for $125,000 and a $300,000 loan so he could buy the rights to a Broadway show, *No No, Nanette* (Frazee was more interested in theater than in baseball). Frazee did not stop there, however. In Rupert and Huston, he had found deep pockets that could bankroll his other interests, and the Red Sox served as the Yankees' personal farm team in the early 1920s. In 1923 the Yankees won their first World Series championship, and the 24-man roster included 11 players that had once played for the Red Sox. The Yankees won four titles in the next decade, and the Red Sox finished in the American League cellar for eight of the next nine seasons. The fact that the Red Sox did not win a World Series title for the remainder of the century is often referred to as the "Curse of the Bambino" because of Ruth's sale. Because that was not an isolated event, it could be more aptly described as the "Curse of Frazee."

On the National League side there were also some multiple winning franchises in the early years of the century, including John McGraw's New York Giants, the Brooklyn Dodgers, and the Chicago Cubs. Numbers of championships can be traced to the number of people living in the metropolitan areas. Benjamin Rader has persuasively argued that the reason for higher population cities producing winning franchises simply can be traced to the gate receipts. More people in a city results in more people going to the games and more revenue for the home team. Owners of smaller-market clubs argued that there needed to be some "revenue sharing" by the larger clubs to offset the disparity. The larger-market owners agreed and decided to share 50 percent of the base ticket prices with the visiting teams. Although this sounded good, eventually reserve and club seating entered into the equation at a higher price, so by the 1930s when smaller club owners could have really used the revenue, they were only getting roughly 21 percent of the total gate receipts of the larger clubs. One way to fight this disparity was devised by **Branch Rickey** in small-market

Members of Baseball Hall of Fame during fundraiser for war bonds at the Polo Grounds in 1943. Front row: Honus Wagner, Frankie Frisch, Babe Ruth, Walter Johnson and Tris Speaker. Back row: Duffy Lewis, Eddie Collins, Roger Bresnahan, Connie Mack, umpire Bill Klem, Red Murray and George Sisler. © Bettmann/CORBIS

St. Louis. Rickey had been a catcher for Ohio Wesleyan University and had played professionally briefly for the New York Highlanders. In 1913 he was named manager and general manager of the St. Louis Browns of the American League. In 1917 he was named general manager of the other St. Louis team, the also-ran and cash-strapped Cardinals. After a brief stint in the Army during World War I (he interestingly served as both Ty Cobb's and Christy Mathewson's commander in the Chemical Warfare Service), he began purchasing direct ownership of various minor league clubs. It was the birth of the **farm system** in baseball. In less than 20 years, the Cardinals' system included 32 different teams and approximately 700 players. If the Cardinals did not use the players for their club, they could benefit financially by selling the players to other clubs. It was a tremendous success, which produced nine pennants over the next quarter century. If they did not win, they were usually in the hunt, finishing second six times. The club's first championship came in 1926 against the vaunted Yankees. The Yankees and other owners at first cried foul and criticized the system but then copied it, and it remains a mainstay for every major league club to this day. The system produced championship teams in the 1930s known as the "Gas House Gang," which was one of the few bright spots in an otherwise dismal decade.

The stock market crash of 1929 brought on the worst economic depression the country has ever seen, and it took a major toll on the national pastime. Baseball attendance hit its all-time high to that point in 1930 with just over 10 million for the season. By 1933 that number had dropped to 6 million, the lowest number since World War I. To bring people back to the ballpark, owners tried a variety of innovations. The All-Star Game was born in 1933, pitting the best players of each league against each other. In 1935 the first night baseball game was played under the lights in Cincinnati. In 1936 the first class of the Baseball Hall of Fame was announced. The Hall opened its doors in Cooperstown, the supposed birthplace of baseball, on its supposed 100th birthday in 1939. The list of five in the inaugural class was heavily represented by "Dead Ball Era" players. The most votes received on that first ballot, surprising many, was Ty Cobb, who edged out Babe

JOE DI MAGGIO
Salutes His Bat

DiMaggio during his 56-game it streak. Image courtesy of Library of Congress

Ruth. The other three were pitchers Walter Johnson and Christy Mathewson and the first great player of the modern era, Honus Wagner. Other than Mathewson, who had died in 1925, they all showed up for the honor, but Cobb refused to be photographed in the official picture due to his ongoing rivalry with Ruth. The new technology of radio had been resisted by owners throughout the 1920s because they thought it would lead to lessening attendance. Owners seemed to change their minds during the 1930s, primarily because stations were able to sell advertising time and thereby pay clubs for the rights to broadcast their games. Thus, in the 1930s, the love affair between fans who may have been hundreds of miles away and their favorite teams blossomed. Although they may not have had enough money to go to a ballgame, through the medium of radio they could be there. The radio was the one appliance Americans had to have during the Depression—it allowed escape from the everyday drudgery.

Despite the various attempts by the owners, the attendance numbers remained low until the outbreak of World War II and the return of some economic activity in 1940. It seemed the entire country was following baseball again during the 1941 season. In what would be the last season before the United States entered the war, two players captured the attention of the nation. Besides the economic struggles, another reason for the decline in the popularity of the game during the thirties was the retirement of the game's greatest and most popular player, Babe Ruth, in 1935. Although there were other great players in the late 30s, none of them seemed to have the magic Ruth did. The player who was supposed to replace Ruth and carry on the legacy of the Yankees was a second-generation Italian American from San Francisco named **Joe DiMaggio**. DiMaggio debuted in centerfield for the Yankees the year after Ruth retired. On May 25, 1941, he went one for four and then proceeded to get a hit in each of his next 55 games until the streak came to an end in Cleveland on July 17. The old American League record was 41 games by George Sisler, and the old major league record was 44 by "Wee" Willie Keeler. What is amazing is that DiMaggio would hit safely in the next 17 games, which meant he hit safely in 73 of 74 games all told—also a major league record. During the streak he hit .408 with 15 home runs and 55 runs batted in. When DiMaggio's streak ended, the attention turned to another great young player for the Boston Red Sox, **Ted Williams**, who was also having a tremendous season. Also hailing from California, Williams joined the Red Sox at the age of 20 in 1939 and wanted to be the best hitter that ever played the game. In 1941 he was in the process of doing something no player had done since Bill Terry in 1930—end the season with an average of .400 or better. As the season progressed, Williams's average continued to stay above .400, and in mid-September it got to as high as .413 before it started to slip. Going into the final day of the season, a day in which the Red Sox were scheduled to play a doubleheader with Connie Mack's Philadelphia Athletics, his average stood at .39955, which would have rounded up to .400. Although his manager asked him if he wanted to sit out the games, Williams refused and took the chance on dropping below the mark. Instead he went six for eight and finished the season at .406. Had the current sacrifice fly rule been in place in 1941 (sac. flies now do not count against a player's average), he would have batted .416. In the 70-plus years since that season, no player has hit over .400, and the closest any player has come to DiMaggio's 56-game hit streak was Pete Rose's 44 games in 1978.

Two months after the 1941 baseball season ended, the Japanese bombed Pearl Harbor, and the United States entered World War II. Unlike the First World War, which many Americans believed was not theirs to fight, this war involved a direct attack on American soil, so it was viewed differently by most Americans, and the impulse to sign up and take part in the fight was overwhelming. Many baseball players joined the armed forces, including both DiMaggio and Williams. We often hear about the violation of the civil liberties of Japanese Americans during the war as they were sent to internment camps for fear they might aid in an attack on the West Coast. What is sometimes forgotten is that other Americans with other heritages experienced a disruption in their lives as well. Italy was also an enemy in the war, and many Italian Americans experienced hardship due to this, including Guiseppe and Rosalia DiMaggio. Their son was in the Army and arguably the most famous American at the time. Yet they were classified by the U.S. government as "enemy aliens" and forced to carry identification with them at all times. They were unable to travel more than a five-mile radius from their home, and Guiseppe's boat was confiscated and his livelihood taken away, as he was barred from fishing in San Francisco Bay. Both of Joe DiMaggio's parents became American citizens before the end of the war.

U.S. postage stamp of FDR.
Image © catwalker, 2013. Used under license from Shutterstock, Inc.

Prior to the 1942 season, baseball owners were not sure if they should even play baseball, so they appealed to the commander-in-chief for advice. President Franklin Roosevelt said that baseball would be good for the morale of the nation, "even if the actual quality of the teams is lowered by the greater use of older players."[31] So baseball went on uninterrupted, but Roosevelt's prediction proved correct, as the quality of play did suffer throughout the war years. The *Sporting News* reported that in 1944 had only roughly "40 percent of those who had played in 1941 were still in the starting lineups."[32] Not one of the starting nine from the 1941 World Series Champion Yankees was playing by 1944. The players who were playing were either those who came out of retirement or were rejected from the army due to physical ailments. Things got so bad that the Saint Louis Browns actually had a one-armed man on their roster. They won their one and only American League pennant in 1944.

Conclusion

The game of baseball underwent amazing transformations in the first half of the 20th century. It had essentially divided itself in half at the beginning of the century to save itself. The establishment of the American League by Ban Johnson, although opposed by many National League owners, actually was the best thing that could have happened because it established competition and the ever-popular World Series. The style of the game also went through a metamorphosis during these years. The first two decades of the century produced some of the great pitchers of all time, and offensive strategies designed to scratch out runs wherever and whenever they could. The emergence of Babe Ruth in the 1920s changed everything. The age of the home run was born, and it changed not only offenses but also pitching strategy. Prior to Ruth, pitchers would usually only have to bear down and worry about runs being scored when teams had runners on base. Now there was a danger of runs being scored at any time. Upon Ruth's retirement and the economic downturn during the 1930s, the game suffered. With a temporary return of popularity just before the country entered the war, the war years were not a good time for the quality of the game or for attendance. The average attendance for a baseball game during the war years was 7,500. The public's attention was elsewhere, including on a professional women's baseball league. No one knew the future of the game after the war ended in 1945. Would it return to its glory days? Would it be able to compete with other entertainment in a postwar America? Most important, would it finally allow everyone to compete for a roster spot, regardless of their heritage? This last question would be answered very soon after the war in large part due to the war itself.

Notes

1. Dean Sullivan, ed., *Early Innings: A Documentary History of Baseball, 1825–1908* (Lincoln: University of Nebraska Press, 1995), 272.
2. Harold Seymour, *Baseball; Vol. 1* (New York: Oxford University Press, 1960), 308.
3. Ibid., 309.
4. Ibid., 313.
5. Ibid., 314.
6. Quoted from the *Spalding Guide* in Ken Burns' *Baseball* series, *Second Inning, Something Like a War* (1994).
7. A. G. Spalding, *America's National Game* (Lincoln: University of Nebraska Press, 1992), 335.
8. Harold Seymour, *Baseball; Vol. 2* (New York: Oxford University Press, 1971), 151.
9. Ken Burns' *Baseball* series, *Second Inning, Something Like a War* (1994).
10. Ibid.
11. Benjamin Rader, *Baseball, A History of America's Game* (Urbana: University of Illinois Press, 2008), 104.
12. Seymour, *Baseball, Vol. 2*, 107.
13. Ibid., 110.
14. Ibid.
15. Rader, *Baseball*, 107.
16. Ibid., 106.
17. Ibid., 100.
18. Al Stump, *Cobb: A Biography* (Chapel Hill, NC: Workman Publishing, 1994), 150.
19. Rader, *Baseball*, 99.
20. Ibid., 98.
21. Ibid., 113.
22. Ibid., 125.
23. Stump, *Cobb*, 294.
24. Ibid.
25. Burns, *Baseball*, "Fourth Inning: The National Heirloom," 1994.
26. Rader, *Baseball*, 133.

27. Ibid., 132.
28. Richard O. Davies, *Sports in American Life* (Malden, MA: Wiley-Blackwell, 2012), 98.
29. Ibid.
30. Burns, *Baseball*, "Fourth Inning: A National Heirloom."
31. Rader, *Baseball*, 172.
32. Ibid., 173.

CHAPTER Six

CHAPTER

Seven

Professional Football

It was a cold November day in Pittsburgh in 1892 when the Alleghany Athletic Association was battling the Pittsburgh Athletic Club for football bragging rights in the Steel City. The cold weather kept the crowd down to an estimated 3,000 people, who watched a typical, low-scoring, defensive tussle in which neither offense was able to move the ball with much success. What most of the crowd did not know was the fact that the game almost did not take place. In the days leading up to the contest, both squads bickered and fought over various players and which team had claims on which players. The accusations of each team toward the other's use of "ringers" and paying them plus the amount of wagering on the game led to the cancellation of the game on the very day it was to be played. Eventually, not wanting to disappoint the thousands of people who had shown up for the game, the two sides came to a truce on the rosters as well an agreement that no wagers would be placed, and the game was played. The AAA won the game when William Walter "Pudge" Heffelfinger picked up a PAC fumble and rumbled 25 yards into the end zone for the only score. The game was not widely reported at the time outside Western Pennsylvania and would not be of much note today except for the widely held belief that **Pudge Heffelfinger** may have been the first professional football player in American history. For what the AAA had actually done prior to their game with the PAC was outbid the PAC for Heffelfinger's services. He was reportedly paid 500 dollars to play in that one game—an incredible amount of money for the time. Heffelfinger was probably worth it—he was viewed as one of the best lineman in the country. He was named to Walter Camp's first All-American team when playing for Yale in 1889 and followed that up with two more stints as an All-American in 1890 and 1891. With his eligibility for Yale exhausted, by 1892 he was ready to play for the highest bidder, and that was the Alleghany Athletic Association. For years it was believed the first professional player (to be paid an actual salary as opposed to just expenses, which was common) was James Brallier of Latrobe, Pennsylvania, in 1895 because he was very open about his professionalism. Heffelfinger, for obvious reasons at the time, kept his professionalism a secret. It was not until the 1960s that a researcher unearthed the truth about Heffelfinger and that he had never owned up to being paid by the AAA. He must still be referred to as "probably" the first professional because there may very well have been others who were paid prior to him but also kept it a secret.

The First NFL

As the competition for winning football squads became fierce between athletic clubs in the 1890s, professionalism became more prevalent and widely known. Because of its payment of players, the AAA was eventually banned from playing other "amateur" clubs by the Amateur Athletic Union

(AAU), which led to the AAA not fielding a team in 1895. By 1896, however, there were enough acknowledged professional teams in Western Pennsylvania that the AAA came back and fielded what is believed to be the first all-salaried professional football team. Pro ball was spreading beyond the confines of Pennsylvania, and after the turn of the 20th century, the first professional league was formed. It was called the **National Football League (NFL)**, and it was modeled after professional baseball. In fact, it was started by magnates of major league baseball. The idea was hatched by Latrobe newspaperman David Berry, who approached the owners of both Philadelphia baseball clubs to form the football version of the Phillies and Athletics. Berry would be in charge of the Pittsburgh franchise as well as serve as the league's president. He had hoped to have teams from Chicago and New York represented in the NFL to show as its name suggested that it was a more "national" league as opposed to merely a Pennsylvania league. Unfortunately for Berry and the NFL, the financial backing for both the Chicago and New York clubs fell through, so the league for the 1902 season would only consist of the three Pennsylvania teams. The teams were evenly matched, but Berry's team signed more well-known players, including New York Giants pitcher Christy Mathewson, who had played fullback and kicker for Bucknell College. The teams played other clubs from outside their association during October as preparation for league play in November. Berry's Pittsburgh team, referred to as the "Stars" by local newspapers, took on the Athletics on Thanksgiving Day for the first championship of the NFL. The game ended in a scoreless tie, so a rematch was staged for the following Saturday. This time the Stars won 11–0, and Berry declared his team the champion. What he could not declare was that the season had been successful. Attendance at the championship games and other league games was disappointing. Money was a major problem. Athletics manager Connie Mack refused to allow his team to take the field until the $2,000 he was promised was paid by Berry. Although he did not have the money, it was produced by the president of Carnegie Steel, William E. Correy, who was a fan of football. It was so bad that most of Berry's players were not paid the salaries they were promised. Although his team was the champion of the NFL, Berry had to admit defeat as a league, and the first incarnation of the NFL folded after one season.

One month after the death of the NFL, New York sports promoter Thomas O'Rourke launched the first of what would become known as the Garden Tournaments open to both professional and college football teams held indoors over the Christmas and New Year's holidays in Madison Square Garden. When no college teams accepted his invitation, the first tournament became a battle of professionals. There were the obvious candidates from the now-defunct NFL, but O'Rourke worried about attendance problems that would be posed by Pennsylvania teams playing in New York. His answer was to combine some of the best players from the NFL and dub them the "New York" squad (even though none of them came from New York). He also recruited three local athletic clubs to play along with a team from Syracuse. Although the former NFL players (New York) and Syracuse were easily the two best teams, he decided to match them up in the first round. He most likely was hoping the Syracuse team would be defeated and set up an all-New York City championship for a greater gate. This did not happen, however, as Syracuse, led by Glen "Pop" Warner, defeated New York on December 29. On New Year's Eve they defeated the Knickerbocker club by the embarrassing score of 36–0. They produced that identical score in the championship game on January 2 against another overmatched local New York club to take the trophy. Although O'Rourke had not filled the Garden, attendance had been good enough to warrant another tournament the following year. The 1903 tournament was a larger one. He decided to invite local high schools along with athletic clubs and professional teams. There were 15 games played over six days. O'Rourke believed that this way there would always be a local team playing, and he would not have to "set up" a New York championship. Unfortunately for O'Rourke, the attendance of the 1903 tournament was much lower than it had been the previous year. It probably did not help that the two best professional teams in the tournament were not from New York City. Eventually, a team from Franklin, Pennsylvania, defeated a team from Watertown, New York, in the championship. The best attended game of the tournament was game between local high school all-stars. Apparently New York City was not yet ready for a steady diet of professional football. O'Rourke must have sensed this, as he abandoned the Garden Tournament after the 1903 installment. It would take some time before the nation's largest city would embrace the professional version of the sport. In fact, unlike baseball, football grew first in the smaller towns and cities. The reason for this, contends Marc Maltby in his book, *The Origins and Development of Professional Football,* was that pro football had not won "broad support" in the cities, and it was always going to suffer from the debate over the "evils of professionalism." Smaller communities could "overlook any suspicions of pro football because for them the maintenance of their community's identity was more important" than the moral debate on the subject.[1]

Professional Football in Ohio

It was in those smaller communities of Pennsylvania and also Ohio that the game was gaining wider acceptance during the first two decades of the 20th century. Two towns in Ohio emerged as the best in the state—possibly the country—by 1905. Massillon had won the state championship in 1904, but a team from Canton was making all the headlines in 1905, including racking up over 100 points in two consecutive games against sailors from the *USS Michigan* and the Dayton Athletic Club. Massillon was also getting some impressive wins, including an 88-point victory over a Cleveland Athletic Club—again showing the dominance of smaller towns over the bigger cities. It was clear both Massillon and Canton had cornered the market on talent, and they dominated the "Big 6" league of Ohio professional football that had been established the previous year. The two towns were in a fierce competition to get the best talent from the East. Although they succeeded in acquiring the talent, they also had to pay a huge financial price. Because most people were not interested in watching lopsided affairs like most of their games were, attendance dwindled unless they played each other (which only occurred once in the regular season and again in the championship). The championship game of 1905 drew the largest crowd of the season—approximately 6,500. The game was played in Massillon, and the team owner decided to raise the ticket prices to one dollar (a large sum for the time). The Cleveland *Plain Dealer* reported that "speculators" were "asking $3 and $4" a ticket, which was possibly the first case of ticket scalping for a professional football game.[2] Massillon won the game that day 14–4, but they did not win the financial battle. They had to give Canton 40 percent of the gate (which was the custom for every game), and after paying its players and figuring in other expenses, the undefeated champion Massillon Tigers, despite playing 9 of its 10 games at home, lost $15.87 for the season. Things were actually worse for Canton—for example, that 40 percent of the gate for the championship came to about $2,600, but the team's salary for just that game came to over $3,000. The teams seemed to have not learned their lesson the following year because in 1906 they again commanded stellar, high-paid rosters and even beefed them up to prepare for each other. Each team even raided the other's roster to improve their own. Not surprisingly, they again met in the championship at the end of the season. They played a two-game series, and in the first game Canton finally got a win against Massillon, but the celebration was short-lived, as Massillon came back with a victory in the second game. Plenty of controversy swirled around this series, including charges of fixing the games for gamblers. The controversy had a detrimental effect on professional football not only in Ohio but also across the country. Both Canton and Massillon dropped their teams after the 1906 season, and any talk of new leagues disappeared with them. All the progressive reformers of the time who were decrying the evil of the professional game now had their prime example to point to.

During the second decade of the 20th century, professional football had a resurgence largely due to the emergence of the game's first superstar, and it came ironically in Canton. When last we discussed Jim Thorpe in Chapter 5, he was playing football for the Carlisle Indian School and defeating Army in 1912. After his eligibility was exhausted at Carlisle, Thorpe tried his hand at professional baseball as an outfielder for John McGraw's New York Giants. By 1915 after several run-ins with McGraw and Thorpe's "intermittent dedication" to the team, along with a sagging batting average, he was sent down to the minors and eventually ended up quitting baseball and returning to football.[3] He first resurfaced as an assistant coach for the University of Indiana and later was coaxed back into a player's uniform by the reincarnated Canton Bulldogs. It had been almost a decade since the original Bulldogs had been disbanded after the gambling controversy, and the new version was under completely different management from the first team. When Jack Cusack announced that he was taking command of this new team as its secretary–treasurer in 1912, he made it clear that things would be different when he proclaimed that the inaugural season would be "the Renaissance year for professional football."[4] He went so far as to rename the team the "Professionals" as opposed to the original "Bulldogs." It was really not until the 1915 season and the emergence of Thorpe that the "renaissance" Cusack was looking for occurred. By then the old nickname had returned, and so had Canton's archrival. Massillon was back, and their new team seemed to pick up where the old team had left off. In a two-game series with Canton in 1915, they defeated the Bulldogs in the first game 16–0, completely shutting down Thorpe. Massillon had a big-name player of their own by signing the former Notre Dame standout Knute Rockne. After coaching the Irish on Saturdays, he would travel to Ohio on Sundays to play for the Tigers. In the second game with Canton, Rockne had apparently scored the tying touchdown late in the game, but after a spectator ripped the ball from his hands and a Canton player fell on it, it was ruled a fumble, and Canton was deemed the winner. Even though there was a fierce protest from Rockne, the call was not changed.

Jim Thorpe. Image courtesy of
Library of Congress

Although the presence of Jim Thorpe did not always guarantee a Bulldog victory, it did guarantee a healthy gate attraction, and Canton became the team to watch. When the two teams met again in 1916, the crowd in Massillon, a town of only 1,600, swelled to nearly 15,000. There was talk that Thorpe might not play football that season as he had returned to baseball, playing for an American Association team in Milwaukee. Much to the relief of Canton and all professional football, he did return after missing only the first two games of the season. That huge crowd saw an ugly contest that ended in a scoreless tie. The weather was horrible, as it rained and the wind blew, and Thorpe's athletic talents were nullified by the elements. One week later in Canton, a slightly smaller crowd saw a much better performance by Thorpe and a lopsided Canton victory of 24–0. America's entrance into World War I in April of 1917 did not stop the pro football season from commencing that fall, but it did hamper attendance and talent. There were also rumors that the aging superstar Jim Thorpe was planning to retire.

The rumors proved not to be true, as Thorpe would play for many more seasons for Canton as well as other teams and not retire until his early forties. There was also a rumor in 1917 that there was going to be another attempt by baseball owners to organize a professional football league similar to the 1902 league. Although that rumor was unfounded, 1920 would prove to be a monumental year for professional football, as the first independent league organized by football owners would emerge. On September 17, Ralph Hay, owner of the Canton Bulldogs, called a meeting in his Canton automobile showroom for just such a purpose. Fourteen representatives of 10 professional football teams met and founded the **American Professional Football Association (APFA)**. Hay refused the presidency of the new league and suggested that because of the need for publicity that they needed a star for that position, so he nominated Jim Thorpe, and it was agreed.

Thorpe would essentially be the figurehead for the organization while Hay was actually in control. The group agreed to charge a fee of $100 to member teams. The fee turned out to be more for an "appearance of financial stability" than anything else. One of the owners at the meeting was George Halas of the Decatur Staleys, who later stated, "I can testify that no money changed hands. Why I doubt if there was a hundred bucks in the whole room."[5] Halas had played football at the University of Illinois prior to World War I, and after entering the armed forces as an ensign, he was assigned to the Great Lakes Naval Training Station, which featured a powerful football squad that actually won the 1919 Rose Bowl. Upon leaving the service, he turned to baseball and was accomplished enough to play outfield for the New York Yankees during the 1919 season. It was sometimes reported that Halas was replaced by Babe Ruth in 1920 when Ruth came over from the Red Sox, but in actuality, Halas had left the Yankees before the 1920 season and had gone to work for the Chicago, Burlington, and Quincy Railroad. During that time, he went back to football and was contacted by the Staley Manufacturing Company about starting a company team in Decatur, Illinois. Halas agreed and quickly established a powerful team that was a charter member of the APFA. His inaugural team compiled the second-best record in the league, and in 1921 he decided to move the club to Chicago for a bigger fan base. A. E. Staley, owner of the company, agreed to help finance the move if Halas kept the Staley name for one more season. Halas agreed, and the Chicago Staleys won the APFA championship that season. In 1922 Halas changed the name of the team to the Bears, and the American Professional Football Association changed its name to the National Football League.

George Halas in Yankee baseball uniform. Image courtesy of Library of Congress

The "New" NFL

In 1919 the Notre Dame administration was made aware that one of its football players had played professionally on Sundays during the 1918 season. Because this was a violation of school policy, the player was expelled from school. The player went back home to Green Bay, Wisconsin, where he had been a standout multisport star athlete for Green Bay East High School. The star athlete was **Earl L. (Curly) Lambeau** and, on returning home, he got a job with the Indian Packing Company. In August 1919, he had assembled his own professional football team of which he was owner, coach, and player. He convinced his boss, Frank Peck, to put up $500 to sponsor the team, which included paying for 20 jerseys with the company name on them, shoulder pads, and 12 footballs. In honor of that sponsorship, Lambeau agreed to name the team the **Green Bay Packers**, and the storied franchise was born. Lambeau played halfback for the Packers for 10 years and was the team's head coach for 30. Lambeau teamed up with George Calhoun, sports editor for the Green Bay *Press-Gazette*, to build a strong squad from the start. Calhoun served as the publicity man for the team and was responsible for helping recruit not only players but also spectators, and it was his duty to collect money from the fans at halftime. He kept the money until the end of the season, at which time he divided the cash among the players. Although Lambeau had a small roster (he carried only a few substitutes on his squad as he put it, "in case somebody got killed or something"), the total payoff per player amounted to only about $17 by the end of the season.[6] That inaugural season may not have been a financially successful one, but it was certainly successful on the field. Lambeau and Calhoun assembled a strong team that won all 10 of its games and faced off against the Fairbanks-Morse Company of Beloit for the state championship of Wisconsin. The Packers lost in a close and extremely controversial game. Lambeau and Calhoun were convinced the officials had been paid off. Perhaps they were struggling to accept the fact their only loss of the season was to a team known as the "Fairies."

The season was not successful enough apparently to warrant an invitation to join the inaugural season of the AFPA in 1920. In 1921, after another good year, the Packers were invited and joined the league. When the name of the league officially changed to the NFL before the 1922 season, three franchises currently still active can truly claim they were there at the beginning: the Chicago Bears, the Chicago Cardinals (later moved to St. Louis and currently of Arizona), and the Green Bay Packers. Although many clubs came and went in the early years of the league, few smaller clubs survived. Even the team in the town that started it all lost their franchise in 1924. The Canton Bulldogs were sold to a Cleveland sports promoter who owned the Cleveland Indians football club—he changed the name to the Bulldogs and invited many of the better players from Canton to join the team. Canton was rewarded for its contribution to the league by having the NFL Hall of Fame dedicated in Canton (albeit almost 40 years later). The coming of the Great Depression in the 1930s sounded the death knell for smaller clubs and almost doomed the Packers. The difference-maker for Green Bay was its quality of play. In the first 10 seasons of the NFL, the champion was awarded on the basis of the team's record—there were no playoffs. The Packers consistently finished among the leaders in the league throughout the 1920s. In 1927, the Packers finished with the second-best record in the league to a team in its third season, the New York Giants. It was the first of the Giants' eight championships prior to 1967 and four after the advent of the Super Bowl. Weeks after the crash of the stock market in October of 1929, the Packers enjoyed their first NFL title by finishing the season undefeated just ahead of the Giants, whose only loss of the season was to the Packers. The championship was especially sweet for Curly Lambeau, who was playing in his last season for the team he founded. At 31, he decided to retire as a player to concentrate on his coaching duties. In 1930, the Packers again finished one game ahead of the Giants for their second championship. They wrapped up their third straight in 1931 with a 12–2 record. Winning those three consecutive championships probably saved the franchise.

In 1932 the Packers' streak ended due to the rule of ties not counting toward the final standings. Ties today are rare, but if they occur they count as a half-win, half-loss. The 1932 season ended with both the Chicago Bears and Portsmouth Spartans having 6–1 won–loss records, but the teams had six and four ties, respectively. The Packers finished 10–3–1—a record that would have given them a fourth consecutive championship had current rules been used. Because ties did not count, Chicago and Portsmouth had better winning percentages. But they had identical winning percentages—so what was the answer? A playoff game was scheduled—the first in league history. Originally to be played at Wrigley Field on December 11, it was later decided to be played in Chicago Stadium (home of the Chicago Black Hawks hockey team) when temperatures dropped below zero outside. The field was shrunk due to the space constraints (60 yards long instead of 100, and 45 yards wide as opposed to 55), but over 11,000 fans packed the stadium—an estimated 10 times the amount that would have braved the frigid cold of Wrigley Field. The game was a defensive struggle, and the winning score was disputed by the losing team. With the score tied 0–0 in the fourth quarter, the Bears were on the Portsmouth two-yard line, and it was fourth down. The best player the Bears had was their all-NFL fullback Bronislau (Bronco) Nagurski, and it was expected he would get the ball and try to smash through the line for the score. Although he did receive the ball, he faked the run and dropped back and passed the ball to a wide-open Red Grange in the end zone. The problem with the play was that rules required passes to be thrown from at least five yards behind the line of scrimmage. The Portsmouth coach protested that Nagurski was not five yards behind the line when he let go of the ball. Without instant replay, officials had to rely on their judgment; they judged that it was indeed a touchdown, and the Bears were awarded the touchdown and eventually the championship. Although controversial, the game was a success, and it ushered in a new era and new rules in the NFL beginning in 1933.

After the AFPA's initial season in 1920, it became apparent that Jim Thorpe was not cut out to be an administrator. It was also clear that he had been named president of the league for his name identification to give the league some credibility. When league owners discussed a change in the office in 1921, Jim Thorpe showed no interest in keeping his job—in fact, he was not even at the meeting. The league instead turned to Joseph Carr, manager of the Columbus Panhandlers. Robert Peterson, in his book *Pigskin*, wrote that "Joe Carr should be credited with bringing the beginnings of order out of the shambles of the APFA in 1921 . . . Carr's good judgment and willingness to make decisions carried the NFL through the shoals of adolescence."[7] As for Carr, he would later say that his nomination for the post "was much against my will, and while I was out of the room."[8] Although he had little executive experience, he quickly gained the confidence of the owners and held the post until his death in 1938. One of the first decisions he made was to establish uniform contracts for all players based on major league baseball contracts. He also said that teams could not approach players under contract with other teams unless they were free agents and established the policy of territoriality for scheduling games—teams could not schedule games in other teams' "territory." Carr first published standings of the teams so fans could know where they stood. It was Carr's idea to have the first playoff game in 1932, and he was behind the **rules changes of 1933** that led to the modernization of the league. Most of the changes were a direct result of that 1932 game. The disputed play from Nagurski to Grange begged the question: Why not let the ball be passed from anywhere behind the line of scrimmage? In 1933 the rules were changed to reflect that, and it led to a more wide-open, exciting style of play. It also led to more scoring. Another rule change that helped produce more points was moving the goalposts up to the goal line from the back of the end zone to make field goals and extra points easier (albeit making the game more dangerous with two large posts sometimes getting in the way of players trying to score). The increase in points was also designed to decrease the number of ties (remember, the Bears had finished first in the standings with only seven wins because they had six ties). It had the desired effect immediately, as the number of ties was cut in half in 1933 from the previous year. The playing of the playoff game itself had an effect on the future of the game—Carr decided to split the league into two divisions and have the winners of each division play in a championship game at the end of the season. Never again would the champion of the NFL be decided by the standings alone. To further enhance the passing game, the shape of the ball itself was changed in 1934. The ball could no longer be no more than 21½ inches around at its widest point (one and a half inches thinner than it had been before), making it easier to throw.

The 1930s not only marked the time that the league began to modernize but also a number of teams joined the league that are still in existence today. In 1932 George Preston Marshall became part owner of the Boston Braves (named for the National League baseball team in Boston—later moved to Milwaukee and currently in Atlanta). Possibly to differentiate from the baseball team, Marshall changed the name to the Redskins in 1933, and in 1937 he moved the team to Washington. The year 1933 also brought into the NFL two Pennsylvania franchises that are still in the league today. **Bert Bell** had a football pedigree that extended back to the foundation of the game. His father had been Pennsylvania attorney general and served with Walter Camp on the Intercollegiate Rules Committee. Bell himself played for and later coached at Penn. Much of the family fortune was lost after the stock market crash in 1929, but he married into some money, and it was his wife who financed the $2,500 purchase of the defunct Frankford Yellow Jackets and turned them into the Philadelphia Eagles. **Art Rooney** had a background as a player and coach growing up in Pittsburgh. He also had a reputation as an excellent handicapper of race horses. The rumor (although he always denied it) was that he started the Pittsburgh Pirates football team with the winnings he acquired during a very good day at the track. Rooney would change the name of the team to the Steelers in honor of the city's nickname "Steel City." It is not a coincidence that both of these teams emerged just as Pennsylvania became one of the last states to eliminate its blue laws, which did not allow for many Sunday activities. Neither Pennsylvania team enjoyed much success in the 1930s. In the later stages of that decade, in an attempt to produce a more talented team, Bell and Rooney proposed a merger of the two teams into one named the Keystoners—it was not allowed. During World War II because of the loss of men going into the armed forces, many teams were forced to merge temporarily, including the two Pennsylvania teams. For one season they were known as the Phil-Pitt Steagles. Although Bell eventually left the Eagles, he was later named to the position of commissioner in 1946 (which replaced the office of president after Joe Carr's death in 1939).

The 1930s marked the beginning of one of the greatest rivalries not just in football but in all sports. When the league was split into two divisions in 1933, the Western Division would come to be dominated by George Halas's Chicago Bears and Curly Lambeau's Green Bay Packers. Between 1933 and 1939, each team won the division three times—the only year they did not was 1935, when the Detroit Lions edged out the Packers by one game. The Lions had moved to Detroit from Portsmouth, New Hampshire, in 1934, marking the departure of the last smaller-city franchise outside Green Bay. Of the nine NFL teams in 1935, only the Brooklyn Dodgers, named in conjunction with the baseball franchise, do not still exist today in some form. The keys to the Bears' and Packers' successes can be attributed to two dominating players—Bronco Nagurski in Chicago and **Don Hutson** in Green Bay. Nagurski was the powerful fullback that threw the winning touchdown in 1932 and dominated defenses throughout the decade. Hutson used the new pass-friendly rules of the 1930s to become the game's best receiver. Even with the increased popularity of the pro game, many college players did not enter the NFL after graduation. A stark example of this is the implementation of the first NFL draft in 1936. Two of the first three draft picks never played in the NFL—including the top pick Jay Berwanger from the University of Chicago, who also was the first Heisman trophy winner the previous year. In fact, the first three Heisman winners did not choose to play professionally. Most players believed they could make more money in other professions. Each team had nine picks in the first draft, and of those 81 picks, fewer than half signed contracts. Those who did sign contracts could only do so with the team that drafted them, which greatly reduced their negotiating power, and that kept salaries down. George Halas later admitted this was one of the arguments owners used to implement the draft, but he said eventually it was a good thing for the game as well as the players: ". . . time proved that by leveling the clubs, the draft system heightened the attractiveness of the sport. It created bigger audiences, which brought bigger revenue, which brought higher salaries for all players."[9]

The late 30s were also a period in which a number of minor leagues sprang up—all called the American Football League (or AFL). Between 1936 and 1941, there were three AFLs, and the NFL eventually absorbed one of the better of the minor league teams—the Cleveland Rams, which joined the Western division of the NFL in 1937 and evened the two divisions at five teams each. The team was not at the level of the better NFL teams early on, however, and routinely finished in the cellar of its division for years. When the Rams left, they were replaced by the Los Angeles Bulldogs which became the first West Coast team to host Eastern and Midwestern teams. Interestingly, the Rams would eventually move to Los Angeles, and the NFL became the first professional team sport to have a franchise on the West Coast. The decade did not end before the brand-new technology of television was attempted in the NFL. On October 22, 1939, the first ever television broadcast of a football game took place in New York between the Brooklyn Dodgers and Bert Bell's Philadelphia Eagles. It followed the first-ever sports broadcast the previous spring, when a baseball game between Columbia and Princeton was telecast. The first televised games were in New York because that is where all the broadcast equipment was and where all the television sets were, albeit very few. The number of people seeing the game probably numbered a few hundred, and even they were not able to see much in the 5- to 12-inch screens through the black-and-white snow. Few could predict the importance this new technology would have on the sport and American culture in general in the second half of the century. It is surprising to note that the first television broadcast (although very much local) actually preceded the first nationwide radio broadcast, which came at the end of the 1940 season when the Chicago Bears crushed the Washington Redskins 73–0 in the NFL championship. It was the first exposure to the game for perhaps millions of Americans. The Bears continued their dominance the following season by defeating the Giants 37–9 on December 21—exactly two weeks after the bombing of Pearl Harbor by the Japanese, which hastened the American entrance into World War II.

WWII and the Pro Football War

December 7, 1941, was a game day for the NFL, and although the attack took place just before 8 a.m. Hawaii time, most games were underway, as it was nearly 1 p.m. Eastern time. News of the attack began to filter across the country and was announced at NFL stadiums. The NFL would not feel the effects of the country's entrance into the war until the following season, when the league learned that 112 of the 346 NFL players (almost one-third) had joined the armed forces. Elmer Layden, one of Notre Dame's famed Four Horsemen from the 1920s, who had taken over the reigns of the NFL after Joe Carr's death, was the first to hold the title commissioner. He noted that this high number of players fighting for their country was a positive thing: "Naturally, we're proud of that record," Layden said, "and I believe it's additional proof of the worthwhileness of football."[10] By the end of the war, 638 active players had served, 69 had been decorated, and 21 had been killed in action or training exercises.[11] The loss of all this talent did take its toll on the talent level of the teams as well as the number of spectators showing up to see them play. The 1942 season saw the number of total fans dip below 900,000 and remain there through the 1944 season. When the war ended in the summer of 1945, players began to return to teams, and fans began to return to the stands. The 1945 season had nearly 2 million fans, which averages just under 30,000 per game, and that was a respectable number. Football was back, and Commissioner Layden announced that a tradition began during the war would continue after the war—the playing of the national anthem prior to the games. "It should be as much a part of every game as the kickoff," Layden said. "We must not drop it simply because the war is over. We should never forget what it stands for."[12]

After the war ended the NFL experienced its own war in the late 1940s. There was the first real challenge to its supremacy in professional football by the All-America Football Conference (AAFC) beginning in the 1946 season. The AAFC first attempted to meet with the NFL and work out an agreement with the league, but Commissioner Layden flat refused, saying, "Let them get a

Coach Paul Brown of the Cleveland Browns. © Bettmann/CORBIS

football and play a game, and then maybe we'll have something to talk about."[13] Because the AAFC was snubbed by the NFL, they felt they had the right to go after any players they wanted, including current NFL players. Jimmy Crowley, one of Layden's fellow Four Horsemen, was named commissioner of the AAFC and made that point when he said, "We originally resolved not to tamper with National League players, but since the NFL snubbed us we see no reason why we can't hire their players."[14] What resulted was a war for players that naturally drove up salaries across the board. Layden was blamed for this escalation and was ousted by the owners even before the 1946 season began. He was replaced by Eagles founder and owner Bert Bell.

Although the AAFC was a short-lived league, it produced a team and coach that would eventually be a storied franchise and innovative mind in the NFL. **Paul Brown** and his Cleveland Browns (named after the coach by a contest of fans) were part of the inaugural season of the AAFC in 1946. It is probably not surprising that Brown became involved in professional football, as he was a native of the Massillon–Canton area, where the first major professional football rivalry started. Although of small stature (weighing only 140 pounds), Brown starred as Massillon High's quarterback and then played the same position for Miami University of Ohio in the late 1920s and early 30s. After graduating from college, he went back to his alma mater in Massillon and taught and coached football for nine years, where he compiled an impressive record of 80 victories against only eight losses and two ties. His success did not go unnoticed in the college ranks, and when Ohio State suffered a humiliating defeat to its archrival Michigan, 40–0, in 1940, the administration decided to fire its coach and hire Brown to take the helm for the Buckeyes for the 1941 season. Brown wasted little time producing a winner, as his team went 9–1 that season and was named college football's national champion. After the 1943 season, Brown entered the military (although already in his mid-thirties). After being commissioned into the Navy, he spent the next two years stationed at the Great Lakes Naval Training Center near Chicago, where he coached the very successful football team there. It was while he was there that he was approached by the leaders of the AAFC about starting a team in Cleveland. He was reluctant at first, but after the Ohio State athletic director seemed to balk at inviting him back to coach postwar, he decided to go the professional route. He received a very lucrative and powerful deal, as he would be not only the Browns' coach but also the general manager and have complete control of signing players and coaches. He commanded an impressive $25,000 a year salary and also five percent of the earnings of the team, as he was part owner as well.

The AAFC was extremely competitive when it came to the player war. Of the 60 players on the college all-star team in 1946, 44 decided to play for the new league. Roughly 100 former NFL players jumped to the AAFC. One of the problems with the new league was that seemingly the best players played for the same team. Of the four seasons the league was in existence (1946–49), the Cleveland Browns won the championship each year. Probably the best season was 1947, when there seemed to be more parity among the teams and most of the teams did well financially. One of the exceptions to this was the Brooklyn Dodgers football club. After making news earlier in the baseball season by being the first team to sign an African American player, Jackie Robinson, general manager Branch Rickey decided to try his hand at football. A receiver on that team, Dan Edwards, recalled the problems that the franchise faced that season: "(the Dodgers) were a total wreck! We weren't getting very big crowds . . . by the end of the season all the players recognized the trouble we were in. We were lucky to get paid."[15] At the end of the season, Rickey also recognized the trouble the team was in and turned over the rights of the franchise to the AAFC. The league decided to merge it with the other New York team (the Yankees), and the players were dispersed among the remaining seven teams for the 1949 season. By 1949 the AAFC and NFL were both hurting financially, and it was obvious some sort of peace would have to be made. In December 1948, representatives from both leagues met for the first time, but no agreement was made. After the 1949 season, the NFL agreed to take three of the teams from the AAFC—the two best teams, the Browns and the San Francisco 49ers, and one of the worst, the Baltimore Colts. The 49ers had emerged as the one challenger to the Browns, and they actually defeated Cleveland by the lopsided score of 56–28 during the regular season before losing to them 21–7 in the championship. The Colts finished last in the final season of the AAFC in 1949, but they would build a winning team in the coming years and actually win an NFL championship before the 1950s ended. The remaining four teams in the AAFC (the New York Yankees, Los Angeles Dons, Chicago Hornets, and the Buffalo Bills) were disbanded, and their players put into a special draft pool for the NFL. The one team that truly believed they should have been included in the NFL was the Buffalo Bills. They had built a strong following in upstate New York, and they had also built a strong team—considered third best in the league after the Browns and 49ers. Buffalo would have to wait until another professional league emerged in the 1960s—the American Football League— before it would have another professional football franchise. By taking the 49ers, the NFL effectively neutralized another minor league—the Pacific Coast Football League—because the NFL now had a presence in two California cities (Los Angeles and San Francisco), so by the 1950s, the NFL effectively had a monopoly on professional football.

The 1950 season was important for the NFL not only because it opened a new decade but also because the wars with other leagues were over and because football emerged as *the* television sport. The Los Angeles Rams were the first team to allow all of their games to be televised. Although it turned out to be a short-term mistake (the Rams' attendance dropped off dramatically), it did portend the future of the importance of the medium to the sport. Another reason the 1950 season was important was that it marked the first time the league adopted the free substitution rule, which essentially set up separate defenses, offenses, and special teams. In the early days of football, most players played on both sides of the ball, but colleges began to implement free substitution in the 1940s. By the '50s most players coming out of college played one way or the other. It allowed for both offenses and defenses to improve because players could concentrate on their specialties. A coach who was especially adept at this was Paul Brown. He was the first coach to implement playbooks and classroom instruction in pro football. He also administered intelligence and psychological tests to his players. He was also the first head coach to hire full-time assistant coaches who were employed by the team year-round, and he would sometimes put those coaches in the press box to get a bird's-eye view of the game. There was no mistake who was in charge of the Browns, however, and Brown was the pioneer of coaches calling the plays from the sideline—prior to him, the quarterback called all the plays. Brown was also a pioneer in another aspect of coaching—what coaches today would call "bulletin board material" to be used to motivate his players. For the entire time the AAFC was in existence, the NFL treated its members as second-class citizens, and owners and coaches were not shy about making their feelings known. An example of this was Redskins owner George Preston Marshall saying of the AAFC: "The worst team in our league could beat the best team in theirs."[16] Browns' quarterback Otto Graham remembered later that "for four years Coach Brown never said a word. He just kept putting the stuff on the bulletin board. We were so fired up we would have played them anywhere, anytime."[17]

The anytime came sooner than anyone expected, as Commissioner Bert Bell scheduled the Browns to play the defending NFL champion Philadelphia Eagles on opening day of the 1950 season. Brown's motivating tactics apparently worked, as Otto Graham passed for over 300 yards and three touchdowns, and the Browns buried the Eagles 35–10. To prove that the win was no fluke, the Browns compiled a 10–2 record and in the NFL title game defeated the Los Angeles Rams 30–28 on a last-second field goal by placekicker Lou "The Toe" Groza. It was the first of three championships for the Browns, and they proved they not only belonged in the league but they were among the best of it. The decade to come would also prove that the NFL was here to stay. The average attendance at a game in 1950 was 25,000. By 1960 that average was over 40,000. The latter number is even more impressive when it is juxtaposed against the attendance numbers of yet another rival pro football league that emerged in 1960. The AFL averaged over 16,500 a game in their inaugural season of 1960. Although the 1950s were a successful decade for the league, the decades to come would prove to be even more beneficial financially. The "golden age" of professional football was about to begin, and many point to a game in 1958 as its origin.

NFL Commissioner Bert Bell talks to reporters in 1947. © Bettmann/CORBIS.

The 1958 Championship Game Kicks off the NFL's Golden Age

The Baltimore Colts were one of the worst teams in the AAFC for the league's four-year existence. For some reason, the NFL decided to bring over the franchise when the league folded in 1949—perhaps because it wanted a presence in Baltimore. That presence did not last long, however, as the team only won one game in 1950, and owner Abraham Watner turned the franchise back over to the league after the season. Following World War II, there had been two mass population movements in this country: One was from the inner cities to the suburbs, and the other was from the cities of the North and East to the Sun Belt of the South and West. As Sun Belt cities grew in population, there was a demand for all the benefits the old cities had, and one of those benefits was professional sports teams. Cities in Texas were a prime example of this. In 1952 Dallas entered the NFL with its first franchise—the Texans. Unfortunately for fans in Dallas, they were no more successful than Baltimore had been in 1950, and the Texans only won a single game. The franchise disbanded and was ironically reorganized in Baltimore. The 1953 season marked the reincarnation of the Baltimore Colts, but the new Colts seemed to be no better than the old version winning only three games in both 1953 and 1954. Although they improved to five wins the next two seasons, they were still a sub-.500 team. The year 1956 would prove to be a turning point year for the Colts when they signed a quarterback named **Johnny Unitas**. Unitas had been drafted in the ninth round of the 1955 NFL draft out of Louisville by the Steelers, but they had cut him before the season started. No other team picked him up that season, so he worked construction in Pittsburgh and played semipro ball for the Bloomfield Rams, earning $6 a game. The Colts were actually looking at a Rams lineman when they had Unitas come in for a tryout, and they signed him for the 1956 season. Although he did not play much in 1956, he took over as the Colts starter in 1957, and he led the league with 2,550 yards and 24 touchdowns. He also led the Colts to their first-ever winning season (7–5) and was named the league MVP. It was quite a jump from working construction to NFL Most Valuable Player in less than two years. He would help the Colts make an even bigger jump the following year.

In 1958 Unitas proved he was no flash in the pan when he put up even better numbers. He passed for almost 2,900 yards and 32 touchdowns. The numbers the Colts fans were most im-

pressed with was the 9–3 record he led them to, which was enough to win the Western Conference and meet the New York Giants for the NFL Championship. The repeat MVP of the league, Unitas helped Baltimore to a 14–3 halftime lead, but the tide turned in the second half, as the Giants came back to take the lead 17–14 in the fourth quarter. In the waning minutes of the game, Unitas, as so many defenses had come to dread, calmly marched the Colts 62 yards down the field and, with seven seconds remaining, Steve Myhra kicked the tying field goal. As time ran out, the NFL would invoke the sudden-death overtime rule for the first time in a championship game. The Giants won the coin toss, but failed to move the ball and had to punt. Once again, Unitas took the Colts down the field—this time 80 yards, culminating with an Alan Ameche one-yard dive for the winning touchdown. This game is often referred to as the NFL's arrival in the modern age, partly because it

Colts scoring winning overtime touchdown in 1958 NFL Championship game. © Bettmann/CORBIS

was such a great game—it was almost immediately dubbed "the best game ever played." The other reason was the fact that so many people were tuned in to the game on television. The medium had grown greatly from its humble origins nearly 20 years before, where only a few sets were available, and they were nearly all in the New York area. Ironically, because the NFL had a blackout rule that did not allow telecasts in the area the game was being played, the only people in New York who were supposed to see the game were the 64,000 who showed up to Yankee Stadium to watch it. As it turned out, some sets in New York were able to pick up the game. Reporter Jack Gould of the *New York Times* wrote: "Thanks to the vagaries of television waves, which sometimes shoot beyond the horizon, station WRCA-TV in Philadelphia—penetrated the New York area for most of the game . . . the picture was badly speckled and streaked but even with the visual handicaps the game was the sports spectacle of the TV year."[18] Those in New York were part of an estimated 10.8 million homes that were tuned into the game that year. Had the game not been as good as it was, who knows if it would have been such a springboard for the popularity of the sport in the years to come.

In 1959 Unitas won his third consecutive MVP award, and the Colts repeated as champions again defeating the New York Giants—this time the game was not that close—31–16. The year would be an important one for the future of the league because of two things that happened off the field. The first was the hiring of **Vince Lombardi** to coach the Green Bay Packers. The once-proud franchise had fallen on hard times after World War II. Due to financial difficulties, the team could not attract the good players it once did and by the 1949 season only managed one win. Curly Lambeau, founder of the franchise, decided to step down as head coach after that season, and the next decade became a carousel of hiring and firing of coaches, with none of them managing to put together a winning season. The low point was 1958, when Ray MacLean was fired after one season when the team sunk to the cellar with a league-worst record of 1–10–1. The 46-year-old Lombardi had been looking for a head coaching position since becoming an assistant coach for the New York Giants in 1954. His only head coaching experience to that point had been St. Cecilia High School in Englewood, New Jersey. Lombardi recognized he had talent, however, and felt he could bring out the best in the team. His workouts were rigorous and done with military precision—no doubt reflecting his days as an assistant at the Military Academy at West Point. The team he inherited already had quarterback Bart Starr and 1956 Heisman Trophy winner and number one draft pick of the 1957 NFL draft, Paul Hornung. Hornung had played quarterback for Notre Dame, but Lombardi converted him to halfback, and he and Starr would prove to be the backbone of the vaunted Packers offense during the 1960s. It did not take long for Lombardi to find success—the Packers finished 1959 with a 7–5 record, its first winning season in 12 years, and Lombardi was voted the Associated Press' Coach of the Year. In 1960, the Packers won their conference and met the Philadelphia Eagles for the championship. On the day after Christmas, the Packers lost to the Eagles 17–13, and Lombardi promised his players, "This will never happen again. You will never lose another championship."[19] The coach was true to his word, as the Packers came back in 1961 to compile an 11–3 record (the league schedule was expanded from 12 to 14 games), and the Packers won their first championship since 1944 by demolishing the New York Giants 37–0 before a home crowd in Green Bay on a frigid New Year's Eve. The victory was especially sweet for Lombardi, who had grown up in New York and coached for the Giants. The 1962 rematch was much closer. Even though the Packers only lost one game during the regular season, they defeated the Giants at Yankee Stadium 16–7. A third consecutive championship run was thwarted in 1963 when the Chicago Bears finished with only one loss just ahead of the Packers, who had two losses. Paul Hornung was suspended for the entire season after it was learned he wagered on football (betting on the Packers). The year 1964 was a season of injuries for the Packers, as the team struggled and only won eight games. They came back for a title run in 1965 with a 10–3–1 record. The Baltimore Colts had an identical record in the same conference, and because there were no tiebreaker rules at the time (the Packers defeated the Colts in the regular season), a playoff game was scheduled in which the Packers won 13–10 in overtime. They then went on to defeat the Cleveland Browns 23–12 for the team's third NFL championship in five seasons.

In addition to Lombardi being hired by Green Bay in 1959, the other important event occurred on October 11, when Commissioner Bert Bell was attending an intrastate matchup between his former team, the Philadelphia Eagles, and the Pittsburgh Steelers. Bell dropped dead of a heart attack and was replaced on an interim basis by league treasurer Austin Gunsel. The big fireworks occurred at the January 26, 1960, meeting of the owners, when they could not decide on a replacement for Bell. It took nine days and 23 ballots until a compromise and somewhat surprising candidate emerged. The owners turned to 33-year-old Los Angeles Rams General Manager **Alvin Ray "Pete" Rozelle**. It turned out to be an excellent choice. In three seasons he had turned the Rams into a profitable (if not winning—their 1959 record was 2–10) franchise. In his nearly 30 years as commissioner, he would do the same for the league and preside over its "golden age." The first thing he had to deal with was another rival league that emerged for the 1960 season. Earlier, Commissioner Bell had refused to expand the league when he was approached by two millionaire Texas businessmen, Lamar Hunt and K. S. "Bud" Adams, who wanted to establish franchises in the NFL. Hunt and Adams decided to take matters into their own hands and establish a new league—another **American Football League**, which began competition in 1960 with eight teams: Boston Patriots, Buffalo Bills, Dallas Texans, Denver Broncos, Houston Oilers, Los Angeles Chargers, New York Titans, and Oakland Raiders. Adams and Hunt owned the

NFL Commissioner Pete Rozelle and Steelers President Art Rooney holding the Super Bowl trophy in the 1970s. © Bettmann/CORBIS.

Houston and Dallas teams, respectively, and hoped for a regional rivalry between the two. Another owner had hoped to start a team in Minneapolis, but when Rozelle took over as commissioner, he reversed his predecessor's ruling on expansion, and franchises were awarded conveniently to Dallas (Cowboys began play in 1960) and Minneapolis (Vikings began in 1961). The inaugural season for the new AFL was not financially successful. Teams played before much smaller crowds than attended NFL games (10,000–20,000 at AFL games and 50,000 at NFL games), and the league lost around $3 million in 1960. The New York franchise did particularly poorly, and eventually owner Harry Wismer had to sell it. The new ownership renamed the team the Jets in 1963. Prior to his selling of the team, Wismer contributed to the league in a very important way by persuading the other owners to negotiate a deal with ABC for the television broadcasting rights to the league. Although it was not the most lucrative deal ever made, it allowed for each team to share equally in the television profits of the league, and it kept the league going.

In 1961 Commissioner Rozelle negotiated a similar contract with CBS for the NFL. This time, however, a federal judge struck down the deal saying it violated federal antitrust laws. The argument was that the NFL and other sports leagues would have monopoly power over their sport, and competition would be stifled. The NFL and other sports decided to go to Congress to have a new law written. In front of a congressional committee, Rozelle argued that it was imperative for the competitiveness of teams for that league to negotiate broadcasting rights for the teams as a league. If each team negotiated its own deals, it would greatly benefit the larger population franchises and hurt the smaller. Equal revenue sharing, Rozelle said, was a key to a successful sports league, and the result was the **1961 Sports Broadcasting Act**, which quickly passed both houses of Congress and was signed by President Kennedy. The act essentially exempted professional sports leagues from federal antitrust when negotiating broadcasting rights laws, and the result was extremely good for the teams in the league, players, and the league as a whole. Revenues began to rise, and so did players' salaries. Rozelle instituted a "league think"[20] mentality in the NFL not only in these negotiations but in everything that was done. He believed by putting the NFL above the individual teams and players, eventually everyone would benefit from a strong and successful league. The owners bought into this mentality, and for over a quarter century professional football enjoyed its "golden age." Beginning in the 1960s, American men began to have something to do on fall Sundays as opposed to just yard work or high-brow entertainment on television, and they tuned in to pro football in great numbers. New technologies like instant replay and slow-motion first used by CBS in 1963 also helped the growth of the game and enhanced the fans' knowledge of the game. For the first time, ratings for football passed the old national pastime, baseball.

By the mid-1960s, Rozelle knew that to "league think" there could and should be only one league. As always occurs when there is a rival league, there was a war for players between the NFL and AFL. In its inaugural season, Bud Adams and his Houston Oilers signed the 1959 Heisman Trophy winner Billy Cannon from LSU. Although that was a coup for the new league, nothing compares to the prize it won in 1965, when **Joe Namath**, quarterback from Alabama, was signed by the New York Jets for $400,000 and a new car. It was the highest price ever paid for a collegiate football player, and it dwarfed the average player's salary, which was around $25,000 at the time. The year 1965 was also one in which the AFL had reached a point where they were thinking about expansion. Ranklin Smith, a businessman from Atlanta, approached the AFL about starting a franchise in that city, and it was agreed that he would be awarded a team. When the NFL learned of this, they made Smith a better deal, and the Atlanta Falcons entered the NFL in 1966. Not to be deterred, the AFL decided to award Joe Robbie a team in Miami, and the Dolphins became the first AFL expansion team also beginning play in 1966—a turning-point year for professional football. In April, the controversial owner of the Oakland Raiders, Al Davis, became commissioner of the AFL, and he decided instead of simply trying to outbid NFL teams for players that he would, true to his team's namesake, "raid" active NFL rosters. In two months he persuaded seven NFL quarterbacks to come to the AFL. The combination of the Namath signing and the Davis raids led to secret meetings between the two leagues in the spring of 1966. The NFL decided it was not going to be able to beat the AFL, so they might as well join them. On June 8, 1966, it was announced that there would be a **merger**. Under the terms of the agreement there would be a common draft, a common commissioner—Pete Rozelle—a championship game between the two leagues at the end of the season, and the leagues would become two conferences in the NFL beginning in 1970. There was concern that the merger would not stand up under antitrust laws, but again, Commissioner Rozelle went to Capitol Hill to get Congress to introduce a bill that would exempt the merger from such laws. Particularly important to getting the bill passed was Sen. Russell Long and Rep. Hale Boggs, both from Louisiana. Three weeks after the bill was signed into law by President Lyndon Johnson in 1967, New Orleans was awarded an NFL franchise, and the Saints became the league's 16th team.

The "Super Bowl"

The first two championship games (not called "Super Bowl" until the third installment in 1969) were not good for the AFL. When last we left the Green Bay Packers, they had won the NFL championship in 1965, and they did so again in 1966. Super Bowl I (as it was retroactively titled two years later) took place on January 15, 1967, and it was not much of a contest. The Packers demolished the AFL champion Kansas City Chiefs 35–10. The Chiefs were formerly Lamar Hunt's Dallas Texans, but Hunt had moved them to Kansas City in 1963, believing two teams were too many for the Dallas area. The win reinforced the prevailing opinion that the NFL was an overall better league than the AFL. Even Vince Lombardi was quoted after the game saying, "I do not think they (Chiefs) are as good as the top teams in the National Football League."[21] The second

Super Bowl was not much better, as the Packers destroyed the Raiders 33–14. Most fans viewed the NFL championship game between the Packers and the Cowboys two weeks earlier as the *real* championship. It was known as the "Ice Bowl" because of the frigid temperatures in Green Bay that dipped below zero, but the outcome of the game warmed the partisan Packer fans, as Bart Starr dove over the goal line in the waning seconds to preserve the game and the championship 21–17. It was Lombardi's third consecutive championship, equaling the earlier record of Curly Lambeau (1929–31) and also his last, as he retired to become the Packers' general manager in 1968. The third Super Bowl (the first to actually be called by that name) was a watershed year for the AFL. The Joe Namath–led New York Jets won their first AFL championship, and they would meet the NFL champion Baltimore Colts. No one gave the Jets much of a chance, including the odds makers, who made the Colts an 18-point favorite.

Joe Namath. © George Tiedmann/ GT Images/Corbis

Namath was apparently tired of hearing that they were going to lose, and three days before the game guaranteed a Jets victory. His team backed him up, and they shocked the football world by defeating the Colts 16–7. Jets coach Weeb Ewbank later joked that he could have shot Namath for the "guarantee," but it had to be a sweet win for Ewbank, who had coached the Colts to the 1958 and 1959 championships but had been unceremoniously fired three years later. Ewbank's quarterback in 1958 was Johnny Unitas, and 10 years later Unitas was injured prior to the season and replaced by Earl Morrall, who had his greatest season ever leading the Colts to the championship. However, in Super Bowl Morall struggled with three interceptions and was replaced by the aging legend Unitas. Unitas led the Colts to their only score but did not lead them to victory.

Super Bowl III was a passing of the torch from the old, conservative NFL to the new, young AFL. The contrasts were stark—Namath with his long hair and white shoes represented the youth counterculture of the late 1960s, which was breaking away from their parents' generation represented by Unitas with his crew cut and black high-top shoes. The youth of the time became known as the "me" generation because they were mainly interested in themselves and had no use for authority—especially authority that could send them off to die in a foreign country. The old NFL was also seen as representing that old authority, and no one person embodied that authority more than Vince Lombardi. When Lombardi was dying of cancer in 1970, a little more than a year after the Jets won Super Bowl III, he was reported to have said in his sleep, "Joe Namath! You're not bigger than football. Remember that."[22] For years Lombardi lamented that everything in the rebellious sixties were "aimed at strengthening the rights of the individual and weakening the state, the church and all authority."[23] He had personified all that into one person, Joe Namath, and apparently he was one of the last things Lombardi was thinking about before he died.

As Lombardi lay dying, the NFL–AFL merger was becoming complete, and 1970 became the first season in which the two leagues would compete against each other during the regular season. In 1968 the AFL had grown to 10 teams with the addition of the Cincinnati Bengals. Art Modell became the majority owner of the Cleveland Browns in 1961, and he and Paul Brown had a rocky relationship from the start. By 1963 they were incompatible, and Modell fired the team's namesake. Brown asked for and got the AFL franchise in Cincinnati five years later. Those 10 teams joined the original 16 from the NFL and became a 26-team league. The 10 AFL teams formed the American Football Conference (AFC), and they were joined by three original NFL teams to make the conferences even. Art Modell volunteered to move his Browns to the AFC, foreseeing an intrastate rivalry with Brown's Bengals. Modell convinced their archrival Steelers to also make the move to continue the rivalry in the same conference. The third team to make the move was the Colts, as they wanted to separate from the Redskins because both teams competed for the same television market. The conferences were divided into three divisions with each division winner making it to the postseason plus a "wild card" from each conference also making the playoffs. That would be the team with the best record that was not a division winner. This doubled the teams in the post-season from four to eight. As the league expanded (and television revenue increased), so did the number of teams in the postseason, as eventually six teams from each conference would make the playoffs. The old AFL teams proved to be the equal, if not better, of the old NFL teams, as they held their own in the Super Bowls during the coming years and would actually have a better record during the season in interconference play during the 1970s and 1980s.

Professional football was increasing in popularity by the 1970s, and the merger only seemed to enhance that. Teams were playing before sold-out stadiums, and television ratings were also on the rise. In 1967 an average pro football game had 11 million viewers; by 1977 that number had almost doubled to 20 million. It was also in the early 70s that the traditional game-day Sunday was joined by Monday. **Roone Arledge** became the director of sports programming for the ABC television network, which was a distant third in the overall television ratings behind CBS and NBC. Arledge believed that by improving the way sports are covered, it would improve the ratings not only for sports but also for the entire network. He thought he could introduce drama and increase the amount of entertainment so that even if a viewer "didn't give a damn about the game, they still might enjoy the program."[24] He introduced ABC's *Wide World of Sports* in 1961, which "spanned the globe" every week in search of strange and interesting sports from various cultures. His plan worked, as ABC became the top overall network by the 1970s. In 1970 he introduced what would

Monday Night Football camera.
Image © catwalker, 2013.
Used under license from Shutterstock, Inc.

be his greatest triumph when he got the rights to broadcast one NFL game per week on primetime, and *Monday Night Football* was born. He also brought in as color commentator for the games the controversial announcer **Howard Cosell**, who was famous for, in his words, "telling it like it is." That meant no one escaped his wrath, including players, coaches, referees, or even owners. Cosell became the guy everyone "loved to hate," and the ratings soared. People would actually schedule their Monday nights around the telecast. By the early 1980s the NFL was on a roll, as Commissioner Rozelle had expanded the league to 28 teams with the addition of Tampa Bay and Seattle in 1976, and he signed a television deal in 1982 that guaranteed every team in the league over $14 million a season. Everyone was still "thinking league" above everything, and as long as they did that, it seemed the "golden age" would never end. Little did the commissioner or anyone else know that the golden age was about to end.

End of the Golden Age and the Beginning of a New Century and New Golden Age?

In 1982 the first sign of a crack in the structure of the NFL was evident when an owner went against the "think league" mentality and did something on his own. Not surprisingly, this "rogue" owner was Al Davis of the Oakland Raiders, who had served briefly as the commissioner of the AFL and, during his tenure, pardon the pun, encouraged "raiding" of NFL rosters by AFL teams. Now he asked the league if he could move the Raiders to Los Angeles because of his failure to get improvements made to the Oakland Coliseum. Rozelle announced he was against the move, and the owners voted 22–0 (with five abstaining) to not allow it. Davis went to court to sue the league for violation of antitrust laws. The federal courts upheld Davis's right to move, and he did so. The Raiders officially moved to Los Angeles for the 1982 season to play in the LA Coliseum and took the place of the Rams, who had recently moved to Anaheim. That same season had a 57-day players' strike that shortened the season to nine games, and the league decided to allow eight teams from each conference into the playoffs, which allowed two teams with losing records to make the postseason. In 1984 the owner of the Baltimore Colts, Robert Irsay, moved the team to Indianapolis. Although he had the approval of the league, he did not have it from the Maryland Senate, which gave the city of Baltimore the right to seize the team through eminent domain. As the legislation was being debated in the Maryland House of Representatives, Irsay worked out a deal with the mayor of Indianapolis, Richard Lugar, to make the move. The legislation was set to pass on the morning of March 29, so Mayor Lugar called his friend, John B. Smith, who was CEO of Mayflower Trucking, and had him send 15 semitrucks to the Colts' training facilities at 2 a.m. on the 29th, and by 10 a.m. the team's belongings had been entirely removed from Baltimore. The 15 trucks each took a different route out of Maryland to not be noticed by the Maryland State patrol. When the trucks crossed into Indiana, they were given a police escort to Indianapolis. Baltimore fans felt, justifiably so, that their team had been stolen from them in the dead of night. Baltimore would be without football for a little more than a decade until 1995, when Browns owner Art Modell decided to move the Browns to Baltimore after a stadium dispute. Ironically, Modell had been very critical of Irsay after his move. The move set off a series of legal maneuvers, which finally allowed Modell to take his players and organization to Baltimore, but he had to leave the team name and colors with the city of Cleveland. Although his team was exactly the same, it was considered an expansion team, and the Ravens began play in the fall of 1996. The Browns returned to Cleveland three years later with new ownership.

The year 1987 brought another strike by the players, but this one actually involved the playing of games with what the league called "replacement" players. The players were actually "scabs" who had crossed the picket line to play in place of actual NFL players. Eighty-five percent of players refused to play, and those that did were not nearly the caliber of the original players. It led to new nicknames for teams such as the Chicago Spare-Bears, Los Angeles Shams, and the San Francisco Phoney-Niners. It also led to a feeling of betrayal among players that Rozelle and the league would allow these games to go on. The five-year competitor league known as the United States Football League (USFL), which folded in 1987, also led to another player salary war, which drove up salaries and frustrated owners. By the late eighties another scourge had descended on the league—drugs. The many drug scandals that broke during the decade seemed to be the last straw for Rozelle, who decided to retire as commissioner in 1989. With his retirement came the end of an incredibly long golden age for professional football. Recent problems aside, Rozelle left the league much more successful and profitable than he found it. It would take a few years but eventually the league would emerge from the problems of the '80s as America's game.

New commissioner Paul Tagliabue had a tough act to follow, and he also had a tough time in which to do it. It took a number of years before the NFL regained lost fans after the labor and drug problems of the 1980s, but slowly it did recover. During the '90s television ratings inched upward, and the league expanded again with teams in the Sun Belt cities of Jacksonville, Florida; Charlotte, North Carolina; and Houston, Texas (the Oilers moved to Nashville in 1997 and became the Tennessee Titans). As the league entered a new century, it now boasted 32 teams and was ever-growing in popularity. A prime example of this would be the labor dispute of 2011. When the owners and players could not come to a collective bargaining agreement, the owners locked the players out of team facilities and shut down operations beginning in March. As the lockout dragged on through the summer months, the beginning of the season and certainly exhibition games were in jeopardy. Finally, after 18 weeks, the two sides came to an agreement, and the lockout ended in late July. Although many fans complained of the unseemliness of millionaires fighting over millions of dollars during a deep economic recession and some claimed they would not watch the NFL during the season, the fact is the ratings were only slightly down from the previous season. In fact, the 17.5 million viewer average per game of 2011 and the 17.9 million of 2010 were the highest ratings since the 1980s. Also 37 NFL telecasts had more than 20 million viewers, which topped the previous high of 35 also from 2010. Although the numbers do not reach the 20 million viewer average of the late 70s, it must be remembered that there were essentially only three networks before the proliferation of cable television in the ensuing years. The 17.5 million per game in 2011 is the equivalent of double or maybe even triple that in 1970s numbers. To put it in perspective, of the top 25 rated television programs in *all* formats during the fall of 2011, 23 of them were NFL games. Although baseball may still be the national pastime, football had emerged as America's favorite game, and as the NFL approached its second century, it appeared to be entering a new "golden age."

Conclusion

Professional football has come a long way since its beginnings a little over a century ago. It took years to step out of the shadow of its more popular counterpart—college football. The public had to overcome its inhibitions of men being paid to play the game versus the collegiate model of amateurs playing for the fun of it. The professional version does have its older counterpart to thank for dealing with much of the struggles and changes of the game during the 19th century. By the time the professional game was gaining in popularity, the rules had been refined to make the game safer and more exciting. The violent nature of the game, which threatened its very existence at the beginning of the 20th century, has never left it. Even in the early part of the 21st century there have been rules changes to help protect the players from serious injuries. When a scandal broke during the 2011 season that the New Orleans Saints had implemented a "bounty" system in which players were given cash bonuses for knocking opposing players out of the game, Commissioner Roger Goodell (who took over for Paul Tagliabue in 2006) came down very hard on the head coach of the Saints, Sean Payton, whom he suspended for a full year, and the individual coach who had instigated the system, Gregg Williams, was suspended indefinitely. Although not the first bounty system to be used by a coach in football, it came at a particularly sensitive time for the NFL and its image due to recent scientific discoveries of the dangers of concussive hits in the game. Violence had always been a part of the game, and it always will be. Take away that, and you probably take away its popularity. The NFL will be walking a very tricky line in the future: the line between protecting its players while also protecting its product—a product that has been carefully cultivated in American culture for almost a century.

Notes

1. Marc Maltby, *The Origins and Development of Professional Football* (New York: Garland Publishing, 1997), 196.
2. Ibid., 94.
3. Ibid., 131.
4. Ibid., 119.
5. Ibid., 185.
6. Ibid., 162.
7. Robert Peterson, *Pigskin: The Early Years of Pro Football* (New York: Oxford University Press, 1997), 76.
8. Ibid.
9. Ibid., 120.
10. Ibid., 138.
11. Ibid.
12. Ibid., 146.
13. Ibid., 148.
14. Ibid.
15. Ibid., 161.
16. Ibid., 192.

17. Ibid.
18. Ibid., 203.
19. David Mariness, *When Pride Still Mattered; A Life of Vince Lombardi* (New York: Simon and Shuster, 1999), 265.
20. Michael Oriard, *Brand NFL: Making and Selling America's Favorite Sport* (Chapel Hill: University of North Carolina Press, 2007), 12.
21. Steve Silverman, "The 'Other' League." *Pro Football Weekly* (7 November 1994).
22. Oriard, *Brand NFL*, 28.
23. Ibid., 29.
24. Benjamin Rader, *American Sports; From the Age of Folk Games to the Age of Televised Sports*, 6th ed. (Upper Saddle River, NJ: Pearson-Prentice Hall, 2009), 248.

CHAPTER *Seven*

CHAPTER
Eight

Golf and Tennis

$\mathcal{O}$n March 6, 1457, a decree came down from King James II of Scotland, which stated,

Item, it is ordained and decreed . . . that football and
golf be utterly condemned and stopped and that a pair
of targets be made at all parish kirks and shooting be
practised each Sunday. . . .[1]

Football being banned by a monarch was nothing new at this time (23 times between the 14th and 17th centuries as was mentioned in Chapter 1), but it was the first time the game of golf was mentioned. The "shooting" that James was referring to was archery. The Hundred Years' War had just ended, and Scotland fought on the side of France against England. James worried that his country was going to not be ready if attacked by Britain or any other country. It's apparent that the game of golf had become popular enough to warrant a banning by the king. Historians have recently questioned whether the game James was banning was the game of golf we know today or a more violent, team-oriented stick and ball game more closely resembling hockey. There were two more bans on the sport in Scotland by two more King Jameses before the end of the 15th century, and by the time of the 1491 decree, historians are in relative agreement that it is the game of golf we know today. Although it is often believed the game of golf originated in Scotland, at least two other countries lay claim to it. Part of that claim can be traced to the name itself: The Scottish term **gouf** is believed to be an alteration of the Dutch word *colf*, meaning stick or club. The Dutch claim they played the game as early as the 13th century. Recent scholarship has linked the Chinese to the game as early as the 10th century during the Tang Dynasty. A spokesman for the Royal and Ancient Golf Club of St. Andrews, Scotland, does not necessarily disagree that other nations had games that bore some resemblance to the game, but he is quick to point out: "Stick and ball games have been around for many centuries, but golf as we know it today, played over 18 holes, clearly originated in Scotland."[2]

The Royal and Ancient

Wherever or whenever the game was "invented," it clearly took hold and was most popular in Scotland. For years it was believed the first set of rules for the game was established by the Golf Club of St. Andrews in 1754. It was not until the mid-20th century that an older rule book was discovered, and the Honourable Company of Edinburgh Golfers was given credit for establishing their club and rules a full decade earlier in 1744. The St. Andrews Club (named the **Royal and Ancient** by King William IV in 1834) became the dominant force behind the game as it grew during the

First hole at St. Andrews. Image © Terry Kettlewell, 2013. Used under license from Shutterstock, Inc.

Gutta ball. Image © Tony Magdaraog, 2013. Used under license from Shutterstock, Inc.

19th century. Queen Victoria came to the British throne in 1837, and her reign spanned the remainder of the century until her death in 1901. The era would come to be named for her as the "Victorian Age," which is examined earlier in this book. What is lesser known about Victoria is that she helped usher in an enthusiasm for everything Scottish when she built Balmoral Castle in Scotland in the 1850s. To accommodate the queen's trips to Scotland, the railroad was brought to the country, and Scottish tourism boomed along with the thirst for knowledge about its history and culture. A large part of that was the game of golf. About the same time new equipment was introduced to the game, including a new ball called the "**Gutta**" or "**Gutty**" **ball**, which was made with the sap from a Gutta-Percha tree. This material acted as a natural latex, and the balls were initially made solidly with this substance, were much more durable, and travelled a greater distance than the previous leather-covered, feather-centered balls. This change revolutionized the sport because the balls were cheaper to make and easier to mass-produce. It also led to new clubs because the older clubs were not built to withstand the hardness of the gutta balls. Initially all the clubs were made of wood and had wooden faces, but in the second half of the 19th century, iron-faced clubs (commonly referred to as "irons") were introduced to the game. Before the clubs were numbered as they are today, they had colorful names like "mashie" (comparable to mid-irons of today—probably would most closely resemble a 5-iron); "niblick" (short irons like the wedges of today); and wood-faced clubs like the "brassie" (2-wood) and "spoon" (3-wood). Steel-shafted clubs were not introduced until the end of the century, at least partially in response to another change in the makeup of the balls. The "Haskell" ball was beginning to be used in the 1890s in which only the outer cover of the ball was made from gutta-percha, and it covered the inner core, which was a tightly wrapped ball of rubber string.

The early club makers were also the best players in the game. Willie Park Sr. and Tom Morris Sr. (known as "Old" Tom Morris when his son—"Young" Tom Morris—began playing) were two of the most well known club makers in Scotland. **"Old" Tom Morris** began his career in the 1830s at the Old Course in St. Andrews as an apprentice to **Allan Robertson**, who is widely considered to

Old Tom Morris. Image © annie greenwood, 2013. Used under license from Shutterstock, Inc.

be the first professional golfer. Robertson often asked Morris to play with him in challenge matches, and the team was considered unbeatable. The two parted ways in 1851 when Robertson fired Morris after seeing him playing with one of the new "gutty" balls (Robertson also had a "feathery" ball business). Morris then helped design and become "keeper of the greens" at a new course in Prestwick, Scotland. It was at Prestwick that Morris and others decided to stage the first ever Open Championship in 1860. The first "Open" was actually only open for professionals, and eight of them entered—all from Scotland. The second Open could truly be considered that because eight amateurs joined 10 professionals in the field. Morris finished runner-up to **Willie Park Sr.**, who scored somewhat of an upset over Morris on his home course. Park began his career as a caddie and club maker. He, Morris, and Robertson were considered the greatest players of the 1850s and 1860s. Morris returned the favor in the second Open by finishing just ahead of Park for his first championship. The first 12 Opens were held at Prestwick, and either Park or Morris won seven of them (usually with the other being the runner-up), with the final four being won by "Young" Tom Morris. "Old" Tom seemed to hand the reins of the championship over to his son after 1867, which was his final win at age 46 (still a record for the oldest winner of the championship). Allan Robertson died in 1859, and the Royal and Ancient membership begged "Old" Tom to return to St. Andrews, which he did in 1864. In 1871, with the urging of "Old" Tom, the administration of the Open Championship was joined by the Honourable Company of Edinburgh Golfers and the Royal and Ancient of St. Andrews. The tournament would be rotated every year to different courses around Scotland. There was no tournament held in 1871, primarily because there was no trophy available ("Young" Tom was given the championship belt to keep because he was the first to ever win the championship three consecutive years). The championship returned in 1872 with a new trophy known as the Claret Jug, which is still awarded to the winner to temporarily hold until the next champion is crowned. The first winner of the Claret Jug? "Young" Tom Morris is still the only player to ever win the championship four consecutive times. In September of 1875, the Morrisses were playing a match against Willie Park Jr. and his brother, Mungo Park, when "Young" Tom Morris received word that his wife had gone into labor with their first child. He quickly returned home to find out that both his wife and newborn baby had died. He went into deep despair, and on Christmas Day of that year he died at the age of 24. The official cause of death was a heart attack, which can be literally termed a broken heart.

Other than Willie Park Jr., who won the Open Championship twice in the 1880s, the most dominant golfer in the first part of that decade was Bob Ferguson, who won it three times in a row from 1880–1882. By the 1890s the game had grown beyond the borders of Scotland and was especially gaining popularity in England. There were more than 50 courses in England by 1890, and that number ballooned to 1,000 by the eve of World War I in 1914. Its growing popularity in that country led to the emergence of great players. The year 1890 marked the first time a non-Scottish winner was crowned the winner of the Open when Englishman John Ball won the tournament. It also marked the first time the winner was an amateur. There was a clear distinction, especially in Britain, between professionals and amateurs. The amateur was seen as a gentleman who played the game for enjoyment and not for his livelihood, so he received no payment for his winning. The professional was just another employee of the club, and he did play for the money. In 1892 another amateur won the Open—Englishman Harold Hilton. His score of 305 strokes was much higher than the previous year's winning score of 166, but it was this year that the number of holes played doubled from 36 to 72 holes. The initial tournaments were three rounds of 12 holes each—by the 1890s courses were uniformly 18 holes, and the Open increased to four rounds. In 1896

Englishman Harry Vardon, who was a professional, won the first of his still-record six Open Championships. Vardon would come to be the first dominant player in golf during the new 20th century.

Golf Invades America

By the turn of the century, golf courses had been built all across Europe and especially throughout the British Empire in countries like Australia, New Zealand, South Africa, and Canada. In its former colonies, the United States, golf was also beginning to catch on. Although versions of the game were known to be played as far back as the Revolutionary era of the 1770s, the game really did not become an organized sport until the latter stages of the 19th century. Not surprisingly, a Scottish immigrant to the United States is often credited with being the "father" of American golf. **John Reid** hailed from Dunfermline, Scotland, and his adopted hometown of Yonkers, New York, would lay claim to the first modern country club, which Reid christened St. Andrews in 1888, after Reid purchased his clubs from Old Tom Morris at the original St. Andrews. Other clubs also could lay claim to being pioneers in the American game, including the Country Club of Chicago, Brookline Country Club in Boston, and Shinnecock Hills in Southhampton, New York. The last of those was designed by Scotsman Willie Dunn, who was brought to the United States by wealthy investors to design a seaside course in the tradition of the great links courses in the old country. Dunn employed 150 members of the local Shinnecock Indian reservation to help build the course and even incorporated their ancestral burial grounds into the layout and in return named the course after the tribe. In December of 1894 representatives from the four clubs already mentioned were joined by the Country Club in Newport, Rhode Island, to form the **United States Golf Association (USGA)**. The USGA was established to produce uniform rules for the game and oversee both the U.S. Amateur tournament (open only to amateurs) as well as the U.S. Open tournament (open to amateurs as well as professionals). Both of these tournaments began in the summer of 1895 and soon joined their British counterparts to become the four major golf tournaments in the world. Interestingly, it was the definition of "amateur" that caused the USGA some early problems in its definition of the rules. In its initial 1895 rulebook, an amateur was defined as someone "who has never made for sale golf clubs, balls or any other article connected with the game, who has never carried clubs for hire after attaining the age of 15 years and who has not carried clubs for hire at any time within six years, and who has never received any consideration (money) for playing a match or for giving lessons in the game."[3] Two years later they amended the definition of an amateur as excluding anyone who had "laid out (designed)" or "taken charge of any golf links for hire," or "who after January 1, 1897, had within the jurisdiction of this association played a match game against a professional for a money bet or stake," or "played in a club competition for a money prize or sweepstakes."[4] The amendment showed how the definition of amateur was evolving into someone who played the game for the enjoyment of it as opposed to monetary benefit. This distinction between the amateur and professional would dominate the sport on both sides of the Atlantic for almost a half century.

Rules were not all that occupied the USGA's time and attention—the number of clubs the organization oversaw was growing at an incredible rate. By 1900 every state in the union had at least one course, and most had several. New York boasted the most with 165, but Massachusetts was not far behind at 157. In 1901, *Harper's Weekly* estimated that there were approximately 1,200 private golf clubs in the country with around 120,000 members. The same article estimated that an additional 30,000 people were "hacking away on public links."[5] Although that was a sizable number, the majority of those who played the game were well off financially. They were the ones who could not only afford the costs of the game but could also travel from Northern climates to the many

Southern resorts in the winter months. The game had not reached the masses yet. A good example of this would be outgoing president Theodore Roosevelt warning his successor William Howard Taft, an avid golfer, in 1908 to not be photographed playing the game for fear it would hurt him politically. Roosevelt wrote Taft during the 1908 campaign: ". . . I have received literally hundreds of letters from the West protesting about it (Taft playing golf). I myself play tennis, but that game is a little more familiar; besides, you never saw a photograph of me playing tennis. I am careful about that; photographs on horseback, yes; tennis, no. And golf is fatal."[6] For all the Americans playing the sport in the late 19th and early 20th centuries, the quantity did not apparently translate into quality, and Scottish and British players dominated the four major championships. Although Chicago Country Club founder and USGA vice president Charles B. MacDonald was the first winner of the U.S. Amateur Championship in 1895 (he was actually a Canadian by birth), the next three winners were from Scotland. Only one American before 1926 won the British Amateur (Walter Travis in 1904), and no American won the British Open until 1921. It was not until 1911 that an American would win his own Open Championship, when John McDermott won the first of his two consecutive championships.

1913 U.S. Open

Many point to the U.S. Open in 1913 as a turning point for American golf. The tournament took place at one of the oldest clubs in the country—many believe it to be *the* oldest—the Country Club at Brookline in Boston. The tournament had all the ingredients for what makes good sports drama: there was the amateur versus professional angle; there was nationalism involved—American versus British; and there was a David versus Goliath aspect. The David in this case was 20-year-old American **Francis Ouimet**. There were many Goliaths—the two-time defending champion John McDermott along with many great players from Britain, including the biggest name of them all, **Harry Vardon**. Vardon was 43 in 1913, and the best of his career was behind him. He had already won the British Open a record five times along with the U.S. Open in 1900—the only previous time he had competed in it. It is safe to say he was golf's first international superstar. Oiumet was born in 1893 in Brookline—in fact, he lived across the street from the Country Club, where he caddied in his youth. His father was a French-Canadian immigrant who was a member of the working class and could not understand his son's fascination with this game. Arthur Ouimet had no

Francis Ouimet. Image courtesy of Library of Congress

Harry Vardon. Image courtesy of Library of Congress

problem with his son working at the club, but he did not want him to waste his time playing a game that would bring in no money. Francis continued to hone his game nonetheless and became one of the best junior golfers in the state of Massachusetts. By the time he was in high school, he was captain of his golf team, but when he turned 16 in 1909, he had a decision to make. If he continued to caddy at Brookline, he would lose his amateur status (remember the USGA rule, which stated caddies were considered professionals if they worked beyond the age of 15). To save his status yet keep the needed money coming into the Ouimet household, Francis decided to quit school and go to work at a Boston dry goods store. By the time he was 18, he found a better job at a sporting goods store owned by George Wright. He was the younger brother of Harry Wright and had played major league baseball with his brother in Cincinnati and also Boston. George Wright also had a link to the game of golf by laying out the country's first public golf course after his baseball playing days were over in 1890. Ouimet was encouraged by Wright to enter the 1913 Massachusetts State Amateur tournament, which he won. In early September he entered the National Amateur Championship in which he lost to the eventual winner Jerome Travers, but his great play caught the eye of USGA President Robert Watson, who extended a special invitation for Ouimet to play in the U.S. Open to be held at his home course two weeks later. Ouimet had to get some extra time off from his boss to prepare for the tournament, which Wright granted.

To play in the main tournament, Ouimet first had to play in the qualifying round on Tuesday, September 16. Even before that he had to find a caddy. He ended up using Eddie Lowery, the 10-year-old brother of a friend of his who was playing hooky from school that day. So now "David" was joined by an even smaller, younger "David," and the legend grew. Ouimet shot a 152 in the 36-hole qualifier and finished fifth, which was good enough to enter the Open, which was to be a 72-hole event played on Thursday and Friday. Eddie would have to skip school again, which he had no problem doing. After struggling to a 77 in his opening round, he came back with a respectable 74 in his second for a 151 total. He found himself only four strokes behind the leaders, Harry Vardon and Englishman Wilfred Reid. Friday's final two rounds were played in a driving rainstorm, and the scores reflected the horrible conditions. Vardon finished with a 304 total (8 over par), which was tied with reigning British Open champion Ted Ray for the lead. The only other player that could catch them was Ouimet, but he would have to play the final four holes one-under par to get to the 304 total. He had two amazing pars on 15 and 16 and then sunk a 22-foot putt on 17 for the birdie he needed. He then sunk a knee-knocking five-foot putt for par on the final hole to tie Vardon and Ray. The three would compete in an 18-hole playoff on Saturday. The rains continued during the playoff, but it seemed to bother the veterans more than the youngster as Oiumet shot an astounding two-under par 72 to Vardon's 77 and Ray's 78. Ouimet himself seemed to grasp the enormity of this win for his country and the future of the game here when he said after the victory: "I simply tried my best to keep this cup from going to our friends across the water—I am very glad to have been the agency for keeping the cup in America."[7] The *New York Times* proclaimed the victory an "awful blow to British golfing pride." Not everyone "across the water" thought the outcome was a bad thing—at least one British writer proclaimed that "America has graduated now as a first-class golfing power. I am glad of it; it is all for the good of the game, and Francis Ouimet, besides having achieved immortal fame among golfers, has done something splendid for the good of that game."[8] The Anglo–American rivalry would continue to grow in the coming years. Although the Americans would come to the aid of Britain on the fields of France in the First World War, postwar challenges would lead to permanent competitions. George Herbert Walker, president of the USGA in 1920, and great-grandfather and namesake of the 41st president of the United States, began the rivalry between American and British amateurs known as the Walker Cup. The cup was competed for annually until 1924, when it became a biannual event. In 1927 the Ryder Cup, named for British golf promoter Samuel Ryder, who donated the gold trophy for the competition, began as the Walker Cup's professional counterpart. Because of the eventual dominance of the

Americans, the British were joined by the rest of continental Europe in 1979. There was also something very American about a young kid who grew up on the "wrong side of the tracks" winning against the very class-conscience British. Ouimet's victory came in front of the largest crowds the U.S. Open had ever witnessed, and it was a portent of what was to come in the very near future.

Professional versus Amateur: Walter Hagen and Bobby Jones

Walter Hagen. Image courtesy of Library of Congress

Finishing in a tie for fourth place in 1913 only three strokes out of the playoff was another 20-year-old American named **Walter Charles Hagen**. He was an unknown at the time, but it would not be long before his was a household name in the world of golf. He was born in Rochester, New York, and his father was a blacksmith of German ancestry. He started playing golf at age four and caddying at the Rochester Country Club at seven. He was an excellent all-around athlete and even had a chance to try out with the Philadelphia Phillies, but golf was his first love. He dropped out of school at 12 to concentrate on the game, and when he was 15, the head professional at Rochester promoted him from caddy to assistant pro. This gave him the opportunity to make and repair clubs, supervise the course, and most important, improve his game. In 1912, at the age of 19, he competed in his first professional tournament, the Canadian Open, where he finished in a respectable 11th place. After his fourth-place finish in the 1913 U.S. Open, he was determined to come back and play even better the following year, which he did—winning it in 1914. He again won the U.S. Open in 1919, the first time it was held post–World War I. He was also the first native-born American to win the British Open in 1922. In 1921, Jock Hutchison won the Open, and although he lived in the United States, he was born in St. Andrews, Scotland—the birthplace of the game. Hagen followed up his 1922 victory with three more before the decade was over (1924, 1928, and 1929), and although Ouimet's victory in the 1913 U.S. Open announced the coming of age of the American golfer, Hagen's four British Open victories in the 1920s cemented the arrival of the Americans. The *New York Times* dubbed Hagen in 1922 as "indisputably the finest overseas player who ever contested for the British Open Championship" and added that his win was "an American victory outright."[9]

Hagen was also a perfect match for the decade in which he recorded most of his victories. The "Roaring" twenties was a time of conspicuous consumption and having a good time all the time and so was Hagen. He was known for his showmanship and his aggressive style, which is what the public wanted in the decade. He was also known for his stylish dress and his playboy ways. He was not just flash, though; he also was a great player who added five PGA Championships to his four British Opens and two U.S. Opens. Four of his PGA titles came consecutively from 1924–27. The combination of his style and success led sportswriter Grantland Rice to proclaim that "Hagen is better known today outside the United States than Babe Ruth."[10] He also did much for changing the perception of the professional golfer. Being a professional from a young age, he never really knew any other way, and he was unapologetic about it. At the time, the amateur was viewed with greater reverence than the professional—in fact, professionals were not even allowed in most clubhouses. They were viewed as just another employee of the club. Hagen did his best to break down those barriers. A prime example of this was after he won his first U.S. Open at the Midlothian Country Club in Illinois, he waltzed into the clubhouse and made himself at home. Because he was so young, he claimed he didn't know the tradition, and because he was so charming, he was able to do things like this that other professionals would not dare try. Although he did not change perceptions overnight, he started the ball rolling in that direction. He was not only unapologetic about being a professional but also about making money at the sport. He was the first professional to make a good living based on his winnings from exhibition matches and tournament purses. It is estimated he earned more than $1 million during his career.

Most players had to supplement their golfing careers with other employment. Although Hagen was the most well-known professional during the decade, there is no doubt who the most famous amateur was. **Robert Tyre Jones** made his living as an attorney, but as an amateur golfer, he had no equal. Bobby Jones was born in 1902 in Atlanta, Georgia, and his father was a successful corporate attorney. Beginning in 1907 the Jones family began renting a summer home near Atlanta's East Lake Country Club, and young Bobby began his love affair with the game. By the age of nine he won the junior championship of the Atlanta Athletic Club and quickly became a child prodigy. Reading about the exploits of Francis Ouimet in 1913 and 1914 only spurred Jones on, and he won the Georgia State Amateur title in 1916 (when he was only 14). He then qualified for the U.S. Amateur, where he made it to the third round. During the first World War, Jones used his fame to travel around and raise funds for the American war effort (he was too young to join the armed forces). In his younger days he often let his temper get the best of him, and it probably cost him winning major championships. The *New York Times* described the 1920 Bobby Jones as "a fretful, impetuous youth—golf's bad boy, a lovable, forgivable bad boy," who was "a headstrong, petulant youth, easily provoked and prone to fly off the handle at any minute."[11] Something changed for Jones in the early 1920s—perhaps he simply grew up and matured—it was also at this time that he started his higher education pursuits that would culminate with an undergraduate and master's degree in engineering from Georgia Tech, another bachelor's degree from Harvard, and eventually a law degree from Emory University, which enabled him to pass the bar and practice law in Georgia. The discipline of his studies translated to the golf course because by 1923 he had gotten control of his emotions, and he won his first major championship at the age of 21—the U.S. Open. In 1924 he won the first of his five U.S. amateur championships.

Bobby Jones. Image courtesy of Library of Congress

When Bobby Jones first played the Old Course at St. Andrews, he did not like it. It was 1921, and he had completed only 11 holes when he walked off the course and tore up his scorecard, effectively disqualifying himself (this was obviously before his "maturing"). He announced his disdain for the course, and the people of St. Andrews reciprocated by calling Jones "just a boy, and an ordinary boy at that." As previously mentioned, that "boy" grew up and learned to appreciate the history of the game and developed a love for the Old Course. In 1927 he won his second consecutive Open Championship. In 1930 he won his only British Amateur Championship at St. Andrews. In 1958, long after his playing days were over, Jones was made a Freeman (honorary citizen) of the city of St. Andrews—joining Benjamin Franklin as the only other American to be so honored. St. Andrews had forgiven the "ordinary boy," and the mutual love between the people and the player blossomed. After Jones won the British Amateur, he traveled to England to win the Open Championship at Royal Liverpool. He then came back home to a hero's welcome and even a ticker-tape parade in New York City. Jones was not finished, however; he then followed up his overseas feats by winning both the U.S. Amateur and Open for what at the time was considered the "**Grand Slam**" of golf—winning all four major championships in a single season. He then shocked the world by announcing his retirement from the game at the young age of 28. He had accomplished all that a golfer possibly could in a relatively short time: Between 1923 and 1930 Jones captured five U.S. Amateur Championships, four U.S. Opens, three British Opens, and one British

Amateur. His 13 major wins would set the standard until Jack Nicklaus eclipsed it almost a half century later.

When Jones retired, he effectively gave up his amateur status because he signed a contract to make golf instructional films, and he began designing his masterpiece. In 1933 the course was completed and christened Augusta National Golf Club in Augusta, Georgia. He wanted to invite all the best players in the world to his course to play in a new tournament, so in 1934 the Augusta National Invitational was born—it would later be known as the "**Masters Tournament**." Jones unwittingly took part in the de-emphasis of amateur championships, as the Masters tournament would eventually become a major championship. The PGA Championship, born in 1916 when the Professional Golfers Association of America was formed, was the brainchild of wealthy department store owner Rodman Wannamaker, who put up the $500 prize money and diamond-studded gold medal that went to the winner. The current trophy presented to the winner of the PGA Championship is called the Wanamaker trophy. The PGA would be the strictly professional counterpart to the more amateur-based USGA, but eventually they would work in tandem as amateurism took a backseat to professionalism. There is no agreed-upon date when the PGA and Masters supplanted the British and U.S. Amateur Championships as majors—some say as early as the 1940s; others argue it wasn't until 1960 and the arrival of television. Whatever the case, there was no doubt that amateurs stopped winning the Open Championships in the early 1930s. Jones's victory in the 1930 British was the last for an amateur. Only one amateur won the U.S. Open after Jones, and that was Johnny Goodman in 1933. No amateur ever won the Masters tournament. Jones came out of his retirement to play in the Masters from 1934 to 1948, when he had to quit the game completely because of a debilitating illness that eventually confined him to a wheelchair until his death in 1971. He never won his own tournament.

It would be negligent to leave out one other golfer's name from this era, and that would be the winner of the second Masters in 1935—**Gene Sarazen**. Sarazen was born into an Italian immigrant family the same year as Bobby Jones, in 1902. His birth name was Euginio Saracini, but he Americanized it when he began his golf career because he felt his name "looked and sounded like it should be on a violin, not a golf club."[12] Like Jones, he was inspired by Francis Ouimet, but Sarazen became a professional making money in exhibition matches and signing an endorsement deal with Wilson Sporting Goods in 1923. He set a record for the longest-running endorsement deal for any athlete because he held that endorsement until his death in 1999 (76 years). At the age of 20 he won both the U.S. Open and the PGA Championship. Because he was not an amateur, he never played in any of the amateur championships, but he was the first player to win all four of the modern major championships (career Grand Slam). When he won the 1935 Masters, he added that to his three PGA Championships, two U.S. Opens, and one British Open for a total of seven. Only four other players have accomplished the feat since Sarazen (Jack Nicklaus, Gary Player, Tom Watson, and Tiger Woods). Although the 1930s were a difficult time for golf as with every other part of American society that was in the grips of the Great Depression, there were some positives for the sport. Although many clubs went bankrupt across the country, those that stayed in business greatly improved the quality of their courses. The equipment was also improved during the decade. Gene Sarazen himself contributed to the improvement by inventing a new club—the sand wedge. He is said to have created it in his garage and kept it secret until he debuted it in tournaments during 1932. The old hickory shafts were replaced by steel, and the combination of the improvement in equipment and course conditions led to improvement in scores.

World War II and After: Hogan, Nelson, and Snead

The year 1912 was apparently the one to be born if you wanted to grow up to be a great golfer. Two born in Texas that year were named William Benjamin Hogan and John Byron Nelson; the other was from Virginia, and his name was Samuel Jackson Snead. All three would turn pro and begin winning tournaments in the 1930s, but the Virginian would have the longest and most prolific career of the three. **Sam Snead** won his first tournament the year he turned pro in 1936 and his last on the Senior Tour in 1982 at the age of 70. In between he amassed a total of 165 total wins, including 82 on the PGA Tour (most ever). He won 14 tournaments on the Senior Tour (those over 50 are eligible), and he can lay claim to being the only male to ever win an official title on the Ladies Professional Golfers Association Tour (LPGA). In 1962 when Snead was 50, he was the lone male to enter the Royal Poinciana Plaza Invitational, which was allowed by the rules at the time, and he won by five strokes. He won seven career majors (three PGA Championships, three Masters, and one British Open). The one missing tournament from his resume that haunted him his whole career was the U.S. Open. He came very close numerous times, including four runner-up finishes, but something always seemed to prevent him from the title. The 1939 U.S. Open was a classic example—he was leading by two shots with two holes to play, and after getting a bogey on the 17th hole, his lead shrank to one, but he mistakenly thought he was tied and in need of a birdie on the final hole for the victory. He took unnecessary risks on the hole, which led to a triple-bogey eight on the par five. Snead was quoted as saying, "If I'd shot 69 in the last round of my Opens I'd have won nine of them."[13] Snead's swing was self-taught: He would use sticks he would pick up and hit rocks and apples in fields near his boyhood home in Virginia. He taught himself well because his smooth swing was often emulated by others, but no one could seem to master what some described as his "perfect swing." The swing also enabled him to hit the ball farther than the other players of his day—often exceeding 300 yards on drives, which, for the equipment of the time, was incredible. Because of his drive length, he earned the nickname "Slammin' Sammy." His talent combined with his folksy charm (early in his career he was shown a picture of himself playing in a tournament that appeared in the *New York Times*, he said, "How'd they ever get my picture? I ain't never been to New York.")[14] also earned him legions of followers who were looking for another golf icon after the retirement of Jones.

Golf fans did not have to look for long because they not only had Snead but quite often during the late thirties and forties Snead's constant challenge came from a Texan by the name of **Ben Hogan**. Hogan and Snead could not have been more different. Snead was nearly six feet tall and had a very upright swing, whereas Hogan was just over five feet, eight inches (often referred to as "Bantam Ben") and had a flatter swing. Snead talked a lot on the course, but Hogan was often silent—concentrating on every shot. His concentration and steely demeanor earned him other nicknames like the "Hawk" and in Scotland, the "Wee Ice Mon." Some, including his biographer, have attributed his introverted personality to a tragedy when he was nine years old—his father's suicide. It has been speculated that his father shot himself in the chest in front of his son, but that is not known for certain. What is known is that it had a major effect on young Ben. The family moved to Fort Worth, where Ben became a caddy and worked on his skills. He dropped out of high school in 1930 to become a touring pro, but did not have success throughout the 1930s. He went broke several times, but stuck it out and eventually won his first tournament in 1940 and was the leading money winner on the tour from 1940–42. The Snead–Hogan rivalry was something the game needed. It was just heating up, however, when the Japanese bombed Pearl Harbor, and the United States entered World War II. Both Snead and Hogan joined the Army and missed three years in the primes of their careers. Many thought that golf was such a frivolous game in the shadow of a world at war that the tour should cease during the war years, but both the USGA and PGA convinced the federal government that the tour should continue, as other professional sports like baseball did. They did use tournaments as fund-raisers for the war, and golf became a way to not only raise money for the war effort but also as an example of how to stay in shape in case you were called to service. The tour did cut back on the numbers of tournaments and even cancelled the U.S. Open and the Masters between 1942 and 1945 and the PGA Championship in 1943. For obvious reasons, the British Open had not been played since 1939 and would not return until 1946.

One player who took advantage of the tour remaining viable during the war was **Byron Nelson**. Nelson grew up in Fort Worth and actually caddied with Ben Hogan and defeated him in a caddy tournament in 1927 when they were both 15. Nelson turned professional in 1932 and won his first tournament in 1935 and his first major (the Masters) in 1937. Nelson is often credited with developing the "modern swing," which followed the shift from hickory to steel shafts and involved more leg turn and power coming from the lower half of the body. Nelson is probably most remembered for the 1945 season in which he won over half the tournaments held that year (18 of 35), including an incredible 11 in a row. Although the competition was probably not what it once was due to the war, winning that many tournaments (especially the 11 consecutive) is a record not likely to be broken. In Nelson's defense, many of the better players, including Snead and Hogan, played at least a partial schedule in 1945. Nelson surprised the golf world when he essentially retired from the game after the 1946 season. He had always said he wanted to make enough money to buy a ranch, and when that happened, he walked away from the game. Although he would play in various events, broadcast tour events on television, and lend his name to a tour event in Fort Worth that still bears his name, he did walk away from the game at the young age of 34. Many tried to get him to come out of retirement, including Snead and Hogan, but he preferred to work on his Texas ranch. Because of the brevity of his career and the fact that there were relatively few majors played during the prime of his career, he finished with only five (two PGAs, two Masters, and one U.S. Open). However, he did win enough tournaments (52) to be sixth on the all-time PGA win list.

After the end of the war and the retirement of Byron Nelson, the stage seemed to belong mainly to Hogan and Snead. On the foggy morning of February 2, 1949, that stage appeared to lose one of the players, when the car Hogan was driving collided head-on with a Greyhound bus on a bridge near Van Horn, Texas. Hogan threw himself across his wife's body in the passenger seat to protect her—a selfless act that saved his own life because the steering column went right through the driver's seat where Hogan had been sitting. The accident resulted in Hogan fracturing his pelvis, collarbone, and left ankle. The doctors did not think Hogan would walk again, much less play golf. He surprised everyone by not only walking out of the hospital less than 2 months after the crash but by playing in the Los Angeles Open a little over a year after the accident. He lost in a playoff to—guess who?—Sam Snead. That summer he completed his comeback by winning the U.S. Open. He won six of his nine major tournaments after the accident, including arguably his greatest season in 1953, when he won the Masters, U.S. Open, British Open, and two other tournaments. The season is often referred to as the "Hogan Slam" because probably the only reason he did not win the PGA that season is that he did not enter it. The PGA was scheduled the week following the British Open, and trans-Atlantic air travel was not yet common, so he was unable to get back in time by ship to play in the tournament. By the mid-1950s, both Snead and Hogan were in their forties and nearing the ends of their careers. The game was looking for a new superstar and, in 1954, he arrived.

The Age of Television: Palmer and Nicklaus

At the relatively advanced age of 25, **Arnold Palmer** joined the PGA Tour after winning the 1954 U.S. Amateur. His first tournament win came at the 1955 Canadian Open, and his "arrival" as a great player came when he won the first of his seven majors at the 1958 Masters. Palmer was from the small town of Latrobe, Pennsylvania, near Pittsburgh. His father, Deacon, was a teaching professional and greenskeeper at the Latrobe Country Club. Growing up, Palmer learned the difference between the amateur and professional golfers firsthand when his father was not treated as the equal of the club members—he was not allowed in the clubhouse, and young Arnold was not allowed to play on the course because his father was merely an "employee" of the club. His father did instill in him a love for the game, and Arnold showed an incredible talent early on not only for golf but other sports as well. The memory of his father not "belonging" never left Arnold, and someday he would do something to make the game of golf much more inclusive. Arnold was a great all-around athlete in high school, and he was built more like a football halfback than the normal golfer build. He could have played other sports collegiately, but he wanted to play golf, so he went to Wake Forest on a golf scholarship. After a stint in the Coast Guard in the early fifties, he decided he wanted to turn professional for the 1955 season. Something was different about Palmer from the beginning—he did not have the technically accurate swing of Hogan or the beautifully rhythmic swing of Snead—he had more of a power swing. He looked as if he were attacking the ball on every swing. He hit the ball extremely far and not always accurately, which made his recovery shots all the more impressive. Fans fell in love with his style and his game—he was a quick, confident player that fans always appreciated. He also made time for the fans, which not all players did. As a result, his followers became fiercely loyal to him, and those that followed him at tournaments became known as "Arnie's Army." There were two things Palmer did not have in the late 50s: the exposure of the modern player and a rival. As a new decade dawned, he would get both.

Arnold Palmer. Image © Debby Wong, 2013. Used under license from Shutterstock, Inc.

The 1960 U.S. Open is often referred to as a crossroads tournament because it marked two beginnings, an ending, and a coronation. It also marked the greatest comeback in U.S. Open history. Arnold Palmer trailed Mike Souchak by eight strokes after the second round and seven strokes after the third round. After a sportswriter told him he was out of the tournament, a furious and determined Palmer stormed to the first tee box and drove the par-four first green at Cherry Hills Country Club in Denver. He then proceeded to birdie the first three holes on his way to a six-under 65 (still the best final-round U.S. Open score in history) and a two-shot victory. Palmer became known as "the King" after that victory. His two-shot victory came over a 20-year-old amateur by the name of **Jack Nicklaus**. Nicklaus's runner-up finish was the best by an amateur since Johnny Goodman in 1933. This was essentially the beginning of the illustrious career of one who is now considered the greatest golfer of all time. It was also an ending for Nicklaus's playing partner that day—48-year-old Ben Hogan was in contention for his fifth U.S. Open and actually tied for the lead with two holes to play but put it in the water on both the 17th and 18th holes to finish four shots back. Hogan would never again come so close to a major victory. The other "beginning" this tournament saw was the beginning of a decade in which the new medium of television would play a crucial role. At the beginning of the decade, there might be six to eight hours of professional golf televised during an entire *season*. By the end of the 1960s, viewers could expect that much coverage on the average weekend.

Jack Nicklaus. Image © Barry Salmons, 2013. Used under license from Shutterstock, Inc.

Many attribute that increase to one man: Arnold Palmer. It could be argued, however, that it was the coming of a rival for Palmer that really led to the increased popularity and coverage of the sport.

The rivalry really heated up after Nicklaus turned professional for the 1962 season. The 1962 U.S. Open was in Palmer's backyard at Oakmont Country Club in Pennsylvania, and the crowd was extremely partisan. After the final round, Palmer and Nicklaus were the only players under par, tied at one-under. They played an 18-hole playoff in which the crowd was extremely harsh to Nicklaus—making reference to his larger build (he was often referred to as "Fat Jack" in the early days of his career). Nicklaus withstood the taunts and beat Palmer by three strokes. Palmer later said he was embarrassed by the treatment his rival received and sorry for it. He was also probably sorry that Nicklaus's arrival meant it would never be as easy for him to win a tournament again. Palmer would only win two major championships after that U.S. Open (the British Open later that summer and the Masters in 1964).

Jack Nicklaus was born in Upper Arlington, Ohio, in 1940. His father, Charlie, was a pharmacist who had been a great all-around athlete and played football for Ohio State and later for a semiprofessional team. Charlie had been a good golfer and tennis player in his youth, and it was obvious from an early age that his son had a talent for the game. He won the first of five consecutive Ohio Junior Championships when he was 12. He attended Ohio State University as his father had and won two U.S. Amateur Championships while attending (1959 and 1961) and also an NCAA Championship in 1961. Jack thought about retaining his amateur status like his hero, Bobby Jones, but after getting married and realizing he would soon need to support a family, he turned professional in late 1961. By the end of the decade he had won seven majors and the career grand slam. By the 1970s, he was the undisputed best player in the game, but he never gained the popularity that was afforded to Arnold Palmer. Palmer seemed very human—Nicklaus almost seemed like a machine. There was also the fact that Americans like risk takers, and that's what Palmer was. Nicklaus always played the percentages—Palmer always went for it, which may have led to more failures than successes, but the fans appreciated that more.

There was no doubt that the combination of Palmer and Nicklaus led to more people taking up the sport, and it would lead to more competitors for Nicklaus as Palmer's career wound down in the 1970s. Golf had always been an "upper-class" sport, but Palmer changed that, and players from all classes began to be successful. A good example of that would be **Lee Trevino**, who was born into a lower-class Mexican immigrant family in Dallas, Texas. He started as a caddy and was self-taught in the game. He emerged as one of Nicklaus's greatest rivals after Palmer and ended up winning six majors from the late 60s to the early 80s. Nicklaus just kept winning, and between 1970 and 1980 (when he turned 40), he won 10 more majors. In 1978 he won the British Open for a third time and became the only player in history to win the triple career grand slam (winning each of the majors at least three times). By the early 1980s, it appeared his career was winding down, and he had no more major wins in him, but as it turned out, he had one more up his sleeve. In 1986 Nicklaus came to the Masters, having won the tournament more times than anyone else (five), and it was a special tournament to him because it was started by his hero, Bobby Jones. Jones had lived long enough to see Nicklaus play and, after watching him win the 1965 Masters, Jones reportedly said, "He plays a game with which I am not familiar." If there were any tournament where he could muster the old magic, it was at Augusta National. He had read the press reports that he was washed up, and much like his rival Palmer back in 1960, it spurred him on to shoot a final round 65 to defeat many players who were half his age and to become the oldest major winner at 46. By that time he was more beloved by the public, and he was loudly cheered around the grounds that day. He had long since grown into his nickname of the beloved "Golden Bear." He made one more improbable run at a seventh Masters Championship 12 years later at the age of 58, when he finished sixth. His 73 PGA wins are second only to Sam Snead, and his 18 major championships (some say 20 if you add his two amateur titles) stand alone at the top of the record books. Both seemed unapproachable until a young player came along at the end of the century who idolized Nicklaus and vowed to break his records.

Wandering in the Desert and the Arrival of a Tiger

With the end of the domination of the game by Nicklaus there seemed to be a search for that next great player. Some emerged to challenge Nicklaus like Americans Johnny Miller and **Tom Watson** (he would tie Harry Vardon for the most British Open Championships won and keep Nicklaus from winning at least two more majors in the late 70s and early 80s) and international players like South African Gary Player and Spaniard Seve Ballesteros, but by the 1990s no one player emerged as *the* dominant player in the game. Beginning in 1968 the *World of Professional Golf Annual* published its rankings of the best golfers in the world, and according to those rankings, Jack Nicklaus held the title of world's greatest golfer from 1968 to 1977. Tom Watson held it from 1978 to 1982 and Seve Ballesteros from 1983 to 1985. In 1986 a ranking system began based on points from tournaments played that ranked the best players in the world on a weekly basis. Between 1986 and 1999, 11 different players held the title of number one player in the world for at least one week. The player who held the title for the most weeks during this time period was Australian **Greg Norman**, who was in the top spot for 331 weeks (roughly half the period). Norman was a charismatic star known as the "Great White Shark." Although he won two British Open championships (1986 and 1993), he became more known for the tournaments he did not win. He finished as a runner-up in two U.S. Opens, two PGA Championships, and three Masters. Probably the most painful was the 1996 Masters, when he held a six-shot lead going to the final round and melted down beginning on the ninth hole with three consecutive bogeys, and then a double-bogey on the 12th turned his six-shot lead into a five-shot loss to Englishman **Nick Faldo**. Although Faldo held the top world ranking for a much shorter time during the period (97 weeks), he got the better of the major championships by winning six of them (including three Masters). Beginning on July 4, 1999 (appropriately), one American held the number one ranking for all but 33 weeks for the next 11 years.

Greg Norman.
Image © Tony Bowler, 2013.
Used under license from Shutterstock, Inc.

Eldrick Tont "Tiger" Woods was born on December 30, 1975, to former Green Beret and Vietnam War veteran Earl Woods and his wife, Kutilda. Earl was a mix of African American, Native American, and Chinese descent, and Kutilda was originally from Thailand but also has Dutch ancestry. The couple met in Thailand when Earl was there on a tour of duty in 1968. The mix would eventually prompt the younger Woods to describe his heritage as "Cablinasian" (a mixture of Caucasian, Black, American Indian, and Asian). Eldrick was nicknamed "Tiger" early in his life in honor of a friend of his father's with whom he'd served in the military. Earl, who played college baseball and was a single-handicap golfer, started Tiger playing the game at the age of two. He quickly became a child prodigy and appeared on the *Mike Douglas Show* two months before his third birthday in 1978 to putt against comedian Bob Hope. He first broke 80 at the age of 8 and 70 at 12. While attending high school he won the first of his three U.S. Junior Championships at the age of 15 (youngest ever up to that point). In 1994 he became the youngest winner of the U.S. Amateur Championship at the age of 18. He also won three consecutive U.S. Amateurs (1994–1996)—the only player to ever do that. After attending Stanford University for two years and winning an NCAA individual championship, he decided in 1996 it was time to turn professional. That same year Earl Woods said in an interview with *Sports Illustrated*: "Tiger will do more than any man in history to change the course of humanity . . . he's qualified through his ethnicity to accomplish miracles. He's the bridge between East and West . . . he is the Chosen One . . . the world is just getting a taste of his power."[15]

His father taught Tiger early on what the records in the game were and that he would be the one to break them. The main record Tiger was after was Nicklaus's record 18 major championships, and although it was a tall order and his father's seemingly insane proclamation of his son being the "Chosen One," Tiger seemed to be able to handle the pressure. The first step on his journey came quickly when he won the first major he competed in as a professional—the 1997 Masters. He not only became the youngest winner of the tournament ever at 21 but he crushed his competition by 12 strokes. The memorable bear hug he received from his father after leaving the 18th green seemed to signal that this was just the beginning—and indeed it was. Tiger shot to number one in the world that summer—the most quickly any player has done that. Although he slipped out of the top spot in 1998, he regained it the following year and held it for five consecutive years. Arguably his best and most dominating year came in 2000 when he became the youngest player to win the career grand slam (24 years old) and almost won the season's grand slam. When he won the 2001 Masters Tournament, he was the holder of four consecutive major tournaments (even though they did not come in the same calendar year), and it became known as the "**Tiger Slam**." His 2000 U.S. Open win at Pebble Beach was called by *Sports Illustrated* "the greatest performance in golf history."[16] He set or broke nine records and won by an incredible 15 strokes. By the time Tiger had turned 30, he was over halfway to his goal and had won 10 majors. In May 2006, Earl Woods died at the age of 74. The loss of Tiger's mentor and best friend was understandably difficult, and he took two months off before returning to the U.S. Open, where his rustiness showed, and he missed the cut. At the British Open that July, he got back on the winning track, and that being the first win since his father's death, it was extremely emotional for Tiger, as he broke down at the conclusion of the tournament. It spurred him on to win six consecutive tournaments, including the PGA Championship for his 12th major. He repeated as PGA Champion in 2007, and his incredible performance with an injured knee at the 2008 U.S. Open showed he could play hurt and still win major championships—this was his 14th. Little did anyone know at the time it may have been his last.

Tiger Woods. Image © Debby Wong, 2013. Used under license from Shutterstock, Inc.

Tiger immediately recognized that golf was turning into big business, and he played a role in making it even bigger business. He signed his first endorsement contract when he turned 21, and many more lucrative endorsement deals followed, including one with Nike worth $105 million—the largest endorsement deal for an athlete ever. He was known as the most marketable athlete on the planet. By his early thirties he was a family man with a wife and two kids, and advertisers played that angle up as well. Golf was obviously good for Tiger, but Tiger was also good for golf. The game had reached new heights in popularity during his decade of dominance on the tour. When he missed the remainder of the 2008 season and part of the 2009 season after knee surgery, television ratings dipped. When he returned, so did the ratings, but he failed to win a major in 2009 for the first time since 2004. He was looking forward to a brighter 2010 when news broke over the 2009 Thanksgiving weekend that he had been in a car accident. The accident had been minor, but it was later learned that it stemmed from an altercation with his wife Elin, who had learned of his infidelity. As the media had a field day and dug deeper, it turned out this seemingly loyal family man had had dozens of affairs. Companies began to drop him, and he was forced to go on television in February of 2010 to issue an apology. He returned to the golf course at the 2010 Masters, and although he finished fourth in the event, the remainder of the season did not go well—he failed to win a single event, and he fell out of the top spot in the world rankings for the first time since 2005. The year 2011 was not much better, as he again failed to win *any* tournament, and his ranking fell to an all-time low of number 58 after more injuries forced him to miss several tournaments. In 2012 he won his first official PGA event since 2009 when he won the Arnold Palmer Invitational in March. At the time of this writing (June 2013) he has failed to win his 15th major. He has also been listed on some of the most hated celebrity polls, and although some of his endorsements and fans have returned, his dominance of the game has not. Contemporary golfer Tom Weiskopf once said of Jack Nicklaus: "Jack knows he's going to beat you and you know he's going to beat you. Most importantly, Jack knows you know he's going to beat you." Nicklaus had supreme confidence on the golf course and so did Tiger Woods—and the other players knew it. Tiger no longer has that—other players think they can beat him because they have. Will he ever get that back? Time will tell—he remains four major victories away from Jack Nicklaus. At 36 years old, the clock is ticking.

Conclusion

Modern golf was born in Scotland, and the game was dominated by Europeans into the 20th century. With the coming of Hagen, Sarazen, and Jones in the 1920s, the Americans took command of the sport and, with the possible short exception of the late 1980s and early 90s when there was really no dominant American golfer, they ruled it for the rest of the century. The arrival of Tiger Woods at the end of the last century and his continued great play in the first decade of this century promised a continuation of that American superiority. However, in the nearly two years since Tiger relinquished the throne of the world's top player, there have been four different number one players—two from England (Luke Donald and Lee Westwood), one from Germany (Martin Kaymer), and one from Northern Ireland (Rory McIlroy, who, at 23 some are calling the next Tiger Woods). The top three have been Donald, Westwood, and McIlroy for most of that two-year span. Although there are a number of good young American players right behind those three in the top 10 (including a not-so-young 42-year-old **Phil Mickelson** at no. 10, who has probably been Tiger's biggest rival and has four major championships of his own between 2004 and 2010), the prevailing belief is that Europe has better players top to bottom than the United States. An example of this would be the Ryder Cup, which was once dominated by the Americans (held a 21–3 advantage after the 1983 matches). The Europeans have won 9 out of 13 since 1985, and the Americans have won only once in this century (2008). Are we witnessing a return to European dominance of the game? Perhaps—again, time will tell. There are a number of young American players who have asserted themselves recently including Rickie Fowler who won the 2015 Players Championship and the 2015 PGA player of the year Jordan Spieth who won multiple tournaments including both the Masters and U.S. Open.

Phil Mickelson.
Image © David W. Leindecker, 2013. Used under license from Shutterstock, Inc.

Golf seems to appreciate and honor its past better than most sports—maybe because it is a game that can be played for longer than other sports, so newer generations can actually see older generations play the game, where in other sports (baseball, football, basketball) retirements come much younger. The Masters Tournament began a tradition in the 1960s that was meant to honor the past by allowing former greats of the game to hit the ceremonial first tee shots of the tournament. In 1963 two players were chosen who had both emigrated to the United States from the birthplace of golf (probably not a coincidence that they were the first chosen for the honor): Jock Hutchison, who was the first American citizen to win the British Open in 1921, and Fred McLeod, who won the U.S. Open in 1908. Hutchison performed the honor until 1973, when he was 89 and too infirm to do it. McLeod continued until the year he died in 1976 at the age of 94. For five years there was no starter, but in 1981 both 69-year-old Byron Nelson and 79-year-old Gene Sarazen became the starters. They were joined in 1984 by 72-year-old Sam Snead. The three were fixtures on the opening day of the tournament for 15 years until 1999, when Sarazen died at 97. Nelson continued until 2001, when he quit because of health problems, and Snead was left alone to perform

Gene Sarazen, Byron Nelson and Sam Snead.
© Gary Hershorn/Reuters/Corbis

the honor for the last time in 2002, when he died just weeks after the tournament and four days before his 90th birthday. For five years there again were no starters, as the Masters' committee tried to get Arnold Palmer to take the honor, but he refused because he continued to play in the tournament as a former winner. He finally relented after retiring as a regular player and struck the first ball in 2007 when he was 77. Palmer was joined by his long-time rival Jack Nicklaus in 2010, when Nicklaus turned 70. In 2012 they were joined by 76-year-old **Gary Player** from South Africa, who had won nine majors throughout the 1960s and 1970s, and in golfing circles the three men became known as the "Big Three." It was fitting the Masters would bring them together. There is no doubt all players have links to past generations—Nicklaus tried to emulate his hero Bobby Jones; Tiger Woods had all the records of Jack Nicklaus up on his bedroom wall as a kid dreaming he would one day break them. Although he has not yet won as many majors as Jack (14 to Nicklaus's 18) he recently passed him on the all-time tournaments won list for second place (74 to Nicklaus' 73) behind Sam Snead's 82. There is one thing Tiger did that Jack could never do—make golf "cool." Golf was always seen as a country club sport for the wealthy and was often regarded as a "prissy" sport—not in the same league as baseball, football, or basketball. By the early 21st century, that image had changed, and that can be credited in large part to Woods. Another country club sport would also need a makeover to change its image, but it would be a taller order.

Tennis

$\mathcal{W}$hen last we left the game of tennis (in the first chapter), it was the 17th century, and it was known as the "royal sport" played mainly by upper-class Europeans and royalty. It was also beginning to lose its popularity. By the 19th century that popularity had returned, and by the second half of the century, the sport became organized. Tennis was usually referred to at this time as "lawn tennis" because it was played on grass. In 1868 the All England Croquet and Lawn Tennis Club was formed for the game that had just recently been invented. Because the croquet and tennis courts were similar, the sport of tennis became popular at the club. By 1877 it was so popular that a tournament was organized, and the first **Wimbledon Championship** (officially titled *The Championships, Wimbledon*) took place at the All England Croquet Club in July of that year. It was so named because of the close proximity of the Wimbledon train station to the club. The first winner of the championship was Englishman Spencer Gore. By 1882 the club reversed the names of the two sports in the title to show the increasing popularity of one and the waning popularity of the other. In fact, some removed the word Croquet from the title completely, but since 1899, the official title has been the All England Lawn Tennis and Croquet Club. The year 1882 also marked the first in

Wimbledon. Image © Stuart Slavicky, 2013. Used under license from Shutterstock, Inc.

which a men's winner successfully defended his title. **William Renshaw** defeated his twin brother Ernest to win the second of what were to be six consecutive championships (1881–1886). He won his seventh in 1889, and although he was considered a great English champion, he is often not mentioned with the multichampions in the modern era because of the rule in the early days of the tournament that the defending champion had a bye into the championship, so he would only play one match. With the exception of his first (1881) and his last (1889) championship, he had to play only one match per tournament. In 1884 the tournament added both a women's singles draw and a male doubles draw. Women's and mixed doubles were added in 1913. The Renshaw twins teamed up to win the doubles championships five times between 1884 and 1889. After being a runner-up four times (three times to his brother), Ernest finally won his only championship in 1888, but it did not come against his brother, who had lost earlier in the tournament.

Lawn tennis was expanding all over the world and, unlike golf, tennis became organized in the United States simultaneously with the European version of the sport. In 1880 the first recorded lawn tennis tournament in the United States occurred at the Staten Island Cricket and Baseball Club in New York. The following year the **United States National Lawn Tennis Association (USNLTA)** was formed, and it announced they would hold the first national tennis championships at the end of August. **James Gordon Bennett**, the wealthy owner of the *New York Herald* newspaper, had recently been asked to leave his athletic club (The Reading Room) for daring a guest (after copious amounts of alcohol were consumed) to ride a horse up the front steps and into the main hall of the club. After the guest complied, Bennett's membership was revoked, and he decided to build his own club, known as The Casino. Bennett was already an accomplished yachtsman and can be credited with introducing the sport of polo to the country in the 1870s. Now he became a pioneer in the sport of tennis by offering to host the USNLTA's championships at his club. It hosted the first 34 national championships until 1914, when the grounds of The Casino were not large enough to continue to host the tournament. In 1915 the tournament moved to West Side Tennis Club in Forest Hills, New York. The tournament remained in Forest Hills for the remainder of the "amateur era" in which the tournament was not open to professionals. The first championship in 1881 was especially closed because it only allowed players from clubs that were members of the USNLTA so nonmembers of clubs and non-Americans were not welcome. The following year it was open to all Americans, whether they were members of the USNLTA or not. Eventually it opened to any amateurs from around the world who wished to compete (and who qualified). The first seven men's singles championships were won by **Richard Sears**. Although he won the first three going through the complete draw, in 1884 the tournament adopted the similar rule of Wimbledon, and the defending champion automatically qualified for the championship and only had to play one match. Between 1901 and 1911 **William Larned** tied Sears's record by winning the tournament seven times. Just as the early Wimbledon champions who did not have to go through the complete draw, these names are largely forgotten. In 1912 the rule was changed so every player had to advance through the same number of matches to reach the championship.

As with golf (and other sports and culture), a rivalry developed between Britain and her former colonies in America. As early as the 1870s challenge matches were held between the United States and Great Britain, but it was not until the final year of the 19th century that a group of Harvard tennis players decided to challenge Britain to an annual match for bragging rights. One of the Harvard players, Dwight Davis, set up the rules of the tournament and purchased a sterling silver cup (for $1,000) that would be competed for annually between the United States and the British Isles. The United States, with Davis on the team, surprised the British players by winning the first International Lawn Tennis Challenge (it would eventually be known as the **Davis Cup**). In 1905 the challenge was opened to other European countries and Australia. In the century since it started, the United States has won the most Davis Cups with 32, followed closely by Australia, who has won 28 times (they dominated the 1950s and 1960s by winning over half of its cups—15—during that time period). Great Britain is a distant third with only 9 wins—the last coming in 1936. By the 100th anniversary of the first Davis Cup competition in 2000, 129 countries competed for the cup. The Davis Cup is now viewed as the ultimate amateur event in the sport because no players are awarded money for the event—it is played for one's country. It is interesting to note that when tennis was first organized in Great Britain in the mid-19th century, there was a very different definition of the term *amateur* than today. Today it is directly related to monetary compensation, but when the Wimbledon tournament first organized, for example, prize money was awarded to the "amateurs." At the time, amateur mainly was referring to the person's class in society. The men's draw is still referred to as the "Gentleman's Draw" at Wimbledon. To be an amateur one *must* be considered a gentleman. Heiner Gillmeister wrote in his book, *Tennis, A Cultural History*, that the word *amateur* was actually a synonym for "gentleman" and that the term *professional* had the "stigma of a manual laborer. Craftsmen, petty shopkeepers, workers went by the name of *professional*. They were normally excluded from membership in amateur clubs."[17] By the 1890s, largely because Irishman **John P. Mahaffy**, an amateur historian, had uncovered what he believed to be the "prototype of the English amateur in the Olympic athletes of Greek antiquity," the amateur morphed into an athlete who played for the love of the sport and not for compensation.[18] By the 20th century, the amateur tournaments no longer offered money prizes, and the modern idea of the Olympic amateur had been born. The problem was that it was a myth—the ancient Greeks made no differentiation between amateurs and professionals based on compensation, and players in the future would pay for (pardon the pun) Mahaffy's mistake.

"Big" Bill Tilden

The first American to cross the ocean and win the championships at Wimbledon was **Bill Tilden** in 1920. It was his first major win and, as biographer Frank DeFord put it, it was that moment at Wimbledon in which he knew "he had arrived" in the sport.[19] He arrived rather late for tennis at the age of 27. He was tall, angular, and thin—his thinness made him seem taller than his actual six-foot, one-inch frame, hence his moniker "Big" Bill. There was also another famous American player at the time named Bill Johnston, who became known as "Little" Bill to distinguish the two. Tilden began his competitive career in 1915 after his father died (his mother died four years earlier), and he was pushed into the sport by his maiden aunt, with whom he had lived since his mother's death. He lived with her until he was 48. She thought tennis would be a good way to help with his grief at the death of his parents. He was born in 1893 into a wealthy Philadelphia family, and although he started playing the game at the age of five, he was not the best player on his high school team and did not even make his college team at the University of Pennsylvania. It was only after college that he began to dedicate himself to the game, and he got good enough to make his first final at the U.S. Championship at Forest Hills in 1918 and win the doubles championship. After losing the singles title that year and also losing in the finals in 1919, he decided the weakest

Bill Tilden. © Bettmann/CORBIS

part of his game was his backhand, so he tirelessly worked on it that winter and came out in the spring of 1920 a new player. He not only won the first of back-to-back Wimbledon championships but also the first of what would be six consecutive U.S. Championships (1920–25), a feat that has never been duplicated. He ascended to the number one player in the world, where he stayed for most of the decade. In a sports-crazy decade as the "roaring twenties" were, Tilden joined superstars from other sports like Jones in golf, Grange in football, and Ruth in baseball to be a part of what historians refer to as sports' "golden age."

Throughout his amateur career, Tilden had a contentious relationship with the USNLTA (by then referred to as the USLTA) and with other players, line judges, and the press. Veteran sportswriter Al Laney described Tilden as "arrogant, quarrelsome, unreasonable; very hard to get along with."[20] His main problem with the USLTA stemmed from the organization's strict policy on the amateur status of its players. Many players, including Tilden, demanded pay for what was termed "covering expenses,"[21] which could be quite vague and open-ended. The USLTA began to clamp down on these requirements, and in 1928 they suspended Tilden for receiving $25,000 per year to write a newspaper column about tennis. They maintained this made him a professional. The suspension came just before the United States was to play France for the Davis Cup (Tilden had been the leader of American teams that had won seven consecutive teams but had finished second in 1927). He was reinstated in time to play, and although he won an exciting five-set match against Rene Lacoste, the team lost to France, and Tilden was never again a member of a winning Davis Cup team. By 1930 Tilden had enough of the USLTA and decided to turn professional. The pro tennis circuit was in its infancy at the time only beginning in 1927. To be a professional entailed traveling around, playing barnstorming matches and exhibitions and getting paid for them. Professionals would also give lessons, which Tilden did also. There were tournaments that emerged in the 1930s, and where the amateurs had their Grand Slam tournaments, the professionals had what were called Pro Slam events. Three of these events emerged: the U.S., French, and Wembley (played in London). Tilden won two French Championships and two U.S. Championships, his last coming in 1935 at the age of 42. He did not stop there, however. He played until 1946 before finally retiring. He was a semifinalist in 1945 at the age of 52 while at the same time teaming up with his longtime doubles partner, Vinnie Richards, to win the U.S. Pro Doubles Championship in 1945—they had been partners back in 1918 when they won the U.S. Amateur Championship.

Throughout his career rumors always swirled around his personal life. There was talk that his "partnerships" with younger players like Richards (he was 10 years Tilden's junior) went beyond the tennis court. Although Tilden never did much to hide his homosexuality, biographer Frank DeFord does not believe that his relationships with younger players and ball boys early in his career were anything but a teacher–student situation. DeFord wrote that he thought Tilden was looking to fill a role for these kids that he never experienced from his father. These protégés became his "surrogate children, his 'heirs,' his 'successors.' To them he was all (but lover): father, teacher, inspiration, friend."[22] It is important to note, DeFord wrote, that all these protégés spoke highly of Tilden as a teacher and coach. When Tilden's career was ending in 1946, he was arrested on morals charges of "contributing to the delinquency of a minor" when he was seen performing a sexual act on a 14-year-old boy. Although he was advised by his attorney to plead not guilty he decided to plead guilty and hope his name and connections would get him off with a fine and probation. Tilden acted very strangely throughout the trial—a mixture of pomposity and nonchalance—and he did not help himself when he, according to DeFord, lied to the judge when the judge indicated this was probably not the first time he had been involved in something like this. Tilden assured him that it was, and the judge believed he had insulted the intelligence of the court and sentenced him to one-year imprisonment. He served seven and a half months, during which time he was visited by a psychiatrist who believed he was suffering from an "endocrine dysfunction" comparable to menopause in women that caused a "weakness in the inhibitionary functions of the will."[23] Tilden answered by saying that "Sex has never been very important in my life; I have had an outlet through sports."[24] Whether it was an endocrine problem or the fact that his athletic outlet was no longer available—Tilden had another brush with the law in 1949 under similar circumstances. This time he served 10 months. Tilden's life ended sadly in 1953 when his unhealthy eating and smoking habits caught up to him, and he had a massive stroke. Although he had been born into wealth and had made large sums of money during his career, he spent it as fast as he made it. When he died, he was broke and alone.

Postwar Tennis: Jack Kramer, Rod Laver, and the Opening of Tournaments

One of the younger players that looked up to Bill Tilden and wanted to play him was **John Albert "Jack" Kramer**. Born in 1921, when he was a teenager he would cut school to go down to the Los Angeles Tennis Club to play Tilden. According to his biographer, Frank DeFord, Tilden was searching for an "heir" to his throne as the best American player, and he recognized the talent in Kramer, but Kramer had an equally strong personality, and he would not allow himself to "fall under Tilden's dominion." As DeFord put it: "While the two always remained cordial, they drifted apart, Kramer to become undisputed champion of the world, heir to Tilden's title, Tilden to go off searching for an heir."[25] Kramer was national boys champion at the age of 15 in 1936 and again two years later in 1938. During World War II, international tennis, as with most sports, took a break, as most males of athletic competition age served in some capacity of the armed forces, and Kramer did his time in the Coast Guard. Kramer's first major championship came in the first U.S. championship after the war and, ironically, the year Tilden retired in 1946. He followed that up with a repeat U.S. win and a win at Wimbledon in 1947. At the end of 1947 he was challenged to a match by Bobby Riggs, who was in a group of American players that prior to the war were probably the best tennis players in the world. Another player in that group was Don Budge, who won all the grand slam events (French and Australian Opens in addition to the U.S. and Wimbledon) in 1938 at the tender age of 23. Riggs won both Wimbledon and the U.S. Championship in 1939 and the U.S. again in 1941. The war interrupted the prime years of these players' careers, and

Jack Kramer. © Bettmann/CORBIS

after the war they all decided to turn professional (Budge had actually turned pro before the war). After the Riggs challenge Kramer had a decision to make—he decided to also turn professional to play Riggs. Riggs defeated Kramer in that match in front of over 15,000 people who showed up to Madison Square Garden in the worst snowstorm in New York history (23 inches). The two went on tour that winter, and Kramer got the best of Riggs overall, which signaled a changing of the guard, as Kramer became the undisputed best player in the world during the late 40s and early 50s.

Kramer dominated the professional tour until an arthritic back forced him to retire in 1954. At that point he entered his second career—that of promoter of the professional game and making tournaments "open." Kramer had long believed the amateur and professional tours should merge and the major tournaments should be open to both. He believed both sides lost out by not accepting the other—major tournaments lost the prestige of the best players with their absences and, conversely, the players lost out on exposure by not being able to play in the biggest tournaments in the world. With Kramer's pushing, opening the major tournaments to everyone actually came to a vote of the International Lawn Tennis Association (ILTA) in the early 1960s, and it failed by five votes. Open tennis would have to wait—but it would not wait long. One of the things Kramer encouraged younger players to do was to turn professional so the grand slam events would eventually be forced to open. The 1960s were dominated by players from Australia, and the best of them turned professional in 1962—his name was **Rod Laver**. During his brief amateur career, Laver had won two Australian Opens, two Wimbledon championships, and a French and U.S. championship between 1960 and 1962. He encouraged the other great Aussies of the era like Ken Rosewall to turn pro as well, and between 1963 and 1967 the grand slam tournaments as Kramer predicted suffered

Stamp of Rod Laver. Image © AlexanderZam, 2013. Used under license from Shutterstock, Inc.

with the absence of the greatest players in the game. Britain was the first to make the move when they defied the vote of the ILTA and decided to open Wimbledon in 1968. When the French found out about this, they also decided to open the French championships, so officially the French championships were the first to go open in May of 1968 followed by Wimbledon four weeks later. The U.S. championships officially became the U.S. Open that September. Although the five seasons without Laver in the grand slam events helped bring about the opening of tennis, who knows how many titles it cost him? In 1968 he won the first open Wimbledon and his third. The year 1969 was arguably his greatest season, as he started it by winning his home major—the first Australian Open. He then followed by winning every other major for his second season grand slam (he had done it before in 1962). That feat, along with his 18 total victories, had never been accomplished before or since. Although he did not win another major tournament, he played into his forties and retired in 1979 with 11 major victories, which at the time was just one behind his fellow countryman Roy Emerson, who benefited by remaining amateur and winning all 12 of his majors between 1961 and 1967 before the open era began. Laver also was number one in the world for seven consecutive seasons (1964–70), and his record of 200 total tennis titles has never been approached.

The "Open" Era

With the end of the amateur era came the end of the amateur in major tennis. By the 1970s they were gone from competitive tennis. One of Kramer's arguments for the open game in tennis had always been the hypocrisy of amateurism because of the money being paid regularly under the table—it was often referred to as "shamateurism." Now the pay could be out in the open—and that pay was increasing. During the 1970s the game of tennis was growing in popularity not only worldwide but especially in the United States. The decade of Australian dominance was over, and great young American players were emerging on the scene. This led to more Americans wanting to attend tennis tournaments and watch it on television. Between 1970 and 1973, the television networks tripled the amount of tennis they covered. It also led to more people taking up the sport and tennis courts, and clubs began to be built everywhere during the decade—tennis was the "in" sport during the 1970s. Chicago, for example, had one indoor tennis facility at the beginning of the 1960s, but by the mid-70s there were 43. Jack Kramer was not finished with his contribution to the sport. In 1970 he created the Grand Prix of tennis, which awarded points as well as money to those who played and those who accumulated enough points during the season qualified for the season-ending tournament for large cash awards. Kramer believed, rightly so, that this would encourage the best players to play as many tournaments during the year as they could. In 1972 Kramer helped found the Association of Tennis Professionals (ATP), which was the governing body for pro players and looked out for their best interests. Kramer served as the organization's first executive director, with South African Cliff Drysdale as its first president.

In 1972 a 19-year-old American named James Scott Connors would turn professional. **Jimmy Connors** had grown up just outside East St. Louis, Illinois, and he had become an all-American at

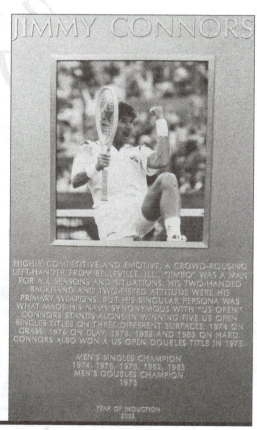

Jimmy Connors plaque. Image © Leonard Zhukovsky, 2013. Used under license from Shutterstock, Inc.

UCLA in the early 70s. When he began his professional career in 1972, little did even he know at the time it would span nearly a quarter century. From the beginning Jimmy Connors showed he was different from the "normal" model of the gentleman's game. With the possible exception of Bill Tilden, he was tennis's first bad boy. He wore his emotions on his sleeve and argued with anyone and everyone if he thought he was being wronged. He also showed himself to be a maverick when he refused to join the newly formed ATP. Maverick and bad boy aside, he was a tremendous player, and 1974 was his breakout year—he won the Australian, Wimbledon, and U.S. Opens and rose to number one in the world at the end of the year. He held that position for the next five years. He went on to win eight grand slam tournaments (including five U.S. Opens) during the 1970s and 1980s. As the 1990s dawned, it appeared his career was over, but then he put together one more improbable run at glory during the 1991 U.S. Open when, at the age of 39, he defeated players literally half his age on his way to the semifinals before finally succumbing to Jim Courier. Connors played one more U.S. Open the following year when he turned 40, and he lost in the second round. He did not officially retire until 1996, when he was 44. In his later years he eschewed his bad-boy image and became a respected elder-statesman in the game.

The mantle of bad boy was handed over to **John Patrick McEnroe**. Seven years Connors's junior, McEnroe burst onto the scene at the 1977 Wimbledon Championships when he qualified as an 18-year-old amateur and made it all the way to the semifinals before losing to Connors. He then attended Stanford University, where he helped the team win the NCAA championship in 1978, after which he joined the ATP. In 1979 he captured his first grand slam by winning the U.S. Open at age 20. One of his great rivals in his early career was Swede **Bjorn Borg**, who had already won six grand slam tournaments when McEnroe joined the tour (three French Opens and three Wimbledon Championships). They first met on center court Wimbledon during the 1980 final. Borg was going for his fifth straight title, which had never been done. The crowd was clearly behind Borg, and they booed McEnroe incessantly throughout the match. This mainly stemmed from the semifinal matchup between Connors and McEnroe in which McEnroe had verbally abused linesmen, the umpire, and even Connors. The final was a classic match often referred to as the best Wimbledon final ever—Borg won 8–6 in the fifth set. McEnroe got his revenge later that year by defeating Borg in the U.S. Open final, and he took from Borg the mantle of the world's number one player. The following year he returned to Wimbledon, and his behavior did not improve. He received fines throughout the tournament and first uttered what would become his catch-phrase, "You cannot be serious!" at several different line calls that did not go his way. Whereas that kind of behavior would cause most players to lose their focus, it almost seemed to bolster McEnroe's play, and he made it back to the finals to once again take on Borg. This time Borg was denied his place in history of winning Wimbledon six times in a row, and McEnroe won his first Wimbledon.

John McEnroe. Image © Gustavo Fadel, 2013. Used under license from Shutterstock, Inc.

Because of his behavior, McEnroe was nicknamed "Superbrat" in the British press, and he was not offered an honorary membership at Wimbledon, which is normally given to a player upon his first victory there (he received a membership after his second victory there in 1983). The taciturn Borg could not have been more different than the fiery McEnroe, but McEnroe never lost his temper when playing Borg. When asked why, McEnroe said he had too much respect for his rival to lose control like he did in other matches. Apparently, he did not have as much respect for Jimmy Connors because they seemed to squabble every time they played, including the 1982 Wimbledon final, when they almost came to blows. Connors won that match, but the two played 34 times between 1977 and 1991, and McEnroe won 20 of those meetings. The Borg–McEnroe rivalry was cut short when Borg decided to retire in the early 80s when he was only in his late 20s. In fact, he was the same age (27) as Bill Tilden was when he won his first major championship. McEnroe admitted he missed not having Borg on the tour, and it may have even cut his own career short, as he only had one more great year—1984—when he won both Wimbledon and the U.S. Open and came very close to winning the French Open. Those were his last major triumphs, and he was only 25. He finished with four U.S. Opens and three Wimbledon Championships. As both Connors's and McEnroe's careers waned in the late 1980s, there were no outstanding American players, and the future of American tennis did not look bright. Few would predict that a new golden age of American men's tennis was about to dawn.

John McEnroe should also be given credit for reviving American interest in the Davis Cup. For all his behavior issues (some blame McEnroe's antics and others during the 1980s for a dropoff in the popularity of the sport), McEnroe always believed playing for his country was extremely important. In the years following World War II, the Davis Cup had been won by either the United States or Australia (between 1946 and 1973 Australia won it 16 times and the U.S. 12 times). By the middle of the 1970s, other countries (like South Africa, Sweden, and Italy) began to break the stranglehold on the cup. Leading American players during the mid-70s had not put as much emphasis on Davis Cup—for instance, Jimmy Connors would rather be paid when he played. McEnroe played in his first Davis Cup in 1978 and helped the team win the first cup since 1972. He went on to play on 12 of the next 15 teams, bringing home the cup five times. He set records for most matches played (30), most singles victories (41), and most singles and doubles wins combined (59). At the end of his career, playing on Davis Cup teams afforded McEnroe the opportunity to mentor the younger American players coming up. Four players born between 1970 and 1972 provided the backbone for this resurgence in American tennis during the 1990s. The first to burst on the scene and win a major was 17-year-old Chinese-American **Michael Chang**, who shocked everyone by becoming the youngest ever to win a grand slam event when he won the 1989 French Open. He quickly vaulted into the top five in the world, and although he would never again win a major championship, he did reach the finals at both the Australian and U.S. Opens in 1996 and was always a difficult draw for anyone who played him until his retirement in 2003. Another great American player during the 1990s was Jim Courier. Courier quickly emerged as a tough competitor and winner, as he won the 1991 French Open and backed it up by repeating the feat in 1992. He did the same in back-to-back years at the Australian (1992 and 1993) for his four grand slam wins. He reached the finals at Wimbledon in 1993 and the U.S. Open in 1991 after dispatching Jimmy Connors's final run. He was also the first American since McEnroe a decade before to ascend to number one in the world in 1992.

Pete Sampras. Image © maxphoto, 2013. Used under license from Shutterstock, Inc.

The year 1992 was John McEnroe's final one on the tour, and it was the last time he played on a Davis Cup team. The United States won that cup, and McEnroe played doubles with a 20-year-old named **Pete Sampras**. Sampras became the greatest player of his generation and some say all time. He defeated world number one Jim Courier in the 1993 Wimbledon finals for his first grand slam title. He then dominated Wimbledon like no other player ever has by winning six of the next seven years between 1994 and 2000. He added to that five U.S. Open titles between 1990 and 2002 and attained the world number one ranking in 1993 and held it for a majority of the decade. Although he never won a French Open (clay was not his best surface), he did win two Australian Opens for a total of 14 grand slam victories, which passed Roy Emerson for most all-time. He had 13 titles going into the 2002 U.S. Open and had lost his number one ranking. At 30 he was a step slower and was reaching the end of his career. Most experts gave him no chance in the Open. He made it to the finals, however, and faced long-time rival **Andre Agassi**. Similar to the rivalry between McEnroe and Connors of the 1970s and 1980s, Sampras and Agassi met 34 times going back to 1990, and Sampras held a 20–14 advantage. Sampras won this last one as well and announced his retirement the following year before the U.S. Open so there could be a special ceremony honoring Sampras's accomplishments. Both Agassi and Sampras acknowledge how the rivalry helped both of their careers.

Agassi had turned pro at the young age of 16 in 1986 and won his first tournament in 1987. He had the reputation of being something of a rebel with his long hair style when few players wore their hair that way. He also was famous for wearing wildly colored clothes, which got him in trouble at places like Wimbledon, which had an "all-white" dress code. In fact, he refused to play Wimbledon until 1991 and did not go to the Australian Open until 1994. Ironically, it was at Wimbledon that Agassi first broke through and won in 1992 after defeating former champions Boris Becker and John McEnroe along the way. He won his first U.S. Open in 1994 and his first Australian in 1995. After those two wins, he temporarily wrested the number one ranking away from Sampras, but it was not to last. In 1996, Agassi failed to make any grand slam finals, and in 1997 he hurt his wrist and played few tournaments. He later admitted in his autobiography that he had failed a drug test and was on methamphetamines during this period—the lowest of his career. By the end of 1997, his ranking fell to 161 in the world, and most thought his career was near an end. To Agassi's credit, he quit meth and rededicated himself to making another run at the top of tennis—1998 began his major comeback. He won five tournaments that season (although no majors) and vaulted back up to world number six by the end of the year. In 1999 he was back in the win column for grand slams, as he won his first and only French Open. This win also entered him into the history books as being one of only five players to win all four grand slam events in his career (the other four being Rod Laver, Roy Emerson, Don Budge, and Fred Perry). Later that summer his comeback was complete when he won the U.S. Open. He won two more major championships, both at the Australian Open (2001 and 2003). He continued to play until 2006 when he was 36, and after losing to Spaniard **Rafael Nadal** at Wimbledon, Agassi announced he would retire after the U.S. Open. He lost in the second round and received a four-minute standing ovation from an appreciative crowd.

Andre Agassi. Image © Photo Works, 2013. Used under license from Shutterstock, Inc.

Conclusion

Nadal did not win Wimbledon that year, but he came back and won it in 2008 and 2010. He also won nine French Opens between 2005 and 2014. With his Australian Open victory in 2009 and his first U.S. Open in 2010, and followed it up with another in 2013 he joined Agassi and the others earlier mentioned as winning all four majors in his career. Nadal was not without his own rival, however. In 2001, Pete Sampras's 31-match win streak was ended by a player from Switzerland named **Roger Federer**. It was seemingly the passing of the torch because Federer won Wimbledon five consecutive years from 2003 through 2007 and again in 2009. He also won five consecutive U.S. Opens between 2004 and 2008, four Australian Opens, and a French for a total of 16 grand slam titles, passing Sampras. Nadal and Federer emerged as the two best players in the world during the first decade of the century. Also joining and eventually surpassing those two is Serbian Novac Djokovic who won his 10th Grand Slam title in 2015 solidifying his top ranking in the world. What was missing from this was an American element. With the retirement of Agassi and Sampras, American men's tennis again seemed to drift into a dark age. The last American to win a grand slam event was Andy Roddick's 2003 U.S. Open

Roger Federer. Image © Neale Cousland, 2013. Used under license from Shutterstock, Inc.

win. Roddick and Federer played some classic matches at Wimbledon and the U.S. Open, and some tried to make it into a rivalry to which Roddick replied after his loss in the 2004 Wimbledon finals: "I'm going to have to start winning some of them to call it a rivalry."[26]

Similar to golf, tennis emerged as a popular spectator sport in the United States in the 1920s and continued to be popular throughout the remainder of the century. But it seems to have had a more difficult time shaking the image as an "elite" or "country club" sport than golf has. Even currently, tennis is still somewhat viewed in a different category than other sports—even golf. Although players are bigger, are stronger, and hit the ball with incredible power and speed, it is viewed in some circles as a "prissy" sport. The 1970s helped change the image, if not temporarily, as a resurgence in the popularity of watching, attending, and playing the sport took place. Although the popularity of the sport waned a bit at the end of the century, there were great American players during the 1990s, and American tennis seemed strong. The new century has seen a drop in the number of dominant male players. Interestingly, it has seen a surge in popularity on the women's side. Although Andy Roddick has held the mantle of American tennis on his shoulders for most of the decade, he turned 30 later in 2012 and retired after the U.S. Open that year. Who is next to take the mantle? That is a question that remains to be answered. At the end of 2011 the highest-ranked American player was Mardy Fish at number eight. Fish had never made it farther than a quarterfinal of a major tournament, and he is actually a few months older than Roddick. American tennis seems to be in a period similar to the late 1980s with no dominant players on the horizon, but we know how quickly that can change. It is still a fairly popular recreational sport, and time will tell if there will be another "golden age" of American tennis.

Notes

1. *A History of Golf in Britain* (London: Cassel & Co., 1952), 45.
2. "Sports Beat," *Seattle Post-Intelligencer*, 11 January 2006.
3. George B. Kirsch, *Golf in America* (Urbana: University of Illinois Press, 2009), 7.
4. Ibid., 8.
5. Ibid., 6.
6. Ibid., 60.
7. Ibid., 50.
8. Ibid.
9. Ibid., 87.
10. Ibid.
11. Ibid., 89.
12. Ibid., 87.
13. Ibid., 121.
14. Herbert Warren Wind, *The Story of American Golf* (New York: Albert Knopf, 1975), 275.
15. Kirsch, *Golf in America*, 197.
16. John Garrity, "Open and Shut," *Sports Illustrated*, 26 June 2000. http://sportsillustrated.cnn.com/2005/golf/specials/tiger/2005/06/09/tiger.2000usopen/index.html. Retrieved August 15, 2007.
17. Heiner Gillmeister, *Tennis, A Cultural History* (New York: New York University Press, 1998), 194.
18. Ibid.
19. Frank DeFord, *Big Bill Tilden* (New York: Simon and Shuster, 1975), 13.
20. Richard O. Davies, *Sports in American Life* (West Sussex, UK: Wiley-Blackwell, 2012), 143.
21. Ibid., 144.
22. DeFord, *Big Bill Tilden*, 219.
23. Ibid., 250.
24. Ibid., 251.
25. Ibid., 220.
26. Source: redOrbit.

CHAPTER
Nine

The Modern Olympics

Pierre de Coubertin.
Image courtesy of
Library of Congress

*O*ne of the most identifiable aspects of Greek antiquity was the ancient Olympic Games that were held for over 1,000 years in Greece. There are disagreements on when the games officially began and ended, but it is known their origin was sometime after 800 B.C., and they lasted until the late 4th or early 5th century A.D., when they were suppressed by Greek leaders as they attempted to impose Christianity as the state religion. It would seem Greek leaders believed the games had pagan influences that had taken on their own religious following. In the years following the end of the ancient games, various local attempts were made around the world to revive the games—especially during the Renaissance period when everything Greek was being venerated. Britain's festive culture even had its own version of them that they called the "Olympics" in the 17th and 18th centuries. It was not until the late 19th century that a revival of the Games participated in by the entire world was proposed by a French nobleman. **Baron Pierre de Coubertin** was born in 1863 and in his youth witnessed his country's loss to the Germans in the Franco-Prussian War of 1870. Coubertin believed the loss was due to the Germans being more physically fit, and throughout his youth his ideas about the importance of exercise grew. Because of his high station in French society, he was able to put his beliefs into action and have some influence on his countrymen. In 1890, he established an organization to help foster the positive elements of sports in his country that he believed were already present in Germany, England, and elsewhere in the world. The Union des Societes Francaises de Sports Athletiques (USFSA) became be the organization that Coubertin chaired and used as his platform for organizing a revival of the Olympics. He first made the announcement of his intentions in 1892 to French and foreign delegates. His proposal was not met with universal acceptance or even understanding for that matter. Eventually they, and the world, learned that Coubertin was serious, and he began to travel around the world and enlist powerful allies like Theodore Roosevelt in the United States, who saw Coubertin as a kindred spirit who understood his belief in the "Strenuous Life." By 1894 Coubertin had formed a committee to plan the games made up of representatives from seven different nations—it became known as the **International Olympic Committee (IOC)**. Coubertin believed, and the committee agreed, that the first games should take place in Athens as a nod to the home of the ancient games.

Coubertin was adamant that the IOC be as impartial and free from politics as possible. He asked the members to be "ambassadors *from* the committee *to* their respective countries." He also said that in meetings of the committee, "it was the man that mattered, not the country."[1] Although it was hoped that the IOC would stay free from nationalistic politics, it was never believed that the games themselves would. The argument that is often heard is that politics and the Olympics should be separate—the reality is that has never been the case. Coubertin himself used the argument that the games could help heal rifts between nations when he was selling the idea. While the ancient

Olympics were discontinued due to religious reasons, Coubertin believed "Olympism" could be a valuable kind of religion. Although religion had been the cause of so much bloodshed over the years, the Olympics, he argued, could be a shared "modern secular faith based on good sportsmanship and fair play."[2] Coubertin was a true 19th-century liberal in that he believed individual liberty was always the most important thing. He also, however, believed that one's nationality was an important part of that individual's identity so no competitors were allowed to take part in the Olympics without representing a nation. There was also the issue of the new definition of amateurism that was discussed in the previous chapter. The British definition of an amateur essentially was defined on a class basis—only a gentleman could be an amateur—and was now the accepted definition. Although this went against Coubertin's liberal ideas by essentially eliminating a whole class of people from competing, his hands were tied, and the "myth" of Greek amateurism (the ancient Greeks drew no distinctions between class and wealth in relationship to who competed in the ancient games) was allowed to continue to bring about the modern games.

The Revival of the Olympics and the Early Modern Games

At the first meeting of the IOC in June of 1894, the committee agreed unanimously that the first games would be held in Athens and that the first president of the IOC should be Greek, so Demetrios Vikelas got the honor. He was not that thrilled because, frankly, his country was not that thrilled at the idea. In fact, by the end of 1894, Greece was making noises that they wished to change the venue of the games, mainly because they believed that cost of the games would prove to be too much for the Greek economy. By early 1895 the funds were raised, and the Greeks began to warm to the idea. When the opening ceremony of the **first modern Olympics** occurred on April 6, 1896, 80,000 people were packed into Panathinalko Stadium to welcome 14 nations to the competition. It was the largest ever gathering for an international sports competition to that date. For 10 days the countries competed in nine different sports, including athletics (what would be called track and field today), cycling, fencing, gymnastics, shooting, swimming, tennis, weightlifting, and wrestling. Medals were only given to the top two finishers in each event, but the IOC later retroactively awarded the modern tradition of gold medals for first, silver for second, and bronze for third; and the host country took the most medals with 46, which was probably more due to volume of competitors in more events than the strength of the Greek team. The United States was probably the strongest team in Athens and edged out Greece for the most gold medals (11 to 10) but finished a distant second in overall medal count with 20. The Germans were third with 13 medals, and the French fourth with 11. Apparently the American fans made themselves known at the games, much to the annoyance of the Greeks—the official report on the games referred to the "absurd shouts" of the Americans, and there were complaints that American fans were "like overgrown children."[3]

By all accounts the 1896 Athens games were a success. The Greeks, who were reluctant to bring the games to Athens, now lobbied to make the games a permanent fixture in their country. Coubertin took over as president of the IOC immediately after the Athens games ended, and he wanted the games to be rotated among different countries—he was also determined to have the 1900 games in his home country. His countrymen were no more enthusiastic about hosting the second Olympics than Greece had initially been about the first. In fact, Coubertin's own creation, the USFSA, voted against the idea. His influence and determination won the day, and it was announced that Paris would host the second Olympiad. The 1900 games were very different from 1896 in many ways. More countries took part (24 instead of 14) and more sports were included (19 instead of 9). There were no opening or closing ceremonies, as the games were organized in conjunction with the 1900 World's Fair, so the games began in May and did not end until October. As a result, more events were contested, but many of them fell short of being considered Olympic sport status. Because the games were held in conjunction with the World's Fair, spectators were often unaware that events were being staged, so attendance was not good. One other major difference was that women were allowed to compete in Paris, and they had not in Athens. Once again the host country captured the most medals, when France won 101. The United States was again second with 47, but this time Great Britain came in third with 30. At least two of the French medals were in dispute when three American marathon runners claimed the Frenchmen who came in first and second had taken a shortcut. American Arthur Newton finished fifth but insisted no one had passed him the entire race, and the two Frenchmen in question were the only runners who finished with no mud on their uniforms. The race was not well marked, and several runners actually became lost during the race. Despite the marathon problems and the large shadow cast by the World's Fair, the Paris Olympics were successful enough to keep the games alive.

Coubertin had traveled to the United States twice, and both times he had visited Chicago and had pictured the games someday being hosted by the Windy City. That day appeared to arrive when Chicago was given the 1904 Olympics. Henry J. Thurber was put in charge of the planning of the event, and although he was enthusiastic at the outset, he eventually tired of the process when he realized how involved it was. Eventually he looked to get out of the job or get the Olympics out of Chicago. His prayers were answered when a delegation from St. Louis approached him about moving the games there to coincide with a 100-year commemoration of the Louisiana Purchase, which would also be staged in 1904. Although the IOC was not happy about this move, they realized that Chicago no longer wanted the games, so in December of 1902, the committee voted to officially move the games to St. Louis. As with the 1900 games, the 1904 installment was held over a multimonth period to coincide with the celebration and that coupled with the distance from Europe led to very few athletes outside the United States competing in the third Olympiad. Of the 554 athletes who competed, 432 were Americans. Not surprisingly, the medal count was incredibly skewed toward the United States: The Americans won 239 medals, and Germany finished next with 13. The games were essentially a national championship for the Americans. Although the local press dubbed the games a success, the international opinion of the Olympics was much more negative. Allen Guttmann noted that the games after 1904 were "close to disaster," and the St. Louis games could have been the last.[4] Fortunately for Coubertin and the IOC, there was to be what were called the "intercalary games" (games held between the Olympics) held in Athens in 1906, which were given as a concession to Greece after they were not allowed to be the permanent site of the games. Coubertin was against the intercalary games and did not attend them, but they certainly did not hurt the cause of the Olympics when there was almost double the number of athletes of who showed up in St. Louis. Historians have struggled to know how to treat these games—most have not considered them part of Olympic history. The intercalary games were supposed to occur every four years in Athens—they were never held again.

The Olympics did survive, and Coubertin lobbied to have the fourth Olympiad in Rome. Next to Athens, Coubertin believed Rome held the highest symbolic importance for the games, and he thought that was especially important after the failure of the 1904 games in St. Louis. Unfortunately for Coubertin and Italy, a natural event occurred in 1906 that would change the venue of the games. Mt. Vesuvius erupted in April, killing thousands and devastating the city of Naples. Funds that were to go to the Olympics were needed for the rebuilding of Naples, so it was announced that the 1908 games would move to London. The games in London are probably best remembered for two things that were, at least in part, related: An intense nationalism surrounded these games culminating with an apparent snub of the British royal family by American athletes, and the length of the marathon was forever altered. The Athens intercalary games introduced for the first time athletes parading in an opening ceremony behind the flags of their respective countries. The stadium was also adorned with the flags of all the countries of the world, but the American flag was absent—this did *not* go unnoticed by American fans or athletes. When the athletes passed the box of King Edward VII, who officially opened the games, the flag bearer was supposed to dip the colors. Every country did this except for Ralph Rose, who was holding the Stars and Stripes. Now this action or rather lack of action has become legend in the past century. Beyond the absence of the American flag in the stadium and the obvious history between England and her former colonies as a backdrop to this incident, there was also the religious issue between Protestant England and her rule over Catholic Ireland. The American Olympic team had a large contingent of Irish Americans on it, and at least one of them, Martin Sheridan, was supposed to have supported Rose with the oft-quoted "This flag dips to no earthly king."[5] Although there are no 1908 sources that support Sheridan making this remark, it seemed to sum up the attitude of the Americans, and it has become tradition that the American flag not be lowered during the Olympics and it has remained so ever since. In fact, in 1942 it became more than a tradition when Congress passed Public Law 829, which stated, "That no disrespect be given to the flag of the United States of America, the flag should not be dipped to any person or thing."[6]

What was the reaction of the British to the "snub" in 1908? On the surface there did not appear to be much of a reaction at all in the press or elsewhere, but if you ask the American athletes, there was a reaction in how they were treated both by fans and especially officials. American athletes complained that British officials were biased in their decisions, and there were numerous protests of those decisions. It got so bad that the IOC recognized the problem of "local officials," so it announced after the conclusion of the games that the officials for 1912 should be as "international as the athletes."[7] The laying out of the marathon course appeared to also be a reaction to the snub, as the normal 25-mile layout was lengthened to 26 miles so the course would start at Windsor Castle and finish in the stadium—and the additional 385 yards were added when officials believed that needed to restore the dignity of the monarchy after the opening ceremonies and ensure the finish line was directly in front of the royal box. Marathon races have been 26 miles, 385 yards ever since. For the fourth consecutive Olympics, the host nation garnered the most medals with 146, much to the chagrin of the Americans, who again finished second with 47. Sweden, who hosted the next Olympiad, was third with 25.

The other legacy of the 1908 games was a rededication of American athletes to the international competition. The slights of the British, whether real or imagined, seemed to galvanize the Americans in their training and their view on the Olympics. The Americans as a whole had not taken the competition as seriously as other nations—that changed in 1912. The American team in 1912 was made up of names that would become well known in future years, including **Avery Brundage**, who later became longtime head of the American Olympic Committee and eventually president of the IOC. Brundage described the 10-day trans-Atlantic trip as a workout because of the track and pool that were installed for the athletes to train. He did note that the exercise and sea breeze seemed to overstimulate some of the athletes' appetites: "Exposure to the unlimited menus on shipboard was fatal to some and several hopes of Olympic victory foundered at the bounteous dinner table."[8] Future general George S. Patton competed in the Pentathlon—but it was the winner of that event that stole the show in the 1912 games. **Jim Thorpe** not only won that event but also won the decathlon and prompted the King of Sweden to say when he met Thorpe, "You sir are the greatest athlete in the world." His short answer, "Thanks, King," may have been apocryphal but his performance was not.[9] The tragedy for Thorpe came after the games, when it was learned by the IOC that he had been paid to play summer professional baseball while a student at Carlisle Indian School. The definition of amateur had been fairly loose during the first four Olympics, but the IOC decided to strengthen it for the fifth, and being paid to play sports was a definite violation. Thorpe was stripped of his medals. The action has often been viewed as a racist act because of

Jim Thorpe stamp. Image © catwalker, 2013. Used under license from Shutterstock, Inc.

Thorpe's American Indian heritage, but Allen Guttmann, in his history of the Olympics, argued against this, citing the fact the Thorpe incident was not isolated, and the IOC also stripped other athletes whose amateurism was deemed violated. For Thorpe, it was a lifelong struggle to restore his status as winner of those events. He died in 1953 without getting the satisfaction; but his family picked up the fight, and after being rebuffed for years by Olympic officials, including former teammate Avery Brundage, the IOC determined in 1982—70 years after the event—to reinstate Thorpe's amateur status and restore his medals. Because the original medals had been stolen, replicas of the medals were presented to Thorpe's children.

Despite the later controversy the 1912 games were a tremendous success, and the host country was given credit. The organization of the games was lauded as the best ever, and there was little controversy regarding officials compared to 1908. There was also the improvement of technology on display in the form of electronic timing of events for the first time. Coubertin may have had other reasons for the location of the 1912 games; when he announced the location in 1909 he said, "Of all the countries in the world, Sweden is at the moment the best qualified to host a great Olympic Games."[10] The nationalism of the 1908 games and the growing tension in Europe based on the various alliances worried Coubertin. Having the games take place away from the cauldron of a simmering Europe seemed like the best idea to soothe tensions. It may have also been why the IOC for the first (and only) time allowed athletes to compete independent of national representation. This also led to the medal count won by nations to be the lowest ever. The United States' rededication to the events almost resulted in the host nation *not* winning for the first time. Although the Americans took the most gold medals (25 to Sweden's 24), Sweden edged out the United States in total medal wins 65–63. In what was viewed on this side of the Atlantic as vindication after 1908, Great Britain finished a distant third with only 10 gold medals and 41 total. Coubertin announced the 1916 games would be in Berlin—back into the cauldron.

The Games between the Wars

The whole world changed in the summer of 1914. Although athletes trained in preparation for the 1916 games, an assassination in Sarajevo ignited a war like the world had never seen. The entangling alliances that nearly every country in Europe had entered into drew nearly the entire continent into the conflagration. By 1915 there were bigger things to worry about than the future of the Olympic movement, but it was obvious the 1916 games would not take place, and the future was uncertain. With the Western front where most of the fighting and dying was taking place being located in France and the possibility of the Germans overtaking Paris, Pierre de Coubertin decided it was time to move the Olympic headquarters (and himself) to a safer spot. In April of 1915 he officially made Lausanne, Switzerland, the administrative headquarters of the Olympics, where it remains today. After the war officially ended on November 11, 1918, Coubertin went into action to revive the games. The first problem to arise was within the IOC membership itself, when British member Theodore Cook demanded that the German members be removed from the committee. When his resolution was defeated, he resigned. When it was decided the games would continue in 1920, the next decision was where they would take place.

The IOC decided it would be a symbolic gesture to award the games to Belgium—the country that was neutral at the beginning of the war and was first invaded by the Germans on their way to France. The next question was would the defeated powers (Germany, Austria, Hungary, Bulgaria, and Turkey) be invited? The IOC decided to leave it up to the host country, and although they did not forbid Belgium from inviting the teams, they encouraged them not to. Whereas all the countries except for Germany returned to competition in 1924, Germany was not represented at the Olympics until 1928—10 years after the end of the war. Those wounds took a long time to heal. What did not take a long time was the period between the announcement that the games would be held in Antwerp, Belgium, and the opening ceremonies—a little over a year. Because of the short preparation time and the devastated condition of the host country, the 1920 games are not remembered as being spectacular. In fact, it's almost a miracle they happened at all. There was also the fact there was an Olympic-like event staged in 1919 called the Allied Games, which featured athletic teams from the victor nations in the war. This may have taken a bit of the steam out of the Antwerp games because they occurred only a year later. The stadium was unfinished and, except for soccer, there was very little fan interest. The games lost money, and although accommodations were abysmal, most athletes recognized the special situation and realized that lesser games was better than no games at all. During the war years, Coubertin had designed a new Olympic flag—the five interlocking Olympic rings representing the five continents so recognizable today was first flown at the 1920 games. The year 1920 also marked the first Olympics in which the host country did not win the medal count—that honor went to perennial runner-up, the United States with 95. Sweden was second with 64, Great Britain next with 46, and Belgium fourth with 36.

Pierre de Coubertin stamp. Image © rook76, 2013. Used under license from Shutterstock, Inc.

In 1921 Pierre de Coubertin announced his retirement from the presidency of the IOC and that the 1924 games would be his last. As a favor to himself, he asked for the 1924 games to return to Paris. However, before he left, another round of controversy enveloped the IOC—the first from the Italians, who were irate that the games would return to Paris a second time before Rome would get their first games. The Italian delegation walked out of the meeting. Coubertin next had to deal with the movement by Scandinavian countries to establish a separate Winter Olympics. Ice skating had been allowed at the 1908 games, and 1920 had included ice hockey, but this was the first time there had been a motion for a separate Winter Olympics. There was much dissension, including the by United States, who argued that due to the climate needed for winter sports, only a limited number of countries could host and compete. With the support of Britain and France, the motion for a separate Winter Games passed, and it was agreed that the first games would take place in January and February of 1924, just months prior to the Paris summer games. Not surprisingly, the Scandinavian countries of Norway and Finland dominated the medal count with 17 and 11, respectively. Although against the idea of the games, the United States fielded a team and performed well enough to tie Britain for third with four medals. The winter games took place the same year as the summer games up until 1992—since then they have been held during the off–even years of the summer games. The Americans did much better in Paris in the summer of 1924, winning three times as many gold medals (45) as the country in second—Finland (14). Three of those gold medals were awarded to American swimmer **Johnny Weismuller**, who set an Olympic record in the 100 meters and a world record in the 400 meters. He also won a bronze medal as a member of the U.S. water polo team. He won two more gold medals in the 1928 games and during his entire career won 52 U.S. national championships and set 67 world records. After his swimming career ended, he signed a movie contract and became more famous for portraying Tarzan in 12 movies between 1932 and 1948. The medal total of 99 for the United States in 1924 marked the second Olympics in a row that the Americans achieved that honor. Unfortunately for Coubertin, his countrymen could only muster a distant second with 38 medals, just ahead of Finland with 37.

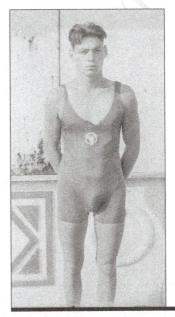

Johnny Weismuller. Image courtesy of Library of Congress

By the 1920s Finland had made its presence known on the international sports scene, and it led many to speculate how a country with such a small population could compete with the larger nations of the world. Many theories were proposed, including the diet of the Finns (raw fish, rye bread, sour milk) to another that said they were direct descendants of a "wild Mongol strain" that made them tough.[11] Whatever the reason, they continued their success into 1928. The 1928 summer games were awarded to Amsterdam, even though the United States thought it was time to bring back the games after the less-than-successful 1904 St. Louis games. Amsterdam had bid for both the 1920 and 1924 games, so it was essentially their "turn." The Americans were appeased when it was announced that Los Angeles would host the 1932 games. The year 1928 would be the first Olympics without the direct involvement of Pierre de Coubertin. He was replaced by Belgium's Comte Henri de Baillet-Latour, who held the post until another world war interrupted the games in the 1940s. He presided over a fairly uneventful Olympics as once again the United States took home the most medals with 56. Germany returned to the competition to finish second with 31 (much to the dismay of Finland, who probably would have finished second but had to settle for a tie for third with their fellow Scandinavian neighbor, Sweden, with 25 each). The United States was now the undisputed leader in the sports world, and many equated this with the greatness of the nation, including General Douglas MacArthur, who reported to President Calvin Coolidge on behalf of the American Olympic Committee after the success of the 1928 games that he believed athletics to be "most characteristic of our nationality."[12]

Knowing that the 1932 games were being planned for Los Angeles, the American Olympic Committee watched the 1928 games very closely and wanted to make the 1932 games the biggest ever. The modesty of the 1920 games in Antwerp had prompted every host city after to try to outdo the one before, but 1932 was really going to take it to another level. A problem intervened in 1929 when the New York stock market collapsed and so did not only the American economy, but a worldwide depression ushered in the 1930s. Countries began to back out of the games due to financial difficulties, and some thought of actually cancelling the games, but Los Angeles stepped up in a big way. The city came up with a $1.5 million dollar bond issue, and voters in California approved an additional $1 million dollars in state funds to be used for the construction of a 105,000-seat stadium (the Los Angeles Coliseum), a 10,000-seat indoor facility, a 12,000-seat swimming facility, and the first-ever Olympic Village to house the athletes. Although only roughly half the athletes who had competed in the 1928 games were financially able to make the trip, those that did were treated to a spectacular event. Los Angeles promoted the games extremely well, and even though the country was in the midst of a horrible economic depression, the public came out in big numbers. It helped to have Hollywood "royalty" like Gary Cooper, Bing Crosby, Cary Grant, and the Marx brothers in the stands. The one citizen who refused to attend was the leading citizen in the country. President Herbert Hoover was in a reelection campaign against Franklin Roosevelt, and he did not think it would be a good public relations move. Perhaps he should have attended—he lost to Roosevelt in a landslide that November. As for the games themselves, the Americans once again took the most medals with 103, Italy was second with 36, and Finland was third with 25. The star of the American team was on the women's side: **Babe Didrikson**. She won two gold medals in the javelin and hurdles, and she won a silver medal in the high jump. Women had come a long way in the Olympic movement, and it was not without controversy. Women had not competed in the Athens games in 1896, and Coubertin had been against women's participation. Although women slowly began to be added to events starting in 1900, it was not until after Coubertin retired that they enjoyed close to full participation. In 1928 women were allowed to compete in track and field for the first time. Even in 1932 women were limited in how many events they could enter—the belief was that they could not physically handle as many as men (who were unlimited). Didrikson could have competed in more events, but she was limited to three. The dean of American sportswriters, Grantland Rice, declared the games the "greatest sporting pageant in world history."[13] Most people agreed—if there is one thing Los Angeles can do, it is to put on a show, and they did in 1932. It even turned out to be more successful financially than most Olympics. The state of California was actually paid back over $200,000 after the games. The 1936 games would have to be quite the spectacle to compare with these.

The announcement of the site for the 1936 games was made before the Los Angeles Olympics. In May of 1931 Berlin was chosen to be the host, and at the time the chancellor of Germany was Heinrich Bruning, who represented the dying centrist coalition of the Weimar Republic. Less than two years later the National Socialists (Nazis) had taken power, and their leader, **Adolf Hitler**, had become chancellor and declared himself *fuhrer*, which meant leader, and would later have the negative connotation associated with Hitler and his policies. One of his policies centered around his belief in the Aryan race (which was Germanic in origin) being superior to all other races. The Olympic ideal (at least theoretically) of race, religion, and ideology not mattering on the athletic field was an anathema to the Nazis. A Nazi Party spokesman had condemned modern sports because they were "international" and "infested with Frenchman, Belgians, Pollacks, and Jew-Niggers."[14] Many Nazi publications in Germany called for limiting the games to white athletes. This was not what the IOC had in mind when it awarded the games to Berlin, and it was, quite frankly, their worst nightmare. Before the IOC could meet to decide what to do about the games, Hitler announced that preparations were underway for the games, and they would be open to all athletes who qualified. Joseph Goebbels, Hitler's minister of propaganda, had convinced the Fuhrer that this would be an excellent opportunity to show the world not only the superiority of the German athlete but also the organizational skills of the new regime. Hitler spared no expense and was willing to provide the organizers with whatever they needed to make this the greatest Olympic spectacle ever produced. They built a 100,000-seat stadium and various other gymnasiums and arenas. Although the technology of television was in its infancy, a closed-circuit version of it was installed throughout the grounds so spectators could follow all the action. Radio broadcasts of the events were strong enough to reach 41 nations. Hitler commissioned Leni Riefenstahl to create a documentary film about the games. Her $7 million film, titled *Olympia*, was considered cutting-edge for cinematography at the time.

All this pageantry did not allay the fears of the IOC or other Olympic committees around the world. There was still great trepidation concerning the Nazi racial policy and the anticipated treatment of black and Jewish athletes. In Great Britain, France, Canada, and the United States, a movement was begun to boycott the games. It was first proposed as early as 1933, but it really picked up momentum in 1935 when the Nazi government passed the Nuremburg laws, which stripped German Jews of their citizenship. A 1935 Gallup poll showed that 43 percent of Americans favored a boycott of the games. The two camps (those in favor and those against) were represented by American Olympic Committee President Avery Brundage, who was against the boycott, and Amateur Athletic Union President Judge Jeremiah Mahoney, who was in favor of it. Mahoney had succeeded Brundage as the leader of the AAU, and they had been friends. The battle over the boycott ended that friendship, as it got nasty and personal. Brundage took a fact-finding trip to Germany to see if the claims of Nazi atrocities were as bad as some were claiming. He returned after being assured that the Germans would abide by Olympic law and allow anyone to compete in the games who qualified, including Jews on the German team. Although it is true that 21 German Jews were invited to a tryout for the team, amazingly, none of them were selected. Brundage's reaction to those in favor of the boycott was that it was a Jewish-Communist conspiracy: "Jews and Communists," he wrote, "threatened to spend a million dollars to keep the United States out of Germany . . .".[15] Mahoney, though not Jewish, was Roman Catholic and based his opposition to the Nazis not only on their anti-Semitism but also on their paganism and persecution of Catholics. Mahoney answered Brundage's charges that there had been no instances of Jewish athletes being discriminated against in Germany with a long list of violations by the Nazis against Jewish athletes, all

Jesse Owens. Image courtesy of Library of Congress

of which have been substantiated. As Allen Guttmann put it in his chapter on the 1936 games in his book, *The Olympics,* "Mahoney had the facts, Brundage had the votes."[16] The boycott was voted down at the annual meeting of the AAU in 1935 by 2½ votes—the Americans would field a team in Berlin in 1936.

Most of the athletes were in favor of competing, not surprising considering the time and effort they had devoted to training for the event. Black athletes, for the most part, were against the boycott. Black newspapers were split— some thought their training should be rewarded with an appearance at the games, and others supported the boycott. Some argued showing up and winning would be the best way to prove Hitler's policies wrong. There was also a darker side to some blacks' response to Hitler's policies. Historian David K. Wiggins has argued that some black Americans were anti-Semitic. "They frequently stereotyped Jews and blamed them from economic exploitation to murder."[17] One of the black members of the American team was **Jesse Owens**. It would be Owens who would do more to disprove the Nazi belief in Aryan superiority than anyone or anything else. In the 1935 Big 10 track championships, Owens ran as a sophomore for Ohio State. He broke four world records and was the Americans' best hope in Berlin. He did not disappoint, as he set a world record for the 100 meters at 10.3 seconds and an Olympic record for the 200 meters at 20.7 seconds. In the long jump he posted 8.06 meters and helped set another world record in the 400-meter relay. In all, he finished with four gold medals. Another black American, Mack Robinson, finished just behind Owens for the silver medal in the 200 meters. He was the older brother of Jackie Robinson.

As for the treatment of the athletes, the Nazis seemed to bend over backward in their treatment of foreign athletes. "There was absolutely no discrimination at all," Owens later said.[18] Hitler and other Nazi leaders were always quick to deflect American accusation of racial policies by pointing out the rampant discrimination in the United States. It is the sad truth that during the year prior to the Berlin Olympics, there were 26 lynchings of black men in the United States. The German press was effusive in its praise of Owens and recognized that he was the star of the games. Ironically, his treatment was better in the German press than in Southern American press. The Atlanta *Journal-Constitution,* for example, printed no pictures of Owens or any other black athletes during or after the games. A famous story that emerged from the games was that Hitler had been so upset that he refused to shake Jesse Owens's hand. In truth, although Hitler congratulated some of the early winners, including the first German victors, he left the stadium before Owens was finished with his events. The following day when Hitler returned, he was cautioned by a German IOC member that he should either congratulate *all* the victorious athletes or *none* of them. Hitler chose the latter and only congratulated the German winners at a private party following the games. It would seem the only charges of anti-Semitism during the games were directed at the American track coaches. Two Jewish members of the American track team had chosen to boycott the games but the remaining two, Marty Glickman and Sam Stoller, were removed from the 400-meter relay. Glickman's time was faster than Foy Draper, who replaced him. In defense of coach Dean Cromwell, who made the change, he had coached Draper at USC, and it was probably more loyalty to him than anti-Semitism against Glickman. Other than the obvious glitch of Owens's excellence, the 1936 games served as what Hitler had wanted them to be—a showcase of German advancements in technology, organization, and even athletic achievement; although Owens stole the show, the Germans took home the most medals—89. The United States was second with 56. Just before the Berlin games began, German troops marched into the Rhineland, an area that had been demilitarized at the end of the First World War. This blatant violation of the Versailles Treaty did not interrupt the preparation for or the games themselves, but it turned out to be the first step in Hitler's

AMERICAN *Sports*

plan to dominate Europe. By 1939 he had occupied both Austria and Czechoslovakia, and when he attacked Poland, the rest of Europe seemed to wake up to his actions; both Britain and France declared war on Germany and Italy, and the Second World War began.

Olympics and the Cold War

It is somewhat amazing regarding the similarities between the two World Wars and their effect on the Olympics. Berlin was supposed to have hosted the 1916 games, but they were cancelled because of World War I—a war in which Germany was seen as one of the aggressor nations. Japan had joined Germany and Italy to become a member of the Axis powers during World War II—and was also viewed as an aggressor nation, especially after the unprovoked attack on the officially neutral United States in December 1941. Where was the site supposed to be of the cancelled 1940 games? Tokyo. The IOC seemed to sense that the militarism of the Japanese might lead to problems, so they had a contingency plan of Helsinki, Finland. By 1938 so many nations were threatening a boycott if Japan were allowed to host the games that the committee decided to implement plan B. When the war began in 1939 the Olympics were cancelled altogether. Because the war was still being waged in 1944, those games were cancelled as well, becoming the first time ever that two consecutive Olympiads were not held. After the war ended in 1945, the IOC decided to award the 1948 games to London. Similar to Antwerp following World War I, London was rewarded for the price it paid during the war. Also similar to Antwerp, London had been devastated by the constant bombing attacks of the German Air Force, so the 1948 games became known as the "Austerity Games" because of the lack of luxuries in Britain due to postwar rationing. The British were trying to rebuild their shattered economy (just as most countries in Europe following the war), and because of that no new venues were built for the 1948 games. Athletes stayed in existing structures as opposed to an Olympic Village, which had become the norm since the 1932 games. Despite all this, a record number of athletes (over 4,100) and nations (59) appeared. The one nation that was noticeably absent was the Soviet Union. Although they were an ally of the United States during World War II, the two nations had emerged from the war as the two superpowers in the world with very different ideologies and ways of life. The resulting rivalry between the two nations became known as the **Cold War**, and it lasted for the next four decades. The shadow of the Cold War was felt everywhere, including the Olympics. The first effect was in 1948 when, although they were invited, the Soviets decided not to send any athletes. The Americans were back on top of the medal count in 1948 with 84, but it would not be so easy after that as the Soviets did send a team in 1952, and the Cold War competition was on.

The year 1952 not only marked the beginning of the struggle of the superpowers on the athletic fields but it also marked the beginning of Avery Brundage's presidency of the IOC. Brundage had been linked to amateur athletics and the Olympics going back to 1912, when he competed as a track athlete in the fifth Olympics at Stockholm with Jim Thorpe. He was later president of the AAU and then the American Olympic Committee, leading the fight against the boycott of the 1936 Berlin games. He then became a member of the IOC and impressed the rest of the committee with his hard work and dedication to the cause. He so impressed them that he moved his way up through the ranks to become second and then first vice president during the 1940s. Although he had to fight the anti-American bias of a committee that was founded and run by European aristocracy beginning with Coubertin and continued with his successor, de Baillet-Latour, his reputation won the day, and he was elected by a 30–17 vote of the committee to succeed Sweden's Sigrid Edstrom in 1952. Edstrom had been president in the postwar years after de Baillet-Latour's sudden death during the war, and Edstrom had endorsed Brundage to succeed him when his term expired. It's not surprising that Brundage would have wanted the Americans to compete in the 1936 games despite the rise of Hitler and the Nazis—Brundage was a true believer in Coubertin's Olympic ideal that athletics should be separated from politics. He announced before the Berlin games that "the AOC must not be involved in political, racial, religious or sociological controversies."[19] Just a short time later as a member of the IOC, he responded to the proposed boycott of the 1940 Tokyo games by various countries by asking of them, "Why do the athletes meddle in politics—have they no foreign office?"[20] Ironically, for someone who thought the Olympics should be separate from politics, in his two decades as IOC president, Brundage presided over some of the most politically charged games in history.

The Soviet Union (USSR), since its formation after the Russian Revolution and the communist takeover, had not applied for membership to the IOC and had avoided Olympic competition since the 1920s. Czarist Russia had competed but not been a serious contender in the early Olympics up to and including the 1912 games. At Stockholm, for instance, they had not won a single medal. After World War II they were again extended an invitation to join the IOC but refused. It's not that the Soviets did not believe sports to be important (they had held their own athletic competitions over the years), but they just did not want to compete in what they considered to be the "bourgeois" international games of the Olympics. International athletes (and probably the Soviet athletes themselves) wanted the Soviets to be included because, to be the best in the world, you want to compete against the *entire* world; and that would include the Soviet Union. By the early fifties the Soviets began to warm to the idea of showcasing their talent to the world, and they finally did join the IOC. The IOC then had to deal with two major issues—amateurism and Eastern Europe. Many of the Soviet athletes had violated Olympic rules by receiving compensation. Although Brundage and other members were committed anti-Communists, they were also committed to the Olympic ideal of allowing everyone to compete regardless of politics, so they wanted the Soviets to compete. They also did not want to cause an international incident by refusing to allow the "professional" Soviet athletes to compete, so they simply ignored the rules. This became a bone of contention for the Americans and others for the next 30 years. The other issue was the countries that had fallen behind the "**iron curtain**" of Soviet domination by the early fifties like Poland, Hungary, and Yugoslavia. They had competed in all the Olympics previously and wanted to continue to be recognized as independent nations and compete as such. Although the Soviets allowed that to happen, what eventually occurred was that all the nations of Eastern Europe became satellite states of the USSR, and their votes on the IOC became parroted votes of the USSR. It became so comical at the meetings of the IOC that Brundage thought about skipping the countries, knowing what their vote would be. The other issue the IOC had to deal with at the beginning of the Cold War was China. In 1949 the Communists under Mao Tse Tung had taken over and banished Chiang Kai Shek (former leader of China) to the island of Taiwan, where he set up a government and ruled "Nationalist" China. The United States only recognized Chiang's China, and of course, the USSR only recognized Mao's China. The question for the IOC was, who would it allow to compete in the Olympics? The answer was both. In an ingenious move, the IOC decided not to recognize either country but to invite both to send athletes to the 1952 games. The athletes would only compete in events governed by the international federation that recognized their side—this would ensure they would not compete against one another. In the end it did not matter because when the Nationalists found out the Communists would be there, they boycotted the games. It was during this time that the idea of a "**sporting ideology**" emerged for the United States. Americans had always prided themselves on values like democracy, freedom of speech, press, and religion. Now sports became a way they identified themselves and differentiated themselves from other cultures. Sports were now viewed in a positive light by most Americans and they helped contribute to the "us vs. them" mentality. The first "them" were the Nazis in the 1930s and 40s but by the post-war years the "them" became the Soviets.

The 1952 games were held in Helsinki due to the fact that the 1940 games were supposed to be there and they were cancelled. Much to the chagrin of Brundage and the IOC, the games turned into a major nationalistic competition between the Soviets and the Americans. When the Americans found out the Soviets would be in Helsinki, there was an extra urgency to their training—doing well against the other superpower would not only bolster American self-confidence but also respect among American allies and a demoralization of the Soviets. Athletes began to view themselves as "surrogate warriors" in the superpower struggle. Decathlon champion (usually indicative of the best athlete in the games), American Bob Mathias, was quoted as saying: "There were many more pressures on the American athletes (in 1952) because of the Russians than in 1948. You just loved to beat 'em. You just had to beat 'em. It wasn't like beating some friendly country like Australia."[21] In the end the Americans did "beat 'em," but it was close. The Americans almost doubled the gold medal count of the USSR (40–22), but the overall medal count was much closer, with the Americans edging the Soviets 76–71. The USSR could probably take some pride in that one of their satellite nations, Hungary, finished third with 42 medals. The 1956 games in Melbourne, Australia, was a repeat of the Helsinki games in terms of nationalistic rivalry. The games themselves were threatened because of international politics. Weeks before the games were to begin, Hungarian Prime Minister Imre Nagy announced that his nation wished to renounce its alliance with the USSR. He had received assurances that he would receive American support in this effort. The Soviets were not about to let their power recede, so they moved into Hungary with tanks and troops, and although Americans had promised support, the support given was limited to words and not actions. The Hungarians were kept behind the Iron Curtain by force and violence— an estimated 5,000 Hungarians were killed by the Soviet troops, and many others defected across the border into Austria. Not surprisingly, Brundage believed what happened outside the games should have no effect on them. Brundage could believe that that all he wanted, but anyone who witnessed the semifinal water polo match between the USSR and Hungary could not deny the Hungarians seemed to be playing for something more than just themselves. The Hungarians dominated the match, and it got so rough that eventually the water began to turn red from the blood literally spilled in the pool. Instead of giving the Hungarians the satisfaction of winning the match outright, the Soviets eventually forfeited. It was one of the few events in which the USSR did not win a medal because they captured the most gold medals (37; with the United States in second with 32) and the overall medal count for the first time with 98 to the Americans' 74. Because of the crisis in Hungary, the Hungarians were not able to repeat their third-place medal performance because many of the athletes being either dead or in another country. They did win the gold in water polo after their very symbolic victory over the Soviets in the semifinals.

Following the 1956 games a noticeable thaw began in the Cold War relations between the two superpowers—at least on the athletic fields. In 1957 track officials in both the United States and USSR agreed to yearly events between the nations to be hosted by each country beginning with Moscow. Rome had been trying to host an Olympics since the eruption of Mt. Vesuvius cancelled the 1908 games, and they were finally rewarded in 1960. The goodwill between the superpowers continued, and the athletes of the two countries, many of whom had gotten acquainted because of the yearly track events, openly socialized together in Rome. The chairman of the Soviet Olympic Committee, Constantin Andrianov, was even quoted as saying, "Politics is one thing, sport another."[22] Brundage surely concurred with that statement. It helped that there had been no major crises between the nations since the Hungarian crisis of 1956. That did not mean that the competition and rivalry had dissipated because when the Soviets dominated the Rome games (besting the United States in gold medals 43–34 and overall medal count 103–71), it prompted the Americans to rededicate themselves to athletic excellence. There was a feeling the United States was falling behind the Soviets in everything from missiles to technology to education and athletics. To combat the last of these, President John F. Kennedy expanded the President's Council on Physical Fitness in 1961 to make sure children were trained in athletics in schools across the country. The American Olympic Committee also rededicated itself to making sure the United States did not slip too far behind the dominating Soviets. In 1964 the games were awarded to Tokyo, who had lost the 1940 games due to World War II. The rededication of the Americans appeared to work, as the United States captured more gold medals than any other nation with 36 (six more than the second-place Soviets) and only trailed the USSR 96–90 in the overall medal count. The relatively issue-free Olympics in the early sixties gave way to some of the most controversial of all the games in the late sixties and early seventies. Issues of race came to a head in the 1968 games after black American athletes dominated the games in 1960 and 1964. Future heavyweight champions Cassius Clay (later Muhammad Ali) and Joe Frazier won gold medals in 1960 and 1964, respectively. Wilma Rudolph was called the "fastest woman in the world" after she won three gold medals in sprint events in 1960. Future NBA Hall of Fame members Walt Bellamy and Oscar Robertson led the United States to its fifth consecutive gold medal in basketball in 1960, and future NFL Hall of Fame wide receiver Bob Hayes equaled a world record in the 100-meter dash. This was before the height of the civil rights movement in the United States, but the 1968 games fell right in the middle of it.

Race, Religion, and Tragedy: 1968 and 1972

The United States was not the only country where racial attitudes were becoming an issue that would affect the Olympics—South Africa's policy of apartheid replaced the U.S.–Soviet Cold War rivalry as the major political issue the IOC had to deal with in the early 1960s. **Apartheid**, which was a racial segregation policy in South Africa, began after World War II. Although there had been racial strife in the country prior to that, the elections of 1948 officially ushered in the policy through government policy and legislation. Protests both internally and externally mounted throughout the 1950s, and enough pressure was put on the IOC to make a decision on the inclusion or exclusion of South Africa. As early as 1959, it was apparent that South Africa was not allowing black athletes to compete for a spot on its Olympic team. The South African National Olympic Committee (SANOC) claimed there was no discrimination because their Olympic team was composed of their best athletes (who just happened to be all white). It was a difficult accusation to prove, so South Africa was allowed to send a team to the 1960 games in Rome. It became easier to exclude South Africa when they began to be open and unapologetic about their policy, as in 1962 when their Interior Minister Jan de Klerk said essentially that the races should not be mixed—off the field or on it. The IOC gave SANOC the ultimatum that government policy must change by the end of 1963 or their invitation to the 1964 games would be rescinded. When no such changes were made, they were banned from the games in Tokyo. After promising to reform prior to the 1968 games in Mexico City, South Africa was again invited back to the Olympics. Brundage proudly announced in January of 1968 that South Africa was sending a "multiracial team of individuals selected by a multiracial committee."[23] When it became apparent that was *not* the case, countries began to voice their opposition to South Africa's participation, and in March when the Soviet Union announced its intention to boycott the games, the IOC met in a special session and voted 47–16 to withdraw South Africa's invitation. They were not allowed to participate again until 1992, when the Apartheid policy finally was ended.

As for black Americans, the Civil Rights movement during the mid-sixties (1964 Civil Rights Act, 1965 Voting Rights Act, 24th Amendment to the Constitution banning the Poll Tax) had changed many of the racial policies, but there was still much to accomplish to undo centuries of discrimination, and many in the movement were losing patience. The Civil Rights movement had been based on nonviolent protest under the leadership of Martin Luther King since the mid-fifties, but when he was murdered in April of 1968, that seemed to signal a transition to more violent means to achieve equality. Race riots took place in most of the larger American cities in the spring and summer of 1968. The more radical "Black Power" movement began to gain followers in the late sixties. Although King's approach had de-emphasized race in an effort to gain equality between the races, the Black Power movement in many ways sought to emphasize the differences between the races to establish a black identity. Black athletes had long stayed out of political movements and even the Civil Rights movement for fear taking sides would hurt their chances to advance in their respective sports. In 1967 sports sociologist Harry Edwards proposed a boycott by black American athletes of the 1968 Mexico City games to call attention to the basic inequities between the races in American society. Some athletes favored the boycott, but most did not. When a vote was taken, fewer than half wanted to pass up the games—similar to the proposed boycott of 1936, most felt they had trained too hard to pass up this chance at glory. Edwards decided to make the boycott optional, and informed the athletes who went to Mexico City that they should protest in their own way. UCLA basketball star Lew Alcindor (later Kareem Abdul Jabar) decided to skip the 1968 Olympics. Sprinter **Tommie Smith** had originally supported the boycott but later decided to go to the games. He remained defiant when he told reporters, "I don't want Brundage presenting me any medals."[24] After Smith won the gold medal in the 200-meter relay, he and fellow American **John Carlos**, who had won the bronze medal, mounted the podium, and when "The Star Spangled Banner" began, they bowed their heads and raised their fists covered by black gloves in a Black Power salute. Avery Brundage was furious at this obvious political statement at a place where he believed it did not belong, and he immediately suspended both men from the American team, barred them from the Olympic village, and gave them 48 hours to leave Mexico City. Not all of the black athletes supported the actions of Smith and Carlos. Boxer George Foreman, although understanding their motivations, believed it did not make sense to protest in an arena that had been less racist than most. Almost as memorable as the iconic pictures of Smith and Carlos was that of Foreman waving a tiny American flag after his winning the gold medal in the heavyweight division. After all the controversy and dust cleared, the Americans were back on top of the medal count

Carlos and Smith's Black power salute at '68 Olympics. © Bettmann/CORBIS

with 107 ahead of the USSR's 91. Hungary finished third with 32, and just edging out East Germany (25 medals) for fourth was West Germany, with 26. It was the first time since the country's separation in 1955 that they had not competed together.

Brundage's term was ending as IOC president in 1968, and some believed he should step down. One of Edwards's terms to lift the boycott was for Brundage's ousting as president. Others believed he was too old (he had passed 80), and it was time for him to retire. Kenya's IOC representative, Sir Reginald Alexander, told him: "Avery, you're eighty; you're on the top . . . Move now, and history will record you as one of the greatest."[25] Stubborn Brundage refused to step down, and he was reelected by a wide margin, but he also made it known that the 1972 games would be his last, and he would step down at the age of 85. His final Olympics would prove to be the most tragic in the history of the games. The **1972 Olympic Games** were held in Munich, West Germany, the first games held in Germany since the 1936 Berlin games. West German Olympic officials were eager to distance themselves from the Nazi regime and showcase their democratic and optimistic country to the world. They even gave the event the official motto of "the Happy Games." For the first 10 days of the games, the name seemed appropriate. The events went smoothly, and everyone seemed to be having a good time. The Americans had a hero in swimmer **Mark Spitz**, who won seven gold medals—setting a world record with each win. His record for most gold medals in a single Olympics stood until 2008, when Michael Phelps won eight. The biggest controversy occurred on the basketball court, when the Americans were playing the Soviets for the gold medal; when the clock ran out, it appeared the Americans had won 50–49. For some inexplicable reason the head of the international basketball federation decided to put three seconds on the clock and awarded the USSR the ball, and they proceeded to make a last-second shot to win 51–50. The Americans protested, and both the timekeeper and one of the referees, Italian Renate Righetto, agreed with the Americans. Righetto said that the additional time was "completely illegal and an infraction of the rules of the basketball game."[26] An international jury who heard the official protest rejected the

Americans' claim. The three communist countries on the jury (Cuba, Hungary, and Poland) voted against the protest. The Americans refused their silver medals, and they are still in a vault in Lausanne, Switzerland.

On the morning of the 11th day of the games, everything changed. The basketball controversy paled in comparison to what happened on September 5. Early that morning six Palestinian terrorists climbed the wall of the Olympic village and were joined by two more Palestinians who had been working inside the village. They began knocking on doors—they were looking for the athletes representing Israel. They found nine of them and took them hostage along with two coaches and two doctors. When two of them fought back, Moshe Weinberg and David Berger, they were killed. The terrorists, who called themselves Black September, demanded the release of 234 Palestinians held in Israel. To show officials they were serious, they tossed Weinberg's mutilated corpse out the window. Negotiators moved in to talk to the terrorists and managed to get the two doctors released, but otherwise, they could only postpone the terrorists' deadlines. Eventually that evening, the Palestinians were allowed to take the nine hostages to an airfield, where they were told they would be provided a plane to take them to an unspecified Arab country. Munich police then planned to ambush the terrorists as they boarded the plane. Unfortunately, the police underestimated the number of terrorists. When they opened fire, they did not get them all, and the remaining terrorists killed every Israeli hostage. In the end, nine athletes, two coaches, a West German police officer, and five of the terrorists were killed. The question for the IOC was what to do next—should the remainder of the games go on or be cancelled? Brundage made his feelings known quickly that cancelling the games would be giving in to the terrorists. The IOC decided to have a memorial service the following morning and halt the games for 24 hours and then resume. Israeli Prime Minister Golda Meir thought the games should be continued. Brundage announced at the memorial service that "we cannot allow a handful of terrorists to destroy this nucleus of international cooperation and good will we have in the Olympic Movement." Irish IOC member and successor to Brundage after the 1972 games, Lord Killanin, who was no admirer of Brundage said, "his stubborn determination saved the Olympic Movement one last time."[27] The games took on an understandably somber tone for the remaining four days of competition, and the Soviets ended up back on top of the medal count with 99 total to the Americans' 94, with East and West Germany finishing third and fourth with 66 and 40, respectively.

Age of the Boycott, Miracle on Ice, End of the Cold War, Abandonment of Amateurism

Beginning with the 1976 games in Montreal, boycotts over political issues dominated the next three Olympics. Avery Brundage would have hated the mixture of international politics with his "pure" Olympic Movement, but perhaps mercifully, he had died in 1975 at the age of 87. Allen Guttmann points to an Egyptian athlete to illustrate the frustration that must have been felt by many who were affected by the boycotts. Shot-putter Youssef Nagui Assad tried out for the Egyptian Olympic team in 1968 at the age of 23. He failed to qualify by two centimeters. In 1972 he made the team but was ordered home by his government after the massacre to show solidarity with the Palestinians. He again made the team in 1976, but Egypt decided to boycott the games to protest New Zealand's rugby ties with South Africa, and they again brought their athletes home from Montreal. In 1980 when he was 35, he made the team in what would be his last chance at Olympic glory, but his government again boycotted the games to protest the USSR's war in Afghanistan.

Days before the 1976 Olympics were to start in Montreal, it was brought to the attention of the IOC that the New Zealand rugby team had toured South Africa, which was still being punished by the IOC for their apartheid policies, and many countries demanded that the New Zealand be barred from the games. IOC president Killanin said the IOC had no authority over rugby, which was not an Olympic sport, so it did nothing. As a result, 28 African countries ordered their teams home in protest. The Soviets amassed an incredible 125 medals that year, with the Americans picking up 94 and the East Germans taking 90. Those three countries would not compete again in the Summer Olympics for 12 years. In 1979 the USSR invaded Afghanistan, and the United States led a boycott of the 1980 games in Moscow. A total of 65 nations boycotted the games, which left only 81 to compete—the fewest since 1956. Not surprisingly, the Soviets and East Germans dominated the medal count with 195 and 126, respectively. Four years later, the Soviets and their allies got their chance at revenge when they boycotted the 1984 Los Angeles games. With no Eastern bloc countries competing,

US Hockey vs. USSR in 1980 Olympics. © Bettmann/CORBIS

the Americans dominated. This included **Mary Lou Retton**, who became the first gymnast outside Eastern Europe to win the all-around competition. **Carl Lewis** equaled Jesse Owens's 1936 record of four gold medals in the exact same events: 100 and 200 meters, 4 × 100 meter relay, and the long jump. Michael Jordan and Patrick Ewing helped the United States win the gold medal in basketball. Weightlifting suffered the most by the Soviet boycott—94 of the top 100 weightlifters in the world were absent. The United States captured 83 gold medals in 1984 and 174 medals overall.

Although the two superpowers did not compete in the 1980 and 1984 summer games, they did during the winter games. This chapter has mainly been concerned with the summer games, but something happened in Lake Placid, New York, in 1980 that must be mentioned. With the only exception being the 1960 Winter Olympics in Squaw Valley, California, when the American hockey team won the gold medal, the sport had been dominated by the Soviets since the 1950s. That domination was expected to continue in February of 1980 when the winter games came again the United States, this time in upstate New York at Lake Placid. Just days before the Olympics were to commence, the U.S. team was manhandled 10–3 by the Soviets in Madison Square Garden. The Soviet coach later said this caused his team to underestimate the Americans. Apparently many countries did because, in the opening round, the United States scored a goal to tie heavily favored Sweden with 27 seconds left and then defeated Czechoslovakia 7–3. Those were the two toughest opponents they would face before the medal round, and they then reeled off three victories against Norway, Romania, and West Germany. With a 4–0–1 record, they qualified for the medal round, and their first opponent would be the USSR. The United States had long been at a disadvantage due to the IOC allowing the Soviets to essentially have professional athletes on their Olympic teams since they first joined Olympic play in 1952. The American team in 1980 once again was made up of college players and other amateurs. To show the caliber of the Soviet team, they played nine exhibition matches against National Hockey League (NHL) professionals and won five, lost three, and tied one. The previous year this team defeated a group of NHL all-stars 6–0. No one gave the Americans much of a chance in this matchup—in fact, ABC television did not even cover the game live when they played on February 22. Although the Americans fell behind early, they kept the Soviets within reach and only trailed 3–2 going into the final period. The fears of the Soviet coach seemed to be borne out in the final period, as they seemed complacent when trying to hold on to win, but the Americans scored the final two goals of the game to win 4–3. In 1980, the United States was mired in an economic recession and a crisis of confidence both at home and internationally—it seemed we were behind the Soviets in everything, and this improbable win in

1992 Dream Team. © Dimitri Iundt/TempSport/Corbis

the Olympics was much needed by the American people. Most Americans believed that win got the United States the gold medal, but they had to defeat Finland in the next round. They trailed 2–1 in the third period but again came from behind to score three goals and win the gold medal 4–2. As the clock ticked down the final seconds of the win against the USSR, ABC's Al Michaels uttered the now-famous phrase, "Do you believe in miracles? Yes!" The win in Lake Placid by the Americans is forever remembered as the "**Miracle on Ice.**"

The 1988 Summer Games were played in Seoul, South Korea. These games marked the first and last of many things. They marked the first time since 1976 that both the Soviet Union and the United States participated in a summer games. They also marked the first time there had really been no major boycotts of an Olympics in 20 years. They also marked end of the Soviet–American rivalry, although that was not known at the time. It was also the end of amateurism. Spain's Juan Antonio Samaranch had succeeded Lord Killanin as IOC president when his term ended in 1980. Samaranch had advocated doing away with the old amateur rule and opening the games to all as early as 1981. By the Seoul games in 1988, the only athletes ineligible for participation were professional boxers, soccer players over the age of 23, and National Basketball Association (NBA) players. After the Seoul games, the IOC decided to allow each country's Olympic committee to determine eligibility for its team. In 1992 the American Olympic Committee ruled that NBA players were eligible, and what became known as the "**Dream Team**" was formed. The team was anchored around three of the greatest basketball players of all time: Michael Jordan, Magic Johnson, and Larry Bird. The only player on the roster with no professional experience was Christian Laettner, who had just won back-to-back national championships with Duke University. He beat out Shaquille O'Neil for the last roster spot. The average margin of victory for the American team was over 43 points—the closest game was their gold medal victory over Croatia 117–85. There have been versions of the original since but it is widely agreed that was the greatest basketball team ever assembled. So much changed in the world between 1988 and 1992—the Berlin Wall, the great symbol of communist exclusion since 1961, came down in 1989. Then there was the breakup of the Soviet Union. The 1992 games in Barcelona, Spain, saw a unified Germany compete for the first time since 1964. Some countries formerly in the Soviet Union competed independently, but 12 former Soviet nations band together to compete for what was called the "Unified Team." That team won the most medals at Barcelona (112) just ahead of the United States (108), and the unified Germany finished third with 82.

Conclusion

In the two decades since the 1992 games, American interest in the Olympics (with the exception of 1996, when the games were in Atlanta) has been on a steady decline. Although the Americans have been on the top of the medal count in every Olympics beginning with 1996, something seems to be missing. The end of the Cold War also brought an end to a great athletic rivalry. Since the terrorist attacks on the United States in 2001, Americans have been fighting a "War on Terror," which is very different from the Cold War—terrorists are a nameless, faceless enemy. The Soviets were identifiable—Americans knew who their enemy was, and victories against them were made all the more sweet. As Bob Mathias said in 1952 referring to the Soviets, "You *had* to beat them." When looking at the Olympic Movement from an international standpoint, it has survived wars, terrorist attacks, and boycotts, and it has grown—from its inception in 1896, when 14 nations sent 241 athletes to Athens to compete in 43 events in 9 sports, to the London games in 2012 when 204 nations sent almost 11,000 athletes to compete in 302 events in 26 sports. Pierre de Coubertin would be amazed at what his dream has become—but he probably wouldn't always be pleased. He shared Avery Brundage's concern with politics mixing with athletics and would have been appalled with the boycott movements of the 1970s and 1980s. Brundage's other concern was with the commercialization of the games, which also began in the 1970s and has continued unabated until the present day. Host cities of Olympics for years knew they would lose money on the venture, but with the advent of television revenue, that changed—it became a financial boon for cities to get the Olympics. NBC, for example, paid $300 million for the rights to televise the Seoul Olympics in 1988. The influence of multinational corporations on the Olympics could also be felt beginning in the late 20th century. Peter Ueberroth, organizer of the 1984 games in Los Angeles, persuaded many companies to donate giant sums of money to the event and, in the end, the games actually made $200 million. Allowing professionals to participate would probably have been something Coubertin would have (and Brundage did) argue against, but it was an argument they most likely would have lost. Coubertin worried about nationalism entering into the games but it (and all the politics that go along with it) has been a part of the movement from the beginning. In the end, that is probably what made the movement a success because people want to cheer and marvel at great athletes—but they will cheer a little harder and with more emotion when it's a great athlete from home.

Notes

1. Allen Guttmann, *The Olympics; History of the Modern Games* (University of Illinois Press: Urbana and Chicago, 1992), 15.
2. Ibid., 3.
3. Ibid., 18.
4. Ibid., 27.
5. Bill Mallon and Ian Buchanan, "To No Earthly King . . .," *Journal of Olympic History*, September 1999.
6. Ibid.
7. Guttmann, *The Olympics*, 31.
8. Ibid., 33.
9. Ibid., 34.
10. Ibid., 32.
11. Ibid., 43.
12. Ibid., 48.
13. Ibid., 52.
14. Ibid., 54.
15. Benjamin Rader, *American Sports* (Upper Saddle River, NJ: Prentice Hall, 2009), 208.
16. Guttmann, *The Olympics*, 61.
17. Ibid., 60.

18. Ibid., 68.
19. Ibid., 59.
20. Ibid., 74.
21. Rader, *American Sports*, 301.
22. Ibid.
23. Ibid., 126.
24. Ibid., 131.
25. Ibid., 121.
26. Ibid., 138.
27. Ibid., 140.

CHAPTER
Ten

Basketball

With everything else that was happening in Berlin during the 1936 Olympics, going almost unnoticed was the fact that a lesser known (at least internationally) sport was making its debut as an Olympic event. The first-ever medals for basketball were presented to the teams by an elderly gentleman who had to be the proudest man in the room for two reasons. The presenter was **Dr. James Naismith** who invented the game 45 years earlier when he was a 30-year-old athletics instructor at the international training school for the YMCA in Springfield, Massachusetts. He must have been proud to see how far his game had come in less than half a century and also because the silver medals went to his native country Canada and the gold medals were won by his adopted home country the United States. The bronze medals went to Mexico; and although the sport was seen as a North American game, it would soon spread worldwide to become one of the most popular sports on earth.

Birth of the Game

James Naismith and his peach baskets
Image courtesy of Library of Congress

James Naismith was born in 1861 in Ramsay Township, Ontario. Growing up he played various sports and was a gifted athlete. One of the sports he played was "duck on a rock," which was a medieval game where the participants tried to knock small stones off a larger rock with other rocks. Naismith quickly learned the best way to knock the stones off was with a high arching, soft toss of the rock as opposed to lower, harder throws. After playing football, rugby, soccer, lacrosse, and gymnastics for McGill University in Montreal, he received a Bachelor of Arts degree in physical education. He then served as McGill's first athletic director before leaving to go to the YMCA training school in 1891. One of the first tasks he was given in the fall of 1891 by his boss, Luther Gulick, was to devise a game that would accomplish two goals: one, span the time between football ending and baseball beginning during the long New England winters, and two, "restore order in an unruly gym class of hypercompetitive types who were bored with gymnastics."[1] Naismith believed there had to be a ball involved to keep interest up but knew it would have to be a lighter ball (Naismith settled on a soccer ball); and, because it was in an enclosed space, there should be no bats, sticks, or rackets involved. To move the ball, players would have to use their hands to pass the ball to each other, but to eliminate roughness in the sport, he thought there should be no running with the ball (because that is where the violence stemmed from in other sports). Remembering the childhood game of "duck on a rock" he thought the goal should be elevated so balls would have to be lofted in the air over players to count as a score instead of through or around them like lacrosse or soccer. When unable to find boxes the correct size, he found two peach baskets and fastened them to the bottom of the elevated track around the gym which were about 10 feet off the floor. The first game was played on December 21, 1891, and it was an immediate hit. There was no name for the game and one of the students, Frank Mahan, suggested "Naismith Ball" in honor of the inventor but Naismith refused. Mahan then turned to the goals themselves and offered the name "basket ball." The name stuck and students took the game home that Christmas break and introduced it to their hometowns.

In January 1892, the Springfield College's newspaper, *The Triangle*, published Naismith's original 13 rules for the game and "basket ball" was a secret no longer. Many of the original rules remain part of the modern game including the first three that stated the ball could be thrown or batted in any direction but that it should never be punched with a fist and that a player cannot run with the ball. Rule 13 indicated the winning team was the side that had scored the most goals when the time expired. The nine rules in between have been modified or dropped altogether. Naismith laid out what constituted a foul in rule 5: "no shouldering, holding, pushing, tripping, or striking in any way the person of an opponent shall be allowed."[2] Rule 10 gave power to the referee (or in Naismith's term "umpire") to not only determine if a player had been fouled but also to disqualify a player when he received three fouls and to award the opposing team a goal. That rule has been modified to five fouls (six in the NBA) and the opposing team given the opportunity to score from the free-throw line (free-throws were not part of the original rules). The biggest addition to the rules that revolutionized the game was the addition of "dribbling" (bouncing) the ball. Initially it was introduced as a defensive maneuver in 1893 when players were allowed to "pivot" on one foot; but, in 1896, Yale employed the dribble as an offensive strategy in 1896, and for the next 30 years there were efforts to curtail or even ban its use. Restrictions such as disallowing the overhead bounce, dribbling with both hands, and the double dribble were put into place by the end of the decade. Between 1901 and 1908 official rules did not allow the dribbler to shoot the ball. Finally, in the late 1920s, the dribble was completely outlawed by the joint committee of college coaches by a close vote of 9–8. They felt passing the ball was the more pure form of the game that Naismith had in mind. They later reconsidered their vote and the dribble has been part of the game ever since. The one unintended consequence of a Naismith rule was with rule number 9. It had to do with the inbounding of the ball in which the rule stated: "When the ball goes out of bounds, it shall be thrown into the field of play by the person first touching it."[3] The unforeseen result was what Naismith was trying to avoid—violence and injury. There was a mad dash to the ball every time it went out of bounds between players trying to be the first to touch the ball and, therefore, keep possession of it for his team. In 1913 the rule was officially changed to award the ball to the opposing team of whichever player *last* touched it before it went out of bounds.

The game spread at an amazing rate throughout the country during the 1890s. Naismith himself had something to do this because his classes would prove to be so popular that they overflowed; and when passersby heard the excited shouts of the students playing the game, they would come in to see what the excitement was all about. Naismith quickly realized this was not only a popular sport with the participants themselves but it could also prove to be a great spectator sport. It was also a sport that he believed should not be limited to males. Early on there were teams of girls organized and one of the players who was part of that inaugural girls' team was Maude Sherman. Maude must have caught the eye of the teacher for more than just her athletic ability because she would eventually become James Naismith's wife. Naismith took a team on the road to play exhibitions throughout New England and upstate New York in 1892. Naismith originally had nine players on each side because he had 18 students in his class, but by the mid-1890s most teams settled on five players per side because nine made for an overly crowded floor. One of Naismith's colleagues at Springfield was Amos Alonzo Stagg, who went to the University of Chicago to become its legendary football coach in 1892. He

Amos Alonzo Stagg.
Image courtesy of Library of Congress

CHAPTER *Ten*

also introduced basketball to the college and would later become its basketball coach for a short period of time in the 1920s while still coaching football. While many colleges did introduce the sport on their campuses, it was really the YMCA that can be credited with its spread. Graduates from the Springfield training college fanned out all over the country and organized teams far and wide. By 1896 there was a national basketball tournament set up by the YMCA to determine the best teams in the nation. Basketball so overwhelmed other sports at YMCAs that some Y's actually banned the sport—the Philadelphia YMCA being one example. This did not lead to the game's demise but quite the contrary—independent teams were organized and the game was played in abandoned warehouses and dance halls.

According to Neil Isaacs in his book, *All the Moves,* by the turn of the 20th century, there were four types of basketball games being played across the country. The first was a cage game where the court actually had a cage built around it so there was no out of bounds and the play was continuous. The second was a game that had no restrictions on dribbling. The third was a passing game with restrictions on dribbling and the fourth was a "recreative" game in which the court was divided into sections in which players would have to stay in their sections to prevent "massing."[4] This was a problem when there were no limits put on the numbers of participants (it is believed the record number of participants occurred at Cornell when a gym class of 100 was divided into two 50-person teams). Eventually the first three versions merged into one and the cage was removed (although cages were still part of some versions of the game as late as the 1920s). The fourth version would be part of women's basketball for a large portion of the 20th century. Iowa and Oklahoma girls' high school basketball, for example, played six on six games in which three players would always play defense on one side of the court and the other three would always play offense on the other side of the court. Iowa abandoned the practice in 1993 and Oklahoma in 1995.

College Basketball

At some point in its first decade of existence the name of the game was changed from two words to one because in 1901 the new name was evident when the *Reach Official Basketball Guide* began publication. In 1905, the Spalding Company joined the fray when it published its *Official Collegiate Basketball Guide* covering primarily the Ivy League schools. Although Eastern schools provided the leadership much as they had in football, basketball spread to the Midwest and West much more quickly than football had so the Ivys did not get the chance to dominate the sport like they had in football. One Midwestern school that would become a college basketball power would be the **University of Kansas**. Once again, James Naismith can be given some credit for this future power as he took a job in 1898 as not only the university's chapel director (he would eventually be ordained as a Presbyterian minister in 1915) and physical education instructor but also its first basketball coach. He coached for nine seasons (until 1907) and, ironically, would be the only coach in the school's history with a losing record (55-60). Although he invented the game, he was never a real student of it—he viewed it as a diversion and thought other sports like gymnastics were better for physical fitness. He once said, "You can't coach basketball; you just play it."[5] One of his protégé's proved that statement wrong—**Forrest Clare "Phog" Allen** played for Naismith's last three teams and then succeeded him as coach in 1907. In 1909 he left to pursue a medical degree in osteopathic medicine and returned after World War I to coach Kansas from 1919 to 1956. He compiled a record of 746 wins and 264 losses. Although there were not official national champions crowned until the 1930s, it is believed that two teams he coached in the early 1920s were the best teams in the country. The first was in 1922 and the second was in 1923. Playing for both of these teams was **Adolph Rupp** who followed in Allen's coaching footsteps and became the head coach at the University of Kentucky in 1930 and coached until 1972, winning four national championships.

Allen's last national championship team was in 1952 and on that team was a player named **Dean Smith**. Smith became the head coach at North Carolina in 1961. When he retired in 1997, he had won two national championships and was the winningest college basketball coach of all time followed by Rupp in second and Allen in third. Those three schools remain among the college basketball elites to this day. The branches of the Kansas "coaching tree" are some of the strongest in the history of the game.

In the early part of the 20th century, basketball was for the most part an unorganized, regional sport in which most games were of the "pick up" variety in driveways and gymnasiums. The YMCA did organize games and played local high schools and colleges, but college basketball was by no means a national phenomenon. Most colleges did not have large enough gyms to hold people who wanted to watch games so it was really not a spectator sport as late as the 1920s. It was in that decade that arenas were built in the East to accommodate the newly found popularity of another sport—boxing. With the coming of the Great Depression in the 1930s, there was a declining interest in boxing; so owners of these large arenas began looking for ways to fill their seats. Basketball became one way to do that. In 1931 New York Mayor Jimmy Walker asked a group of sportswriters to put together basketball tripleheaders in one of these arenas—Madison Square Garden. The proceeds raised from these games would benefit the city's depression relief fund so they became known as the "Relief Games." The games filled the Garden to its 16,000-seat capacity and were a tremendous success for the three years they were held. In 1934, one of the sportswriters who helped organize the games decided to take it upon himself to start his own tournament. **Edward S. "Ned" Irish** decided to rent the Garden and host his own tournament, and whatever profits were left over would go to him instead of the relief fund. He reduced the tripleheaders to doubleheaders and renamed them the "**Garden Games**." The games became extremely successful and important for nationalizing college basketball. Irish would usually schedule popular local teams against the best teams from around the country. An example of this occurred in 1936 when Irish invited Stanford University and its star **Hank Luisetti** to play Long Island University which had won 43 consecutive games. Luisetti was the star of the game scoring one-third of Stanford's points (15) and leading them to a 45–31 victory that ended Long Island's win streak. More important for the future of the game, however, was how Luisetti scored. Up to that point the common way to shoot the ball was the two-handed set shot with both feet on the floor. Luisetti shot with one hand and was a pioneer in what would become the "jump shot" with the player's feet leaving the floor. Not everyone was impressed with the new style—City College coach **Nat Holman** said "That's not basketball. If my boys ever shot one-handed, I'd quit coaching."[6] Much to Holman's dismay, the new style was the future of the game. When it was combined with elimination of the center jump after each basket in 1937, the offensive part of the game was enhanced.

The "Capital" of College Basketball

New York City was the capital of college basketball in the 1930s and 1940s not only due to the Garden Games but also because there was a group of sportswriters who decided to organize a tournament that would crown a national champion on the court instead of by votes of committees. The Metropolitan Basketball Writers Association began the **National Invitational Tournament (NIT)** in 1938 with the writers inviting what they considered to be the best teams in the country with the winner being considered that season's national champion. The first tournament only consisted of six teams with Temple winning title. In 1941 the tournament expanded to eight teams and after the war, as the number of quality teams across the country expanded, so did the number of teams invited to the tournament. By 1950 there were 12 teams in the NIT. In 1939 the NCAA began its own postseason tournament with eight teams but it was not until the 1950s that the NIT was surpassed by the NCAA tournament in prestige when it expanded to 16 teams and it became *the* tournament to be invited to. Teams could play in both tournaments and three that did so between 1940 and 1950 (Utah in 1940, Kentucky in 1949, and City College of New York (CCNY) in 1950) won both tournaments and were crowned the national champion. In 1970 the NCAA disallowed teams from playing in any other postseason tournaments if they were invited to the NCAA tournament. The NIT was eventually relegated to the "next best" tournament for teams that did not make the NCAA invitation list. As with all sports, college basketball suffered during the World War II years with most college-aged men joining the service. Following the war, Ned Irish decided to expand the Garden Games to Philadelphia and Buffalo so teams travelling east would be guaranteed games in three cities. He also increased the number of doubleheaders being staged at the Garden to 25 and, during the 1950 season, the Garden drew over 600,000 spectators to watch college basketball games. You knew you had arrived when you were invited to play at the Garden. The future of college basketball in New York appeared bright but that all changed in 1951.

In the spring of 1950, as mentioned earlier Coach Holman's CCNY team won both the NIT and the NCAA tournaments to be named the national champion for that season. In January 1951, New York District Attorney Frank Hogan arrested seven men including three of the star players of that CCNY team for "**point-shaving**" basketball games for gamblers. The point spread was a recent innovation that allowed gamblers to bet on the outcomes of games based on how many points the winning team won by. For example, if a team is favored by 10 points but they only win by 9, those who bet on the losing team actually win the bet. Prior to the point spread, a gambler would have to bet on teams based on odds and the less-talented teams (with essentially no chance of winning) would rarely have anyone wager on them. This change allowed gamblers to tempt players on very good teams to "shave" points for money meaning they would still win the game but not win by the point spread because the good teams usually were favored by a large number and could afford to "take it easy" on opponents and still win. There had been rumors for years that this was going on but it was not until Hogan's formal investigation using sting operations to infiltrate teams did the rumors prove to be true. Eventually the scandal spread as 32 players from seven schools were implicated. In his final report, Hogan accurately pointed out that the cause of this problem ran deeper than just a few kids trying earn some quick money: "Underlying the scandal was the blatant commercialism which had permeated college basketball. What once had been a minor sport had hippodromed into a big business."[7]

The long-range effect on college basketball was a shift from the big city arenas back to the college campuses. New York bore the brunt of the shift as the Garden Games ended because colleges refused to send teams to New York City. Although New York continued to host the NIT, it would not host an NCAA tournament game for over 30 years. New York became the symbol for corruption and a paranoia that was enveloping the entire nation during the early 1950s. The Red Scare had everyone afraid of a communist infiltration of the country and any scandal fed that fear. New York colleges themselves were affected because, even though the administrative leaders were not to blame (Coach Holman, for instance, was never implicated in the scandal), many of the schools either de-emphasized basketball or dropped the sport altogether. As a result, schools began building fieldhouses on their campuses that would hold enough people who still wanted to see their schools play the sport. A good example of this is Allen Fieldhouse on the campus of the University of Kansas that began construction in 1952; but because of a postwar limit on use of steel for construction, it was not completed until 1955 (after there was a loophole in the federal law found where if they constructed a room that could store guns and ammunition they could call the building an "armory"). The building cost $2.5 million (almost $22 million in today's money), seats 17,000, and was named for the legendary current coach at the time, "Phog" Allen. Although Allen only coached in the building for one season before his retirement in 1956, the building has become a symbol of home court dominance over the last half century as the Jayhawks have amassed a winning percentage of .865. A banner that hangs in the building sums up the difficulty for opposing teams that reads: "Pay Heed All Who Enter: Beware of the Phog."

One of the greatest players to ever play home games at Allen Fieldhouse (or any other arena) was **Wilt Chamberlain**. A member of Allen's freshman team during the 1955–56 season, he joined the varsity following Allen's retirement. Chamberlain was born in 1936 in Philadelphia and was already 6 feet, 11 inches tall when he entered high school (he would eventually reach 7 feet, 1 inch) and was a dominant player for his high school team. In his three seasons, his team won two Philadelphia city championships only losing three games. He averaged 37.4 points per game, once scoring an incredible 90 points in one game. Over 200 schools were interested in the seven-footer upon his graduation in 1955. Chamberlain wanted to venture away from the East Coast, and he ruled out the South because of its continued racial segregation. He settled on KU after being recruited by Allen and visiting the campus. He always had the utmost respect for the legendary coach and was extremely disappointed when Allen retired after Chamberlain's first season. His biographer, Robert Cherry, believes that he probably would not have gone to Kansas had he known of the coach's impending retirement. In retrospect he probably should have known as Kansas had a mandatory retirement policy when an employee reached the age of 70. James Naismith had hoped height would not be a great factor in the game which is why he included his eighth rule which stated: "A goal shall be made when the ball is thrown or batted from the grounds into the basket and stays there, providing those defending the goal do not touch or disturb the goal. If the ball rests on the edges, and the opponent moves the basket, it shall count as a goal."[8] This was the forerunner to the defensive goaltending rule that was codified in 1944 to also include touching the ball by a defender while on the rim or on its downward arch toward the basket. World War II had some effect on the revolution of the height of players because some branches of the armed forces would not accept men of a certain height so they were left at home during the 1940s and many of them went to college and played basketball. The average height of college teams began to creep up in the 1940s. In addition to the goaltending rule, other rules were added to the game attempting to negate height advantage—in 1945 offensive players were given only three seconds to stand in the lane (shaded area under the basket) and in 1956 the lane was widened from 6 feet to 12 feet. In addition, the two spots closest to the basket must be occupied by a member of the opposing team of the free throw shooter to prevent easy baskets after a missed free throw. The following year offensive goaltending was also banned, and grasping the rim was deemed unsportsmanlike conduct.

These later rules were put in place as a direct result of one player: Wilt Chamberlain. It did not seem to have the desired effect because he was as dominant in college as he had been in high school. In his first game for the varsity team he scored 51 points and grabbed 31 rebounds—both Kansas school records. He led the Jayhawks to the conference title and to the championship game of the NCAA tournament in 1957. They met North Carolina in the championship game and coach Frank McGuire implemented many unorthodox tactics like triple-team defense on Chamberlain which did not seem to affect him, but it rattled his teammates as they shot a dismal 27 percent from the floor. As teams often did, North Carolina got the lead in the second half and stalled (which was possible before the advent of the shot clock) and won the game. Despite scoring 23 points and getting 14 rebounds in the game and being voted the tournament's outstanding player, Chamberlain later said it was the most difficult loss of his life. The following season was even more difficult as he ran into triple-teams and stalls against almost every team they played. When Kansas failed to win the conference title in 1958 (only conference winners were invited to the NCAA tournament at the time), Chamberlain decided he had had enough of college basketball and decided to turn professional before his senior season. The NBA had a rule at the time that stipulated that only

Wilt Chamberlain. Image courtesy of Library of Congress

players who had earned their degree could come directly into the league so Chamberlain signed a contract to play for the Harlem Globetrotters, which he did in 1958–59, before joining the NBA. Chamberlain was not the only big man to star in the college ranks in the early post-war years. **George Mikan** (6' 10") had been the first as he was named the NCAA Player of the Year in both 1944 and 1945 and helped DePaul University win the NIT tournament in 1945 including scoring 53 points against Rhode Island which equaled the scoring of the *entire* Rhode Island team (DePaul won 97–53). A contemporary of Chamberlain was **Bill Russell** (6' 10") who played for the San Francisco Dons and, although they never played against one another in college (Russell graduated in 1956 before Chamberlain started on the varsity squad), they would establish an intense rivalry in the NBA that is examined later in this chapter.

Walton, Wooden, Jabbar.
© Villafuerte/AP/AP/Corbis

The UCLA Dynasty

Two dominant big men of the next generation would help establish college basketball's first great dynasty. The **UCLA Bruins** were not a college basketball powerhouse when **John Wooden** became their coach in 1948. Wooden had been a great player in his own right as an all-America guard on three Purdue teams—his senior season Purdue was named the national champion in 1932. After serving in the Navy during World War II, he returned to his home state to become head basketball coach at Indiana Teachers College (later Indiana State) and, after two seasons there, was named head coach of the University of California Los Angeles. Although the Bruins only managed an 11–12 record the year before he arrived, Wooden's first team went 22–7 and won a conference title. By the 1950s UCLA was a regular invitee postseason tournaments but it was the 1960s in which something special developed for Wooden. In the 1963–64 season, UCLA did not lose a game going 30–0 and won its first national championship. The following season the team, although losing two games during the season, repeated as national champions. The 1966–67 season saw the emergence of a 7-foot 2-inch center named **Lew Alcindor** for the Bruins who dominated the game over the next three seasons and helped UCLA win three consecutive national championships. He still holds several UCLA records including highest career scoring average (26.4 points), season scoring average (29 in 1967), most points in a season (870 in 1967), and most points in a single game (61). Alcindor would later convert to the Muslim faith and change his name to **Kareem Abdul-Jabbar**. Picking up where Alcindor left off was another big center named **Bill Walton** who joined the Bruins in 1971. He was always listed at 6 feet, 11 inches but it is believed he was over seven feet tall but did not want to be classified as a seven-footer. Walton helped the Bruins to two more championships in 1972 and 1973, during which time UCLA won an NCAA-record 88 consecutive games; but, in 1974, not only did that streak end but so did the consecutive championship streak going back to 1967 when they lost in the semifinals in 1974 to North Carolina State. Walton always said it was the biggest disappointment of his career. The next season would be Wooden's last and his team gave him a retirement present of his 10th national championship. With his retirement came the end of an incredible dynasty as UCLA would not win another title for two decades. In retirement Wooden became the "grand old man" of the game writing several books on his philosophy and being the sage whom everyone went to for advice. He dispensed this advice for a long time as he lived until 2010, dying four months shy of his 100th birthday.

March Madness

UCLA won its championships before college basketball really emerged as a television sport (the first nationally broadcast college basketball game did not occur until 1968 when the Alcindor-led Bruins faced the Houston Cougars in front of over 50,000 at the Astrodome—a game in which UCLA actually lost). It was not until the late 1970s that regular season games were regularly televised—early rounds in the NCAA tournament were not even televised until the early 1980s. The tournament field was expanded to 48 teams in 1980 and in 1982 CBS allowed a new cable station called ESPN to broadcast early games, and it was the network's first contract to cover a major NCAA event. The popularity of the tournament soared during the decade largely due to ESPN's coverage and the expansion of the tournament to 64 teams in 1985. By 1991, CBS wanted exclusive coverage of the

Final 4. Image © Pierre E. Debbas, 2013. Used under license from Shutterstock, Inc.

tournament and it elbowed ESPN aside. The event was now a miniseries that was spread out over a period of three weeks in March and was dubbed "**March Madness**" and television revenues tripled between 1987 and 1994 from $49 million to over $150 million. Because of this, CBS signed the largest television contract ever when it agreed to pay $1.7 billion for the rights to telecast the tournament through 2002. During the decade of the 1990s the "**Final 4**" (the final weekend of the tournament in which the semifinals and championship game occur) moved past baseball's World Series in television ratings. Current revenue from the tournament amounts to over $500 million annually.

Since the NCAA tournament began in 1939, the school with the most titles is UCLA with 11. Second is Kentucky with 8. Tied for third is North Carolina and Indiana with 5 each. Three of Indiana's championships came during the tenure of head coach **Bob Knight** (1971–2000). Nicknamed the "General" both because of his coaching at Army (1965–1971) as well as his stern and occasionally bombastic coaching methods, when Knight retired in 2008 he had amassed 902 wins—more than any other coach in history. During the 2011–12 season, Knight was passed on that list by one of his own. **Mike Krzyzewski** was one of Knight's players at West Point and was then one of his assistants. After taking over as head coach of Army during the 1970s, he became the head coach at Duke in 1980 where he built one of the true powerhouse programs of the last 30 years. During Krzyzewski's tenure at Duke, they have won four NCAA tournaments (fifth most all-time) and, going into the 2015–16 season, have won 945 games. In 2015 He became the first Division I coach to win over 1,000 games in his career. Every season it seems Duke is in the national championship conversation. College basketball's coaching trees indeed branch out everywhere and now "Coach K," as he is known, has numerous former players who have found success as head coaches throughout the country.

Coach K. Image © Aspen Photo, 2013. Used under license from Shutterstock, Inc.

Professional Basketball

When the subject of the history of professional basketball is broached, the conversation usually begins in 1949 with the establishment of the National Basketball Association (NBA). As Robert Peterson pointed out in his book, *Cages to Jumpshots, Pro Basketball's Early Years*, men were playing basketball for money not only prior to the Second World War but even before the First World

NY Original Celtics. Image courtesy of Library of Congress

War. As early as the 1890s, there is documentation of players being paid to play the game. Trenton, New Jersey, is often given credit with fielding the first all-paid team during the 1896–97 season. The team was originally organized at the local YMCA, but Trenton was part of the movement discussed earlier to remove basketball from the YMCA during the middle part of the decade so they moved into the Masonic Temple. The court was enclosed with what is believed to be the game's first cage—a 12-foot high wire mesh fence with doors on opposite ends to allow access by the players. There are three theories as to why the court was enclosed with a cage—the first two deal with the rules of the time. As mentioned previously, James Naismith's original rule of the first team to touch the ball out of bounds gets possession of it was still in effect so the cage would eliminate the battle among the spectators. The cage would also keep the game going continuously as there would be no stoppage of play for the ball going out of bounds. The third theory for the cage comes from a quote made by the sports editor of the local newspaper. After he watched a practice by the Trenton team he said, "They played like a lot of monkeys and should be put in a cage."[9] Although the court was negatively referred to as "Trenton's monkey cage,"[10] when the first professional league was formed in 1898, the cage was made mandatory for all teams. The cage never caught on with high school or YMCA teams but professional leagues particularly in the East continued to use the cage even after the out of bounds rule was changed. Some professional teams used the cage as late as the 1930s. The cage would live on for generations in the sports pages as writers would continue to refer to basketball as the "cage game" and players as "cagers" well into the second half of the century and it is even sometimes referred to by those names today.[11]

In the first two decades of the 20th century, at least a dozen professional leagues are known to have existed; but it was not until after World War I that college players began to turn professional on a regular basis. It was also not until the 1920s that newspapers began to cover professional basketball with some regularity. This is perhaps due to most newspapers not containing sports pages until that decade. Once the papers had a page devoted entirely to sports they had to fill it with something and, being the golden age of most sports, that was not usually a problem. Although not on the same level as names like Babe Ruth, Red Grange, Bill Tilden, or Bobby Jones, some names from professional basketball began to join them on the sports pages. The first team to be known nationally was the New York Celtics—later referred to as the "**Original Celtics**." The Celtics formed prior to World War I but did not become a dominant force in the professional game until the early 1920s. The team was part of various leagues over the years but gained the most fame when they were an independent barnstorming team

Nat Holman in his Celtics jersey. © Underwood & Underwood/Corbis.

travelling around the country taking on all comers. During the 1923–24 season, for example, they played 141 games winning 134, losing 6, and playing to a 32–32 tie with Mt. Vernon. The tie was unusual given most basketball leagues by this time had a provision for overtime periods. It is believed that the Celtics would often intentionally play to a tie at the end of regulation and then demand more money from the locals to continue the game. Perhaps Mt. Vernon in this case refused to pay them more. Most of the time the crowds would not reach the numbers that college games did (usually the Celtics would draw a few hundred spectators) but sometimes when they played in larger arenas like Madison Square Garden, they could draw numbers as high as 10,000.

The main reason for their success was the longevity of the Celtics core group of talented players who played together for years. They often made each other better and even devised plays that would be integral to the future of the game. One of their star players Nat Holman, who would go on to later success as the legendary coach of New York's City College, claiming it was the Celtics who perfected the "give and go" as well as the "pivot play" in their offense: "The Celtics made constant and important use of the play in which one man moved slowly across the foul-line territory near his own basket, received a pass and made a quick return play (give and go). However, the player moving across the court . . . finally came to a stop at the foul line where he stationed himself firmly . . . and made himself the central point in the offensive orbit. Thus was introduced the pivot play. The Original Celtics . . . developed this into the most damaging scoring play ever devised and did much to bring the play to its present state of comparative success."[12] The first professional league that could be truly considered a "national" league arrived in 1925 when the American Basketball League formed. It had teams stretching from as far east as Boston to as far west as Chicago. The ABL gained prestige when the Original Celtics joined its ranks in 1926 and won two consecutive championships. The Celtics so dominated the league that, after its second championship in 1928, the ABL ordered the Celtics broken up and its players distributed to the other teams. The Celtics decided instead to go back out on the barnstorming circuit and left the ABL. Although the team would continue to tour throughout the 1930s, it was never quite at the level it had been up to 1928 mainly because that core group began to get older and leave the team and the players that replaced them were never at the same level. The absence of the Celtics and the arrival of the Great Depression caused attendance at ABL games to plummet and the league to eventually fold in 1931.

The Harlem Globetrotters

Another barnstorming team that formed during the 1920s was **The Harlem Globetrotters**. In 1927, a young promoter from Chicago named Abraham Saperstein took a core group of black basketball players known as the Savoy Big 5 and renamed them the New York Harlem Globetrotters. Although the entire team was from Chicago, the headquarters for black culture at the time was Harlem and the name would add a mystique to the team and also announce that its membership was entirely black. The name Globetrotters implied that the team had travelled around the world (which would not be true until decades later). For the first few years before Saperstein could recruit new players, he suited up himself as a substitute which must have been an odd sight to spectators to see a 5' 5" white Jewish guy take the court occasionally. The early years were difficult for the Globetrotters as they would play in front of small crowds and not make much money. There was also the inherent racism of the country that made it difficult to find places to eat and sleep. In the early years they would usually stay in the homes of sympathetic black families. The Globetrotters would eventually develop into a team more known for their showmanship than their serious

Harlem Globetrotters. Image © Laszlo Szirtesi, 2013. Used under license from Shutterstock, Inc.

basketball abilities. In the early years they were a serious barnstorming team and would take on any challengers. At the height of their talent, the Globetrotters would win a World Basketball Championship in 1940. Legend has it that the showmanship began one cold night in Williamsburg, Iowa, when William "Kid" Oliver got too close to a pot-bellied stove along the baseline and his shorts caught on fire. He went squealing across the floor trailed by a smoky trail and the crowd erupted with laughter. Although the "act" was accidental, it gave Saperstein the idea that adding things like this to the games would only help bring more people in to watch them. The team would continue to play hard and try to win, but they would increasingly introduce "razzle-dazzle" plays into their games. The 1930s were difficult economic times for the country, but the Globetrotters grew in popularity and over the next two decades they would become the world travelers that Saperstein had envisioned when naming the team. The organization would also provide the only opportunity for black players to play the game professionally until the game became more integrated in the 1950s.

In the midst of the Great Depression, the seeds of what would become the NBA were sown when a small circuit of professional teams from Ohio, Michigan, Indiana, and Pennsylvania formed the Midwestern Basketball Conference in 1935. As with early professional football teams, most of the teams were sponsored by companies (with two teams from Akron, for example—one named the "Goodyear Regulars" and the other named the "Firestone Non-Skids"). Most of the players were employees of the company; and, although they may not have been paid to play basketball, their "job" was to play basketball for the company. Others were paid on the side in addition to their full-time job. The first season was not very organized as one player, Gene Scholz, who played for the Columbus Athletic Supply Club, remembered: "I didn't even know we were in a league. I didn't know what was going on. I was just picking up a few bucks on the side playing basketball."[13] Two years later the league changed its name to the **National Basketball League (NBL)**. Although the member teams were essentially the same, the name change occurred both because they were getting confused in the sports pages with the Big 10 conference of Midwestern college teams and also because adding the word "National" seemed to give the league a more geographically widespread feel. The league stayed together during World War II but began losing men and teams to military service. In its initial season (1937–38) the NBL had 14 teams—by the 1943–44 season the league was down to four. One of the little-known effects of the shortage of players during the war was the integration of the league—at least temporarily—during the war. Two teams decided in 1942 to allow black players on their rosters—the Chicago Studebakers and the Toledo Jim White Chevrolets. Toledo owner Sid Goldberg later recalled, "I went to the league and told them, 'I don't know what you fellows are going to do, but if you want me to stay in'—and they wanted my team—'I'm going to use blacks.' Some of them didn't relish it, I suppose, because they thought it would bring problems, but I don't think any of them objected."[14] Unfortunately the four black players he signed must not have had the greatest skills because his team was forced to disband after four games (all of which they lost) when more players left for the war. The Chicago team finished the season but only managed an 8–15 record. The experiment seemed to fail and the league would not have black players again for four years—after Jackie Robinson signed to play baseball with Brooklyn.

After the war ended, the NBL got its first big-name player when the Chicago American Gears signed George Mikan from DePaul in 1946. That same year another professional basketball league began play when the **Basketball Association of America (BAA)** was formed. The league was put together by arena owners and managers in the larger cities like Ned Irish, who made enough money in his Garden Games that he formed the New York Knickerbockers and became principal owner of them, and Walter A. Brown of the Boston Garden who started the Boston Celtics. Unfortunately for Mikan, the Gears' owner decided to pull his team out of the NBL in 1947 and start a different league that folded before it began, so the NBL took ownership of the team and parceled the players out to different teams for the upcoming season. Mikan was the big prize that the Minneapolis Lakers won. In 1948, Mikan helped the Lakers win the championship of the league as well as the World Tournament in Chicago (since it was open to all the leagues in existence, its winner was thought of as the best team in the world). It was widely agreed that the NBL had the best players and the BAA had the biggest arenas to fill and populations to draw from. Not surprisingly, in 1948, four teams decided to defect from the NBL to the BAA (Indianapolis, Ft. Wayne, Rochester, and Minneapolis). The Lakers won the last championship of the BAA in 1949 because by that summer the two leagues had decided to merge and form the **National Basketball Association (NBA)**.

The NBA

The NBA began its inaugural season in 1949 with 17 teams in three divisions (Eastern, Central, and Western). In addition to the Celtics and Knicks in the East, the only other current team that was part of that first season was the Denver Nuggets in the West. The division winners with the two best records met in a seven-game playoff at the end of the season to decide the league champion. In the first season the Minneapolis Lakers picked up where they left off by defeating the Syracuse Nationals four games to two. The Mikan-led Lakers could be considered the NBA's first dynasty as they added three more championships in the next four years before Mikan retired due to injuries in 1956. It is often said that Mikan carried the fledgling league on his back for the first years and he is credited with keeping the league going. Two other factors also contributed to the success of the league in the early years: the point-shaving scandal in college basketball in 1951 and the addition of the shot clock in 1954. The scandal and resulting refusal of colleges to send teams to the larger cities led to the collapse of the Garden Games and other college tournaments, which left a void for basketball fans in the cities. For urban fans in the 1950s it was the NBA or nothing. The boring style of basketball that the early rules allowed for (getting a lead and then holding the ball and stalling) was done away with when the 24-second shot clock was introduced. An offensive team now had 24 seconds to shoot or they turned the ball over to the opposition. Offensive numbers jumped and a more exciting style ensued.

The Celtics Dynasty

Just as the Mikan Lakers dynasty was ending, another dynasty was getting started. The Boston Celtics were born with the BAA in 1946 and took their name both as a tribute to the original Celtics from New York as well as a nod to the large percentage of Irish Americans in the Boston populace. They played in Walter Brown's Boston Garden but they did not play very well. In the three seasons the BAA was in existence, the team went 67–101 and never managed a winning season. The worst season came in their first in the NBA—the Celtics were 22–46 and Brown decided he needed to make a change. He removed head coach Doggie Julian and replaced him with 32-year-old **Harold "Red" Auerbach** in 1950. Auerbach began his coaching career at Roosevelt High School in Washington, DC; and after joining the Navy during World War II, he coached the Naval team at Norfolk, Virginia. After the war he was hired as the Washington Capitals' first head coach. He compiled the best record the team ever had (49–11) but resigned after his third season when the Capitols owner refused to allow him to make some trades to rebuild the team. He then coached one season with the Tri-Cities Blackhawks but again resigned after the owner traded away his favorite player. Brown gave Auerbach all the power for the Celtics. He was the only coach and also acted as general manager for the team—overseeing all draft picks and trades. One of the first things Auerbach did was draft Chuck

Bob Cousy. Image courtesy of Library of Congress

Cooper—the first black player in the NBA. The league did not officially have a color barrier as other sports leagues did, but there had been no black players on any of the league's 17 teams during its first season. The other thing he did during that draft was ignore point-guard **Bob Cousy** who was a local legend in New England after becoming an all-American at Holy Cross in Worcester, Massachusetts. In those days of the NBA draft, teams were allowed one "territorial" pick which meant they could have taken Cousy, but Auerbach thought he was "too flashy" and chose to not draft him—much to the disappointment of Boston fans and the local press which savaged Auerbach for the move. As it turned out, Auerbach got Cousy anyway because although he was drafted by Auerbach's old team, the Tri-Cities, he demanded a salary of $10,000 a year and when he was only offered $6,000 he refused to report. His rights were then sold to the Chicago Stags which promptly folded. The players on the Stags were parceled out to different teams and the Celtics got Cousy. When this news was given to Auerbach he gruffly replied, "He'll have to make the team."[15] Make the team he did and for the next eight seasons he led the league in assists. He was named to the all-league team for 10 consecutive seasons and made 13 all-star games. Auerbach quickly realized his mistake and would later say, "Every kid who can dribble a basketball gets called another Cousy. Well I've got news for you. There ain't nobody as good as Cooz. There never was."[16]

With the help of Cousy, Auerbach quickly turned around the fortunes of the Celtics. In his first season, the team went 39–30; and, by the 1952–53 season, they amassed the best record in the history of the franchise (46–25) and had turned the team into championship contenders. They made the playoffs every season between 1951 and 1956 but always failed to make the championship series. Something was missing and Auerbach believed he knew what that something was. His teams seemed to tire down the stretch—they needed a dominating center who would not only be a force on offense but more importantly on defense to give the rest of the team a break and save their energy for the end of games. Boston was also known as the best fast break team in the league but one of the worst defensive rebounding teams in the league. "I had to have somebody who could get me the ball,"[17] he later said. That somebody turned out to be Bill Russell. The 6' 10" center from the University of San Francisco was known as the best defensive rebounder in the college game, but most scouts did not think his shooting was good enough for the NBA. Auerbach did not care about that—he had been following Russell's college career for at least two years and wanted to get him in the 1956 draft. The problem was the Celtics picked sixth and he knew of at least two teams ahead of them who wanted Russell. The team drafting first was Rochester and they passed because they could not afford Russell's asking price. The other team that wanted him was Minneapolis who needed a center because of the retirement of Mikan. Auerbach put in a call to the owner of the St. Louis Hawks that drafted second (just ahead of Minneapolis). Auerbach offered a trade for the rights to Russell. Ed Macauley had been a great player for the Celtics, but he was nearing the end of his career and wanted to return home to St. Louis. Hawks owner Ben Kerner wanted one more player and he got Cliff Hagan who had been all-American forward at Kentucky before entering the Army. The Celtics owned the rights to him when he was discharged from the Army. Auerbach made the deal and got Russell. Had Minneapolis drafted Russell (which they certainly would have with the next pick), the Lakers dynasty might have continued into the 1960s. As it turned out, the team did not even stay in Minneapolis past 1960. With dwindling attendance, the Lakers moved to Los Angeles beginning in the 1960–61 season. Had Auerbach not made that move, Russell could have joined four of the best centers ever to play the game that wore the Lakers jersey (Mikan, Wilt Chamberlain, Kareem Abdul-Jabbar, and Shaquille O'Neil). By making that move (along with picking up future hall of famer forward Tom Heinsehn and guard K.C. Jones in the same draft), Auerbach began a dynasty that would see 11 championships in the next 13 seasons. His first championship came in 1957 and, beginning in 1959, the Celtics won an unprecedented eight consecutive championships. After the 1966 championship, Auerbach retired and Bill Russell became player-coach for his final three seasons. He was the first black coach in league history and the first to win a championship (which he did in both 1968 and 1969).

The ABA

In the 1950s the NBA had absorbed or forced other professional basketball leagues to fold, but in 1967 a new league sprang up to challenge them. The **American Basketball Association (ABA)** was formed in the same year the AFL and NFL merged and the founders hoped for the same result for the ABA. For this to happen they would need to sign a national television contract and for that to happen they would need great players. In the early days the players they signed were at a lower level than those in the NBA. They did have a former great player as their first commissioner. George Mikan introduced some changes from the NBA, notably the three-point shot from beyond 25 feet; a 30-second shot clock instead of 24; and, perhaps most infamously, the red, white, and blue basketballs. Some derisively called the ABA the "beach ball league."[18] Getting that television contract proved to be very difficult for the ABA—it was also difficult for the NBA which lost its national television contract with NBC in 1962 who simply dropped the league's games due to lack of ratings. The league desperately needed a big-name player, and they tried to get Lew Alcindor in 1969 after he graduated from UCLA. Although not able to get him, the Virginia Squires did sign **Julius Erving** out of the University of Massachusetts in 1971. "Dr. J" as he became known was an exciting player who is credited with bringing the "slam dunk" into the game. It was not allowed at the time in the NCAA or the NBA (referred to as the "Alcindor rule" to prohibit such an easy score), but because the ABA allowed it, the NBA was forced to allow it by 1975 to compete with the excitement it generated in the ABA. The NCAA followed suit the next year. Many credit Dr. J with keeping the league alive longer than it should have but even he could not keep it going forever, and without a television contract it was forced into a merger with the NBA. The NBA only took four of its teams when the merger occurred in 1976 (Indiana Pacers, Denver Nuggets, New York Nets, and the San Antonio Spurs). The Nuggets had been an original NBA team but was forced to disband after one season. There were some lasting effects of the ABA on professional basketball including the three-point shot, allowing teams to draft college players before their eligibility was exhausted (the ABA allowed it, the NBA had not prior to the merger) and the skyrocketing salaries of players which was brought about by the competition of the other league. Fortunately, the multicolored ball was not one of the legacies of the rival league (except in the three-point contest during the all-star break).

The NBA's "Golden Age"

ABC picked up the NBA's television contract in 1962 when NBC dropped it, but it too dropped the contract after one decade. When CBS took over the coverage in 1973, they were taking a bit of a risk as the league now had a rival (ABA) and ratings had never been consistently good. CBS would be glad it signed the contract with the league, but it would take awhile before it paid off. While attendance at NBA games had increased from around 2 million annually in the early 1960s to nearly 10 million by the end of the 1970s, that had not translated to television ratings. There are various theories for this including the style of basketball being played (a more playground, individualistic style that did not play well on television), as well as no great dynasties or rivalries in the 1970s. There were eight different teams that won NBA championships during the decade. Competitive balance does not always guarantee television numbers. Little did CBS know that a college game it covered in 1979 would not only change its fortunes but the fortunes of the NBA over the next decade. Michigan State defeated Indiana State for the NCAA title that year and the two stars for their respective teams, **Ervin "Magic" Johnson** and **Larry Bird**, would help usher in the most successful era the NBA had ever seen. Taking advantage of the new drafting rules, Celtics

Magic Johnson, David Stern and Larry Bird. Image © lev radin, 2013. Used under license from Shutterstock, Inc.

General Manager Red Auerbach drafted Bird in the 1978 draft not knowing if he would play his senior season or not. After he did play his senior year, the Celtics retained his rights and were able to sign him. The rule has since been changed so teams cannot draft a player and then wait a year to sign him—they lose the rights if he does not play right away. It is known as the "Bird Rule." Johnson was drafted by the Los Angeles Lakers, and both players made an immediate impact on their teams. The Celtics were 29–53 the year before Bird's arrival and improved to the league's best record of 61–21 during his rookie year. Although Johnson had a strong rookie campaign also, Bird was named the league's Rookie of the Year in 1980. Bird may have won that award, but the Lakers had the league MVP, Kareem Abdul-Jabbar, and with the addition of Magic Johnson, the Lakers defeated the Philadelphia 76ers led by Julius Erving (who defeated the Celtics in the Eastern Conference finals) for Magic's first NBA championship. The following season, the Celtics added center Robert Parrish and forward Kevin McHale to its lineup to help Bird and produce one of the best front-courts ever assembled in the NBA. The Celtics again met up with the 76ers in the conference championship but this time defeated them (coming back from 3–1 down to win three consecutive games by two points or less) in thrilling fashion. They then defeated the Houston Rockets in six games to capture the franchise's 14th championship and Bird's first.

The rivalry was on and the Celtics or Lakers would win every championship during the decade except for two (Julius Erving's one and only championship with the 76ers in 1983, and the Detroit Pistons thwarting the Lakers' attempt at a "three-peat" in 1989). The first time the two teams faced each other in the NBA finals was in 1984. Bird got the best of Magic in this series, winning seven games for his second championship; 1984 was also an important year for the league because of two other figures, one on the court—the other, off. **Michael Jordan** joined the Chicago Bulls that season and **David Stern** became NBA commissioner. Jordan quickly established himself as the most exciting player in the league, and Stern embarked on a marketing plan that helped bring the league into its "golden age." Jordan himself would have a large role in this when he joined the Nike Corporation and marketed basketball shoes known as "Air Jordans." The combination of great marketing and the rivalry between Bird and Magic seemed heaven-sent for the NBA, and the results were tremendous increases in both attendance and television ratings. Things had gotten so bad for the NBA on TV by the end of the 1970s that CBS broadcast both the 1980 and 1981 NBA finals on a tape-delay basis. In 1982, CBS paid just under $92 million for a four-year contract to broadcast the league. In 1986 that contract nearly doubled when they paid $173 million for the next four years. In 1990 CBS lost their contract when they were outbid by NBC who decided after dumping the NBA nearly 30 years before that they wanted a piece of the action to the tune of over $600 million for the next four years. Nielson ratings measure the number of households that are watching a particular broadcast and a rating point indicates just under 1 million homes. Rarely had NBA basketball broadcasts garnered ratings out of the single digits but, beginning in 1984, the ratings for the entire finals series steadily increased from 12.3 to a then-all time high of 15.9 when Bird and Magic met for the final time in a championship in 1987. Games 4 and 5 in the 1987 finals drew 18.9 ratings; game seven in 1984 reached over 19, and Game 7 in 1988 actually hit the astronomical number of 21.2. Only one NBA game has ever surpassed that number since—Game 6 of the 1998 finals hit 22.3 which was Michael Jordan's last game in a Bulls uniform.

The golden age seemed to culminate with the 1992 Olympics in Barcelona when the "Dream Team" was assembled. It was a chance for the three greatest players in the game (and arguably of all time) to play together. Jordan, Bird, and Johnson were joined by other greats in the game like Charles

Barkley, Karl Malone, John Stockton, David Robinson, Scottie Pippen, and Patrick Ewing. The team easily won the gold medal but shortly after the Olympics ended, Larry Bird announced his retirement from the game. A year earlier, Magic Johnson also announced his retirement because he had contracted HIV. The end of the rivalry left Michael Jordan alone as the game's greatest player, and he had just won his first championship in 1991. Jordan was acknowledged as the best player in the game by the late 1980s but he did not have the talent surrounding him for a championship. That changed in the 1987 draft when the Bulls got both small forward Scottie Pippen and power forward Horace Grant. When they picked up 7' 1" Bill Cartwright in 1988, all the pieces seemed to fall in place; and after they defeated the Lakers in Magic's last finals appearance in 1991, they won two more consecutively to achieve the "three-peat" that Magic was never able to get. Jordan then surprised everyone by retiring before the start of the 1993–94 season. Some say his change in direction was due to the murder of his father that happened in July of that year—he seemed to lose his desire after that. He shocked the sporting world again by signing a minor league baseball contract with the Chicago White Sox. When that career move did not pan out, he came back to the Bulls and won three more consecutive championships (1996–98). When he left the game again after that season (although he would return briefly to play for the Washington Wizards from 2001–2003), he had won six championships, been the finals MVP every time he played in them, won five league MVPs, won 10 scoring titles, and was widely considered the greatest basketball player of all time.

Conclusion

The golden age of professional basketball seemed to end when Michael Jordan left the Bulls after the 1998 season. The ratings for the 1998 finals were the highest of all time (18.7), but they dropped to an 11.3 in 1999; and, in the first decade of the 21st century, they have never gone above 12.1. Not even a renewal of the Lakers–Celtics rivalry in the finals in 2008 and 2010 could bring back the old "magic" in the ratings (9.3 and 10.6, respectively). In 2010 when LeBron James joined Chris Bosh and Dewayne Wade to play for the Miami Heat as the self-proclaimed "Big 3," there seemed to be a renewed interest in the NBA—if nothing else to cheer against the apparent arrogance of these players (who announced they would win multiple championships in Miami). When they lost to the Dallas Mavericks in the 2011 finals, it garnered a 10.2 rating—when they won their first championship in 2012, the rating was only a 10.1. Part of the reason the ratings were down in 2012 was due to an NBA lockout which delayed the start of the season until Christmas. Millionaires arguing over millions of dollars while not playing does not do a sport any good, and it was something the NBA could not afford during this decline in popularity. Can the NBA make a comeback? There might be some hope as the 2015 NBA finals between

LeBron James. Image © Domenic Gareri, 2013. Used under license from Shutterstock, Inc.

the Golden State Warriors (with its sharp-shooting guard Stephon Curry) and the Cleveland Cavaliers (where LeBron James had returned) garnered a 13.9 rating, the highest since 1998. It will probably take a return of a rivalry between players like a Bird-Magic to bring the NBA back to the levels it hit in the 1980s and 1990s, if that is even a possibility. College basketball, however, seems to still be in its golden age. Attendance and ratings have never been better, and championship games routinely rate in the 20- to 30-point Nielson range and sometimes even higher. There is no doubt about the overall popularity of the sport. James Naismith would be amazed to know that if all levels of basketball are combined (pickup games, high school, college, professional) that it is the most participated in and watched sport in the country by far. Not bad for a game that started with two peach baskets and a P.E. teacher just trying to keep his class interested over the winter.

Notes

1. Neil D. Isaacs, *All the Moves: A History of College Basketball* (New York and Philadelphia: J.B. Lippincott Co., 1975), 19.
2. Usabasketball.com: "Dr. Naismith's Original 13 Rules of Basket Ball."
3. Ibid.
4. Isaacs, *All the Moves,* 22.
5. Zukerman, Earl, "McGill grad James Naismith, inventor of basketball". *Varsity Sports News.* McGill Athletics. http://athletics.mcgill.ca/varsity_sports_article.ch2?article_id=110. 17 December 2003.
6 Benjamin Rader, *American Sports; From the Age of Folk Games to the Age of Televised Sports*, 6th ed. (Upper Saddle River, NJ: Pearson-Prentice Hall, 2009), 286.
7. John D. McCallum, *College Basketball, U.S.A., Since 1892* (New York: Stein and Day, 1978), 94.
8. "Dr. Naismith's Original 13 Rules of Basket Ball."
9. Robert Peterson, *From Cages to Jumpshots, Pro Basketball's Early Years* (Lincoln and London: University of Nebraska Press, 1990), 33.
10. Ibid.
11. Ibid., 34.
12. Ibid., 77–78.
13. Peterson, *From Cages to Jumpshots,* 125.
14. Ibid., 130.
15. Glenn Dickey, *The History of Professional Basketball Since 1896* (New York: Stein and Day, 1982), 78.
16. Ibid., 79.
17. Ibid., 82.
18. Ibid., 134.

CHAPTER

Eleven

Modern Baseball

*T*he 1941 season is often referred to as the greatest season in major league baseball history. Perhaps that is more nostalgia than fact because it was the last season before the United States entered World War II, but there is no arguing the fact that there were two incredible individual accomplishments that occurred that season. Joe DiMaggio's 56-game hitting streak and Ted Williams' batting .406 are marks that have not been matched since. Both men played during the 1942 season (although Williams was drafted into the military in January he appealed his draft status to a presidential board which granted him a reprieve to play baseball on the basis he was the sole supporter of his family) and Williams had one of his best seasons and won the American League triple crown (highest batting average, .356; most home runs, 36; and most runs batted in, 137). Within months of the end of the 1942 season, both of these great stars had entered the armed forces. Williams had taken some criticism for his earlier avoidance of the draft so in early 1943 he enlisted in the Marines and became an aviator. DiMaggio entered the Army Air Force and served mainly as a physical education instructor and also played baseball. Neither player served any time overseas; however, Williams would later fly 39 combat missions in Korea in 1952–53. When the war ended in 1945, both players returned to their respective teams secure in the knowledge that they would probably pick up their great careers right where they left them. What was less certain, however, was whether or not the game of baseball was still the country's "national pastime." During the war and the decade leading up to it, the popularity of the game had been steadily declining and no one was sure what the future held.

First Modern Era (1946–68)

Post-War Struggles for Baseball

The early post-war years were an uneasy time for Americans. Returning soldiers were unsure if there would be jobs waiting for them and political leaders as well as citizens wondered if the terrible economic times of the Great Depression would return. After some initial hiccups, the American economy roared back to life in the late forties and fifties. The American government helped by passing the GI Bill of Rights, which provided many returning soldiers with a college education thereby making them more viable in the job market. There were also federal programs through the new Federal Housing Administration (FHA) and the Veterans Administration (VA) that offered low-interest loans to soldiers to buy a home. The returning soldiers filled those homes with children at a record pace, producing what would be known as the "**baby boom**" which produced the greatest population growth spurt in American history. Although the birthrate had consistently declined for the previous century, there were more babies born between 1948 and 1953 than the 30 years before combined. Most of these growing families were inhabiting a new demographic known as the "**suburbs**." There was in the postwar years not only an incredible population growth but also a population shift from the inner cities to the "outskirts" of cities. This movement into the suburbs and the focus being put on those areas left the downtown areas of cities to fall into a decline. With that decline came an increase in crime and the inner cities became a dangerous place to be. This decline would have a major effect on sports in general and baseball in particular.

The families of the suburbs not only were hesitant to make the trek into the cities (where most ballparks were located) to attend a professional baseball game where they (as well as their vehicles) could be in danger, but there were also other diversions for the post-war family that may not have existed before. "Why should a guy with a boat in the driveway, golf clubs in the car, bowling ball and tennis racket in the closet, a trunkful of camping equipment, two boys in little league and a body full of energy left over from shorter working hours pay to sit and do nothing but watch a mediocre game?" asked W. Travis Walton in a letter to *Sports Illustrated* in 1958.[1] Along with other sports (including the sports of their children), yard work, and PTA meetings that might occupy the time of the average suburbanite, there was also a brand new technology that would capture the attention of the entire country within a decade of the end of the war: television. In 1947 there were 7,000 television sets in the United States and by 1950 that number had increased 100-fold to over 7 million. By the end of the 1950s nearly 90 percent of all homes had at least one TV set and many had more than that. Early television hurt baseball in a dual way—eventually programming provided one of the alternatives to attending games and its poor reception and camera angles did not lend itself well to coverage of the sport. As a result, attendance at major league baseball games during the 1950s and 60s dropped to numbers well below that of the late 1940s and certainly below the numbers of the glory days of the 1920s, especially when seen as a percentage of the population. Television ratings for baseball also remained low even after technology improved. Baseball has always been one of the most difficult sports for television to cover—there are often so many things going on that the cameras cannot catch. There was also the problem offered by the long season—very few regular season games seem to matter in baseball. Alternatively, there are so few games in football that each one seems important. By the 1960s, regular season baseball games were seeing its ratings nearly half of those of professional football games. By the end of the 1970s, baseball ratings were fifth on the list of all sports coverage behind professional and college football, boxing, and even, believe it or not, professional bowling. By the second half of the 20th century, the age of baseball being the national pastime appeared to have passed.

The effect of television could also be felt in the minor leagues of baseball. Because of the return of prosperity after the war and the location of most minor league teams in smaller cities and towns, annual attendance almost tripled during the 1940s from 15 million to 42 million. There was also a ban on broadcasting major league games in minor league markets in an attempt to not cut into that attendance. In 1951, the major league owners lifted that broadcasting ban and the result was a drop in attendance back to 15 million by 1957 and even lower to 10 million by the end of the 1960s. If a person wanted to watch a baseball game, it was much easier (and cheaper) to watch it at home on television. Not only did attendance at minor league games drop but the number of leagues in existence also diminished. In 1949, there were 51 minor leagues in baseball and by 1970 there were only 20. Prior to 1961 major league baseball could not negotiate television contracts that benefited all teams. The commissioner's office would negotiate a "game of the week" during the 1950s but it was not until 1961 when Congress passed the Sports Broadcasting Act that the league could negotiate television packages that benefited *every* team in the league—not just those that were broadcast the most. The result was a financial windfall for teams that reached $4 million per team by the 1980s and over $14 million by the end of the century.

CHAPTER *Eleven*

The Domination of the Dynasties

During what is referred to as the first era of modern baseball (1946–68), the powerhouse teams tended to come from the large population centers. The largest city in the country was not only the capital of trade and investment in the modern American economy but it was also the capital of baseball. The only city that could sustain three teams, New York, was the center of the baseball world during the early post-war years. Before the National League Giants and Dodgers left the city to the American League Yankees after the 1957 season, a team from New York was repre-

Casey Stengel. Image © Ffooter, 2013. Used under license from Shutterstock, Inc.

sented in the World Series every year but one going back to 1947 (with the one exception being 1948 when the Cleveland Indians defeated the Boston Braves). Leading the way were the New York Yankees. The post-war Yankee dynasty was really just a continuation of the dynasty that began with Babe Ruth back in the 1920s. Attendance gate money had always helped the Yankees with their payroll, but now there was an additional avenue for funds through television broadcasting contracts. Because of this cash flow, the Yankees were able to get the best players in the league; and manager **Casey Stengel** (managed Yankees from 1949–1960) had the luxury of implementing what became known as the "platoon system." Because left-handed hitters statistically are more successful against right-handed pitchers and vice-versa, Stengel was able to stack his lineup depending on who the opposing pitcher was for that game. It is now a system used by every manager. One of the players he did not have to platoon was the switch-hitting **Mickey Mantle** who was

called up to the Yankees in 1951. Stengel was so confident in the 19-year-old prospect that he gave him uniform number 6 because he thought he was the next in line to carry the dynasty forward (following number 3 Ruth, number 4 Gehrig, and number 5 DiMaggio). He initially struggled and was sent down to minor-league Kansas City, and it was there he contemplated quitting the game. When he told his father, a coal miner from Commerce, Oklahoma, he drove to Kansas City and started to pack his son to bring him back to follow his footsteps in the mines. Mantle remembered later that his father told him he thought he had raised a man, but apparently he had raised a coward. That was all it took to snap the younger Mantle out of his slump as he batted .311 for Kansas City and hit 23 home runs before being once again called up to the Yankees with 40 games remaining in the season. Seemingly recognizing the pressure Mantle was under the first time he came up, this time Stengel gave him the number 7 and he would wear it for the next 18 seasons. The symbolic passing of the dynastic baton occurred when Joe DiMaggio retired after the 1951 season and Mantle took over his position in centerfield. In the only World Series in which they appeared together, Mantle (then playing rightfield) and DiMaggio nearly collided going for a fly ball hit by Willie Mays and, when DiMaggio called him off, Mantle stopped abruptly and got his spikes caught in a drainage cover and twisted his knee. He was carried off the field and was in pain for the remainder of his career.

The pain did not stop Mantle from amassing 2,415 hits, 1,509 RBIs, and 536 home runs (currently 17th all-time) and helping the Yankees win 12 American League pennants and 7 World Series championships 1951 and 1964. During the forties and fifties, there were seven World Series that featured teams from New York. They were referred to as "subway series" and although one of them included the Giants (Yankees winning in 1951), in the other six the National League was represented by the **Brooklyn Dodgers**. The first of these subway series happened in 1947 after the Dodgers had made history by finally breaking the racial barrier set up through the owners' "Gentlemen's Agreement" of the previous century not to hire black players. Dodgers' general manager Branch Rickey's decision to call up Jackie Robinson in April of 1947 would help them win the pennant but not the World Series. The Dodgers would get another chance two years later but would again lose to the Yankees. In 1952 and 1953 the same teams met with the same outcome. The slogan "Wait 'til next year" became the mantra for Brooklyn fans by the mid-fifties. They were lovingly referred to as "dem bums" by the fans, but Rickey and the Dodgers had quietly assembled a solid lineup during the fifties consisting of Robinson, Pee Wee Reese, and Gil Hodges in the infield; Duke Snider and Carl Furillo in the outfield; Roy Campanella behind the plate; and the solid pitching of Don Newcombe and Johnny Podres. "Next year" finally arrived in 1955 when they defeated the Yankees in seven games in the fall classic and the borough of Brooklyn went crazy. Little did their fans know at the time that within two years their beloved "bums" would leave for California.

Relocation and Expansion

Real estate magnate **Walter O'Malley** became majority owner of the Dodgers in 1950 and essentially muscled Branch Rickey out. Rickey moved on to the Pittsburgh Pirates. It became quickly apparent to O'Malley that aging Ebbets Field was in need of repair or a new stadium would have to be built. After deciding repair to the old park was probably not going to work (he did not like the present location of the ballpark anyway), he began to look for a suitable spot to build a new one. He had thoughts of some land in another section of Brooklyn but he wanted New York City Construction Coordinator Robert Moses to condemn the land which would have allowed O'Malley to purchase the land at a less-than-market price. Moses refused to do this but did offer O'Malley a section of land in Queens that would be paid for and owned by the city (eventually Shea Stadium would be built there for the expansion New York Mets a decade later). This was not what O'Malley envisioned so he began to entertain offers to move the Dodgers not only out of Brooklyn but out of New York altogether. Cross-country air travel was becoming much more widely used so the thought of having West Coast teams was not out of the realm of possibility by the mid-fifties. City officials from Los Angeles were looking for either an expansion team or an Eastern team to move west. It was not the Dodgers they first had in mind—they knew Washington Senators' owner, Calvin Griffith, was looking to move his franchise; and they were in talks with him (the Senators would eventually move to Minneapolis in 1961 and become the Minnesota Twins), but it was during the 1956 World Series that they came to New York to talk with O'Malley. During what would be the last subway series until the next century (Yankees got their revenge from 1955 by once again defeating the Dodgers), the idea was floated to move the Dodgers to Los Angeles. O'Malley knew, however, that having only one team in California would not be sufficient so he talked to Giants owner Horace Stoneham about also moving to the West Coast. Stoneham worked out a deal with officials in San Francisco and both the Dodgers and Giants moved out of New York after the 1957 season. Dodger fans were crushed—for this to happen so soon after their first championship seemed particularly cruel. Most of them never forgave O'Malley for what he did to their beloved "bums." As for O'Malley, he and the Dodgers never looked back—he was given the opportunity to purchase the land on which Dodgers Stadium would be built so he would control everything that happened there. In the meantime, the Dodgers played the 1958 season in Los Angeles Memorial Coliseum (built for the 1932 Olympics) and the opening day crowd was nearly 80,000. It did not take the Dodgers long to win in California as they defeated the Chicago White Sox in the 1959 World Series for their first championship in Los Angeles. They would win two more in the 1960s (1963 and 1965) and lose to the Baltimore Orioles in the 1966 Series.

The Dodgers and Giants were not the first to relocate. It began in 1953 with a string of "second" teams in cities featuring two teams. The first "also-ran" team to leave was the National League Boston Braves to Milwaukee. The Braves never could compete with the cross-town Red Sox. The American League got into the act the following year when the perennially awful St. Louis Browns left for Baltimore where they would be renamed the Orioles. The third to go was the once-great Philadelphia Athletics in 1955. The A's moved west to Kansas City. When the Dodgers and Giants left New York after 1957, it left only Chicago with more than one team until the expansion years beginning in the 1960s. Both the American and National Leagues had eight teams going back to the elevation of the American League to a major league, but that changed in 1961. The first to expand was the American League when Washington received a new franchise after the old one moved to Minnesota, but unfortunately they kept the same name and were christened the "new" Washington Senators. The new Senators picked up where the old ones left off—never finishing above seventh place and only once finishing with a winning record. In 1972 the Senators left again—this time to Texas to become the Rangers. The other team the American League added in 1961 was a second team in Los Angeles. The team was owned by singer Gene Autry and was originally called the Los Angeles Angels, but eventually moved to suburban Anaheim and was renamed the California Angels. They are currently referred to as the Los Angeles Angels from Anaheim. The National League expanded the following year when New York added a second team with the Mets, and Houston was given a franchise originally called the Colt 45s and later changed to the Astros. Although there were now 10 teams in each league, no new layers of playoffs were added at the time.

New Era of the Pitcher

Toward the end of the first modern era, baseball made some changes that drastically affected the game. In 1963, Major League Baseball in an effort to speed up games for modern spectators and television, instructed umpires to enlarge the strike zone. The rules committee now said that strikes should be called when a pitch was between the "bottom of the knees (and) the top of the shoulders."[2] The result was a return to the dominance of the pitchers over the hitters not seen in the game since the dead ball era during the early years of the century. Between 1963 and 1966, the Dodgers had the services of two of the greatest pitchers of all time and they were direct beneficiaries of the new strike zone. **Sandy Koufax** and **Don Drysdale** were the one-two punch that led the Dodgers to three National League pennants during those years, including two world championships (1963 and 1965). Koufax, in particular, was impressive during these years. In these four seasons, his record was 97–27 with earned run averages of 1.88, 1.74, 2.04, and 1.73. He also pitched a no-hitter in each of these seasons. Unfortunately for Koufax and the Dodgers, he was forced to retire at the age of 30 after the 1966 season because of arthritis in his arm. Another dominant pitcher of the time was **Bob Gibson** of the St. Louis Cardinals. He helped the Cardinals win the World Series in 1964 and 1967 and in 1968 had arguably his greatest year when he went 22–9, pitched 13 shutouts, and had an incredible 1.12 ERA. In what was dubbed the "year of the pitcher," Gibson was the best of all and once again propelled the Cardinals to the World Series. The year 1968 was also one of racial consciousness for African Americans (including John Carlos and Tommie Smith's Black Panther salute and the Mexico City Olympics that summer) and Gibson identified with the new militant attitude. When asked about the pressure on the mound Gibson answered, "I face more pressure every day just being a Negro."[3]

Don Drysdale, Sandy Koufax and Dodgers Manager Walter Alston. © Bettmann/CORBIS

The "Year of the Pitcher" seemed to wake up Major League Baseball to its mistake. After the initial rule change, offensive numbers immediately dropped. The 1963 season saw run totals fall by 1,681, home runs by 297, batting averages by 12 points, and walks by 1,345. That season proved to be the high water mark for offense over the next five years—by 1968, the American League batting champion was Boston's Carl Yastrzemski with an average of .301, the lowest in major league history.[4] Although there were other factors that contributed to this offensive dropoff—including more night games (harder to hit the ball at night), better equipment including larger gloves, and larger ballparks built in the late 50s and early 60s—it became apparent that it was the change in the strike zone that was the main culprit. Prior to the 1969 season, baseball made two changes to try and even the score between pitcher and hitter. First the pitching mound was lowered from 15 inches to 10. This was in an effort to lessen the success of the slider and curveball. Secondly, umpires were instructed to lower the ***de facto* strike zone**. This meant that although the actual strike zone in the rulebook would not change, the strike zone the umpire would call would be smaller. Instead of extending to the top of the hitter's shoulders or even armpits, strikes would not be called above the belt. Four years later the American League introduced the **designated hitter** which allowed teams to substitute for the pitcher in the batting order. All three of these changes did help lessen the dominance of the pitcher and bring back more offense to baseball, but it took a long time to reach pre-1963 offensive numbers.

Second Modern Era (1969–1992)

First Expansion (Two-Division) Era

The second modern era known as either the "first expansion" or "two-division" era began in 1969. Since the elevation of the American League to a major league in 1903, the team that won its respective league advanced straight to the World Series without any other level of playoffs. That changed during the 1969 season. Although there had been 10 teams in each league beginning in 1962, it was not until 1969 when two more teams were added to each league (Kansas City Royals and Seattle Sea Pilots in the American League, and San Diego Padres and Montreal Expos in the National League) did Major League Baseball decide it was time for realignment. The result was dividing each league into an east and west division consisting of six teams each and the winners would play each other in a league championship series with the winners moving on to represent their respective leagues in the World Series. Two of the new teams in 1969 are worth noting: The first was the team in Seattle known as the "Sea Pilots." Unfortunately for Seattle, the team proved to be a disappointment both on the field and off as they were forced to declare bankruptcy after one season and the franchise was relocated to Milwaukee when a car salesman named Bud Selig purchased the franchise and changed the name to the Brewers for the 1970 season. The other newcomer was the Montreal Expos which became the first non-American city to have a major league baseball team. They were joined by another Canadian club in 1977 when the Toronto Blue Jays joined the American League East. In 1977 Seattle was once again awarded a franchise, but this time it proved a more stable one with the Mariners.

With the addition of those teams, major league baseball had grown from its initial 16 teams to 26 teams in only 15 years. After the championship by the "Miracle Mets" in 1969, the 1970s saw its share of multiple championship winners (Oakland Athletics 1972–74, Cincinnati Reds' "Big Red Machine" 1975–76, and the Yankees 1977–78). The 1980s and early 90s were a period when the dynasties seemed to disappear. During the decade of the 80s only three of the 26 teams did not win at least a division crown. Historians have attributed the parity of this decade to three reasons: more teams, the amateur draft, and the emergence of free agency. With the addition of 10 more major league teams by the late 1970s, the number of players in the league jumped by 250 (25 per team) so talent was spread a little thinner over that many more teams. The talent was spread more equally with the addition of an amateur draft in 1965. Teams could choose players in reverse order of how they finished the previous season (so the teams with the worst records got the first picks in the draft), and this served to offset the age-old advantage of the larger-populated cities. For almost a century, the reserve clause had been the owners' hammer they held over players' heads when negotiating contracts. The reserve clause bound players to their respective teams for one year after their contract expired. Under the clause, players had two options: they could ask to be released from their contracts or they could hold out, refusing to play and thereby forfeiting their pay. The National League adopted the clause from its inception in 1876 and the American League followed suit when it joined the National League as baseball's other major league in 1903. It was a difficult position for the players, but the owners thought it necessary to limit free agency and keep salaries down. There was also a fear by the owners that if the clause ever went away, the best players would go to the teams with the most money and the results would be domination by the dynastic, large population centers. When the reserve clause was modified and free agency by players emerged in the mid-1970s, the opposite appeared to be the case. Major League Baseball became more of an even playing field. How this process played out deserves a closer look.

Curt Flood was an outfielder who came of age in baseball during the early years of integration in the game during the 1950s. For the African American Flood, it was a difficult time in which he remembered feeling "too young for the ordeal" of often being the only black player on a small town minor league club. He said that he often "would break down in tears as soon as he reached the safety of his room."[5] By 1969, he was a 31-year-old veteran who felt like he had paid his dues and deserved to be treated as such. He had played 12 seasons for the St. Louis Cardinals and had become a star earning seven Gold Glove awards and batting over .300 in six seasons. He had even been voted one of the team captains, but after the season he was notified that he had been traded to the Philadelphia Phillies. He refused the trade not wanting to play for a bad team and in front of fans he believed to be racist. Flood convinced the Major League Baseball Players Association's (MLBPA) executive director Marvin Miller that he wanted to challenge the reserve clause in court as a violation of federal antitrust statutes even though it might mean the end of his career. The case went all the way to the Supreme Court and, in 1972 (by this time Flood had sat out the entire 1970 season and although signing with the Washington Senators in 1971 he only played 13 games and retired), the court found against Flood and upheld the 1922 court's decision to exempt Major League Baseball from antitrust law. Although Flood lost, the result was a hardening of the player union's position against the reserve clause and a push for free agency. In 1974 Oakland Athletics pitcher **Jim "Catfish" Hunter** took his owner Charley Finley to arbitration over his salary and the head of the arbitration board, Peter Seitz, ruled that since Finley had not fulfilled the terms of his contract that Hunter was now a free agent. Finley hoped the other owners would remain united and not sign Hunter, but the new owner of New York Yankees **George Steinbrenner** apparently did not get the memo as he offered Hunter a five-year contract worth $3.75 million. The entire baseball world was taken aback from the enormity of this contract and the *Sporting News*, baseball's oldest publication, wrote that "Baseball's establishment will live to regret the Catfish Hunter case and players will live to profit from it."[6]

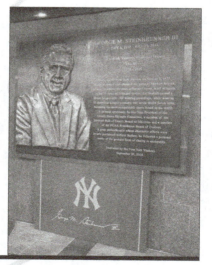

Monument to George Steinbrenner in Yankee Stadium. Image © Daniel M. Silva, 2013. Used under license from Shutterstock, Inc.

The following year two pitchers, Andy Messersmith and Dave McNally, refused to sign new contracts after their old ones expired. They were forced to report to their respective teams anyway under the reserve clause and they both played the 1975 season. Both Marvin Miller and Peter Seitz warned the owners that they needed to revise the reserve clause or there would be problems. The owners refused and, after the 1975 season, Seitz ruled in favor of Messersmith (McNally had retired). The owners appealed the ruling but the courts found in favor of the arbitration board's decision. Now Major League Baseball had to decide on the reserve clause as the courts had essentially declared every player (except those in multiyear contracts) would become free agents simply by playing out the 1976 season. Ultimately, the powers in baseball decided that players who had played for six seasons became eligible for free agency. The combination of the introduction of player arbitration rights in the early 70s, the 1975 decision in the courts, and baseball's free agency decision in 1976 resulted in a major power shift away from the owners and toward the players. It also resulted, as the *Sporting News* had correctly predicted, in an escalation of players' salaries. The average salary for a major league baseball player in 1976 was $52,300. By 1980 that salary had nearly tripled to $146,000. By the end of the 1980s the average had more than tripled again to $589,000.[7] Free agency can also be credited with helping bring parity to the game as it was at least partially responsible for the breakup of the powerful Oakland Athletics teams of the early 1970s and the "Big Red Machine" in Cincinnati during the mid-70s.

The game was also changing on the field as well during the two-division era. Players were bigger and stronger than they had been in earlier times. The average height of the player at the beginning of the century was just under 5 feet 10 inches. In 1990 the average was 6 feet, 3 inches—a full five inches taller. In the 1950s there were very few men in all of major league baseball who weighed more than 200 pounds, but by the end of the century every team had numerous 200-pounders. Increased focus on diet and the growing acceptance of weight training was an important factor in this phenomenon. Although there was not a dramatic difference in offensive output during this period, players will tell you that batters were hitting the ball harder. As a result, infielders would play deeper than they had in the past. Because there was also an increase in speed during the time, infielders and outfielders had to have stronger arms to throw from their deeper positions to get the faster runners out. Phil Rizzuto, who had played shortstop for the Yankees in the forties and fifties and was positioned a few feet behind the baseline, said in 1990, "I couldn't have played the short leftfield that guys do today."[8] The lost art of the stolen base returned as an offensive weapon. After the advent of the power game in the 1920s, the stolen base nearly disappeared in baseball strategy. During the forties and fifties whole teams averaged fewer than 50 stolen bases per season. During the 1960s, that began to change and it was led by black and Latino players. In 1962 Dodgers shortstop **Maury Wills** stole 104 bases, breaking Ty Cobb's 1915 record of 96. As a team the Dodgers stole 198 which broke the record set in 1918. Wills had won the National League stolen base title for six consecutive years when **Lou Brock** of the St. Louis Cardinals broke that streak in 1966. He would go on to win the title eight of the next nine seasons and eventually broke Wills' single season stolen base record in 1974 when he stole 118. Most importantly for the future of the game, both Wills' and Brock's speed helped power their respective teams to National League pennants during the 1960s (Dodgers in 63, 65, and 66; and Cardinals in 64, 67, and 68) so managers began to recognize the importance of this strategy to winning games and championships, and they started to use the stolen base as an offensive weapon. Over the next two decades virtually all stolen base records fell. Brock's single season record stood until **Rickey Henderson** stole an incredible 130 in 1982. When Brock retired in 1979, he had broken Ty Cobb's record of career stolen bases with 938. Twelve years later Henderson would also break that record and go on to steal a total of 1,406 bases by his retirement in 2003.

The other major change in strategy during the era was an increase in the use of relief pitchers. The manager had always been reluctant to let go of what Ben Rader called the "complete game mystique."[9] At the beginning of the century, the starting pitcher completed nearly two-thirds of all games. Managers stuck with the starter unless he really struggled because they often had no one better in the bullpen. An extreme example of this was game seven of the 1925 World Series when the Washington Senators' manager Bucky Harris left Walter Johnson in the game even though he gave up 15 hits and nine runs for the full nine innings. After the Senators lost 9–7, American

League President Ban Johnson asked Harris why he had left the 38-year-old Johnson in the game when he had the best reliever in baseball, Fred Marberry, in his bullpen, he said, "I went down with my best."[10] In other words, even the best reliever in the game was not better than your best starter, tired or not. During the first years after the war, managers began to use their bullpens with more frequency, especially during the pennant races and the World Series, but starters were still completing over 25 percent of games when the two-division era began. By the time it ended (1993), they were completing less than 10 percent. The use of the relief pitcher became so much more widely used that, in 1974, Mike Marshall became the first relief pitcher to win the Cy Young award in the National League. Reliever Sparky Lyle won the American League Cy Young three years later. In 1981, Rollie Fingers not only won the AL Cy Young but also the Most Valuable Player Award. Fingers helped usher in a new phenomenon in pitching known as the "closer." The closer was a pitcher who would come into the game (usually in the ninth inning) and close out the game. He would often be preceded by the "setup" man who would pitch one to two innings prior and, depending on how the starter was doing, there might be a middle or long reliever before the setup man. By the 1980s and early 90s, the bullpen was an integral part of the game. As their importance grew, so did their salaries. The closer would especially command larger salaries, which also led to pressure on the managers to use them. By the 1990s most managers did not expect starters to finish a game and their strategies reflected that. Even if a starter was pitching well into the late innings they would rarely finish the game. Added to that was the new phenomenon known as the "**pitch count**." Toward the end of the two-division era, there began to be a movement to count the number of pitches thrown and limit pitchers to 100 pitches per game. The belief was that a pitcher's effectiveness drops dramatically after that "magic" number. There have been many critics of this idea—some who say that every pitcher is different and there is not a one-size-fits-all solution. Others have argued that it becomes a self-fulfilling prophecy—that the pitcher could be doing great until he realizes he's past the 100 pitch count and then falls apart. The argument behind the pitch count was that it protected the investment of the owner by prolonging the career of pitchers. Critics have complained that it babies the pitcher too much and quite often more injuries emerge as a result of this "babying" than if they had thrown more pitches. Defenders of the policy point to pitchers enjoying longer careers due to the count. As for its effect on the game, some argue it led to more relief pitching; others claim the more relief pitching led to the pitch count. It is somewhat of a "chicken and egg" argument that won't be solved anytime soon. One thing is certain, over two decades after its introduction, the pitch count appears to be a permanent part of the game.

Third Modern Era (1993–present)

Second Expansion; Wild-Card; Steroid Era

MORE EXPANSION

In 1993, major league baseball expanded from 26 teams that had made up its ranks since 1977 to 28 teams with the addition of the Florida Marlins and the Colorado Rockies—both of which joined the National League. After playing one season with the old division format it was decided to realign the divisions and add two playoff spots. There would be three divisions in each league: East, Central, West. The champion of each would make the playoffs plus one wildcard team made up of the next best record in the league. In 1998 two additional teams were added: the Arizona Diamondbacks in the National League West and the Tampa Bay Devil Rays in the American League East. The Milwaukee Brewers also agreed to change from the American League to the National League that year to keep even numbers in each league (14 in the AL and 16 in the NL). The realignment doubled the number of playoff teams from four to eight; and although there was some criticism from baseball purists that it watered down the playoffs and made the regular season less meaningful, others have lauded the move saying it makes sure a championship-caliber team does not get left out at the end of the season. The record over the past two decades appears to bear out that argument. Between 1996 and 2011 there have only been three seasons (1998, 2001, 2009) in which a wildcard team from one or both of the leagues has not at least advanced to the league championship series. In nine of those 16 seasons, a wildcard team has advanced to the World Series, winning it five times. In fact, it apparently was becoming such a common phenomenon that baseball decided to make it a bit more difficult for the wildcard teams to advance when it added an addition step for them in 2012. Starting that season there would be two wildcard teams that would meet in a one-game playoff and the winner would advance to play in the divisional, best of five series. In 2014 the San Francisco Giants defeated the Kansas City Royals in the World Series—both teams had begun the playoffs as wildcards. Unfortunately for baseball, they would have to wait to implement the original wildcard system until the 1995 postseason because there was a work stoppage in 1994. Beginning on August 12, 1994, there were no baseball games played until opening day the following year. For the first time since 1904 there was no world series played that season. Baseball became the first professional sport to cancel an entire postseason and fans were understandably upset by this. The third era of modern baseball was off to a rocky start.

Once an agreement was struck and the 1995 season commenced, many fans were not willing to forgive and forget—many of them simply stayed home. One of the themes of the third era of the modern baseball is its **attendance decline**. The year 1993 was a milestone year for baseball attendance—for the first time total attendance topped 70 million, up from just over 55 million in 1992 (keeping in mind there were two new teams added in 1993, it was still a dramatic increase). Average attendance for the 1993 season was over 31,000 per game. Prior to the strike in 1994, attendance numbers even exceeded that average but in 1995 they dropped dramatically to just over 25,000 per game. Twenty million fewer fans went to baseball games in 1995 than had gone in 1993. The numbers rose slowly and did not top 70 million again until 1998 when expansion added two new teams and there was a dramatic home run chase between Sammy Sosa and Mark McGwire to see who could break Roger Maris' 1961 record of 61 home runs in a single season. It took until 2006 before the average per-game attendance reached pre-strike numbers. That is a long time to hold a grudge and it was costly both financially for baseball and for the popularity of the sport. As it approaches two decades since the strike there are still people who refuse to watch baseball because of what they perceive to be the greediness of the players.

Return of the Dynasty

While the 1980s had seen more parity in the game, beginning in 1995 two teams dominated their respective leagues for the next six seasons. Between 1995 and 2000 the Atlanta Braves and the New York Yankees won their divisions every year, and at least one of the teams played in the World Series in each of these years (save 1997) with the Yankees winning four championships and the Braves winning one (1995). The Yankees defeated the Braves both times they faced each other in the World Series (1996 and 1999). On opening day 1996 the Yankees, despite objections from owner George Steinbrenner, started a 21-year-old rookie at shortstop—the first time a rookie had started at that position since Tom Tresh in 1962. The rookie's name was **Derek Jeter** and that day he hit his first career home run. That season he would hit nine more while batting in 78, scoring 104 runs, and amassing a .314 batting average. He was unanimously voted the American League rookie of the year and led the Yankees to their first World Series championship since 1978. Jeter batted .361 in the postseason and

Derek Jeter. Image © Rena Schild, 2013.
Used under license from Shutterstock, Inc.

picked up the other veteran players for the Yankees who struggled offensively. This would become a seemingly yearly event as Jeter would always produce in the postseason and help the Yankees win four championships in his first five seasons including three in a row beginning in 1998. The 1998 team is often mentioned as one of the best teams of all time, winning 114 games, and finishing off the season with a four-game sweep of the San Diego Padres. When the Yankees won their third straight World Series in 2000, it was especially sweet as it came against the cross-town rival Mets. It was the first subway series (featuring New York teams) since 1956. It was not, however, the first time the two teams played as **interleague play** had begun in 1997, and the schedulers made sure teams from the same city played at least two series per season. Because of interleague play it was not necessary to have an even number of teams in each league so in 2013 the Houston Astros moved from the National League Central Division to the American League Western Division which evened all six divisions with 5 apiece. Since 2013 there must be at least one interleague series happening at all times because of the change.

In 2001 the Yankees were attempting to make it four consecutive championships when the World Trade Center was attacked by terrorists on September 11 and over 3,000 people were killed. The whole sports world seemed to stop and baseball was no exception. Games were postponed for one week until it was decided to start the season again if nothing else to serve as a diversion from the horrible news of the day. Long seen by many as the "evil empire" of baseball, the Yankees with their mega-payroll and yearly trips to the World Series were actually embraced by much of the country and were viewed as a symbol of not only the resiliency of New York to respond from the tragedy but the country itself. Their run through the pennant chase and playoffs seemed to lift the spirits of New Yorkers. Always known as a clutch player, Jeter earned a new moniker during the 2001 World Series when he hit a game-winning home run to defeat the Arizona Diamondbacks in game four, one minute after midnight on November 1. Because of the delay due to the attacks, this marked the first time in history that baseball was played in November and Jeter was dubbed "Mr. November" for his game-winning hit. Unfortunately for the Yankees and their followers, the Diamondbacks won the series in thrilling fashion in seven games. This seemed to mark the end of this incarnation of the Yankee dynasty as they would not win another championship until 2009. Jeter proved that age was not a factor that season as he put the team on his back and batted .355 in the postseason including .407 in the World Series against the Phillies at the age of 35. That season he became the all-time Yankee hit leader (2,772 hits) passing Lou Gehrig on, ironically, September 11. Two years later he became only the 28th player in major league history to get 3,000 hits. He retired after the 2014 season with 3,465 hits which is 6th all-time. His final hit in Yankee Stadium came in dramatic fashion as he slapped a single to right field to drive in the winning run to defeat the Baltimore Orioles. Unfortunately for Jeter and Yankee fans, the team failed to make the playoffs that year for only the third time in his career. The first decade of the 21st century brought not only the first championships of the Diamondbacks (2001) and Angels (2002), but it also saw the breaking of two of the oldest "curses" in baseball history. In 2004 the Boston Red Sox won their first championship since 1918. It was referred to as the "curse of the Bambino" due to sale of Babe Ruth to the Yankees in 1920. The 2004 team also broke another record by being the first team to ever come back from a 3–0 deficit when they won four straight games to take out their hated rival, the Yankees. The following year the Chicago White Sox ended their drought by winning their first championship since 1917. The infamous "Black Sox" scandal of 1919 appeared to have finally been exorcised. Presently the longest World Series drought belongs to their neighbors to the north. The Cubs last won the World Series in 1908. In 1945 the Cubs appeared in their last World Series, and there was a man who wanted to bring his goat into Wrigley Field for a World Series game but was denied access because of the odor of the goat. Legend has it that he put a curse on the Cubs from that day forward. Whether one believes the "curse of the billy goat" or not, the Cubs have never since been to the World Series.

Camden Yards in Baltimore. Image © Heath Oldham, 2013. Used under license from Shutterstock, Inc.

Steroids

The main theme to the third modern era would have to be the incredible surge of power hitters not seen since the 1920s. There is a long list of reasons for this surge from new hitter-friendly ballparks to the dilution of the pitching talent due to expansion to "juiced" baseballs ("Juiced" meaning wound tighter). The 1990s saw a number of ballparks built that were attempts at recapturing the golden age of baseball when the parks were quirky and smaller. The movement seemed to be a reaction to the "cookie cutter" parks that had been built in the 1960s and 70s that had no character. The first of these "retroparks" was Camden Yards in Baltimore that opened in 1992. Although some of the parks were smaller, that did not seem to be the answer to the rising number of home runs by the late nineties. While it is true there were more pitchers due to expansion, that would also not seem to be a viable reason for the skewed numbers and the idea that the balls were wound tighter and would fly out of the parks more easily was never proven. Others pointed to lighter bats being used and umpires reducing the size of the strike zone. Although it did seem as though strike zones were miniscule by the end of the decade, that might be a good argument for higher on-base percentages, batting averages, and maybe a slight increase in home runs—but not to the extent that was seen in the late nineties. The more plausible explanations were an increase in weight training and the use of performance-enhancing drugs.

Although simply looking at the numbers of home runs hit does not answer the entire question, it is telling. As already noted earlier in this chapter, the decade of the 1960s was known as the "age of the pitcher," and home run totals as with most offensive numbers were down. In 1968, the last year before realignment (also known as the "year of the pitcher"), the home run total, not surprisingly, reached its low for the decade with under 2,000 total home runs (an average of 99.75 home

Sammy Sosa being hugged by Mark McGwire. © Stephan Savoia/ /AP/Corbis

runs for the 20 teams in MLB). In 1969 the total jumped to over 3,000 and although there were four more teams added to the major leagues, the number jumped from under 100 home runs per team to almost 130. The number stayed relatively constant over the next two decades inching up slightly (with the exception of 1987 when totals ballooned to over 4,400 or 171 per team). In the first year of the third modern era (1993), the totals were approximately where they had been in the late 70s (143 home runs per team) but things were about to change drastically. By 1996 the total was over 177 per team and by 2000 the total reached its zenith. The 2000 total topped out at just under 190 home runs per team.

The individual home run numbers are perhaps even more telling. Roger Maris broke Babe Ruth's 34-year-old single season home run record when he hit 61 in 1961. Over the next 30 years only three players hit more than 50 home runs (Willie Mays hit 52 in 1965; George Foster matched that in 1977; and Cecil Fielder hit 52 in 1990). Between 1962 and 1992 the average number of home runs hit by the MLB leader was just under 45. Between 1995 and 2002 (the height of the power surge), that average jumped to nearly 60 per year with two players hitting over 70. The first time a player hit 70 home runs was in 1998. That whole summer right fielder **Sammy Sosa** of the Cubs and first baseman **Mark McGwire** of the Cardinals were battling it out for the crown. It was an incredible race that captivated the nation and brought many fans back to the game that had left it after the 1994 strike. McGwire won out with 70 and Sosa finished a close second with 66. What had taken 34 years and 37 years, respectively, with the Ruth and Maris record-breakers only took three years when Giants outfielder **Barry Bonds** hit 73 in 2001. It may have been the short length of time between the records, it may have been the fact Barry Bonds had never hit 50 home runs in a season, or it may have been the fact Barry Bonds' head looked like it had grown at least three sizes since his rookie season (enlarged skulls being a symptom of long-lasting steroid use); but the earlier whispers about performance-enhancing drugs turned to out-and-out accusations after 2001. In 2005, Jose Canseco wrote a tell-all book called *Juiced: Wild Times, Rampant 'Roids, Smash Hits & How Baseball Got Big*, in which he not only admitted his own steroid use but implicated many others including his former teammate Mark McGwire. He went so far as to say he estimated the number of players who used performance-enhancing drugs could have been as high as 85 percent. Most who were implicated denied it but many later admitted using drugs—including McGwire who admitted that he had done so—including 1998 when he broke the home run record.

Barry Bonds' home run swing . Image © Daniel M. Silva, 2013. Used under license from Shutterstock, Inc.

The cloud of steroids hovered over all the players who played during the era and, even if your record was clean, you were inexorably linked with those who used. One player who played his entire career during this era but whose name was never mentioned in the same breath as drug accusations was **Darin Erstad** who played for 14 seasons from 1996–2009. Erstad was the number one draft pick in 1995. He was chosen out of the University of Nebraska by the Angels. He played 11 of his 14 seasons with the Angels including catching the last fly ball of the 2002 World Series which cemented the franchise's first and thus far only championship. After retiring in 2009, he went into coaching and currently is the head coach at his alma mater. He said the steroid era has changed how people look at players who have particularly good performances: "That's part of our sports culture now—a guy does good, the first question is: Why? Are they really that good or is there something else going on?" Although the steroid problem is not limited to baseball, Erstad believes there seems to be a special spotlight on the sport: "Baseball had the sacred records from previous generations like the home run record. Are they going to question a quarterback in football because he is throwing for more yardage and touchdowns? Probably not but the sheer act of hitting a baseball as far as it will go is again something sacred in baseball, and it (the tremendous surge in power) caused a lot of controversy."[11]

Darin Erstad. Image © Aun-Juli Riddle, 2013. Used under license from Shutterstock, Inc.

Erstad said despite claims to the contrary, from his perspective, there were not that many who were using steroids: "To say that it was 80 percent of players (like Canseco suggested) just isn't true. I had suspicions about guys on our team but it was one, maybe two guys and that was it." He said the subject was really never talked about until the home run race in 1998 started to raise eyebrows. The issue was brought up during the players' collective bargaining discussions in 1997, but the players worried that any kind of admission would open up a "Pandora's box" of "Olympic-style testing." There was also the fact that baseball was just emerging from the latest work stoppage and it was worried about its image. The simple fact was the home run race in 1998 and the subsequent power in the game was bringing back fans, and it became easy to look the other way. However, as the accusations and admissions began to mount up, baseball decided to clamp down and get serious about testing and punishment. It took nearly a decade from the collective bargaining agreement in 1997, but, in 2004, it implemented "Olympic-style" testing as Erstad put it, and in 2005 the punishment for violations were increased to 50 and 100 game suspensions for the first and second violations and (appropriately for baseball), for the third strike, you're out—lifetime ban for a third violation. On why it took so long, Erstad said there was plenty of blame to go around: "It was difficult in the beginning because we had been so unified to not give in as a union to owner demands, but eventually common sense came into play and we decided we needed to clean up the game. What we're getting now (testing) is good for the game." In Erstad's opinion, is the game now clean because of the testing? "When there's that much money out there, players will continue to push the envelope as far as what they can get away with. To say the sport's clean? There's no way it's clean . . . there's no way. Chemists are good—they're going to be one step ahead of the testing at every level . . . it's just an ongoing battle."[12]

Conclusion

The game may not be clean—but it seems to be clean*er*. After the new policy was implemented in 2005, there has been a steady decline in power. In 2007 the number of total home runs dropped below 5,000 for the first time since 1997 (and there were two fewer teams that year) and fewer hit in 2008 and 2009. The numbers appear to be returning to a normal level; and although it may not

Roger Clemens. Image © Daniel M. Silva, 2013. Used under license from Shutterstock, Inc.

be as many home runs hit, the ones that *are* hit have a much better chance of being legitimate. Legitimacy seems to be the concern when looking at players from this era. Of the top 12 all-time home run leaders, five of them were active during this era and are, therefore, tainted—including the top of the list Barry Bonds. What would have been considered automatic Hall of Fame credentials for him and the other four (Sammy Sosa, Mark McGuire, Alex Rodriguez, and Rafael Palmeiro) are no longer so automatic. Hitters were not the only players being accused of taking PEDs—pitchers also fell under the scrutiny. One of the greatest of all time, **Roger Clemens**, was accused of using steroids—an accusation he denied to a Congressional committee. He was then charged with perjury but was eventually acquitted. He is number 9 all time with 354 wins and the only pitcher to win the Cy Young award seven times—the steroid stain will probably keep him out of the Hall. With the testing and stricter punishments being enforced, is it possible we're moving into a new era—a post-steroid era perhaps? Darin Erstad is skeptical: "I don't think the steroid thing is ever going away. I think some players will always try to get a competitive advantage."[13]

Notes

1. Benjamin Rader, *American Sports; From the Age of Folk Games to the Age of Televised Sports*, 6th ed. (Upper Saddle River, NJ: Pearson-Prentice Hall, 2009), 258.
2. Benjamin Rader, *Baseball; A History of America's Game*, 3rd ed. (Chicago and Urbana: University of Illinois Press, 2008), 186.
3. Ibid., 185.
4. Ibid., 185–186.
5. Ibid., 168.
6. Ibid., 211.
7. Ibid., 213.
8. Ibid., 230.
9. Ibid., 231.
10. Ibid., 232.
11. Interview with Darin Erstad, 27 June 2012.
12. Ibid.
13. Ibid.

CHAPTER
Twelve

Boxing

*T*he 1920s could be considered the golden age of modern sports and the dawn of the sports hero. The decade could also be considered the time when the nation accepted and even embraced one of the oldest sports in history: boxing. Part of the reason the once-outlaw sport was gaining in popularity was the shift in the culture of the country from the self-restrained 19th century Victorianism to a less-restrained, pleasure-seeking middle class of the early 20th century in which boxing was a better fit. The other reason for its popularity was certainly the hero of the sport and its most well-known champion of the decade: Jack Dempsey. He was the heavyweight champion for a majority of the decade and the personification of this new middle class with his explosive style. The sport's popularity took a hit after Dempsey was defeated by Gene Tunney in 1926 as well as the 1927 rematch. In fact, after Tunney abruptly announced his retirement in 1928, the title of heavyweight champion was vacant for nearly two years. During those two years there were many contenders for the championship, but it came down to four men (Americans Jack Sharkey, William Lawrence "Young" Stribling, Johnny Risko, and German Max Schmeling). After Sharkey defeated Stribling in 1928, Schmeling defeated Risko in the last major match of the decade in November of 1929 setting up the 1930 title bout in which Schmeling defeated Sharkey to take the title. Prior to the Schmeling-Risko fight, a British guest was announced and into the ring stepped Francis Archibald Kelhead Douglas. The Madison Square Garden crowd of 18,000 erupted in an extended standing ovation. Although the name may not have been familiar, his title was—Douglas was the Tenth **Marquess of Queensberry** and the New York fight crowd knew the significance of that title to the history of the sport.

Origins of Boxing

What was interesting is that the Marquess himself did not understand the significance of his title to boxing. As he stood in the ring acknowledging the cheers and applause he had no idea why an American crowd was so effusive in its support for an unknown British nobleman. Douglas was ignorant of the sport as well as his family's involvement in it: "The simple truth is that until that moment it had never occurred to me that it was my duty to have at least a smattering of knowledge of the sport which my ancestors did so much to foster."[1] As a result of this experience, the Marquess did become a fan of the sport as well as an amateur historian of his own family. In 1945 he wrote a history of his family titled, "The Sporting Queensberrys," in which he summed up his and his family's love of boxing as a love of "action." He wrote that "against a ton of words give me an ounce of action."[2] This could have been the mantra of the new middle class of the early 20th century.

It was the fourth Marquess of Queensbury who seemed to begin the tradition two centuries earlier—known as "**Old Q**," he would wager on anything. While he would bet on traditional sporting events such as horseracing, cricket, and boxing, what he really thrived on was setting up situations in which others would take his bets and he would almost always win. "Old Q" was more of a con-man than a gambler because the situations were slanted in his favor. One example is when he announced he could make a letter travel 50 miles in an hour. At the time (1753), 20 miles per hour was the fastest recorded travel speed, so bettors flocked to "Old Q" to take his challenge. To accomplish the feat he enclosed a letter inside a cricket ball and arranged 20 cricket players well known for their skill at throwing and catching in a circle with a circumference of one half mile. The ball made the circle 100 times (50 miles) in less than a half hour—"Old Q" collected again. Another time he bet that a man of his choosing could eat more at one sitting than any and all comers. Old Q was unable to attend the competition, but had a deputy attend and report back to him. Although no records exist of exactly what was consumed, his deputy reported: "Your man beat his opponent by a pig and an apple pie."[3] One of the few wagers that "Old Q" did not collect on was when he bet on his own death. In 1809 he was convinced he was about to die so he pronounced that he was opening up wagers on whether he would live past a certain date. Possibly not being of sound mind considering that would have been a difficult wager to collect on—he did pay out and lived nearly another year dying at the age of 84.

Five years before "Old Q" was born in 1725, a British fighter named James Figg declared himself the champion and "modern" boxing (i.e., boxing record-keeping) was born. Fist fighting goes back as far as human memory can travel—probably back to when humans first discovered their fists, but it was the ancient Romans who developed the first rules. Greek historian and essayist (who later became a Roman citizen) Plutarch, who lived in the 1st and 2nd centuries A.D., is credited with naming the sport ***pugilism***, which derived from the Latin word *pugnus*, meaning fist. It is believed pugilism was introduced to Britain when the Romans invaded in the first century and occupied the island until the 5th century. The sport had trouble gaining acceptance and all but disappeared shortly after. It returned in the 17th century and began to grow in popularity after Figg became champion and opened his own amphitheatre to showcase the sport (along with the more accepted sports of fencing and cudgeling). **Jack Broughton** succeeded Figg as champion and was instrumental in devising the first rules known as the "**London Prize Ring Rules**" in 1743. Figg had been the victim of the earlier lack of rules when he was strangled for half a minute before getting out of the hold. Broughton brought some order with his rules that outlawed hitting below the belt as well as hitting a man when he was down. The first superstar British champion was **Tom Cribb** who was proclaimed British champion in early 1810; and, after defeating the American **Tom Molineaux** (a former slave) later that year, he was declared the first British world champion. Throughout the 19th century, boxing was getting increasingly out of control—so much so that the Broughton rules were amended in the 1830s and 1850s. Eventually it was decided to throw out the old rules and implement new ones. In 1865, the 8th Marquess of Queensbury helped devise the "**Queensberry rules for the sport of boxing**" and they were made public in 1867. One of the main differences with the new rules was rule 8, which stated, "the gloves to be fair-sized boxing glove of the best quality and new."[4] These were the first published boxing rules that required gloves to be worn. While Britain immediately accepted the new rules, American fighters continued the tradition of bare-knuckle fighting for the next two decades, not requiring gloves to be worn until the end of the 1880s. Ironically, American boxers fought under the revised "London Prize Ring Rules" longer than the British boxers did.

Early American Champions and John L. Sullivan

Under the original Broughton rules, not only were bare fists allowed but also legal were what modern fans would consider wrestling moves. There were no time limitations put on rounds. Rounds ended when a participant was knocked or wrestled to the ground or deliberately fell to the ground to avoid further punishment. The fallen participant then had 30 seconds to "come to scratch" or "toe the mark" (the line drawn in the middle of the ring was known as the "scratch").[5] If he did not (or could not) do that, the fight was over. It was this lack of time limit, even more so than the fact no gloves were used, that led to the brutality of the sport at the time. Many fights would take hours to finish and it usually led to one (or both) of the participants being incapacitated by the end. Sometimes the results could even be fatal. One match in 1842 between Christopher Lilly and Thomas McCoy consisted of the two men beating each other's brains in for over two and a half hours before McCoy finally fell to the ground dead. It was these types of stories that led to calls for changes in the rules. Eventually, the Queensberry rules not only put a limit of three minutes per round but also a limit on the number of rounds in a fight (eventually settled on 20 rounds—but later that number was decreased even further, depending on the weight class). It would be years before those rules were implemented, however, and the American champions prior to the Civil War would fight using the Broughton rules. The first American champions tended to be Irish immigrants. The first major American champion was **John Morrissey** who was actually born in Ireland in 1831 and moved with his family to Troy, New York, when he was three. The Irish prided themselves on their ability to fight and Morrissey represented that culture and the working-class boxing fraternity in pre-war America. He first gained fame as a street fighter, but in 1853 he defeated Yankee Sullivan to become the unofficial American champion. Four years later he defeated another son of an Irish immigrant, **John C. Heenan**, who coincidentally was also from Troy. After defeating Heenan again in 1858, he decided to move into the gambling business. He took winnings from his fights and bought a gambling parlor in New York that by the end of the decade was the most successful in the city. After investing on other gambling houses in New York, he moved upstate and built a race track and casino in Saratoga. It was Morrissey who helped turn Saratoga into the Las Vegas of the 19th century. Unlike most former fighters, Morrissey was extremely successful after his boxing career ended and not only amassed a fortune but he also entered politics and served two terms in the House of Representatives before his death in 1878.

Former fighter John Morrissey as a member of congress. Image courtesy of Library of Congress

After Morrissey's retirement, Heenan assumed the mantle as champion and, in 1860; he travelled to London to fight the British champion Thomas Sayers. The fight turned into a 42-round, 2-hour-20-minute bloodbath in which the crowd became so out of control that they poured into the ring, and eventually the police broke up the fight and it was declared a draw. Although American fighters had made the trip to England twice earlier in the century to take on a British champion, hardly anyone had taken notice. The reaction to the Heenan-Sayers fight showed how boxing had grown in popularity over the past 50 years. Heenan was welcomed back to his home country as a conquering hero. There were estimated crowds of 50,000 that greeted him in New York and another 12,000 in Boston. Championship belts were created for both fighters and both nations (not surprisingly) claimed their fighter had been the true victor. Americans especially seemed to feel Heenan had been robbed of the championship by the home crowd and referee and rallied behind him. Historian Elliott Gorn wrote that boxing, while certainly not accepted in all parts of American society, was becoming more acceptable to a growing number of American males. It was those men who could "imagine prize fighters as representative (of) Americans, symbols of national prowess, (and) defenders of the Union against foreign foes. Boxing matches hardly offered a model of Victorian decorum, but Heenan seemed a comparatively respectable champion."[6] Unfortunately for Heenan and other boxing fans, a different fight would break out the following year that would relegate boxing (and about everything else) to the backburner. The American Civil War would put a stop to Heenan's career in the states. He went back to England during the war (a move which brought him some criticism for not fighting for the Union) and he boxed there, finally ending his career by losing a match in 1863.

While there were some organized matches during the Civil War by noncombatants, none of them lived up to the pre-war fights. There were many instances of soldiers staging boxing matches among themselves during the war and, even on at least two occasions, matches were staged with the enemy during ceasefires. One of those matches occurred in 1862 near Fredericksburg when a truce was announced; but not everyone got the word and some Union men shot at some Confederates, and one of the rebels issued a challenge to a fist fight with one of the "Yankees." The two began exchanging punches and eventually there was a large crowd of both Union and Confederate soldiers watching. Eventually the fight was called a draw and the truce was reinstated "ratifying their decision by handshakes all around."[7] Although boxing was popular during the war, it lost some of its luster during the post-war years of the 1860s and 70s mainly due to the sport getting a reputation for corruption. It's probably the easiest of all sports to "fix" or pay a competitor to "take a dive" by losing on purpose for gamblers and that became commonplace. As Gorn put it, "the ideal of a fair fight to the finish had given way to a presumption of corruption."[8] Sometimes it was hard to know who was on the take because it could very well have been both fighters. A championship bout in 1871 between Jem Mace and Joe Coburn went for an hour and 17 minutes with neither fighter landing a punch. All of this was not helped by the fact that boxing was not legal in most states, and it had an unsavory reputation among respectable Victorian society. The decade of the 1880s would usher in a resurgence in the sport due in large part to both an effort to clean it up and the work of one promoter and one fighter.

Richard Kyle Fox took over as owner/publisher of the sensationalistic *National Police Gazette* in 1877 and is considered by many as the father of the modern tabloid. During the heart of the Victorian period, the *Gazette* was famous for its non-Victorian content. It ran stories of scandals, printed pictures of scantily clad showgirls, and even printed advertisements for contraceptives. Fox also promoted various contests of skill but his favorite was boxing. He lobbied for years to bring the sport out of the shadows and make it legal (in most cases he was unsuccessful in that latter goal, but he did succeed in the first part of that goal to some extent). During the 1880s, Fox did his best to find a worthy opponent for the reigning champion, **John L. Sullivan**. Legend has it that early in Sullivan's career he was dining at Harry Hill's saloon in New York—a well-known hangout for boxers, and as Victorian reformers at the time called it, "the most dangerous and demoralizing" place in New York which was "the resort of a low class of prostitutes, and of the ruffians and idlers who support the prize ring."[9] Fox happened to be eating there at the same time and wanted Sullivan to be brought to his table to meet him. Sullivan supposedly replied that Fox "could come to him if he had something to say."[10] From that point on, there was an ongoing feud between the two which did both of their careers a world of good. In fact, as Elliott Gorn put it, "one suspects that their well-publicized enmity quickly became less a personal affair than a business ploy."[11] It became Fox's goal in life to bring Sullivan down but by doing so he gave the champion an incredible amount of publicity.

John L. Sullivan. Image courtesy of Library of Congress

John L. Sullivan was no shrinking violet and he was pretty good at self-promotion. He was born in 1858 in Boston's South End neighborhood to Michael and Katherine Sullivan, both Irish immigrants, and growing up in a tough neighborhood he became tough himself and eventually earned the nickname of the Boston Strong Boy. Throughout his teenage years he attempted different occupations, but quickly found out his penchant for fighting. In December of 1880 he travelled to Cincinnati to fight the "Champion of the West" John Donaldson. It marked Sullivan's first official "prize" fight as a purse of $53 was raised by the 30 spectators in attendance. Sullivan took only 21 minutes to defeat Donaldson and immediately issued a challenge to the boxing world: "I am prepared to make a match to fight any man breathing for any sum from one thousand dollars to ten thousand dollars . . . This challenge is especially directed at Paddy Ryan and will remain open for a month if he should not see fit to accept it."[12] The challenge by the 22-year-old was addressed to the *Cincinnati Enquirer*, but it was reprinted in dozens of papers all over the country. **Paddy Ryan** was the de facto champion at the time (there were no official champions in 1880) and believed to be the best fighter in the country. Ryan did not accept that challenge but did offer Sullivan a challenge of his own to "go and get a reputation."[13] For the next year that is exactly what he did by travelling across the country offering any man 50 dollars if they could stay in the ring with him for four rounds. He had many challengers but none who could last the four rounds. He also defeated some fighters in staged prize fights along the way. By late 1881, the pressure was on Ryan to set up a fight with Sullivan. Richard Fox offered to back Ryan with $10,000, and the *Police Gazette* constantly ran stories pushing for a fight. Eventually, Ryan agreed to fight Sullivan; and the match was set up for February 7, 1882, in the resort city of Mississippi City, Mississippi. The champion was no match for the challenger and the fight only lasted nine rounds. Ryan was quoted as saying, "When Sullivan struck me I thought a telegraph pole had been shoved against me endways."[14] The 23-year-old Sullivan was now the undisputed heavyweight champion of the country.

For the next decade Sullivan was the man to beat, and Fox's *Gazette* did what it could to find someone to beat him. It was a difficult task as Sullivan met all challengers (except Black fighters—many believed Peter Jackson was one of the best contenders of the time, but he never received a chance). Sullivan also went on another tour of the country, this time offering the incredible sum of $1,000 to anyone who could stay in the ring for four rounds. It is reported that of the dozens of men who tried, only one performed the feat. Sullivan could easily afford the $1,000 payout as he went from a young man who could not hold a job in the 1870s to the first athlete to earn over $1

Sullivan-Kilrain fight. Image courtesy of Library of Congress

million by the time his career ended. His career almost ended prematurely in 1888 when he fought the British champion Charlie Mitchell to a draw. He should have defeated Mitchell easily, but years of hard drinking and poor diet were beginning to catch up with Sullivan and he was woefully out of shape. He vowed to get back into shape before his next fight which he did and it was a classic. He fought **Jake Kilrain** (who Fox had earlier proclaimed champion because Sullivan had refused Kilrain's challenge due to the fact Sullivan had broken his arm and was unable to fight). The fight took place on July 8, 1889, outside in the hot summer sun of Richburg, Mississippi. The fight lasted over two hours and 75 rounds in what would be the last championship of the bare-knuckle era. Sullivan-backers were worried in the 44th round when he vomited after being given tea mixed with whiskey. Those who knew Sullivan claimed his "stomach was retaining the whiskey while rejecting the tea."[15] He recovered from that to go on and defeat Kilrain, but his age was beginning to show (he was now in his thirties) and years of hard living aged him even more and he knew it. He did not engage any serious fights for the next two years. Instead, he toured North America in 1890 and Australia in 1891 giving speeches and occasionally sparring with various young fighters.

One of those he sparred with during the tour was **James J. Corbett** from California. When the time came in early 1892 for a title defense he issued his challenge to the world and announced that the fight would be a gloved battle using the Marquess of Queensberry rules. In his challenge he mentioned three fighters by name: Frank Slavin of Australia, Charlie Mitchell of England (whom he fought to a draw four years earlier and said he "would rather whip than any man in the world),"[16] and Corbett. While the first two fighters refused, Corbett accepted; and the fight was set for September 7, 1892, in New Orleans. Corbett was different in many ways than Sullivan besides his age (he was eight years younger than the champion). Corbett viewed himself not as a brawler but as a "scientific" boxer than used strategy in the ring. Although he was also Irish, Corbett was not the street-fighter that Sullivan and many sons of Irish immigrants were in the late 19th century. Known as "Gentleman Jim," he attended college, held a white-collar bank teller job, and his training had not taken place in the backroom of some saloon but in an athletic club. It was the emergence of these clubs that had attempted to bring order to boxing by creating **six weight classes** and training referees to help end the chaos and danger of the old version of the sport. Richard Fox had added legitimacy to these weight classes by promoting the fights in the *Police Gazette* and creating championship belts for each of them. The Sullivan-Corbett fight was not only the first championship to use the Marquess of Queensberry rules, but it was also the first to be sponsored by an athletic club and to be fought indoors under electric lights. During the 1890s major newspapers were battling each other for readers and although earlier fights were condemned by newspapers, this one was actually promoted by them. In fact, the agreement for the fight was actually signed in the offices of the *New York World* newspaper as opposed to the *Police Gazette*, as fight agreements had been in the past. While it was promoted like no fight before it, once it got underway it was no contest. Sullivan was overweight, slow, and showing the signs of being nearly 34. Corbett was 25 pounds lighter than the champion and much quicker. Corbett almost seemed to toy with Sullivan until the 21st round when he "shot his right across the jaw and Sullivan fell like an ox."[17] Sullivan's reign was over and he never made another serious attempt at the title.

"Gentleman" James Corbett. Image courtesy of Library of Congress

Jack Johnson and the Great White Hope

"Gentleman" Jim would be the champion for the next five years until he was defeated by Englishman Bob Fitzsimmons on March 17, 1897 (Fitzsimmons would be the last British heavyweight champion for nearly a century). Although Sullivan had brought some respectability to the sport, boxing entered the 20th century with a bad reputation. It was still illegal in many parts of the country. The gamblers' effect on the sport still was strong and the average American believed most fights to be "fixed" and not legitimate. There was also the problem of some of the best challengers not getting a shot at the title because they were of the "wrong" skin color. Because of the racism prevalent in the country at the time, Black fighters were rarely, if ever, given serious consideration in boxing. The color line was not limited to American fighters, though. Black fighter Peter Jackson, who desperately desired to fight John L. Sullivan during his reign and never got the chance, was from Australia. African American **Jack Johnson** refused to suffer the same fate. Almost from the moment Canadian Tommy Burns won the championship in February of 1906, he was hounding him for a chance to fight him for the title. It took over two

Jack Johnson. Image courtesy of Library of Congress

years, a lot of money and a foreign country to finally give Johnson the chance. In December of 1908, wealthy Australian businessman Hugh McIntosh staged the championship that guaranteed Burns $30,000 win or lose and Johnson would receive $5,000. The amount guaranteed to Burns was by far the most ever awarded to any fighter, and it caught the attention of many including the former champion John L. Sullivan who said, "Shame on the money-mad champion! Shame on the man who upsets good American precedents because there are Dollars, Dollars, Dollars in it!"[18] Part of the reason Sullivan and other white champions followed that "good American precedent" was the fear that the Black fighter might be good enough to beat them; and that is exactly what happened in Sydney, Australia, on the day after Christmas in 1908. Burns was no match for Johnson and the boxing world, whether they liked it or not, was forced to recognize the new heavyweight champion of the world was not of the Caucasian race.

There immediately began a search for someone (white) to unseat Johnson. The challengers became known as America's "**Great White Hope**" to bring the title back to its "rightful" place. In a time of extreme racism in the North and Jim Crow segregation in the South, Jack Johnson was not a quiet champion. In the vernacular of the day, he was known as the prime example of an "uppity Nigger."[19] He was very outspoken in and out of the ring. In the ring he taunted his opponent with a smile on his face. Outside the ring he dressed lavishly and drove fast cars. He was also very open about his love for women—usually white women, which was an extreme taboo at the time. He married three different white women and had sexual relationships with many others. The first challenger white America produced for Jackson was a former champion, **James Jeffries**, who had been the champion from 1899 until 1905. He was the first modern boxer to relinquish the title by retiring. During his decade-long professional career he compiled a record of 19 wins 0 defeats and 2 draws. Jeffries was initially hesitant to come out of retirement—he had enjoyed his post-fighting career and was quite out of shape by 1909 when he began to be approached for a comeback against Johnson. He had ballooned from his fighting weight of 227 pounds to over 330 pounds. As usual, it was money that convinced him. There were many bids made for the fight, but the winner was a relative newcomer to the scene by the name of **George L. "Tex" Rickard**. Rickard had built and lost several fortunes as a professional gambler, saloon owner, gold prospector, and sports promoter. His bid of a total purse of over $100,000 to be split 75/25 between the winner and loser of the fight was by far the most ever offered in the history of prizefighting, and it was accepted by both parties.

The fight was billed as the battle for the racial supremacy of the respective fighters and was set for July 4, 1910, in Reno, Nevada. Jeffries had a lot of work to do to get back into fighting shape, and it appeared on the day of the fight that he had not reached the goal—he was 35 years old and looked, according to some spectators, "big, old and tired."[20] Although Jeffries had no history of animosity toward Blacks, it seems the months of racially charged promotion of the fight had an effect on Jeffries. Before the fight he said, "That portion of the white race that has been looking to me to defend its athletic superiority may feel assured that I am fit to do my very best."[21] Jeffries' "very best" was not good enough, and Johnson pummeled the older and slower fighter for 15 rounds before finally knocking him out. Most of the gamblers' money had been on the challenger (in fact, there was a rumor that Johnson would throw the fight) and when the fight ended, there was silence from the 20,000 spectators. Johnson biographer Randy Roberts in his book, *Papa Jack*, described the reaction of the crowd as similar to "the conclusion of a horse race where the favorite broke a leg and had to be destroyed."[22] Unfortunately, the rest of the country did not react to the outcome in silence. While the Black community erupted in celebration, angry white mobs sparked by the humiliation of the defeat took out its frustration on blacks in which many were injured and at least eight individuals lost their lives.

It was becoming apparent that it was going to be difficult to defeat Johnson in the ring so there began to be a concerted effort to take him down in a different manner. This is where Johnson's reputation did him no service—especially his reputation concerning women. It was the middle of the Progressive Era and reformers were everywhere—including moral reformers. In 1910 Republican Congressman James Robert Mann sponsored a bill known as the White Slave Traffic Act, but it became better known as the **Mann Act** which prohibited women being taken across state lines "for the purpose of prostitution or debauchery, or for any other moral purpose."[23] After defeating

Jim Flynn on July 4, 1912, to retain the heavyweight championship, the mother of one of Johnson's conquests claimed Johnson had violated the Mann Act with her daughter. Johnson was found not guilty on this charge, but it seemed to give those who wanted to bring Johnson down the blueprint on how to do it. Violations of the act were relatively few (2,801 in the 10 years it was in existence between 1910 and 1920—the Department of Justice estimating that 98 percent of those convictions involved the commercialized sex trade, not individual targets).[24] Jack Johnson was part of the two percent as United States District Attorney James Wilkerson brought more charges against Johnson, this time involving a prostitute named Belle Schreiber. She was the government's star witness and was planning on testifying against him (whereas the plaintiff in the earlier case refused to testify). Sensing that this time the case appeared more serious, Johnson first attempted to get in touch with Schreiber to talk her out of testifying (he admitted knowing her but denied the charges). When that failed he made an attempt to escape to Canada but was caught before leaving the country and returned to Chicago to stand trial. His attempted escape (which he denied doing) was not viewed favorably by the court, and he was found guilty and sentenced to one year in prison.

Now believing he could not get a fair hearing in the United States, Johnson made good on his earlier escape plans and went to Canada and eventually Europe in the summer of 1913 while waiting an appeal. At the end of the year he fought another African American fighter also named Johnson (Jim) in Paris which marked the first time two black men fought for the title. Although it was determined to be a draw, he retained the title. In 1914 he again fought in Paris defeating Frank Moran. He left Europe after the outbreak of World War I and knocked out Jack Murray in December of 1914 in Buenos Aires, Argentina. The following year, 1915, would prove to be the year that white boxing fans had been waiting for as there was finally a "Great White Hope" who rose to the challenge and defeated Johnson. His name was **Jess Willard** and he was from

Pottawatomie County Kansas and because of his size (6 feet, 6½ inches) was known as the "Pottawatomie Giant." In Havana, Cuba, on April 5, 1915, Willard knocked Johnson out in the 26th round. There were rumors that Johnson took a dive (spread by Johnson himself) in return for $50,000 and a commutation of his sentence and a return to the United States. Film of the fight seemed to add credence to the rumors as it showed a "knocked out" Johnson apparently shielding his eyes from the sun. What did not add credence to the claim was that Johnson stayed away from the United States for the next five years. He would fight a number of more times in Spain and Mexico before finally returning to his home country in 1920 where he served his sentence at Leavenworth, Kansas. During his incarceration he fought four more times—winning all four. He would continue to fight even into his sixties (two exhibitions were his last in 1945 at the age of 68) but he never again fought for the heavy-weight championship.

Willard knocking out Johnson in Havana, Cuba in 1915. Notice Johnson appearing to be shielding his eyes from the sun. Image courtesy of Library of Congress

Jack Dempsey and Boxing's "Golden Age"

Jess Willard defended his title only once, and it was a "no-decision" against Frank Moran in 1916. After leaving the country when Jack Johnson did, Tex Rickard was back and promoted this fight. Rickard realized Willard was uncharismatic and the sport (and he as a promoter) needed someone who could excite the masses. He found that someone in Colorado named **William Harrison**

Tex Rickard. Image courtesy of Library of Congress

Jack Dempsey and Jack Kearns. Image courtesy of Library of Congress

"Jack" Dempsey. Biographer Nat Fleischer described Dempsey as having "that spectacular . . . dynamic called charisma . . . Jack was not a scientific boxer, but a fighter with a capital F—the slugger par excellence."[25] This was what not only Rickard was looking for but also the new American middle class that was emerging after World War I. They found this kind of hero in Dempsey, Red Grange, and Babe Ruth. Ironically, Ruth and Dempsey were born in 1895. Dempsey was the ninth child of 11 born in Manassa, Colorado, which gave him his life-long nickname of the "Manassa Mauler." Hearkening back to the previous century, he was a fighter with Irish roots, and he was not a stranger to the barroom brawls of his ancestors. He fought low-stakes fights until hooking up with manager **Jack Kearns** in 1917. Kearns was able to get him higher-profile fights with many of the heavyweight contenders who all wanted a shot at Willard. By 1918 Kearns thought his fighter had earned a shot at the title so he went to New York to meet with Rickard. He was introduced by mutual friend Giants baseball manager John McGraw. The meeting did not go well and Rickard, whom Dempsey would later make an even wealthier man, was not impressed with the fighter from Colorado. "He's too small," he said, "He's no match for Jess. Do you want a killing on your hands?"[26]

Rickard was looking at a contender named Fred Fulton to fight Willard which he thought would be a much better match. Kearns did convince Rickard to set up a fight between Fulton and Dempsey on July 27, 1918. After Dempsey knocked Fulton out in the first round, he then proceeded to defeat every contender that could be found over the next nine months save one (he lost in a decision to Willie Meehan in September, but defeated an incredible 13 other fighters in that short time span—11 by knockout). This was enough to change Rickard's mind who set up a championship match between Dempsey and Willard on July 4, 1919. Because boxing was still not legal in New York, the agreement was made across the river in Weehauken, New Jersey (ironically where over a century earlier another illegal match was staged between Alexander Hamilton and Vice-President Aaron Burr— a duel that ended with Hamilton's death). Although this dual would be fought in Toledo, Ohio, it was Willard who issued a death warning to Dempsey when he said: "I want immunity against any injury suffered by Dempsey. Bull Young met accidental death in a battle with me and I don't want a recurrence."[27] Willard should have been more worried about himself than his opponent because Dempsey showed him no mercy as he punished him from the beginning of the fight (he knocked down the champion seven times in the first round) until the beginning of the fourth round when Willard's corner informed the referee that he was not able to continue the fight. Jack Dempsey, whom Tex Rickard had dismissed as "too small," was now the heavyweight champion of the world.

The 1920s dawned with boxing being viewed in a different light by the majority of Americans. Part of the reason for this was its being used as training for American soldiers going off to fight in World War I. It was seen now more as a positive form of exercise and was acceptable to a growing group of Americans who were looking for excitement in their lives. It was no longer that outlaw activity spoken about in hushed tones and fought in backrooms and river barges staying one step ahead of the local authorities but in public arenas being promoted in newspaper sports pages. Evidence of this was seen as one by one states repealed their bans on the sport. The New York legislature made boxing officially legal in 1920 and, in December, the future Mecca of the sport, Madison Square Garden, hosted its first heavyweight championship title defense when Dempsey knocked out Bill Brennan in the 12th round to retain the title. Rickard now looked to reach heights never before achieved in the sport—he wanted a million-dollar gate. Although even the biggest fights in the past rarely brought in more than $300,000, the new popularity of the sport and its champion convinced Rickard it was possible. When he set up a fight between the Frenchman **Georges Carpentier**, who was billed as Europe's best fighter, and Dempsey, he knew this could be a promoter's dream. Carpentier had distinguished himself as a soldier fighting for France during the war and Dempsey, who had not served, had to defend himself against accusations that he was a "**slacker**" (the World War I equivalent of a draft dodger). Formal charges were brought against him, but a jury quickly acquitted him in June of 1920 saying that he received a deferment from the draft because he was his family's only means of support. Despite the acquittal, Dempsey was still viewed by many as shirking his duty during the war; and Rickard planned to play that up in his promotion of the Carpentier fight. The whole country began choosing sides—the American Legion passed a resolution condemning Dempsey while the Veterans of Foreign Wars sided with him. Debate over the fight even reached the floor of the United States Senate—but the important thing in Rickard's eyes was that it was being talked about, and he knew he was going to have a huge gate. He was so sure about it that he financed the building of a 91,000-seat capacity stadium in Jersey City, New Jersey, for the fight. Rickard got what he wanted as over 80,000 showed up on July 2, 1921, and the gross was over $1.7 million for the largest gate of all time up to that point. Unfortunately for those who watched, the "European Champ" had been largely overbilled and it was not much of a contest. Carpentier was battered by Dempsey for three rounds before being knocked out in the fourth.

Rickard had now set the bar pretty high in terms of the gate, and he always claimed that it took at least two years to put together a million dollar fight. In the meantime, though, Dempsey wanted to keep his name out there and capitalize on his growing popularity since the Carpentier fight as well as keep in shape so he fought two "smaller" matches before the next "big" one. Both of them ended in decisions for the champ: the first against Jimmy Darcy in 1922 and the second against Tommy Gibbons in July of 1923. The Gibbons fight turned out to be more difficult than many imagined. In front of a crowd of only 7,000 in Shelby, Montana, Gibbons kept "running and twisting like a coyote" to avoid the savage beatings others had taken from Dempsey. Biographer Nat Fleischer, who attended all of Dempsey's big fights, called Gibbons the "best defensive fighter Dempsey had ever met."[28] The fight went the full 15 rounds and Dempsey won the unanimous decision. The main event was planned for that September at the Polo Grounds (home of the baseball Giants) against Argentinian **Luis Firpo**. When Dempsey defeated Willard who was six inches taller than he was, he had been referred to as "Jack the Giant Killer." Now Rickard had found another giant (or at least one that he could promote as the "Argentine Giant" even though he was only two inches taller than Dempsey), and he believed he could get another million dollar gate with similar promotion and he was right. Over 80,000 turned out, spending $1.1 million (it could have been an even bigger gate but a reported 20,000 were turned away). The fight turned out to be better than the Carpentier match even though it was shorter. The first round was when all the fireworks occurred including seven knockdowns of the challenger and two of the champion. The second of those actually knocked Dempsey completely out of the ring and into press row with his head landing on a typewriter. It took a reported 14 seconds to get him back into the ring with the help of some reporters—had it taken six seconds longer, Firpo would

Dempsey vs. Firpo. Image courtesy of Library of Congress

have become the new heavyweight champion. Dempsey was able to finish the round and, when he came out for the second, he was a new man and knocked Firpo out to retain the title. Although a brief fight, it is often remembered by those who saw it as one of the greatest of all time.

Harry Wills. Image courtesy of Library of Congress

Gene Tunney.
Image courtesy of
Library of Congress

The next three years were eventful for Dempsey outside the ring but not in—he had no title defenses until 1926. His popularity was at an all-time high and he appeared to be in no hurry to return to the ring as he made over half a million dollars a year in endorsements, vaudeville performances, movies, and just being Jack Dempsey. He and his long time manager Jack Kearns separated in 1924 and it was not an amicable parting. Kearns claimed he was owed money by Dempsey and took him to court. Rickard seemed preoccupied with his involvement in the building of a new Madison Square Garden, which he helped to finance and promote and opened in 1926. On top of all of this, Dempsey's wife wanted him to retire. Another factor in Dempsey's absence from the ring was **Harry Wills** who was considered to be the best challenger of the time. The problem was that Wills was black. There is varying information as to why this matchup never took place. Some say Rickard refused to promote a Dempsey-Wills fight either out of racism or worry about race riots, and some say it was Dempsey himself who refused for the same reasons (along with the reason that he might lose). Others say that there were attempts made to make the fight happen by Rickard, Kearns, and Dempsey but that they were blocked by politicians. Dempsey told his biographer Nat Fleischer that the match had been set up to be fought in Jersey City, but the New Jersey governor refused to allow it to take place. Fleischer claims to back this up by referring to a ticket he owns to the fight that never took place and it was dated November 8, 1924.

Whatever the reason, Wills never got a shot at the title and, instead, Rickard set up Dempsey's next title defense against **Gene Tunney** on September 23, 1926. Because the New York Boxing Commission had ordered Dempsey to fight Wills, the match could not take place in New York so it was staged in Philadelphia in front of the largest-ever crowd to witness a boxing match: 120,000. Tunney was regarded by many as a second-rate fighter but he surprised everyone by staying with Dempsey, finishing the fight, and actually receiving a unanimous decision. Almost immediately following the loss, Dempsey and Rickard began to work on a rematch. Dempsey's wife begged him to retire, but Rickard knew he was still the biggest draw in the sport so he first set up an elimination match at Yankee Stadium between Dempsey and Jack Sharkey—considered to be one of the best challengers. In what turned out to be his fourth million dollar fight, Dempsey knocked him out in the second round, and a rematch with Tunney was set for September 22, 1927, at Soldier Field in Chicago. Over 100,000 people saw what became known as the controversial "**Long Count**" match. The source of controversy occurred in the seventh round when Dempsey knocked Tunney down and, after the referee asked Dempsey to retire to his corner, he didn't and the start of the referee's count was delayed. Tunney rose on the count of nine but witnesses say he was down for much longer than that. Tunney stayed upright for the rest of the fight and won by unanimous decision. Dempsey then permanently retired and his popularity continued to grow to even greater heights. Sadly for Tunney, he was never able to reach the popularity of Dempsey—largely because he was more of a scientific fighter than Dempsey had been and the American public craved a dynamic, exciting slugger that Tunney was not. Rickard actually lost $400,000 on Tunney's only title defense against Tom Heenan in 1928 after which Tunney promptly retired. To make matters worse for the sport, Rickard was in the middle of promotion for an elimination series to set up another heavyweight championship when he died of appendicitis on January 6, 1929. There was no one to replace Dempsey and, as it turned out, there was no one to replace Rickard; and the Golden Age of boxing came to an abrupt halt.

Boxing in the Great Depression and Joe Louis

There was not much "golden" about the next decade in or out of sports. The Great Depression affected all corners of American society and, as it spread, the whole world. There were no million dollar gates to be found for the first part of the decade—far from it. Even Tex Rickard himself had he lived would have found promotion difficult during the period. That does not mean, however, there were not heavyweight championships fought during the Depression. German **Max Schmeling** began the decade as the champ after defeating top challenger Jack Sharkey. Sharkey got his chance for revenge after defeating Italian **Primo Carnera**, and he defeated Schmeling in a controversial split-decision on June 21, 1932. Carnera, in turn, defeated Sharkey the following year to become the champion. Sharkey attempted an unsuccessful comeback over the next three years in which he fought seven times, winning only twice and losing four times with one draw. His final fight came against up-and-coming challenger **Joe Louis** in 1936. He lost to Louis and promptly announced his retirement. Sharkey holds the distinction of being the only boxer to fight both Jack Dempsey and Joe Louis (losing to both great champions).

It would be another year before Louis would get his shot at the title. In the meantime, Carnera was defeated by Max Baer in a TKO (Technical Knockout) in June of 1934 to capture the title. In 1935, Baer defended his title against **James J. Braddock** who was seen by Baer's handlers as an easy win for the champ. Baer did not seem to take the fight seriously, and his training (or lack of training) showed it. Braddock trained very seriously and turned out to be a much stronger fighter than his record showed (he lost more fights than he won since 1929 and even quit fighting for a period to work as a longshoreman to feed his family). After Braddock shocked not only Baer but the boxing world in a major upset, sportswriter Damon Runyon dubbed him "Cinderella Man" because he went from working the docks and accepting welfare to being the heavyweight champion of the world. Seventy years later a movie by the same name would bring to life Braddock's incredible story with Russell Crowe playing the title role. With the country needing inspiration, Braddock certainly delivered. One part of his story that always embarrassed Braddock was the fact he took relief money from the government. The first chance he got, he paid back every penny he received. Braddock did not pay back the public with a title defense for over two years.

James Braddock. Image courtesy of Library of Congress

Part of the problem was the best challenger for the title was a black man named Joe Louis. It had been two decades since Jack Johnson relinquished his championship, and not much had improved between the races since then. There was the worry that another black champion would produce similar riots as the last one. Louis was forced to fight 19 times in the two years that Braddock waited for a title defense. Those 19 fights included four former champions (Carnera, Sharkey, Baer, and Schmeling). The Baer fight in 1935 was held in Yankee Stadium and drew more than 80,000 and produced boxing's first million dollar gate in eight years. The only loss in those 19 fights (and Louis' only loss of his career to that point) was to Schmeling in 1936 (also held in Yankee Stadium) so by 1937 Braddock had no choice but to give Louis a shot at the title. The fight happened on June 22 at Comiskey Park in Chicago in front of 45,000. Braddock seemed old and slow (he was nearly a decade older than the 23-year-old Louis). Louis realized early that he could not be overconfident because the champ still had a wicked right cross that knocked Louis to the canvas in the first round. The challenger seemed to wear down the champ and, by the eighth round, knocked him out. Boxing had its first black heavyweight champion in 22 years. Louis was not Jack Johnson, however, and he was embraced by a larger group of Americans—of all races—than Johnson had been. His next big fight would prove that. Louis did not believe Braddock was the best fighter in the world at the time and, on the night of his greatest triumph, he had one man and revenge on his mind when he said, "I don't want nobody to call me champ till I beat that Schmeling."[29]

Louis defended his title three times over the next nine months. Later in 1937 he defeated Welshman Tommy Farr who went the full 15 rounds and Louis won on a unanimous decision. In early 1938, he knocked out Nathan Mann and Harry Thomas, both Americans, in preparation for the main event which was a rematch against Schmeling in Yankee Stadium that June. Many things had changed since they first met back in 1936. For one thing, Louis now had the championship belt and had the aura of a champion about him. Globally, Adolf Hitler had begun his move on Europe by re-arming the Rhineland, taking Austria, and threatening to invade a part of Czechoslovakia that he believed was rightfully German (the Sudetenland). On top of that, Germany joined Italy in backing the attempted fascist takeover in Spain in what many viewed as a preview of an approaching bigger war. Schmeling represented Hitler's idea of the powerful "Aryan" and was seen as his golden boy. After his first defeat of Louis, the Fuehrer sent flowers to Schmeling's wife congratulating her on her husband's victory. Many saw the rematch as a battle between democracy and fascism. The 70,000 that packed Yankee Stadium on the night of June 22 (another million dollar gate) saw a very quick fight that ended with Louis getting his revenge with a knockout in a little over two minutes of the first round. There were no flowers from Hitler this time—in fact, Schmeling was now shunned by the Nazi leadership and eventually fought for the German army once World War II commenced the following year. While Hitler probably would have preferred that Schmeling not come back from the war, he not only did that but he continued to box until his retirement in 1948. In the 1950s he became involved in the Coca-Cola Company in Germany and eventually became a very wealthy man. While both fighters were supposed to hate each other for the sake of their respective nations, they really didn't. There was a mutual respect and eventually a close friendship that lasted until Louis' death in 1981 in which Schmeling helped finance the funeral and was a pallbearer.

As for Louis, his victory over Schmeling proved to the world and perhaps more importantly to himself that he was now the champion of the world. He was also considered the champion of all Americans, not just African Americans. Perhaps it was patriotism due to the looming world war or Louis' more humble nature when compared with Jack Johnson but, for whatever the reason, he was claimed by more than just the black boxing fans and he can truly be considered the first African American sports superstar. The other thing that Americans loved about Louis was that he would take on all comers. He successfully defended his title four times in 1939 and four more times in 1940. In the final year before the United States entered World War II, he fought no less than seven times. In January 1942, he was scheduled to fight former champion Max Baer's younger brother Buddy. After the Japanese bombed Pearl Harbor in December, Louis decided that all proceeds from the fight would go to the Naval Relief Society. He knocked Baer out in the first round and the next day he got his draft notice. Now as a member of the army, he thought it would be a good idea to stage another title defense—this one to benefit the Army Relief Society, in which he defeated Abe Simon in a TKO in the 6th round. He would fight only once more in the next four years and after his discharge from the army at the end of the war in 1945. He was in his thirties now and he was no longer the dominant fighter he had once been. In 1947, he fought Jersey Joe Walcott who fought the champion hard all the way to the end, and Louis fought what he believed was his worst fight. Although he got the split decision, the crowd showed their displeasure. "I wanted to get out of that ring the minute I heard the bell . . . it was worse because the crowd booed when I got the decision. I knew I had to fight Walcott again because I didn't want to retire with that for my last showing."[30] A rematch was scheduled and this time Louis knocked out Walcott in the 11th round. He then retired at the age of 34 holding the record for the longest tenure as champion (140 consecutive months between 1937 and 1949) and most title defenses (26).

1950s: Boxing's New Golden Age?

Nothing showed the changes in the sport more than the two men who battled for Louis' relinquished title in June of 1949: Ezzard Charles defeated Walcott after a 15-round decision (both men were African American). This fight would have never happened 20 years earlier, but many things have changed, including Jackie Robinson's breaking baseball owners' old gentlemen's agreement in 1947 when he took the field for the Brooklyn Dodgers. The breaking of the color line in baseball may never have happened had it not been for Joe Louis. Robinson was charged with striking a white officer in 1944 and was set to be court-martialed which would have resulted in a dishonorable discharge and perhaps jail time. The world may never have heard of Robinson but for Louis who allegedly bribed the commanding officer to make sure Robinson was found not guilty. A year into retirement, Louis was in no position to bribe anyone—in fact he owed over half a million dollars in back taxes to the IRS. He decided the only thing to do was attempt a boxing comeback. Promoters were ecstatic as Ezzard Charles was not the most charismatic of fighters. The Charles-Louis fight was set for September of 1950 at Yankee Stadium but the old draw (and abilities) of Joe Louis was waning. Only 13,000 showed up to the fight and Louis' purse only amounted to $100,000—far less than what he had hoped for. Louis was 36 now and a shell of his former self—Charles seemed to take pity on the old champ and let the fight go the full 15 rounds before a unanimous decision gave Louis only the second loss of his career. Louis could not afford to quit, and he continued to fight over the next year; and, after rattling off eight wins, people were becoming convinced that the 37-year-old had defied time and could possibly regain the championship. In October of 1951 he faced a rising young contender for the title named **Rocky Marciano**. For the first few rounds he seemed to have the Madison Square Garden crowd convinced he was back, but by the sixth round he began to slow and, unlike Charles, Marciano showed no reverence for the former champ and beat him unmercifully until the referee stopped the fight in the 8th round. Louis never fought again. As for Marciano, he became the champion the following year and held it until his retirement in 1956. When he retired he became the only boxer in history to have never lost a professional fight—he was 49–0.

Joe Louis and Rocky Marciano before their 1951 fight.
© Bettmann/CORBIS.

Joe Louis being knocked out by Rocky Marciano.
© Bettmann/CORBIS.

Like every other sport that has been examined in this book, television had a major effect on boxing. As historian Ben Rader put it, "television contributed to a short-term boom and a long-term depression."[31] In 1944, the Gillette Safety Razor company began sponsoring weekly Friday night fights featuring all weight classes in Madison Square Garden. By the early 1950s, the fights had become such a ratings success that fights began to be televised on other nights of the week. It drew droves of new fans to the sport that may have never been exposed to it without TV. It also brought in more participants who wanted to get famous on television. In the mid-fifties the happy union of the sport and the new technology began to unravel. Long time devotees of the sport noticed the style of the sport had changed since the advent of television. Instead of learning the science and strategy of the sport, young fighters wanted to knock out their opponent as soon as possible because that played the best on TV. There was also the problem that once a fighter lost on television, advertisers did not want that fighter to return so there was not an endless supply of fighters to televise. Fight promoter Chris Dundee summed it up when he said, "The sponsors didn't want losers, just winners. And let's face it, the sponsors called the shots during the TV age of boxing."[32] By the end of the decade, live audiences at Madison Square Garden began to dwindle because of television. In the late forties it would not be uncommon for 10,000 to 12,000 people to show up for a fight. By 1957, the average attendance was one-tenth of that. Even smaller fight clubs and training facilities were dealt a blow by television and it's estimated over half of them closed by the end of the fifties. What was really ironic is that what television had created for it-self, it also ruined. By the late fifties there were so many competing programs on TV that ratings for boxing fell off dramatically. In 1952, 31 percent of all television sets were tuned to boxing when there was a fight on; by 1959, that number had shrunk by almost one-third to 10.6 percent.[33] Boxing's second golden age was at an end and something or someone needed to come along to revive it.

Muhammad Ali

Cassius Clay. Image courtesy of Library of Congress

In the 1960 Olympics in Rome, there was one boxer who became more well-known than almost any other athlete at the games and he was light-heavyweight **Cassius Clay**. He was more known for things outside the ring than inside. Clay was born in Louisville in 1942 and, by the time his amateur career had reached its zenith in Rome that summer, the 18-year-old had become known as the "Louisville Lip" because of his penchant for talking. In modern parlance it would be known as talking "trash" because he would say things about and to his opponents, referees, reporters, and anyone else who would listen. During his amateur career, he won 100 fights while only losing five. He captured six Kentucky Golden Gloves and two national Golden Gloves championships along with an AAU national title. Clay was a force of nature and becoming more known in the boxing world, but, in the summer of 1960, he became known to the entire world not only for his talking but also for his incredible boxing ability because he won the gold medal in his division. There had never been a boxer, perhaps any athlete, more suitable for the television age than Clay. After the Olympics he turned professional and many of his early pro fights were televised by the Gillette Company and featured as the "fight of the week." The long-running boxing coverage by Gillette on the National Broadcasting Company (NBC) was dropped because of low ratings in 1960, but it was immediately picked up by the American Broadcasting Company (ABC) and its new director of sports programming, Roone Arledge. Boxing was not at the forefront of Arledge's mind as he was building the ABC sports empire and by 1964 the Gillette sponsorship of fights ended after 20 years and so did ABC's coverage of the sport. Boxing's popularity had seemed to hit a low point for many reasons—since the popular Rocky Marciano's retirement in 1956 there had not been a champion to come along that could capture his popularity, and the sport had once again become mired in a reputation of corruption and even criminal activity. No champion represented that reputation more than **Sonny Liston** who became the champ after knocking out Floyd Patterson (who took over as champion after Marciano) in the first round. Liston had been arrested numerous times and actually started his boxing career in the Missouri State Penitentiary in the early fifties. He was also associated with organized crime figures and this added credence to the rising belief that boxing was a dishonest if not criminal sport.

By 1964, Clay's professional record was 19–0 and he was the top contender for a title shot against Liston and he got it in February. Before the fight, Clay began a tradition of not only naming his opponents (Liston was the "Big Ugly Bear") but also reciting a poem about them. After announcing he would knock Liston into orbit, he told his poem that ended, "Yes, the crowd did not dream when it laid down its money that they would see a total eclipse of the Sonny."[34] Clay was true to his word defeating Liston on a TKO in the eighth round to become the heavyweight champion of the world at the age of 22. There was a rematch scheduled for the following year, and this time he knocked Liston out in the second round. Although the first fight was televised only on a closed-circuit basis, Arledge decided to re-run the fight on ABC's *Wide World of Sports* program in which it received an incredible rating of 13.7, which for a replay of a fight in which the outcome was already known was an incredible rating. Arledge knew he had something here that transcended sports and, although the network dropped the Gillette fights later that year, Arledge made sure he covered Clay whenever he fought; and ABC did for the remainder of his career. As one new boxing fan wrote to a magazine: "Before Cassius Clay came along, I wasn't the least bit interested in boxing. Now you can't keep me away from my TV set when the fights are on—and that goes for the other people I know."[35] After the Liston fights, Clay would be known by a different name for the remainder of his career. He had converted to Islam, and he gave up what he referred to as his "slave name" and would from that point on be known as **Muhammad Ali**.

In his next title defense, his religion would take center stage as former champion Floyd Patterson wanted and got a shot at Ali in November of 1965. The fact that Patterson was a Christian and involved in the Civil Rights movement and the desegregation of the country and Ali was Muslim and in favor of a separation of the races was played up in the promotion of the fight. Patterson refused to call him Muhammad and continued to call him Cassius and Ali called Patterson "Uncle Tom" (a derogatory term for blacks who did whatever whites said). Singer Frank Sinatra, who could not stand Ali at the time, famously said that Patterson would win the title back for America. Recently W.K. Stratton wrote a biography of Patterson and has alleged the treatment of Patterson by Ali was an act designed to promote the fight and make each of them more money. Stratton said that Ali admitted as much in an interview shortly after the fight, and one of the reasons Patterson called him Cassius is that he could not pronounce Muhammad (he had a speech impediment). After the fight Patterson asked Ali if he could call him Cassius and he replied, "Anytime, Floyd." Patterson was reportedly the only person Ali allowed to call him by that name.[36] The other misunderstood part of the fight, according to Stratton, was that Ali supposedly punished and toyed with Patterson before finally getting a TKO in the 12th round when he could have ended the fight sooner. Stratton said that Patterson had injured his back in training, and the fight should have been postponed and Ali knew that. Instead of wanting to hurt Patterson, he was hoping for the referee to stop the fight but he didn't stop it until the 12th round. Credence seems to be lent to this allegation in that Patterson had very little bruising and he admitted after the fight that he had never been hit with such "soft punches."[37] After the Patterson fight, Ali's mouth would get him in trouble when he was asked about the Vietnam War and he replied, "Man, I ain't got no quarrel with them Vietcong."[38] Interpreted as an insensitive comment when Americans were fighting and dying at the hands of the Vietcong, Ali found he was not able to find a welcoming venue in the country for a title defense so, as many fighting-aged men were doing to avoid the draft, he went north of the border.

He fought Canadian George Chuvalo in Toronto. The fight was not a particularly good one. Although Chuvalo lasted the full 15 rounds, he took an incredible beating and after the fight his face looked, according to one reporter, "like it was made up of a number of driving-range golf balls."[39] Ali got the decision, but it was not a good financial payoff nor was it considered a great fight, but two very important things came from this fight. First, ABC got the rights to air the fight three days later and Arledge put all his effort into making it a show instead of just a mediocre fight. The fight was almost secondary to comments by Ali himself and the backstory of his political commentary. The second important thing to happen after this fight was bringing in sports reporter **Howard Cosell** to interview Ali for the show. Cosell was a former New York attorney who had dabbled in radio reporting but went full-time into entertainment on both radio and television in the late fifties. Cosell and Ali were made for each other—they each loved to talk, and they each realized the other was good for their own career. The ratings for the Ali-Chuvalo rebroadcast were great and ABC fought for and got the rights to televise live Ali's next three fights—all scheduled to be fought in Europe. The first was against British fighter Henry Cooper in London, and again ABC's *Wide World of Sports* made a huge production out of the fight and this time, because it was live, Cosell was at ringside calling the fight alongside Chris Schenkel and former heavyweight champ Rocky Marciano. Ali won that fight with a TKO in the 6th round and defended his title three months later against Brian London (also in London) with a knockout in the third round. The third of the title defenses in Europe occurred a very short one month later in Frankfurt, West Germany, when he defeated German Karl Mildenberger on a TKO in the 12th round. The fight was the first to be broadcast live and in color and once again Cosell was there. The two were now inextricably linked and Cosell joked to Ali after the fight: "I made you . . . where would you be without all the shows, without 'Wide World of Sports,' without me doing your fights, without the interviews in the ring? Yes, I made you."[40] What Cosell or Ali did not know at that time is that an Ali fight would not appear on live television again for seven years.

After three more successful title defenses (all back in the United States after finding venues in Houston and New York), Ali refused to be inducted into the United States Army after being drafted. He claimed conscientious objector status because of his religion but that was rejected by the courts, and he was eventually convicted of draft evasion in June of 1967 and was sentenced to five years in prison. As a result of his conviction he was stripped of his title as heavyweight champion and his boxing license was suspended. His attorneys immediately appealed his case, but it took four years before he was eventually cleared of the charges by the U.S. Supreme Court in 1971 and he never spent any time in jail. He did spend three years out of the boxing ring, however, and the loss of revenue took its toll. **Joe Frazier** was now recognized as the heavyweight champion and Ali wanted to fight him. After getting boxing licenses in Georgia and New York in 1970, he fought Gerry Quarry and Oscar Bonavena and defeated them both on TKOs. Much of the boxing world viewed Ali still as the champion so a fight with Frazier was scheduled for March of 1971 to decide it. The fight was billed as the "fight of the century" and to many it lived up to its billing—going the full 15 rounds before Frazier received the unanimous decision. It was the first loss of Ali's career and, as he neared 30, he contemplated retirement. It was a fleeting contemplation, however, as the champ was far from done. Ali rattled off 12 victories over the next two years trying to get another shot at Frazier. In March of 1973, he lost the second fight of his career in a split decision to Ken Norton. A rematch was immediately scheduled for six months later, and this time it was Ali's turn to win on a split decision. These fights marked Ali's return to live television and he finally got his rematch with Frazier scheduled for January of 1974.

Stamp of Ali-Frazier "Fight of the Century." Image © catwalker, 2013. Used under license from Shutterstock, Inc.

This time Ali defeated Frazier on points, but the problem was Frazier had been defeated the year before by **George Foreman** who was now recognized as the champion. A fight between Foreman and Ali was scheduled for October of 1974. It was scheduled for Zaire, Africa, and was billed as the "Rumble in the Jungle." Not many, including Cosell, gave Ali much of a chance against the younger (by seven years) Foreman who had recently beaten both Frazier and Norton much easier than Ali had (in fact he knocked them both out in the second round). During the fight Ali was his usual taunting self, and he employed a tactic designed to tire Foreman in which he used the ropes and covered up while Foreman flailed away at Ali—not really landing punches squarely. The tactic (known as the "**rope-a-dope**") worked and Foreman began to tire by the middle rounds. Ali was able to knock him out in the 8th round and improbably win back the title at the age of 32. He successfully defended his title 10 times over the next three years including one of the greatest fights of all time that took place in the Philippines in 1975, which was dubbed the "Thrilla in Manilla" in which he fought Joe Frazier for a third and final time. The temperatures reached well over 100 degrees and it was such a brutal fight that Frazier's corner stopped after the 14th round because both of his eyes were swollen shut. Ali was quoted as saying the fight was as close to death as he had ever come in the ring, and he paid Frazier a rare compliment that he was the greatest fighter of all times next to Ali. In February of 1978 Ali lost to Leon Spinks and immediately scheduled a rematch with him for seven months later in which Ali won to become the only fighter to win the title on three separate occasions. After retiring in early 1979, he decided to come back to try to win the title for a fourth time but it was not to be. **Larry Holmes** was now the champ and he was scheduled to fight Holmes in October of 1980 when he started noticing his famous speech beginning to stutter and a trembling in his hands. Although he was cleared to fight Holmes, he was showing early signs of Parkinson disease. Holmes was clearly the better fighter and, for the first time in Ali's career, he lost a fight by knockout. Many believe that fight sped up the onset of the disease. Despite his loss, he scheduled one more fight in December of 1981 in which he lost to Trevor Berbick in a unanimous decision. This time he announced his official retirement one month shy of his 40th birthday and never fought again. Over the past 30 years, Ali has transformed into something more than just a boxer—he is often mentioned as the most recognized *person*, not just athlete, in the world. In 1999 ESPN named him the athlete of the century. While alienating some with his beliefs, many others have admired him for his political and religious stands and his charisma and athletic abilities combined to make him a towering figure in the history of sport. Although Parkinson's has taken away his speech and his athleticism, he is still, in his seventies, one of the most admired figures on earth.

Conclusion

Holmes would dominate the heavyweight scene for the first half of the 1980s, but in the mid-80s a young fighter took the division by storm—his name was **Mike Tyson**. He defeated the last fighter Ali faced, Trevor Berbick, by a TKO to become the youngest heavyweight champion of all time at the age of 20. Controversy would follow Tyson throughout his tumultuous career in and out of the ring. He would hold the title until losing to Buster Douglas in 1990. During his comeback, he was accused and eventually convicted of rape in 1991 and 1992. After serving three years of a six-year sentence, he came back to defeat some less-than-stellar opponents before getting his shot at the title again against former champion **Evander Holyfield** on September 11, 1996. Holyfield had defeated Douglas to take the title after Douglas beat Tyson. Now Holyfield defeated Tyson by a TKO, but it was the rematch in 1997 that included one of the most remembered moments in the sport's history. Tyson was issued a warning by referee Mills Lane after biting Holyfield's ear. Tyson later claimed his biting was a reaction to head butts by Holyfield that were not called. When Tyson bit Holyfield's other ear in the third round—this time so ferociously that a piece of the ear was missing and later found in the ring—Lane disqualified Tyson and awarded Holyfield

Mike Tyson. Image © s_bukley, 2013. Used under license from Shutterstock, Inc.

Evander Holyfield. Image © Gustavo Fadel. 2013. Used under license from Shutterstock, Inc.

Ali and Foreman. Image © Featureflash. 2013. Used under license from Shutterstock, Inc.

Sugar Ray Robinson. Image courtesy of Library of Congress

the victory. Tyson's life spiraled after that and he eventually filed for bankruptcy, but he did get one last shot at the title at the age of 35 in 2002 when he met Lennox Lewis (the first British champion since Bob Fitzsimmons in 1899) with Lewis knocking him out in the 8th round. In need of money, he continued to fight until finally retiring in 2006 just shy of 40.

One interesting flashback that occurred during the decade of the 1990s was the return of a former champion. George Foreman who had retired in 1977 decided to make a comeback in the late 1980s at an age when most fighters are retiring. In 1994, at the age of 45, he got a shot to regain the title against Michael Moorer who had defeated Holyfield for the championship. Wearing the same trunks he had worn in the "Rumble in the Jungle" loss to Ali 20 years earlier, Foreman shocked the world by knocking out Moorer in the 10th round. He broke three records with this victory. At 45 he was the oldest champion in history, the 20 years between titles was the longest ever, and the 19 years that separated the two fighters was the most ever. In 1997 he lost his final fight against Shannon Briggs. Although he announced his retirement again at age 48, there were plans made for a fight against Larry Holmes in 1999, which was to be billed the "Birthday Bash" as both turned 50 that year, but the fight never materialized. Foreman reintroduced himself to a new generation as a popular announcer and TV pitchman, especially for his now-famous George Foreman grill which he is arguably more known for than his boxing career.

During the first decade of the 21st century, there appeared to be a disappearance of the heavyweight boxer. In years past when people were asked who the heavyweight champion of the world was, even nonboxing fans could name the individual. Now boxing fans are hard-pressed to do so. Part of the reason could be the lack of great American heavyweights since Tyson and Holyfield—the last American to hold the title was Shannon Briggs who defeated Foreman in his last fight. Another reason could be the difficulty in seeing the fights. During Muhammad Ali's prime, his fights were routinely shown on ABC, but in the last 30 years they have moved to pay cable channels like Home Box Office (HBO) or pay-per-view venues where, if the average fan wanted to see the fights, they would have to pay up to and even exceeding $100, depending on the fight. There is also the emerging popularity of a competitor of boxing: mixed martial arts. Many former boxing fans or younger people who may have never watched boxing are turning to the no-holds barred sport which is less-restrictive than boxing. It is also not limited to men as Rhonda Rousey has shown by going undefeated between 2011–2015 at 12-0 and taking the title of UFC Women's Bantamweight Champion. Another reason for the disappearance of the heavyweight could be the increased popularity of the lower-weight divisions since World War II. The first superstar boxer that was not a heavyweight was **"Sugar" Ray Robinson** who fought as a welter and middleweight. He won the welterweight championship of the world in 1946 and held it until 1950 when he moved up to middleweight and defeated Jake LaMotta (the subject for the movie *Raging Bull)*, and he held and lost the title for that division numerous times over the next decade until finally retiring in 1965 at the age of 44. He amassed an incredible 173 wins over his career and is often called the greatest fighter pound-for-pound in the history of the sport. Following in his footsteps a decade later was Robinson's namesake **"Sugar" Ray Leonard** who also started his career as a welterweight and won a gold medal in that division in the 1976 Olympics. He became the welterweight champion of the world in 1979 and defeated some of the greatest fighters in that division. They also had some of the greatest nicknames like **Roberto "Hands of Stone" Duran** and **Thomas "Hitman" Hearns**. In 1987 he moved up to the middleweight division and won that title after beating **"Marvelous" Marvin Hagler**. To continue great rivalries, both Hearns and Duran also moved up to the division. Leonard lost the title in 1991 to Tony Norris and retired due to an eye injury that doctors said could blind him if he continued to fight. Ignoring the doctors, he came back to fight for the middleweight championship against Hector "Macho" Camacho in 1997 when Leonard was 40. After losing the fight he retired for good. In the last decade, fighters like Oscar De La Hoya, Floyd Mayweather, and Manny Pacquiao have kept boxing fans interested in the lower divisions to the detriment of the heavyweight division and boxing in general. Also some attribute the diminishing popularity of boxing to the growing popularity of Mixed Martial Arts (MMA) in recent years. Only time will tell if there will be a return of the popularity of the heavyweight which most experts agree is needed for a return of the general popularity of the sport.

Sugar Ray Leonard.
Image © s_bukley, 2013.
Used under license from
Shutterstock, Inc.

Notes

1. Francis Archibald Kelhead Douglas, *The Sporting Queensberry's* (Hutchison and Co.: London, New York, Melbourne, 1945), 11.
2. Ibid., 12.
3. Ibid., 70.
4. Ibid., 118.
5. Elliott L. Gorn, *The Manly Art; Bare-Knuckle Prize Fighting in America* (Cornell University Press: Ithaca and London, 1986), 24.
6. Ibid., 158.
7. Ibid., 164.
8. Ibid., 173.
9. Ibid., 183.
10. Ibid., 211.
11. Ibid.
12. Ibid., 210.
13. Ibid.
14. Ibid., 215.
15. Ibid., 234.
16. Ibid., 238.
17. Ibid., 245.
18. Benjamin Rader, *American Sports; From the Age of Folk Games to the Age of Televised Sports*, 6th ed. (Upper Saddle River, NJ: Pearson-Prentice Hall, 2009), 147.
19. Ibid.
20. Randy Roberts, *Papa Jack; Jack Johnson and the Era of White Hopes* (The Free Press: New York, 1983), 103.
21. Ibid., 103–104.
22. Ibid., 107.
23. Ibid., 144.
24. Ibid., 145.
25. Nat Fleischer, *Jack Dempsey* (Arington House: New Rochelle, NY, 1972), 13–14.
26. Ibid., 64.
27. Ibid., 68.
28. Ibid., 120.
29. Barney Nagler, *Brown Bomber* (World Publishing: New York, 1972), 87.
30. Ibid., 159–160.
31. Rader, *American Sports*, 246.
32. Ibid.

33. Ibid., 247.
34. Randy Roberts, "The Wide World of Muhammad Ali: The Politics and Economics of Televised Boxing," in *Muhammad Ali, The People's Champ*, Elliott Gorn, Ed. (University of Illinois Press: Urbana and Chicago, 1995), 41.
35. Ibid., 40.
36. Alex Belth, "Ali-Patterson: The Real Story," an Interview with W.K Stratton in *Sportsonearth.com.* 26 August 2012.
37. Ibid.
38. Roberts, "The Wide World of Muhammad Ali," 44.
39. Ibid., 46.
40. Ibid., 50.

CHAPTER
Thirteen

Postwar College Football

On September 30, 1939, the Waynesburg, Pennsylvania, Yellow Jackets football team travelled to New York City to take on the Fordham Rams. Waynesburg scored first when Bobby Brooks rambled 63 yards for a touchdown, but they did not score again and lost the game 34–7. The game would be long forgotten if not for the fact there was a television camera (only one camera) documenting the game for the National Broadcasting Company. For the first time a college football game was broadcasted on the new medium of television. Not many people saw the game that day as there were only an estimated 1,000 television sets in the New York metropolitan area at the time, and the broadcast signal had only about a 50-mile radius. Undoubtedly, the biggest change to sports in the postwar world was the improvement of the technology and the proliferation of television across the country. Although the first television broadcasts had occurred back in the 1920s, it was not until the 1936 Olympic Games in Berlin that the new technology was used to broadcast a major sporting event. During the war, as with most technological advancements not related to the war effort, television was put on the back burner. At the conclusion of the war, television would become a major part of American culture as it moved into the 1950s. Unfortunately for sports fans, early TV did not lend itself well to team sports like baseball or football. Individual sports like boxing and wrestling transmitted better over the new medium, and it would not be until the technology improved in the 1960s that Americans would see an improvement in the way their favorite team sports were broadcasted on TV.

The Emerging Power of the NCAA

During those early years after the war, college football made some major changes. Although it had been nearly 20 years since the Carnegie Report, the echoes of its findings still reverberated throughout college football. In 1948 the NCAA decided to address at least one aspect of the report when it adopted a policy known as the "**Sanity Code**." The code would allow institutions to pay tuition for athletes as long as they upheld two conditions: first, the student must meet the same academic standards as other students, and second, the student would have to show financial need.[1] To enforce the code, the NCAA formed a committee with the power to investigate violations and punish schools up to and including expulsion from the NCAA. The committee found out in short order that they had a big job to enforce the policy. Schools voiced their complaints about the code especially in regard to the academic portion of the requirement. Many schools simply refused to abide by the code and were placed on a list known as the "Sinful Seven."[2] To show how unpopular the code was, when the seven schools were brought up for expulsion during the 1950 national convention of the NCAA, the needed two-thirds majority was not reached and it was decided to do away with the hated code. In 1952, the NCAA, under new executive director **Walter Byers**, decided to allow schools to award athletic scholarships not based on academic standards, and the scholarships could cover tuition, room and board, books, and even money for living expenses. Byers told schools they should refer to those receiving "full-ride" scholarships as "**student–athletes**," and a new term was born.[3] Byers would serve as the leader of the NCAA for almost four decades, and it was during his reign that the NCAA would grow from a nearly powerless organization to an extremely powerful cartel. All college sports, but especially football, became commercialized; and, by the end of his tenure in the late 1980s, athletic departments resembled more of a professional organization than the amateur ones they were supposed to be. In sharp contrast to the big-time college football represented by the NCAA, a new organization was forming postwar on the campuses where college football began in the previous century. In 1945 eight Eastern schools signed the first Ivy Group Accord, which agreed to "unsubsidized football" and "maintenance of high academic standards for athletes."[4] These schools had been de-emphasizing football for years but, by the mid-1950s, they made it official with the formation of the Ivy League to include Harvard, Yale, Princeton, Columbia, Dartmouth, Brown, Cornell, and Pennsylvania. Recruiting was limited, as was the influence of boosters; athletic scholarships were not allowed, nor were postseason bowl appearances. The only way an athlete could receive a scholarship was academically. At a time when many schools were going the opposite way, the Ivy League seemed to stand alone in its maintenance of high academic standards and less-commercial approach to sports. The Carnegie Foundation would be proud.

1960s' Rules Changes and Beyond

The decade of the 1960s witnessed the already popular spectacle of college football soar to even greater heights. During the decade annual attendance rose from 20 million to 30 million, and by 1980 it was up to 40 million.[5] There were many reasons for this, but chief among them were the pageantry of the game, the proliferation of postseason bowl games, the improvement of television technology to include color and clearer pictures, and, finally, changes in rules that made the game even more exciting. An offensive explosion occurred during the sixties due in part to coaching innovations but also to rules changes made by the NCAA. Throughout the decade various ways to stop the clock were added to the rules, which resulted in an average of 27 more plays per game in 1968 than there had been in 1964. In 1970 there was an average of 40 more plays in college games than in the NFL. The NCAA also adopted a two-platoon system (offensive and defensive players), which ended the old system of players playing positions on both sides of the ball and made offenses more specialized and potent. Coaches began taking more control of the games in the 1960s and developing formations to rack up more yards of offense. Tom Nugent created the "I-formation" at Maryland, which allowed offenses to combine rushing and passing attacks. More ground-oriented formations were created in Texas: the wishbone attack first used by Darrell Royal at the University of Texas and later adopted (and many would say perfected) by Barry Switzer at the University of Oklahoma. Houston's veer formation would also be an attack that would help its offense gain hundreds of yards on the ground. College football also seemed more fun than the professional game. Ironically, at a time when it was becoming more like a business behind the scenes, it seemed less so on the surface. Tailgates, marching bands, cheerleaders, and fan card sections all added to the pageantry of the game, which seemed to not take itself as seriously as its counterpart in the professional ranks.

TV Contracts and the First Conference Realignment

In the early 1950s, the NCAA took control of contracts for the televising of college football games. They quickly limited the amount of televised games to seven per season in different regions of the country because they feared too many games on TV would limit the attendance at games. This was one of the ways the NCAA was becoming an economic cartel because it negotiated the broadcasting contracts and provided revenue sharing to all its member schools. Colleges seemed to not have a problem with this in the early days, but during the 1960s and '70s, as attendance rose and television technology improved, schools knew they could get a better deal than what the NCAA was providing. In 1976 the Big 8 Conference and Notre Dame led 52 other big-time college football programs to form the College Football Association (CFA), which demanded a better deal from the NCAA. The NCAA relented and negotiated a bigger television contract with ABC, which increased its payment annually from $3 million to $29 million. The NCAA also increased the number of televised appearances schools were allowed to have per year. This did not satisfy some of the major football powers who did not like sharing television revenue with the smaller schools. In 1984, the Universities of Oklahoma and Georgia filed suit on behalf of the major powers against the NCAA saying that their television deals violated antitrust laws. The suit was successful, and overnight the major powers were given the rights to negotiate their own deals or have their conferences negotiate. The results were twofold: Major independents like Penn State and Miami joined conferences (the Big 10 and Big East, respectively), and bigger schools began to appear almost weekly on television. An example of this was Nebraska, who, in 1983, went undefeated during the regular season, lost the national title by one point to Miami in the Orange Bowl, and was on television only twice that season, not counting the bowl game. Move forward only a few years, and it is rare for a Nebraska game to *not* be televised in that state. One of the few independents to not join a conference during this time period was Notre Dame. Due to their huge nationwide following, the Irish were able to negotiate their own television contract with NBC. Independents joining conferences weren't the only shakeup in this realignment. Some conferences disbanded and others were formed. A major example of this was the dissolving of the old Southwest Conference in 1994 and its members joining various conferences in the West. The most prominent result of this was that four of its schools from Texas (Texas, Texas A&M, Texas Tech, and Baylor) merged with the Big 8 Conference to form the Big 12.

Nebraska Football

One of the teams that the Texas schools joined when forming the new conference was the University of Nebraska. Nebraska had been playing football since before the turn of the 20th century and was one of the charter members of the Big 8 Conference, but it had only fairly recently joined the elite. With no real major population centers, no professional teams, or any other major universities, Nebraska football became *the* identifying feature for the state. In 1951 the *Saturday Evening Post* recognized this when it wrote, "Football commands much more than the average amount of interest in Nebraska. In this prairie state of great open stretches and small communities, where the average town is only about 375 people, the university's football team is one of the strongest bonds."[6] It was that identifying feature that first emerged on the scene in 1890. The University of Nebraska was founded in 1869 and spent the 1870s and '80s trying to establish itself as a legitimate institution of higher learning. As a young, land-grant college all alone on the sprawling prairie, it searched for ways to compete with the eastern universities; and, by the late 1880s, football had emerged at

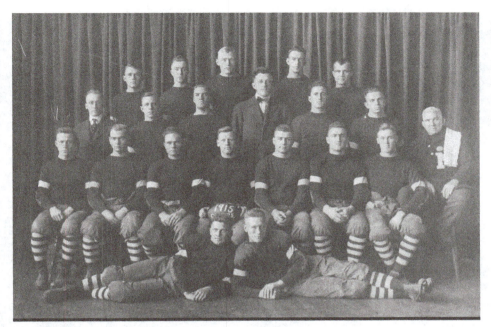

1915 Nebraska Cornhuskers–Jumbo Stiehm's final undefeated team. Reprinted by permission of the Nebraska State Historical Society

those universities as an important part of the "collegiate way." So on Thanksgiving Day in 1890, the University of Nebraska fielded its first football team and defeated the Omaha YMCA 10–0 in its first-ever game. Over the next decade the team would not see a losing season playing under many different coaches and under varying team mascots finally settling on the "Bugeaters." In 1900 it was decided that a change in the name was needed, and sportswriter Cy Sherman suggested the name "**Cornhuskers**." The university's teams have been known by the nickname ever since. The football program came of age during the early part of the century when there were many calling for the game's abolition. That would not have been a popular move for the emerging fan base of the team as the program experienced not only winning seasons during the first decade of the new century but also undefeated seasons under **Walter C. "Bummy" Booth** in 1902 and 1903. Booth compiled a record of 46-8-1 during his six seasons as head coach which was an incredible winning percentage of .845. That record would actually be bested by one of his successors, **Ewald O. "Jumbo" Stiehm**, whose teams only lost two games in his five seasons (1911–1915) and his .915 winning percentage (35-2-3) is the best of all-time at the school. During his tenure he had three consecutive undefeated seasons (1913–1915) including a 34-game win streak. Stiehm won conference championships (Missouri Valley Conference) in each of his five seasons. During the 1920s, six of the Missouri Valley Conference teams (Iowa State, Kansas, Kansas State, Nebraska, Missouri, and Oklahoma) broke away and formed a separate conference (the Big 6). By the 1950s, the six schools were joined by Oklahoma State and Colorado and the conference became known as the Big 8. The Big 8 would last until the first conference realignment in the 1990s when it merged with four Texas schools to become the Big 12.

During the Jumbo Stiehm years, the NCAA made some major changes (discussed in Chapter 5) that brought college football into its modern age. It was also during this period that college football began to be "**democratized**." By this it is meant that the game was spreading out across the nation and more people were playing the game and watching it. Ben Rader points to two fundamental ways that college football was democratized during this period. First, the game "spread

CHAPTER *Thirteen*

Al Zikmund catches a touchdown pass for Nebraska in their first-ever bowl appearance: the 1941 Rose Bowl.
Reprinted by permission of the Nebraska State Historical Society

geographically from the elite Northeastern schools to the lesser-known and less-distinguished state universities and private schools." Second, those who were playing the game and becoming stars were not necessarily the sons of the upper class anymore but "increasingly came from farming and working-class, ethnic families." There were a number of examples of this democratization, including Nebraska, but Rader pointed to the ultimate "symbol of the American melting pot" being Notre Dame.[7] As discussed earlier, Notre Dame not only became a football powerhouse in the Midwest but it also offered a rallying point for the nation's Catholics. Because of its relative proximity to other Midwestern schools, it also became a team that everyone wanted to play (and defeat) for a validation of their own program. Nebraska got its first chance during Jumbo Stiehm's final season in 1915 when the two schools began a series that would develop into a fierce rivalry. It was so fierce, in fact, that after a decade, Notre Dame discontinued the series citing anti-Catholic treatment by Nebraska fans in Lincoln. The initial game in 1915 was especially important for Nebraska because, by defeating them 20–19 in Lincoln, the Cornhuskers essentially announced their arrival as a football program. The Cornhuskers reiterated their membership in the club by defeating Notre Dame four more times during the series including twice during the age of the Four Horseman (Knute Rockne's only two losses in 1922 and 1923). The 1930s were a difficult time for the nation and for college football but during the latter part of the decade Nebraska coach Biff Jones put together a squad that would win two Big 6 conference championships and take the Cornhuskers to their first ever bowl game when it lost to Stanford in the 1941 Rose Bowl. Due in part to the coming involvement of the U.S. in World War II and in part to other factors, Nebraska football slipped into a two-decade period of mediocrity. That would change rather abruptly in the decade of the 1960s.

The late fifties were particularly difficult for Nebraska fans to stomach when Coach Bill Jennings won an average of only three games per season between 1957 and 1961 and was fired after the 1961 season with a final record of 15-34-1. The Nebraska administration looked west to Wyoming where its 46-year-old coach **Bob Devaney** had won 35 games against only 10 defeats during the same period that Jennings was at Nebraska. Devaney turned things around immediately in 1962 when he guided Nebraska to a 9–2 record and its first-ever bowl win when they defeated Miami in the Gotham Bowl. Devaney was also a perfect fit for the emerging television age. He would host a weekly televised program that allowed fans all across the state to get to know their head coach, and they found they liked the Irishman with the quick wit. So did potential recruits as the coach was able to win over players and their families and build a solid foundation for the future of the program. In his second season, he improved on his first by winning 10 games, the Big 8 conference, and defeating Auburn in the Orange Bowl. In Devaney's fourth season, the Cornhuskers went undefeated and found themselves playing perennial power Alabama in the Orange Bowl for the national championship. Although they lost that game, they had proven they were among the best in college football. Coupled with the following season's blowout loss (34–7) to Alabama in a rematch (this time in the Sugar Bowl) and back-to-back four-loss seasons in 1967 and 1968, Devaney decided it was time to revamp his offense and he named assistant coach **Tom Osborne** as his offensive coordinator for the 1969 season. Devaney and Osborne introduced the I-formation which produced a more innovative offensive scheme with an added balance of running and passing. The change produced dividends quickly as the 1969 team went 9–2, including a 45–6 blowout of Georgia in the Sun Bowl. The 1970 team returned many of the starters of the previous year and Nebraska went through the season undefeated setting up a meeting with LSU for the national championship in the Orange Bowl. In an exciting game Nebraska scored a late touchdown for a 17–12 win and the school's first-ever national championship. The 1971 team was arguably even better and after defeating second-ranked and perennial rival Oklahoma 35–31 in what was dubbed the "Game of the Century," Nebraska gave Devaney his second national championship and some revenge for the earlier losses to Alabama and its legendary coach Paul "Bear" Bryant by defeating the Crimson Tide 38–6 in the Orange Bowl. Contemplating retirement, Devaney decided to return for one final season in 1972 to try and become the first coach to ever win three consecutive national titles. Although it did not happen, Devaney finished with a record of 101-20-2 in his 11 seasons. He also won eight conference titles and two national championships.

Bob Devaney. Reprinted by permission of the University of Nebraska Archives and Special Collections.

Before Devaney left coaching to become athletic director he named Osborne as his successor. Although it took him longer before he played for his first national championships (1982 and 1983—both of which were lost) his teams were very consistent and they never won fewer than nine games a season nor finished out of the top 15 in the polls. It was in the early 1990s (much like he and Devaney had done in the late 60s) that Osborne realized he needed to change up his scheme and recruit more speed to be able to compete with the other national powers. After the 1993 season, Nebraska again played for the national championship, falling a missed field goal short losing to Florida State 18–16. The next season he would finally get his first title after 20 years as Nebraska head coach defeating Miami in the Orange Bowl 24–17. The 1995 squad is often considered not only Osborne's best team but arguably the best team in college football history (it was voted as such by an ESPN poll) as the team went undefeated and drubbed Florida 62–24 in the

Tom Osborne. Reprinted by permission of the University of Nebraska Archives and Special Collections.

Nebraska's Memorial Stadium. Image © rthoma, 2013. Used under license from Shutterstock, Inc.

Fiesta Bowl. After winning his third championship in four years, after the 1997 season (defeating a Peyton Manning-led Tennessee Volunteers 42–17 in the Orange Bowl), he decided to step down after 25 seasons as head coach. In his final five seasons his winning percentage was better than Jumbo Stiehm's overall record as Osborne went 60–3 for an incredible .952 average. He was not only voted the coach of the decade (1990s) but in the 2007 ESPN poll that voted his 1995 team the best of all time, Osborne was also voted the greatest college coach of all time. Like he had been selected by Devaney, Osborne selected his offensive coordinator and former Nebraska fullback Frank Solich to continue the legacy. Unfortunately for Solich and Nebraska, it was not meant to be as he was let go after the 2003 season despite winning nine games. Devaney and Osborne had set the bar pretty high and neither Solich nor his successor, former Oakland Raiders coach Bill Callahan, were able to keep the success of the program going. To the contrary, in 2004 Callahan produced Nebraska's first losing season (5–6) since before Devaney and during the 2007 season had a five-game losing streak including an embarrassing 76–39 loss to Kansas in which Nebraska players appeared to quit playing. Athletic Director Steve Pederson, who had hired Callahan, was fired and replaced with the legend Osborne. Osborne, in turn, fired Callahan after the season and replaced him with former assistant coach Bo Pelini. Although Pelini did seem to restore order in his early seasons, he rubbed many people the wrong way with some on and off fileld antics and was fired after the 2014 season even though he won 9 games. One thing that did not need rebuilding was the dedication of the Nebraska fans who began a sellout streak at Memorial stadium during Bob Devaney's first year in 1962 and, as of the end of the 2012 season, it has reached an incredible 321 games over half a century. The fans have gotten used to winning as there are only three schools that have won more games than Nebraska (Michigan, Texas, and Notre Dame) in the history of college football.

Polls, Bowls, and the BCS

Nebraska did finish ahead of Michigan in a different area. Fans could also get used to seeing the Cornhuskers ranked in the polls. Since the United Press International poll (coaches) joined the Associated Press (sports writers and broadcasters) in 1950, many of the same teams could be seen in the polls from year to year. Between 1950 and 2000 perennial powerhouses Nebraska and Oklahoma led the way by finishing in the top 10 over half of those years (27 times). Michigan was next with 22, followed by Alabama and Ohio State with 21, and Notre Dame with 20. The polls led to more excitement in the game because there was something for fans to discuss from week to week and especially at the end of the season. The polls would often not agree on where the teams were ranked and many times that included the top teams. When the polls had different top ranked teams there would be a split decision and two national champions. This happened 10 times during the same period and the controversy caused by these poll discrepancies would eventually lead many to call for a playoff.

Michigan Stadium. Image © Steve Pepple, 2013. Used under license from Shutterstock, Inc.

From their inception in the 1930s (with the exception of the Rose Bowl's 1902 start), postseason bowl games were designed to be a reward for a successful season and a financial boon for the host city and the competing schools. By the start of World War II, five bowls were in existence (Rose, Orange, Sugar, Sun, and Cotton). With the advent of the top 20 polls, other ranked teams wanted to reap the benefits of the bowl games, and other cities wanted to get into the act as well; so the number of games grew to 8 and then 10 by the end of the 1950s, with the additions of long-standing events like the Gator and Liberty Bowls and other more temporary venues. The number remained roughly the same over the next two decades with the coming and going of different bowl games, but it was

Rose Bowl. Image © Byron W. Moore, 2013. Used under license from Shutterstock, Inc.

during the 1980s that the number of games begin to multiply—especially after the 1984 lawsuit. By 1990 there were 19 bowl games, and by 2000 there were 23. After the 2010 season that number had jumped to an amazing 35 games. There were so many games the NCAA felt compelled to step in and make a rule on which teams were "bowl eligible." It was decided teams must have a winning record. In 2006, when the NCAA went from an 11-game to a 12-game schedule (also to fill the expanding roster of bowl games), it relaxed the requirement and said a .500 record (6–6) was good enough. By the 21st century, it seems the original purpose of the bowls to make money was still very much a part of the equation but, instead of a postseason appearance being a reward for a good or great season, it has become for many schools a reward for a mediocre one.

The bowls themselves have long been divided between what are considered the major bowls (usually those played on New Year's Day) and the minor ones (usually played prior to New Year's and often named for a transitory sponsor such as the "Poulan Weed-eater Bowl" or the "Go-Daddy. com Bowl"). The major bowls were, for the most part, the original bowls consisting of the Rose, Orange, Sugar, and Cotton (the Sun, while remaining a bowl, never reached major status). Those four were eventually joined by the **Fiesta Bowl**, which is an interesting story in itself. Most of the bowls had conference tie-ins by the 1970s (winners of the various conferences would go to certain bowls—the winners of the Pac-10 and Big 10 would meet in the Rose Bowl, for example). The Western Athletic Conference had no tie-ins, and its champions in 1968, Wyoming, and 1969, Arizona State, were not invited to any bowls. The last straw for the WAC was in 1970, when its champion, again Arizona State, was undefeated and was invited to a lesser Peach Bowl. Tempe (not-so-ironically), the home of Arizona State, announced they were hosting the first Fiesta Bowl in 1971, and the winner of the WAC would automatically qualify. Over the next decade the Fiesta Bowl grew in prestige, and in 1981 it would be moved to a coveted New Year's Day slot. It really shot to the highest ranks after the 1986 season, when independents Penn State and Miami were ranked number one and two, but were not tied to any bowls, so they were invited to play in the Fiesta Bowl (no longer tied to the WAC), which turned out to be for the national title. It did not always work that way—because of the tie-ins of the conferences, the two best teams did not always meet on the field, and the pollsters decided the "mythical" national champions. By 1998, the drumbeat for a playoff had become so incessant that the members of the six major conferences plus Notre Dame decided to create the **Bowl Championship Series (BCS)**. A computer would calculate rankings based on a combination of the original two polls, AP and the newly constructed USA Today/ESPN Coaches Poll (which took the place of the UPI), strength of schedule, and won–lost record. The winners of the six conferences would join two at-large teams to play in the major bowls, consisting of the Rose, Orange, Sugar, and Fiesta, to determine the national champion. To make it fair to the four bowls, they would rotate the championship among them so every four years they would get to host the championship. Beginning in 2006 two more at-large teams were added, and a separate game titled the "BCS Championship" would be held in addition to the four major bowls (usually one week after the New Year's bowls occur) at the site of the major bowl (rotated between Miami, New Orleans, Tempe, and Los Angeles). Although there has been continued controversy over the BCS, there is no doubt it has been a profitable arrangement for the schools involved and the networks broadcasting it. In 2001, ABC agreed to pay $550 million for the rights to the BCS games through 2005. Beginning in 2006, with the addition of the extra BCS game and the addition of the FOX network, it and ABC paid over $2 billion for the telecasting rights.

Another Realignment, the Coming of a Playoff, and the Penn State Scandal

By the 21st century, college football had become big business in a way that Walter Camp, Knute Rockne, or even the Carnegie Foundation could never have imagined. By the end of the first decade of that century, a new conference realignment had begun in earnest and there was even talk of a long-awaited playoff—talk that would soon turn into a reality. There was also a shocking reminder of the danger of a program becoming so powerful that it would go so far as to protect one of its own and its own reputation and neglect the most vulnerable people in our society.

It is not altogether clear if there were two separate conference realignments that began in the 1990s and continued in the first decade of the new century or if the recent changes are just part of the century-long shifting landscape of college football. Whichever the case, that landscape began to rumble in 1999 when eight teams left the Western Athletic Conference (WAC) to form the Mountain West Conference. The oldest conference in existence (the Big 10) also made it known that they were willing to add a 12th team (after Penn State became the 11th a decade earlier) when it offered Notre Dame a spot but was turned down. With the possible exception of Arkansas leaving the South West Conference to join the SEC in 1990, conferences had never actively pursued teams with other conference affiliations but that changed in 2003. The war began when the ACC raided the Big East and took three of their teams (Miami, Boston College, and Virginia Tech) in order to raise its number to 12 teams. Conference championship games had begun the previous decade and the ACC saw the money made by conferences like the Big 12 and the SEC and wanted to host a championship game of their own. NCAA rules stated that conferences had to have at least 12 teams in order to get that game so 12 became the magic number. After the 2003 raid, things did not look good for the Big East as they were down to four teams; but two years later they conducted their own raid by bringing in three teams from Conference USA (Cincinnati, Louisville, and South Florida) and brought Connecticut up to division one for a total of eight teams.

If the earlier moves were mere rumbles, 2010 and 2011 produced a full-blown earthquake. The Pac-10 and Big 10 were the next major conferences looking to get a championship game and they set their sights on the Big 12. First Colorado accepted an invitation from the Pac-10 and then Nebraska announced it was going to the Big 10. It was not the first time the Cornhuskers were rumored to be heading to that conference as it was widely believed they would replace the University of Chicago when that institution dropped football in 1946. Michigan State would ultimately be that replacement. The Pac-10 next offered Texas the 12th spot in the conference and, when Texas was making its decision, the Big 12 held its collective breath because a departure of Texas would probably mean the death of the conference as other teams would follow Texas' lead and find other conferences. Texas ultimately stayed and so did the conference. Although it would lose both Missouri and Texas A&M (along with one of the greatest rivalries in the history of college football—with Texas) it gained TCU and West Virginia for a total of 10 teams by 2011. The conference lost its championship game but it stayed alive. The musical chairs between the ACC and the Big East continued in 2011 when Syracuse and Pittsburgh both left the Big East and joined the ACC. In late 2012, it was announced that a team from each of those conferences (Rutgers—Big East, and Maryland—ACC) were going to join the Big 10 and bring its numbers up to 14. The first major **superconference** was announced to start play in 2013 when the Mountain West and Conference USA announced a merger and the possibility of up to 24 teams in one conference. The Big East announced in 2011 that it would eventually get the magic number of 12 but it had to go coast-to-coast to do it. They added Boise State, San Diego State, Houston, SMU, and Central Florida. Realignment often did not make much geographical sense as a conference named the Big "East" now spanned 3,000 miles and four time zones all the way to the Pacific Ocean.

Playoff

When the BCS formed, it made the winners of the six major conferences (Big East, Big 10, Big 12, SEC, ACC, Pac-10) what it called "automatic qualifiers"—meaning, they qualified for one of the major bowl games which meant more money and prestige for the university. That was one of the reasons for the realignment of conferences also—hopes to become an automatic qualifier. This was especially the case for the forming of a superconference—two minor conferences merging in hopes of becoming a major one. In the summer of 2012 all that became moot as the automatic qualifiers were thrown out and a **four-team playoff** was approved by an NCAA presidential oversight committee. The four teams will be chosen by a selection committee and the two semifinals will be held at current bowl sites either on New Year's Eve or New Year's Day. The championship game site will go to the highest-bidding city and will occur on the first Monday in January that falls at least six days following the semifinals. The committee will take into consideration win–loss records, strength of schedule, head-to-head results, and whether a team is a conference champion. The loss of the automatic qualifiers seem to hurt the Big East the most as its champions in recent years appear to have been the weakest of the BCS teams and now they will not automatically get a spot in the playoffs. For that matter, no conference has any guarantees in the new system. It is an "open marketplace for all schools," as Big 12 Commissioner Bob Bowlsby said.[8] For years many have called for some sort of playoff. Some have gone so far as propose a 16-team playoff as is done in the lower divisions in college football. The biggest stumbling block for any playoff system has always been the established bowls. The new system promises to continue the use of the bowl games and even the executive director of the bowl association Wright Waters was on board when he announced, "Today is the beginning of an exciting time for the future of college football and we are committed to continuing the rich tradition of the bowls."[9] Whenever there is a committee deciding something there promises to be some controversy. One only has to look at the NCAA committee that picks the field for the basketball tournament every March and invariably the teams that are left out cry foul. To be fair though, there are rarely more than four teams that legitimately can lay claim to being the best team at the conclusion of the regular season so perhaps the decisions will not be that difficult. The toughest decision may be how to seed the teams for the semifinals. As Virginia Tech president Charles Sterger said, "A four-team playoff doesn't go too far; it goes just the right amount."[10] Time will tell—if the first installment is any indication of the future it should be a successful one as Ohio State defeated Alabama and Oregon (who had defeated Florida State) to win the championship. The system is set to run through the 2025 season.

Scandal at Penn State

Joe Paterno. Image © Richard Paul Kane, 2013.
Used under license from Shutterstock, Inc.

Penn State is one of the towering post-war college football institutions and most of that reputation can be credited to one man: **Joe Paterno**. Unfortunately, that towering image took a major hit at the end of his career and his victories will only be part of his legacy. Paterno played college quarterback and cornerback at Brown University for Rip Engle and, after his graduation in 1950, he planned on going into law to follow in his father's footsteps (he was a law clerk) but was encouraged by his former coach to come to Penn State where Engle took over as head coach. Paterno served under Engle until he succeeded him upon Engle's retirement in 1966. Paterno quickly built on what he and Engle had begun and had back-to-back undefeated seasons in 1968 and 1969. Although he would coach five teams that went undefeated, only two of them were named national champions (1982 and 1986). He certainly would have benefited from the new playoff system and became a staunch advocate (not surprisingly) for a playoff over the years.

Paterno would continue to coach into his 80s and became the face, not only for Penn State football but for the University in general and, in many people's eyes, of all college football. The 2011 season, Paterno's 45th at Penn State, started with Paterno chasing Amos Alonzo Stagg's all-time win record for the winningest coach in college football but it ended with Paterno being fired amidst a growing sex scandal.

In November of 2011, long time assistant coach Jerry Sandusky was indicted on 52 counts of child molestation of underage boys between 1994 and 2009. The charges were bad enough, but it was also alleged that many of the molestations took place on university property and even with the knowledge of university officials. As the scandal continued to swirl it began to take down some of these officials including the president of the university, Graham Spanier; vice-president Gary Schultz; and the athletic director, Tim Curley. The big question was whether Paterno knew about the allegations. Assistant coach Mike McQueary testified before a grand jury in 2010 that he witnessed Sandusky molesting a boy in the Penn State football showers in 2002. He also testified that he reported what he saw to both Curley and Paterno. Not only was nothing done but Sandusky (who had retired in 1999 to concentrate on his charity, The Second Mile, which was designed to help at-risk boys) retained an office at Penn State and was allowed access to the athletic facilities there. The calls for Paterno to go became so loud that he offered to retire at the end of the season but that was not enough for Penn State administration who fired him on November 9, 2011. On November 21 it was announced that former FBI director Louis Freeh would lead an independent investigation of the university's handling of the scandal. The Freeh report was released in July of

2012 and it was a stinging indictment of the administration and Paterno. It accused them of "conceal[ing] Sandusky's activities from the Board of Trustees, the University community and authorities." According to the report, the officials were concerned that Sandusky be treated "humanely," but they did not express the same feelings toward his victims. Freeh found that Schultz, Spanier, Curley, and Paterno "failed to protect against a child sexual predator harming children for over a decade."[11] In addition, the report said that the four men "exhibited a striking lack of empathy for Sandusky's victims by failing to inquire as to their safety and well-being." The report stated that the men knew about a 1998 incident but "empowered Sandusky to attract potential victims to the campus and football events by allowing him to have continued, unrestricted and unsupervised access to the University's facilities and affiliation with the University's prominent football program" while the investigation was underway.[12] The report also stated the four men not only made no effort to identify the victim of the 2002 incident that McQueary witnessed, but alerted Sandusky to McQueary's allegations against him, thus potentially putting the victim in more danger. It also stated that Paterno had lied to the grand jury regarding his knowledge of Sandusky's behavior; he had stated at that time that he hadn't known about any inappropriate activity until 2002. In response, Penn State's trustees announced that they accepted the report's conclusions and would implement corrective measures. As for Paterno, he did not live long enough to see the report as he died of lung cancer on January 22 at age 85.

The Sandusky trial began in June of 2012 with 48 of the original 52 counts surviving and Sandusky maintaining his innocence throughout. On June 22 he was convicted on 45 of the 48 counts and on October 9 he was sentenced to a minimum of 30 and maximum of 60 years which is essentially a life sentence for the 68-year-old. Three weeks later former president Spanier was formally charged for his alleged role in the coverup. He faces eight charges, three of which are felonies. As for the other two officials, Curley and Schultz, they have also been charged with grand jury perjury, conspiracy, obstruction of justice, and child endangerment. As of the time of this writing they are all awaiting trial. On July 23 the NCAA stepped in and imposed the following sanctions on Penn State: five years probation and a four-year postseason ban. They were forced to vacate all wins from 1998 to 2011—112 wins in all. This had the effect of stripping the Nittany Lions of their shared Big 10 titles in 2005 and 2008. It also removed 111 wins from Paterno's record, dropping him from first to 12th on the NCAA's all-time wins list. A $60 million fine was imposed, the proceeds of which were to go toward an endowment for preventing child abuse. According to the NCAA, this was the equivalent of a typical year's gross revenue from the football program. There was a loss of a total of 40 initial scholarships from 2013 to 2017. During the same period, Penn State is limited to 65 total scholarships—only two more than a Division I FCS (formerly I-AA) school is allowed. Penn State was required to adopt all recommendations for reform delineated in the Freeh report. Penn State must enter into an "athletics integrity agreement" with the NCAA and Big 10, appoint a university-wide athletic compliance officer and compliance council, and accept an NCAA-appointed athletic integrity monitor for the duration of its probation. Many thought the sanctions were overly harsh and punished student-athletes that had nothing to do with the scandal. Others argued that a message had to be sent that this kind of scandal and coverup would not be tolerated. Those that thought the sanctions were too harsh seemed to be vindicated when the NCAA eventually shortened the postseason ban to two seasons and the Nittany Lions were allowed to play in a bowl game after the 2014 season. They also reduced the number of scholarships the program lost and by 2016 be back to 85 total scholarships which is the full allotment allowed by the NCAA. In early 2015 the NCAA restored 112 wins to the University which gave Joe Paterno a total of 409 and put him back on top of all-time NCAA wins as a coach.

Conclusion

NCAA President Mark Emmert stated that the Penn State sanctions were levied "not to be just punitive, but to make sure the university establishes an athletic culture and daily mindset in which football will never again be placed ahead of education, nurturing and protecting young people."[13] That sounded strikingly similar to the findings of the Carnegie Report of 80 years earlier. The Carnegie Commission was seemingly prophetic in its findings. Since college football became a big-time business in the first half of the 20th century, it has always walked a fine line between being a fun, extracurricular activity for students, players, and fans to being an all-consuming, overly important business that eclipses the importance of student education. The Penn State scandal reminded everyone of how bad it could be when that line is crossed.

Notes

1. Richard O. Davies, *Sports in American Life* (West Sussex, UK: Wiley-Blackwell, 2012), 205.
2. Ibid.
3. Ibid., 206.
4. Ibid., 207.
5. Benjamin Rader, *American Sports; From the Age of Folk Games to the Age of Televised Sports*, 6th ed. (Upper Saddle River, NJ: Pearson-Prentice Hall, 2009), 279.
6. Ibid., 185.
7. Ibid., 189–190.
8. "Playoff to Run Through 2025," by Heather Dinich, *ESPN.com*, 27 June 2012.
9. Ibid.
10. Ibid.
11. Kevin Johnson, Kevin and Mary Beth Marklein, "Freeh report blasts culture of Penn State." *USA Today*. 13 July 2012.
12. Ibid.
13. Colleen Kane, "NCAA punishes Penn State." *Chicago Tribune*. 23 July 2012.

CHAPTER
Fourteen

American Women in Sports

*I*f one's only exposure to American sports history was what has been written in this book up to this chapter, then that reader's conclusion could logically be that athletics is not only a male-dominated arena but that women have not been involved at all. That was neither the intention of the author nor the truth of the matter. However, as sports historian Allen Guttman points out in the first line of his seminal work, *Women's Sports: A History,* "there has never been a time, from the dawn of our civilization to the present, when women have been as involved in sports, as participants or as spectators, as men have."[1] He is quick to point out, though, that women throughout history have never been completely excluded from athletics. In the early chapters of the book, Guttman points to evidence that the ancient Egyptians, Spartans, Etruscans, and Greeks all had examples of female athleticism. Even during the later stages of Britain's "Festive Culture" (16th through 18th centuries) examined in the first chapter of this work, which Guttman calls a "masculine preserve," women could be found engaging in athletic pursuits.[2] As with the 19th century's Victorian counterculture, the British female involvement at that time was largely reserved to the upper and lower classes of British society. There is no denying that there has never been a time in which women were more involved in sports both as participants and spectators than the last half-century. This is largely due to a fundamental change in both the attitude of society toward sports in general and women's involvement with them in particular. This chapter will take a look at those changing attitudes over the years and the resulting participation by women in athletics beginning in the 19th century and continuing up until the present time.

Women's Sports in Victorian America

Women in colonial America could be found engaging in recreational activities and sometimes in what the Puritans referred to as "Lawful Sport," but usually the activities were limited to non-physically competitive pursuits like dancing, fishing, or playing cards. It was not until the 19th century that women began to become more involved in what we would consider today to be competitive sports. As with males, higher education fostered a growth in the popularity of sports with women also. Sports were becoming more a part of the "collegiate way," as detailed in Chapter 4. The problem for women was that they were excluded not only from the collegiate way but also from most colleges for decades during the early years of the republic. Even public high schools weren't opened to women until the 1820s. **Oberlin College** was founded in Ohio in 1833 and was the first college in the United States to allow women and Black students. The first woman to earn a bachelor's degree in the United States did so from Oberlin in 1841. It took the early women's rights movement of the 1850s and the Civil War to open the doors of colleges to women. Prior to the

Civil War, only five colleges were open to women. Because of the shortage of male students during the war, many colleges changed their policies to allow female students; and the Morrill Land-Grant Colleges Act of 1862 created dozens of land-grant colleges throughout the Midwest and West which were open to both sexes. By 1870 nearly one-third of all American colleges were coeducational.

During the Victorian period, there was a strict segregation of the sexes into what was known as "separate spheres," as discussed in Chapter 2, but there was also the idea that women were not only to be confined to the home (the private sphere) but also should be protected and treated as the more delicate of the sexes. This came to be known as the cult of "**True Womanhood**." The idea was that woman was made from "finer clay" than "mortal, sinful man" and exposing her to the "rough contacts" of the male-dominated public sphere would do irrevocable damage to society's view of the "true woman."[3] One of these "rough contacts" was higher education; and although the Civil War and the influx of immigrants that the industrialized American economy was attracting produced some very different women than the society's ideal, the belief in the cult of True Womanhood continued in the late 19th century. Many worried that women attending college would do damage to this ideal. This concern was readily evident in 1875 when the all-female Smith College opened its doors in Northampton, MA. Although founded by a woman, Sophia Smith, with an inheritance she had received, the first president was a man, Laurenus Clark Seelye, who tried to alleviate these worries when he said in his inaugural address: "... *it is neither the aim nor the tendency of higher education to make women less feminine or attractive in those graces peculiar to her sex. It is to preserve her womanliness that this college has been founded; it is to give her the best opportunities for mental culture and at the same time the most favorable conditions for developing those innate capacities which have ever been the glory and charm of true womanhood.*"[4]

Women's exposure to higher education was being attacked on many fronts—including the medical profession. The same year Smith College opened, Dr. Edward C. Clarke published a book called *Sex in Education: or a Fair Chance for Girls*. In it Dr. Clarke produced a theory that overuse by one part of the body takes away energy from other parts. The woman's brain would need more blood flow to the brain to navigate through the difficult challenges of college courses and would, therefore, take blood flow away from her uterus which would cause her to become sterile. This was not some lone quack doctor espousing these theories but a widely held belief in the medical profession and was used as an argument against women attending college. It was also, ironically, an argument that would help introduce physical education into women's curriculum. As a precaution against Dr. Clarke's theory, physical education was introduced into the female curriculum to balance the blood flow so it not only going to the brain but to other parts of the body. Eventually, Clarke's theory was disproven as women were shown to be as capable as men at the rigors of academia but the physical education continued as a source of balance for women. Eventually physical education would broaden into competitive sport. The combination of the athletic component of the "collegiate way" and "muscular Christianity" movement that was more associated with the American male could also be seen with females—especially on college campuses. One of the earliest proponents of what he called "joyous unrestrained activity" for female students was Matthew Vassar, founder of Vassar College an all-female college in Poughkeepsie, NY.[5] Shortly after its founding in 1861, Vassar spoke about expanded physical education for his students beyond calisthenics. Vassar envisioned horseback riding and even "playful games" which were the forerunners of competitive sports that were to come.[6] It is believed that the first competitive sport that was played by college females was basketball when it was introduced by Senda Berenson to her gymnastics class at Smith College shortly after Naismith's invention of the game in 1892. Newspaper accounts show the popularity of the game when the classes of 1895 and 1896 played each other in an interclass game. Berenson described the "whole school turning out with flags and class colors" but there was also the reminder of the cult of true womanhood when she described the "unladylike behavior" of some of the fans during the game and the fact she "limited the cheers to musical ones."[7] From this beginning basketball, as we saw with the male version in Chapter 10, spread to women's colleges all over the country.

Just as competitive sport was spreading, there came new cautionary medical theories. In the 1890s, there were many in the medical field who argued that women who participated in athletics did great damage to her reproductive organs and could be rendered permanently infertile. One of the most fanatical of these theorists was actually a woman named Arabella Kenealy. She agreed with the reproductive organ argument but she went even further and argued that, similarly to Dr. Clarke's earlier argument but in reverse, physical activity denies the brain needed blood flow and can actually result in mental illness and even early death. In her 1899 essay titled, "Woman as an Athlete," she writes that girls that ride bicycles and swing tennis rackets die proverbially young. "Lunatics and other diseased persons frequently exhibit muscular strength which seems almost superhuman."[8] There were others who argued that this was nonsense. Dudley Sargent was a Harvard physical education instructor and had a national reputation for his knowledge on the subject believed that athletics, even competitive sports, were good for females as well as males. Even Sargent, however, was not ready to endorse female participation in the more "manly" athletics such as wrestling and boxing. Despite the arguments against their participation, women became active in more and more sports as the turn of the century approached. In 1930 D. Ainsworth wrote in *The History of Physical Education in Colleges for* Women that there were three phases in the late 19th century that the idea of physical education went through—the first two have been discussed (a balance and a preventative measure against the rigors of academic life) and the last was sport for the sheer enjoyment of it. Interviews with women who played college athletics during this time are rife with this point. Most of them say it was the best part of not only their college careers but the best part of their lives. As the Victorian Age was ending and a new century was beginning, it appeared the "separate sphere" and cult of "true womanhood" was ending also. There was the emergence of what many historians have called the "**New Woman.**" This was a woman who was taking advantage of the new opportunities open to her through higher education and the professional possibilities that might bring—possibilities that heretofore had only been available to men. It was also a woman who, despite all the obstacles stacked in front of her, was entering into an ever-increasing number: athletics.

The Early 20th Century: Gibson Girl to Flapper

Stamp of Gibson Girl. Image © catwalker, 2013. Used under license from Shutterstock, Inc.

In 1890 the artist Charles Dana Gibson painted a tall, slim, athletic-looking girl that would forever be known as the "**Gibson Girl**." He would paint her participating in various sporting events like bicycling, golf, and tennis. Whether knowing it or not, Gibson had created society's ideal woman for the next 30 years. Charlotte Perkins Gilman, the foremost feminist of the time, described the Gibson Girl as "braver, stronger, more healthful and skillful and able and free, more human in all ways."[9] The Gibson Girl was the embodiment of the "new woman" that emerged from the Victorian "cult of true womanhood." This image change helped make athletics more acceptable for the American woman. One of the first competitive sports that benefited from this change was tennis. The sport was first introduced to America by a woman, Mary Ewing Outerbridge, a wealthy American who while vacationing in Bermuda in 1874 first played the game and brought it back to her native New York. Her brother who was the director of the Staten Island Cricket and

Baseball Club had a lawn tennis court installed and the club and American tennis was born. Women were first allowed entry in the Wimbledon Championships in 1884 and the first American women's championships followed in 1887. Like golf, tennis was considered an upper-class sport and only women from the "best families" were allowed to enter the tournaments in the early years. As with the male side of the sport, women's tennis became a spectator sport in the 1920s. Arguably the first international female superstar was French tennis player **Suzanne Lenglen**. She was a child prodigy making it to the finals of the 1914 French Championships at the age of 14. Although she lost that match, she won the World Hard Court Championships, turning 15 during the tournament, which made her the youngest winner of a major tennis championship—a record she still holds. The outbreak of World War I that fall put everything on hold for the next five years including Lenglen's career. The next tournament she would win would be the 1919 Wimbledon championship. She

Suzanne Lenglen. © Bettmann/CORBIS

would win that tournament five consecutive years (1919–1923) and again in 1925. She would add back-to-back French titles in 1925 and 1926. In 1926 she decided to turn professional and went on a tour to the United States promoted by Charles "Cash and Carry" Pyle (agent of Red Grange who promoted a similar tour of Grange and the Chicago Bears the year before). Pyle paid her $50,000 to play matches against Mary K. Browne who had won the U.S. Tennis Championship three consecutive years from 1912–1914. Browne was now 35 and past her prime—Lenglen defeated her 38 times against no defeats on the tour by the time it ended in February of 1927. Much like Grange had been exhausted and injured after his tour with Pyle (many say he was never the same after it), Lenglen's career actually ended with the tour. She was advised by doctors to take an extended rest after the tour—she chose instead to retire.

In one of her last matches as an amateur in February of 1926, Lenglen played against a 20-year-old American named **Helen Wills**. She had already won three consecutive U.S. Championships (1923–1925) but was not yet proven on the world stage (other than a gold medal in the 1924 Paris Olympics). The Lenglen–Wills match in Cannes, France, garnered even more publicity than the Olympics had. Extra stands were built to accommodate the high demand for seats but it was not enough—scalpers reportedly were getting $44 a ticket (to put that in perspective, a seat at the U.S. Championships in Forest Hills that year cost $2). Lenglen won the match 6-3, 8-6 in the only time the two stars met on the court. Lenglen's career was ending and Wills' was just beginning. She would go on to win the U.S. Championship four more times between 1927 and 1931; four French championships between 1928 and 1932; and an incredible eight Wimbledon championships between 1927 and her last in 1938. Where Lenglen was flamboyant and emotional, Wills was stoic and unemotional. Wills was never loved by the public the way Lenglen was—always respected for her talent but never loved. She was hard to identify with for most people—almost inhuman and cold, an "Ice Maiden" as she was often called. Early in her career she was described as a "goddess in the form of an American Girl" who seemed to fit with the "Gibson Girl" image.[10] The problem was that by the 1920s, the image of the ideal woman had shifted from the "Gibson Girl" to the "**flapper**." This was a much less stoic, more outgoing person who wore her emotions on her sleeve. The flapper wore her hair short, danced, and even drank alcohol (which by this time was illegal). The "goddess" Wills did not seem to fit this description. Like her or not, the public could not deny that Helen Wills was the first American female athlete superstar.

Helen Wills.
© Underwood & Underwood/Corbis

Flapper. Image © Gorbash Varvara, 2013. Used under license from Shutterstock, Inc.

Babe Didrikson. © Underwood & Underwood/ Corbis

A woman who fit into the "flapper" mold perfectly was swimmer **Gertrude Ederle**. After the 1924 Olympics, the Literary Digest described her as "the bob-haired, 19-year-old daughter of the Jazz Age."[11] In the 1924 Olympics she took bronze in the 100 and 400 meter freestyle races and a gold medal as a member of the 400-meter relay team. By the end of the year, she held 18 world records in swimming. Two years later, she gained her greatest fame by becoming the first woman to swim the English Channel. She was unable to handle her fame, and she suffered a nervous breakdown and retired from competitive swimming in 1928. Both Ederle and Wills were lucky to have competed in the Paris Olympics in 1924. If the founder of the modern Olympics had his way, women would have not been allowed to do so. Pierre de Coubertin forbade women from competing in the first modern games in 1896. It was not that he was against women's sports per se, he just did not want them competing in public because he felt the "spectators who gathered for such competitions don't show up to look at sports."[12] Much against his urging, women began to compete as early as 1900. Those games allowed women's participation in tennis and golf. Archery was added in 1904 and figure skating in 1912. Women's swimming also made its debut in the Stockholm Games of 1912 much to the horror of many who worried about showing too much female skin to the world. The president of Australia's New South Wales Swimming Association, Rose Scott, was so upset that she resigned her post saying, "I think it's disgusting that men should be allowed to attend."[13] Probably the biggest break for American women came when James Sullivan, president of the Amateur Athletic Union, and even more against women's participation in the Olympics than de Coubertin, died in 1916. In 1928 women were allowed to compete in track and field for the first time. Four years later the games returned to the United States and one of the greatest female athletes of all-time competed—her name was **Babe Didrikson**.

She was born Mildred Ella Didrikson to Norwegian immigrant parents in 1911; and contrary to the popular myth that she earned her nickname after hitting five homeruns in a schoolyard baseball game (which no doubt happened), she had actually been called "Bebe" by her Norwegian mother beginning when she was just a toddler. Although not named for Babe Ruth, she certainly had Ruthian aspirations from a young age. In her autobiography, she wrote that her goal was "to be the greatest athlete who ever lived."[14] Notice she did *not* write the word female between greatest and athlete. In fact, after winning gold medals in the javelin and the 80 meter hurdles and a silver medal in the high jump, she was quoted as saying, "I don't worry about the races with girls."[15] In high school she had played baseball, basketball, volleyball, golf, tennis, and swimming. She must have been spending most of her time in athletics because she eventually dropped out of school without graduating. After getting a job with an insurance company, she helped start a company female basketball team and in 1931 helped that team win an AAU national championship. She also convinced the company to sponsor a track team on which she starred and in 1930 broke three world records. At the AAU national championships in 1932, she won six gold medals and set four more world records. In the 1932 Los Angeles Olympics, she certainly could have competed in numerous events but had to pick three (women were limited to three events). In the javelin she beat the old world record by more than two meters. Although tying a world record with her fellow competitor Jean Shiley in the high jump, the gold was awarded to Shiley because Didrikson dove over the bar. In another world record, she completed the 80 meter hurdles in 11.7 seconds barely defeating Evelyn Hall for the gold medal (some say Hall actually won).

After the Olympics she barnstormed as a baseball player throughout 1933 and 1934 but by 1935 she had decided to enter the sporting arena that would garner her the greatest fame—professional golf. She had actually wanted to compete as an amateur but was denied that status because she had received money while touring with Gene Sarazen as well as continuing to play other sports. In 1938 she entered the Los Angeles Open on the PGA Tour and played against the men. Although she shot an 81 and 84 and missed the cut, she did meet her future husband at that tournament, wrestler George Zaharias. She was told that if she wanted to earn back her amateur status, she would have to play no other sports for three years which she did and in 1942 earned the right to play in amateur events winning the U.S. Amateur in 1946 and the British Amateur in 1947. She formally turned professional after that and was one of the founding members of the Ladies Professional Golfers Association (LPGA) in 1950. That was also her greatest year on tour as she won eight tournaments and held the Grand Slam of women's golf (then consisting of three tournaments: The U.S. Open, Western Open, and Titleholder's Championship). She would win 41 titles on tour including 10 major championships. Although she did not make the cut in the 1938 Los Angeles Open, she tried again in 1945 and this time made the first cut but not the second. She also entered the Phoenix and Tucson Opens that year and made both cuts finishing 33rd and 42nd, respectively. This made her the first (and so far only) female to make the cut in a PGA event. It should be noted that she had to qualify for those tournaments unlike later players Annika Sorenstam and Michelle Wie who received sponsor exemptions into the PGA tournaments they competed in. In 1948 she attempted to qualify for the U.S. Open (male version) but her application was rejected by the USGA that said this was a tournament meant to be played by men. She was diagnosed with colon cancer in 1953 and after surgery made a comeback in 1954 and won her 10th and final major, the U.S. Women's Open one month after having surgery wearing a colostomy bag. Unfortunately the cancer returned in 1955 and she was limited to eight events (winning her 40th and 41st events). She died the following year at the age of 45. She was still a force on the tour at the time of her death so who knows how many more victories she would have amassed had she been given the chance? ESPN named her the 10th greatest North American athlete of the 20th century, and the Associated Press listed her as 9th. In neither poll was the word female used—she would have liked that.

All-American Girls' Baseball League

Although women's baseball was most famously played during and just following World War II, it can actually be traced back to just after the Civil War when some women's colleges attempted to add the sport to its physical education programs. In 1867 the Dolly Vardens were an African-American female baseball team in Philadelphia that were paid to play making them the first professional baseball club in the country (two years prior to the Cincinnati Red Stockings). In the 1880s an entrepreneur named Harry H. Freeman attempted to start a professional women's baseball league but was stopped when it was rumored that he was recruiting the women for a prostitution ring. In the late 19th century most colleges that tried to introduce female baseball were eventually forced to abandon it (i.e., Smith College in 1880) because it was believed the sport was too taxing for females to play. If women wanted to play baseball and were talented enough, they were forced to play on men's teams or barnstorm with coed teams and many did that in the late 19th and early 20th centuries. An example of one of these talented female players was **Alta Weiss**. She was born in 1890 in Ohio and started to pitch for boys' teams at 14 and at 17 joined the semiprofessional Vermillion Independents. Over 1,200 people showed up to see her make her debut in which she gave up only four hits and one run in five innings. She made enough money playing baseball to put herself through medical school, and she was the only female in the Sterling Medical College's graduating class of 1914. She continued to play baseball even after she was a physician—drawing large crowds every time she pitched. While talented women like Alta Weiss and Babe Didrikson were rare in baseball, there was another venue where women began to excel, and that was in the relatively new sport called **softball**. As colleges began to frown on female baseball in the late 19th century, physical education classes started to incorporate something known as "indoor baseball" in which the field dimensions were smaller than baseball (because of the limited space of the gymnasium) and the balls were larger and softer (hence the name) so as not to travel as far as fast or break things when striking them. This activity was seen as perfect for women because they would not exert themselves as much as they would in baseball (baselines were shorter and the pitcher threw underhand as opposed to overhand which had been adopted by virtually all baseball leagues by this time). Softball was very popular in Chicago, and it moved outside after the turn of the 20th century with the advent of the "Playground Movement" which also began in Chicago but soon spread across the country. By the 1930s it had become a spectator sport, and in 1933 the Amateur Softball Association (ASA) was formed and held its first national tournament. The ASA reported in 1935 that there were roughly 2,000,000 "enthusiastic softball players in the United States, more than 60,000 amateur teams and 1,000 lighted ballparks." Although the majority of those players were men, the female numbers were not insignificant. The ASA reported that while the majority of players and parks were in the Midwest, it was expanding. By 1938 there were nearly "1,000 female softball teams in the Los Angeles area alone."[16] By 1943 the numbers rose to almost 3 million players on over 100,000 teams. After the United States entered World War II in 1941, a baseball mogul would look to female softball as a remedy for the predicted shortage of baseball-playing men.

Philip K. Wrigley. © Bettmann/CORBIS

Philip K. Wrigley, the chewing gum king and owner of the Chicago Cubs proposed in 1942 to develop a women's professional softball league in conjunction with major league baseball teams around the country. The only executive to show any interest was Branch Rickey of the Brooklyn Dodgers. Due to that lack of interest, Wrigley and Rickey decided to establish a league composed of smaller Midwestern cities in Illinois, Indiana, and Wisconsin. One of the things Wrigley demanded was a uniform that kept the femininity of the players intact. They were modeled after tennis, field hockey, and ice skating outfits of the time. They included skirts which got progressively shorter over the years to allow more mobility and speed. What was not allowed to be short was the player's hair—Wrigley wanted the girls to continue to look like girls so their hair would remain long. The four original members included teams from Racine and Kenosha, Wisconsin, South Bend, Indiana, and Rockford, Illinois, and were christened the All-American Girls' Softball League (AAGSBL) for the 1943 season. Even before the first season was over, the powers-that-be in the league (mainly Wrigley) began thinking of a switch from softball to baseball. By the end of the first season, sportswriters were instructed to call the league the All-America Girls' Ball League. For the next season the dimensions of the field would change—the baselines were lengthened along with the distance from the pitcher's mound to home plate, and the pitchers would now throw overhand. By 1945 the league had officially changed its name to the All-American Girls' Baseball League (AAGBBL). By then Wrigley had sold his ownership of the league thinking the league would not last past the end of the war. Little did he know at the time but the league would continue for almost a full decade expanding to a high of ten teams in 1948. By the early 50s for a variety of reasons, the league began to lose players, attendance, and teams. By 1954 there were only five teams left and the league folded after the season.

One of the great fears of Wrigley and other leaders was that the players would lose their femininity (this was a common fear throughout American history when women engage in what is thought to be traditionally a male-dominated field—i.e., women who joined the military during World War II found that their uniforms were the same as males except instead of pants they wore skirts). Along with the skirts and long hair required in the AAGBBL, all players were required to attend etiquette classes given by famous etiquette expert Helena Rubinstein. These classes taught the girls everything from table manners to hygiene to how to sit like a lady. Because many of the girls were young and away from home for the first time (and because coaches, managers, and umpires were almost exclusively male) they were provided with chaperones. They were usually physical education teachers or veteran amateur softball players. Beginning in 1950 some veteran AAGBBL players acted as chaper-

Dorothy Harrell, shortstop for the Chicago Collins. © Bettmann/CORBIS

ones. The managers tended to be former major league baseball players the most famous being hall of famer Jimmie Foxx who managed the Fort Wayne Daisies in 1952. The longest-lasting and most successful of all the managers was Bill Allington who managed Rockford for eight seasons and Fort Wayne for two. There were a few examples of players assuming managerial positions (usually when there was a midseason change), but negative fan reaction to and player noncooperation with these female managers caused the league board to ban women managers in 1951. In 1947 all eight teams were brought to Cuba for spring training (Branch Rickey made Havana the spring training home of the Dodgers that year for fear of racial problems they might encounter in Florida because of the presence of Jackie Robinson), and the women's teams attracted over 75,000 spectators during its eight-game exhibition which far outdrew the Dodgers' games. They proved so popular that they inspired the formation of a Latin American Feminine Baseball League that began play that fall (and even brought back some American players for exhibitions). As for the league itself during its 12-season run, the most successful team was the Rockford Peaches who won four championships. While the league was largely forgotten over the next four decades, the 1992 film *A League of Their Own* starring Tom Hanks, featured the formation of the league and largely centered around the play of the Rockford Peaches.

Title IX

There were many reasons why the AAGBBL folded in 1954 beyond internal league difficulties. Social patterns in the country began to shift—away from baseball to other outdoor activities and to activities around the home including the proliferation of the new technology of television. There was also the returning societal belief in the 1950s that a woman's place was not in the workforce or on the ball field but in the home raising the children. The reemergence of the female sphere in the

1950s changed many people's minds about women's involvement in historically male activities like baseball. There was even the growing belief that if a woman did not want to stay in the home there was something wrong with her psychologically or, worse yet, politically. While women who worked in factories during World War II were referred to as "Rosie the Riveter," women who continued working postwar were referred to by some as "Rosie the Red." During the Red Scare of the late 40s and early 50s to be called a "red" or a communist was about the worst name that could be applied to someone's character. Not all women shared this belief that their place was in the home as many women continued to work postwar, albeit usually fewer hours and for less pay than their male counterparts. By the early 1960s there began to be a backlash by many women and the modern feminist movement was born. Some point to the two-year study beginning in 1961 by President Kennedy concerning the "Status of Women" as the beginning of the movement. Still others say it was the publication of Betty Friedan's feminist manifesto called *The Feminine Mystique* in 1963 that got it all started. Friedan, who ironically had graduated from Smith College, had interviewed American housewives who were bored or unfulfilled by their roles in the home and were looking for something more. She originally intended it to be a magazine article; but when no magazine would publish it, she lengthened it and published it book form. She argued women should be given equal opportunities in education, employment, and pay. Part of the 1964 Civil Rights Act was Title VII which banned discrimination in employment based on race, sex, religion, or country of origin. What it did *not* cover was education. In the nearly 100 years since Smith College opened its doors, female enrollment in colleges across the country had been steadily increasing, but it was not yet equal to male enrollment. The other inequality that needed to be addressed was in the professional schools which were nowhere near the level of equity that even the undergraduate levels were. Most professional colleges had arbitrary quotas for the number of women they allowed in and/or had higher academic standards for women than it did for men. The modern feminist movement may have been born in the early 1960s, but it was really in the early 1970s that it had gained momentum enough to get meaningful legislation passed. 1972 was a watershed year for the movement as Congress passed both the Equal Rights Amendment to the constitution that guaranteed equal rights for women in all areas of society and the Education Amendments Act with a 37-word section that became known as **Title IX**.

The 37 words were: "No person in the United States shall, on the basis of sex, be excluded from participation in, be denied the benefits of, or be subjected to discrimination under any education program or activity receiving federal financial assistance."[17] What is interesting is this piece of legislation which is so closely related to equity in women's athletics was not originally passed for that purpose. In fact, most who voted for the bill probably did not even know it was there. Those in favor of gender equity stuck Title IX into the huge bill hoping it would not be noticed and pass along with the omnibus bill and they got their wish. Those supporters wanted to close a loophole that Title VII of the Civil Rights Act had left open—namely discrimination against women in educational institutions. Athletics was not a high priority of the original supporters of Title IX. As Representative Patsy Mink of Hawaii said, "When it was proposed, we had no idea that the most visible impact would be in athletics. I had been paying attention to the academic issue. I had been excluded from medical school because I was female."[18] The immediate effect of Title IX was the ending of things like quotas and higher standards for women, and athletics were not seen as an area under the legislation's purview because athletic departments do not receive federal funds directly. It did not take long for colleges to realize that the law applied to the *entire* institution that received federal funding and all of its programs—including the athletic departments. Almost immediately athletic directors across the country began to worry what the ramifications would be—does it mean teams would have to be coeducational? Does it mean athletic budgets for women would *have* to be equal to that of men? And what effect would it have on the revenue-producing sports for the university—especially football? While "King" Football was seen as the "goose that laid the golden egg" on most campuses, the reality was that football only made money on about 20 percent of college campuses, and they were almost entirely the largest schools with the top programs. It was those schools with the backing of the NCAA which fought for exemption for football from Title IX. Beginning in 1975 and several times since, the exemption for football has been struck down by various courts and has never been upheld. The question of coeducational teams was resolved fairly early in the process when it was decided a better idea was to separate teams by sex in relatively comparable sports (basketball for both, baseball for men, softball for women, etc.). This led to the other perplexing question: What about budgets for the two? Athletic directors breathed a sigh of relief when a compromise was reached in 1975 that instead of athletic budgets being split 50-50 along gender lines, the idea of budgeting based on proportionality of students was agreed to. In the 1970s the average school had a proportionality of 56 percent male to 44 percent female. Little did those administrators realize that those numbers would reverse themselves within a quarter of a century (57 percent female to 43 percent male by 2000) at least partly due, proponents would argue, to Title IX.

As with any major piece of legislation, there are consequences—both intended and unintended. The primary intended consequence of Title IX was evident quite quickly. The number of female collegiate athletes rose dramatically practically overnight. In the 1966–67 school year there was roughly one female student participating in intercollegiate athletics for every ten male students who competed (15,727 female; 154,179 male). By the 1976–77 school year there were over 64,000 females competing compared with 170,000 males. Even more dramatically, the number of girls in high school athletics was even less than colleges—closer to one-twelfth that of boys on the eve of Title IX (300,000 girls to 3.7 million boys). By the end of the decade (1978–79), the number of girls participating had jumped to over 2 million and dramatically closed the gap with the number of boys at 4.2 million.[19] The same year that Title IX was passed, the **Association for Intercollegiate Athletics for Women (AIAW)** was formed as the national membership organization to coordinate the activities of women's sports. The AIAW really came about because the NCAA, women felt, was more focused on men's sports so they felt they had to act on their own behalf. The AIAW sought to do things differently than the NCAA by being less commercial and focusing more on education and the fun of competition. To this end they initially banned the awarding of athletic scholarships (they voted to allow scholarships in 1973). Member schools went from 280 in its initial year to 659 by 1975. As the AIAW and female athletic participation grew, the NCAA began to take notice and wanted in. There was a major battle brewing between the two organizations that played out during the 1970s. Women argued that the NCAA had never been friendly to women's athletics and had fought hard against Title IX so why should they be allowed to be part of women's sports now? Margot Polivy the AIAW's lawyer said, "If the NCAA had started women's programs in the 1960s there would not be any AIAW. But now they say, 'You built a nice house there. We think we'll move in.'"[20] In the end the NCAA proved to be too strong for the AIAW. The AIAW was always hurting financially, a problem the NCAA did not have. The NCAA began to hold national championships for women that competed with the AIAW championships, and they were held at no cost to the schools that competed—something the AIAW could not do. By 1982 the AIAW folded—crushed by the cartel that was the NCAA.

One of the other major goals of the AIAW was to keep women in charge of women's collegiate athletics in both coaching and administration. This was one of the unintended consequences of Title IX: The growth of women's collegiate sports led to more money being spent on those sports and created more coaching positions that were attractive to men as well as women (both in status and salary). That coupled with the NCAA takeover led to fewer and fewer women in positions of power over their own sports. Another consequence (whether intended or unintended) was the loss of "minor" men's sports across the country. When the Department of Education became a cabinet department in 1979, their office for Civil Rights was put in charge of making sure universities and colleges were in compliance with Title IX. The penalty for noncompliance would be withholding of federal funds (which has never happened in the 40-plus year history of the law). They came up with what they called the "three-prong test" for compliance: The first was proportionality of budgets and numbers of athletes between the sexes (which was already mentioned). The other two prongs dealt with "interest" issues on the part of the underrepresented sex, in this case female. Schools would have to show that it had a "history and a continuing practice of program expansion" to meet the needs of women and that the programs could "fully and effectively (accommodate) the interests and abilities of the underrepresented sex."[21] In the 1990s for the first time in two decades, the NCAA began to look at program expansion for women to help schools pass the three-prong test for Title IX. In 1996 it published a list of what it called "emerging sports" for women which included ice hockey, synchronized swimming, team handball, water polo, archery, badminton, bowling, squash, and equestrian. Another emerging sport for women toward the end of the century was crew and it was attractive to schools for a couple of reasons: It was one of the few women's sports which demanded a large roster (for all the boats involved), and that would help balance the numbers with men's football; and it did not take a lot of earlier training—participants could be trained on the collegiate level.

It was that last point that irked some coaches and athletes of the so-called male "minor sports," especially the Olympic sports of wrestling and gymnastics as many of them went onto the chopping block across the country in the interest of proportionality. There are male athletes that have competed in their various sports practically since they could walk, and now they are being told that their program is being cut in favor of something like female crew in which the team members need not have ever picked up an oar or been in a boat before. As one might imagine, that did not sit well with many associated with those "minor" male sports. According to the office of Civil Rights, cutting male sports to comply with Title IX is a "disfavored" way to do it but it has been done. In 1995 Congress held hearings dealing with this issue and T.J. Kerr, President of the National Wrestling Coaches Association, testified that wrestling lost "over 100 programs" due to proportionality compliance or what he called gender quotas. He said his goal was to "end the elimination or reduction of male sports programs to achieve a quota." He called the elimination a "devastating betrayal" to male student-athletes who are promised that they will be part of an athletic program for four years only to have that taken away. It's even worse, Kerr went on, when the student finds out that the "reason for the elimination was Title IX or gender equity." Kerr also talked about the negative effect this will have on high school programs. He said that wrestling is currently the sixth most popular high school sport but that there is now only one college program for every 33 high school programs, and it will only get worse. As more and more college wrestling programs are cut, there will be less incentive for high schools to continue their programs with no future involved. He said this is not only limited to wrestling but also to other sports like soccer, baseball, tennis, and swimming. He then brought up the age-old argument that if kids don't have these sports to play, they will resort to what he called "antisocial behavior."[22] Unfortunately, in the nearly two decades since that hearing the controversy of cutting male programs continues.

The early numbers of increasing female athletic participation continued after the initial years and even into the new century. By 2001 the number of female participants was up to 150,000 while the male number stood at 208,000. The high school numbers are also interesting—girls were up to nearly 3 million in 2001 while the boys' numbers actually dropped from the 1979 number of 4.2 million to around 4 million even. This possibly helps make Kerr's case about the dropping of collegiate programs hurting male participation in high schools across the country. While that may be debatable, there is no debating the incredible strides females have made since the passage of the Title IX in 1972. What some are debating is how much of an effect Title IX has had on those numbers or if it would have happened anyway without passage of the law. While there is no doubt there has been a change in attitude about female athletics over the past forty years, without the passage of Title IX those changes discussed in this chapter would certainly not have happened with the speed it has. There is also the old "chicken and the egg" argument of which came first, the change in attitude or the passage of the law—and did one cause the other? While many argue we have not arrived at true gender equity yet, there is no doubt that female athletes today have many more opportunities than their grandmothers or even mothers did a short time ago. Judith Sweet, past president of the NCAA said in 1993: "I never had the opportunity to be a varsity athlete, and when I talk to the female athletes and try to put that in perspective compared the opportunities they have now, all I get are blank stares. That's positive because they can't relate to what I'm saying."[23]

Professional Women's Basketball

Professional women's team sports had always had difficulty getting off the ground and maintaining leagues for very long with a few exceptions (most notably the decade that the AAGBBL was in existence). With the success of Title IX helping the expansion of more women's collegiate programs in the 1970s and the Olympics allowing women's basketball as a medal sport in 1976, sports promoter Bill Byrne decided the time was right to start a professional league called the **Women's Basketball League (WBL)** in 1978. It began with eight teams playing a 34-game schedule but financing was always an issue, and two franchises did not make it to the end of that first season. Salaries for the players ranged between $5,000 and $15,000 which was not that much (even in the 1970s) but if players wanted to play professionally, it was their only option.

To survive, the league needed some superstars and it recruited one in its third season. **Nancy Lieberman** had been the youngest member of the 1976 silver medal-winning Olympic basketball team and then led Old Dominion University to two UIAW national championships in 1979 and 1980. She had planned on again returning to the Olympics in 1980; but when the United States boycotted the Moscow Games, she decided to drop out of school and join the WBL as a member of the Dallas Diamonds for the 1980–81 season. Nicknamed "Lady Magic" as a nod to Ervin "Magic" Johnson, Lieberman is credited with "masculinizing" the women's game and making it more exciting to watch. She was not only a good shooter but she (like Magic Johnson) was incredibly adept at passing the ball and raising the level of play of her teammates. Her career record of assists (961) while at Old Dominion is a school record that still stands today. Unfortunately for Lieberman and the WBL, by 1981 it was obvious the league was in trouble. Attendance numbers were low (averaging less than 1,500 per contest) and without a television contract to bring in needed revenue there were only three teams that made it through that season (Lieberman's Dallas team, and teams from Chicago and San Francisco). The WBL folded after its third season in 1981 and women's basketball's first superstar Lieberman was left to play on various men's teams including in the semipro United States Basket-

Nancy Lieberman. Image © carrie-nelson, 2013. Used under license from Shutterstock, Inc.

ball League (USBL) throughout the 1980s as well as playing for the Washington Generals (the Harlem Globetrotters' eternally vanquished opponent). In 1996 she was elected to the basketball hall of fame, but she was not done with her playing career quite yet. The following year a new women's professional basketball league was forming and it needed a superstar to help launch it. At age 39, Lieberman became a member of the Phoenix Mercury in the inaugural season of the **Women's National Basketball Association (WNBA)**. She only played one season and then became the general manager and head coach of the Detroit Shock where she coached for three seasons but then left after a sex scandal involving her and her point guard on the team. The scandal

WNBA. Image © Dmitry Argunov, 2013. Used under license from Shutterstock, Inc.

Lisa Leslie. Image © Photo Works, 2013. Used under license from Shutterstock, Inc.

opened up long-simmering arguments of sexuality and lesbianism associated with female athletics that remain part of women's sports to this day. It also ended Lieberman's 13-year marriage to one of her former Washington Generals teammates Tom Cline. After signing a one-week contract to play for the Shock in 2008 at age 50 to break her own record for oldest player in the history of professional women's sports, she became the first woman to coach a men's team in an NBA development league in 2009. She remains probably the most famous woman to ever play basketball and the face of women's professional basketball.

The WNBA was not the first attempt at a professional women's league since the WBL folded in 1981. In 1991 there was the **Liberty Basketball Association (LBA)** in which players, promoters promised, would "be attractive to both in-arena and television viewers" so their uniforms would not be the "baggy, ugly, grotesque" uniforms worn by college players but instead be a "form-fitting spandex unitard."[24] The court would be smaller and the basket shorter (9'2" instead of 10') with hopes the game would be more like the men's NBA. After one exhibition game in which most of the commentary centered around the uniforms (most thought they were too tight) the league was never launched citing financial difficulties. The same year the WNBA formed (1997) the **National Women's Basketball League (NWBL).** Initially it was associated with amateur basketball but in 2001 it formed its own professional league which would play its games during the offseason of the WNBA. In fact, many WNBA players would play on the NWBL also. The NWBL was also not able to be sustained and folded in 2007 which left the WNBA as the only professional women's basketball league in operation. Why did the WNBA survive when so many leagues did not? There are many reasons for this not the least of which is the WNBA was the first professional league that had the backing of the NBA. The original eight teams were all affiliated with an NBA counterpart and played in the NBA arena of that counterpart (they played during the NBA offseason from June through September). The NBA helped also with a television deal with NBC and also had deals with the Walt Disney Company to be televised on ESPN and Lifetime Network. The league also benefited from a much-publicized gold medal run by the American women in the 1996 Atlanta Olympics and an ingenious marketing campaign using three of the star players from that team who all were going to be playing in the WNBA. While Nancy Lieberman may have been the superstar of the past that gave the league some history, the faces of the future were **Rebecca Lobo, Sheryl Swoopes, and Lisa Leslie**. These three would play on different teams (New York Liberty, Houston Comets, and Los Angeles Sparks, respectively), but they would star in an advertisement campaign called "We got next" in which the three players would utter those three words to male basketball players in pickup games all over the country. The ads would be run throughout the NBA season of 1996–97 in anticipation of the upcoming WNBA season. The campaign was successful and the three players did prove to be the face of the league for a long time. Lobo's career was the shortest and most disappointing retiring in 2003 with no championships. Leslie played until 2009 helping win championships for her team in 2001 and 2002 and making the all-star team eight times. In 2002 she earned the distinction of being the first woman to dunk a basketball. Swoopes' career proved to be the longest of the three—known as the "female Michael Jordan" (primarily because she was winning championships when he was) she helped the Houston Comets win the first four championships of the league (1997–2000) she would go on to play until 2012 earning league all-star credentials six times before finally retiring at 41. Even with the exit of these great players the league continued on and in 2014 the league will begin its 18th season with 12 teams—half of which are independent from the NBA.

Modern Professional Women's Tennis

Professional individual women's sports had always fared better than their team-oriented counterparts and the two biggest were golf and tennis. The LPGA formed in 1950 and has been going strong for well over half a century. As the male tennis tour fought for open tournaments (open for both professional as well as amateurs as detailed in chapter eight) the women's side had other fights on its hands. As the "Open Era" began in the late 1960s, the prize money awarded to women was miniscule compared to the male winners. No single individual did more to change this than professional player **Billie Jean King**. She won her first Grand Slam title at Wimbledon at age 23 in 1966 and would win eleven more before her retirement in 1983 including five more Wimbledon titles and four U.S. Opens. Her championships cement her as one of the greatest female tennis players of all-time but what she did for the sport off the court should also be examined. She won the Italian Championship in 1970 and received $600 compared to the male winner receiving $3,500. When she learned that the Pacific Southwest Championships planned to award the male winner $12,500 and the female $1,500 she decided to take a stand and demanded a boycott until there was equality in the prize money. When the United States Lawn Tennis Association (USLTA) refused, she helped start a women's tour sponsored by Virginia Slims cigarettes and financed by the Philip Morris Company. Within three years the tennis circuit boasted a 22-city tour with prize money of $775,000 compared to the male tour of 24 cities and $1.2 million. In 1973 she help found the Women's Tennis Association (WTA) which was the female counterpart to the USLTA. That year, due largely to King's efforts, the USLTA announced that the U.S. Open would award equal prize money to both its male and female winners ($25,000).

Billie Jean King. Image © Featureflash, 2013. Used under license from Shutterstock, Inc.

1973 was also the year of King's most famous match. The women's game had become a much stronger, faster, and more aggressive game than it had been in the early days of the sport, and the inevitable comparisons began about how it compared to the male version and whether a great female player could beat a male player. Bobby Riggs, a former great player in the 1940s and 50s, and now the self-proclaimed "Clown Prince of Tennis" at age 55, boasted that he could beat the best women players in the world. A match was set between Riggs and Margaret Court, the Australian player who had won three Wimbledon and five U.S. Open championships (and would eventually hold the record for most Grand Slam victories for a woman at 24). They played on Mother's Day in 1973 and Court was no match for Riggs who won easily 6-2, 6-1. Riggs then boasted he was the "undisputed, number-one male chauvinist in the world."[25] Although probably more of an act to get more women to play him than his true feelings, Riggs was successful in getting King to schedule a match against him because she felt she had to "do something to redeem the situation."[26] They played on September 20 in the Houston Astrodome in front of 30,000 people in what became known as the second installment of the "**Battle of the Sexes**." After weeks of hype and trash-talk splitting the country in half along gender lines, an estimated 40 million people watched on television as King destroyed Riggs 6-4, 6-3, 6-3. While women lauded the triumph, men excused the loss because of the age of Riggs. In the years since, there have been rumors that Riggs lost intentionally for gambling purposes (he was known to gamble on anything and everything) but Riggs denied it up until his death in 1995 and King herself said she did not believe it. As for his age she said it was not a thrill to beat a 55-year-old former champion, but it was thrilling to bring a new audience to her sport.

Something else she did for her sport was to become the first openly gay professional athlete in 1981. At the time it was not financially wise to do so because most sponsors did not want to be associated with an admitted homosexual. King estimated she lost $1.5 million in endorsements after the admission and had to continue to play on the tour two years after she initially planned to retire. One player who was against King's admission was fellow lesbian **Martina Navratilova**. King's admission and changing attitudes made it much easier for Navratilova to come out a short time later. In the early 1980s King passed the tennis torch to not only Navratilova but also to American **Chris Evert**. The rivalry between Evert and Navratilova would dominate the rest of the 1980s, and it would be more than just on the court. The old question of female athletes being "too masculine" played out between the two. Evert was seen as more of a throwback to the early female tennis players and sexuality played a part in that. She was heterosexual and, therefore, more feminine. Navratilova because of her sexuality and her weight-training regimen (which was something new for female athletes) was thought by some to be masculine enough to play on the men's tour (she did take part in the third installment of the "Battle of the Sexes" in 1992 losing to Jimmy Connors 7-5, 6-2). Every time the two met in a tournament, it seemed to be a battle between a "real woman" and some sort of machine. Even her nickname "Chrissie" was thought to be more feminine. While "Chrissie" held the advantage in the rivalry in the early days, by the time Evert retired in 1989, Navratilova had overtaken her and held a 43-37 advantage in their head-to-head matchups. Navratilova would go on to play singles for another decade (winning her final Grand Slam singles title at Wimbledon in 1990 which tied her, fittingly, with Evert for fourth all-time with 18 titles). In what is arguably more incredible is her Grand Slam doubles career in which she won 31 female doubles titles and added 10 more mixed titles (teaming with a male player) her final one coming in 2006 when she was 47 years old. A player who was just beginning to win championships before Evert retired was the German **Steffi Graf**. She won her first Grand Slam title in 1987 and by the time her career ended in 1999, she had won 21 more putting her second all-time on the list of titles. Two years after her retirement, she married Andre Agassi making their union (if they wanted to be) arguably the greatest mixed-doubles team of all-time.

As a new century dawned, no one in women's tennis envisioned the heights the sport would reach largely because of a pair of sisters. **Venus and Serena Williams** turned professional in the 1990s but became top players in the world during the first decade of the 21st century. Venus was born in 1980 and Serena in 1981 and they were not only close in age but also close friends. They were also something fairly rare in the sport in that they were African-American and from a lower-class background in Compton, California (known mainly for its violent, gang-filled streets during their childhood

Billie Jean King and Bobby Riggs following their "Battle of the Sexes" in 1973. © Bettmann/CORBIS

Martina Navratilova. Image © John Barry de Nicola. 2013. Used under license from Shutterstock, Inc.

Chris Evert. Image © lev radin, 2013. Used under license from Shutterstock, Inc.

in the 1980s and early 90s). The two turned professional in the mid-90s as teenagers, and it was Venus who first made a Grand Slam final in the 1997 U.S. Open at the age of 17 losing to the top seed Martina Hingis. The two would meet for the first time in a Grand Slam event at the 1998 Australian Open when older sister dispatched 16-year-old Serena in the second round. The first Grand Slam title would actually go to Serena who defeated Hingis in the 1999 U.S. Open (after sister Venus lost in a grueling three-set semifinal). Serena became the first African-American female to win a Grand Slam event since Althea Gibson in 1958. Venus would not have to wait long for her first title as she won both Wimbledon and the U.S. Open in 2000. While their singles play was impressive when they teamed up for doubles, they were nearly unstoppable. They would win 13 doubles championships between 1999 and 2012. As of 2014 they are both still playing tennis and younger sister Serena has won 17 Grand Slam singles titles putting her 6th all-time while Venus has won 7. They have met eight times in Grand Slam finals with Serena winning five of those. Their play also elevated their sport to new levels. When they met for the 2003 Australian finals, they had played each other in four of the preceding five Grand Slam

Martina Navratilova and Chris Evert. Image © Debby Wong, 2013. Used under license from Shutterstock, Inc.

finals. Their matches almost always garnered higher television ratings than the men's matches. 50 percent more Americans watched their 2002 Wimbledon Doubles final than watched the male singles final. Their 2001 U.S. Open singles final drew a higher audience than the Nebraska-Notre Dame football game on a competing network. What Tiger Woods had done for golf, the Williams sisters did for women's tennis. What's even more amazing is they did all this in two traditionally white, upper-class sports.

CHAPTER *Fourteen*

Steffi Graf and her husband Andre Agassi. Image © Everett Collection, 2013. Used under license from Shutterstock, Inc.

Venus and Serena Williams. Image © Phil Anthony, 2013. Used under license from Shutterstock, Inc.

Conclusion

"You've come a long way, baby," was the slogan for Virginia Slims cigarettes when they were introduced in 1968. The campaign was directed toward women and the emerging women's rights movement of the time. This was one of the reasons that the company decided to sponsor Billie Jean King's separate female tennis circuit—the two seemed to fit well together. The slogan could aptly describe the history of women's sports in America. In a little more than a century, women have gone from being warned by the American medical profession of the danger that athletic competition posed to their reproductive organs to Lisa Leslie dunking a basketball and being paid to do it. Women *have* come a long way and although some would argue it is not far enough, we are at a place where we can imagine a time when our daughters and granddaughters will not be denied any opportunity whether it is in education, employment, or on the athletic fields—and that is surely something to celebrate. Allen Guttman was correct when he said that women have never been involved in sports to the same degree that men are and perhaps they never will be. However, he stated that over two decades ago, and there is little doubt the numbers are closer now than they have ever been in history.

Notes

1. Allen Guttman, *Women's Sports: A History* (New York: Columbia University Press, 1991), 1.
2. Ibid., 2.
3. Mary-Lou Squires, "Sport and the Cult of 'True Womanhood': A Paradox at the Turn of the Century," from *Her Story: A Historical Anthology of Women in Sports* (West Point, NY: Leisure Press, 1982), 101.
4. Ibid., 102–103.
5. Ibid., 103.
6. Ibid.

7. Ibid.
8. Guttman, 95.
9. Ibid., 125.
10. Ibid., 151.
11. Ibid., 148.
12. Ibid., 163.
13. Ibid., 164.
14. Ibid., 144.
15. Ibid.
16. Merrie A. Fidler, "The Establishment of Softball as a Sport for American Women, 1900–1940," from *Her Story: A Historical Anthology of Women in Sports* (West Point, NY: Leisure Press, 1982), 536.
17. Susan Ware, *Title IX, A Brief History With Documents* (New York: Bedford/St. Martin's, 2007), 3.
18. Ibid.
19. Ibid., 8–9.
20. Ibid., 12.
21. Ibid., 6.
22. Ibid., 102–103.
23. Ibid., 24.
24. Susan Cahn, *Coming On Strong, Gender and Sexuality in 20th Century Women's Sport* (New York: The Free Press, 1994), 273.
25. Guttman, 210.
26. Ibid.

CHAPTER *Fourteen*

CHAPTER
Fifteen

Gambling's Effect on Sports

*R*emember back when you were a child and you were arguing with another child about something and you were sure you were right? After a few back-and-forth exchanges, eventually someone would become so sure of themselves that they would utter the provocative two-word phrase, "Wanna bet?" It was then that the other child (and anyone else who might be listening) knew that person was serious. They were so positive they were right that they would actually risk losing something important to them on the outcome of the argument. The counterpart in this argument would know exactly what that meant and, if they were equally confident, their response would be, "How much?" What these kids were unwittingly doing was revealing the omnipresence of gambling in American culture. These children had to learn this ritual from someone—usually older children or adults—which means that they witnessed it from an early age and, although their parents or older siblings may not have consciously taught it to the kids, they nevertheless picked it up as being important. Nowhere is this ritual more prevalent than in the world of sports. It also seems to be more common among males than females (perhaps since boys seem to gravitate to athletics earlier and at a higher percentage than girls). Wagering on the outcome of sporting events either that they are involved in or watching seems almost second nature to American boys before they even reach their teenage years. Why is this? Possibly because for years they have been taught (usually by their mothers, but in some cases fathers) that gambling is an evil thing (even though the children witness the parents buying lottery tickets every time they go to fill up their car with gas), and we know how children often want to do something that they are told is wrong. While in recent years gambling (whether it be the lottery, March Madness basketball pools, or fantasy sports) has become more acceptable, when the nation was colonized (especially in Puritan New England), it was not viewed with such acceptance. This chapter examines the history of America's view on gambling and, more particularly, gambling's effect on sports over the last century.

America's Views on Gambling Pre-20th Century

Gambling was very much a part of Britain's "Festive Culture" but, as we have learned, when the Puritans broke away to form their own colony in New England in the 17th century, they broke away from everything that had to do with that culture. The Puritans recognized how naturally gambling and sports go together so it was the games that were viewed as leading to gambling that were outlawed. The "lawful sports" that were acceptable were supposed to refresh the participant's mind and body to better perform their daily chores to better society, but they could just as easily have been described as activities that will be least likely to lead to wagering. Time was especially important to the Puritans, and any activities that were viewed as wasting time were also seen as mocking

God. Southern colonists took a different, in some cases opposite, view on gambling. Gambling was an important part of the Southerner's life. From horseracing to cockfighting to card-playing, the Southern colonist was constantly exposed to gambling; and they did not view it as a waste of time but quite the contrary. They viewed the outcome of their gambling as an indication of where they stood in the grand scheme of the universe. If they won they were viewed favorably, and if they lost one might say that God was "mocking" them.

Throughout the colonial period the country tavern was the enclave of the gambler, and it could be found in virtually every region of the colonies. The tavern not only centered on alcohol but also on the games that were played there and the associated wagers that were made. As was mentioned in Chapter 2, tavern patrons would not necessarily need a game to bet on but would wager on anything from how much alcohol would be consumed by an individual to which customer would be the first to pass out. While public drunkenness was a problem that many communities began to try to regulate, with the exception of some New England communities, gambling was not restricted by statute until the 1770s. As the colonies prepared for war with Britain, the Continental Congress thought that the break from the mother country should be so complete that it even issued a proclamation that the colonists should avoid "diversions and entertainments" that included "gaming," which usually means gambling.[1] The two diversions they mentioned by name were cockfighting and horseracing which are both activities that always involve gambling. The horseracing industry took a hit in the early years of the republic but made a dramatic recovery by the 1820s. It was during this period that sports and gambling were again beginning to be viewed in a negative light due to the religious revival known as the Second Great Awakening. The ensuing Victorian Era would also be a difficult time for the majority view on sports and gambling, but it was also during this time (second half of the 19th century) when a counterculture would emerge that would bring sports (and gambling) to new levels.

The Victorian counterculture would put such a premium on sports that they would develop their own fraternities to participate in and display them. The sporting spectacles (organized competitions) would be where this would take place. It was through the spectacles that the fraternity would make money by charging a gate (entrance) fee for spectators, selling concessions, and, yes, betting on one's own team to win. Gambling was a central part of the sporting fraternity and the Victorians hated this because not only were participants being paid to play a game but sometimes that payment was coming from gamblers. That did not stop the gamblers from exerting their influence on the fraternities. This was nothing new in Britain; sporting fraternities and gambling had been common for years, and it was the British rules of wagering that were the example used by the Americans. The most popular of all these fraternities just before and after the Civil War was the baseball fraternity. As we saw in Chapter 3, it did not take long for this fraternity to develop into a business and for professional leagues to form. By the end of the 19th century, professional baseball was in trouble for many reasons detailed in that chapter but also for one that was not: gamblers' influence on the game. Baseball was viewed (with the possible exception of boxing) as the most corrupt of all the sports played in the country. Games would be routinely "**thrown**" (lost on purpose) for the benefit of gamblers (and the players involved). Sometimes games would be purposefully lost not necessarily for the direct benefit of the gamblers. An example of this was the three-game series. Today, teams play a set number of games no matter who wins or loses but, in the late 19th century, the third game of a series would only be played if the first two games were split. Because the players would not be paid for that third game (and owners would not reap the benefits of the gate and concessions) winners of the first game often were "encouraged" to not try as hard in that second game. Although this was not a direct payment by the gamblers, it certainly made it easier for gamblers to make money who were in the know and it led to the growing suspicion that the game was not on the "up-and-up." Although baseball cleaned up its image and emerged in the early 20th century as America's national pastime, the dark cloud of suspicion continued to hang over the sport until it eventually burst in the early 1920s with the "Black Sox" scandal. Baseball was certainly not unique with its gambling scandals as nearly every sport fell under some sort of suspicion at some point during the 20th century. Examples of these scandals are examined in the following pages.

The First Football Scandal

After the first National Football League folded after only one season in 1902, professional football was mainly centered in Ohio and the state's league known as the Big 6. Two of those teams dominated the league: the **Canton Bulldogs** and **Massillon Tigers**. The two teams were natural rivals because of their proximity (only 10 miles separated them) and also because of their talent level. Massillon won the 1904 championship by defeating Akron and then defeated Canton after the 1905 season for its second consecutive championship. The 1906 season was dominated by the Bulldogs and Tigers, and there was no doubt they would again meet in the championship—but this time it would be a series (one game at Canton and the other at Massillon). The first game was won in an upset by the hometown Bulldogs 10–5. In the second game, the Tigers got their revenge 13–6. Prior to the first game, there were rumors swirling that the game in Canton would be fixed to make sure the Bulldogs won the first game. In a setup that hearkened back to the baseball fixes of the previous century, the second game would be fixed so the Tigers won, which would set up a third and deciding championship game to be played in Cleveland where the gate receipts would be greater. The rumors became so pervasive that Massillon manager **Ed Stewart** felt compelled to address them before the first game: "It would be impossible to 'fix' the coming football game," he said. "Such suspicion does discredit to an honest sport and is certainly an injustice to those connected with the teams."[2]

After the games were played, Stewart changed his tune and dropped a bombshell to a reporter from the Massillon *Evening Independent* making a charge of a fix involving the Canton coach **Blondy Wallace**. The accusation was that Wallace had talked to Massillon player **Walter East** with the backing of $50,000 from gamblers to try and recruit other players in the scheme. East spoke with Bob Maxwell and Bob Shiring about throwing the first game. Maxwell and Shiring reported to Stewart what East had tried to do, and Stewart immediately released East from the team. Stewart hoped to make the claim more believable when he also accused East of fixing games in the past when he was a baseball manager in Akron and when he played football for Western University of Pennsylvania. Wallace denied the accusation and initiated a $25,000 libel suit against Stewart. Wallace claimed that he had been "injured in his business and profession and that his good name and professional credit (had) been ruined."[3] Eventually the suit was settled out of court, and although Wallace was not exonerated in a public trial (which is what he wanted), most believe he was innocent of the charge—especially in light of the countercharge that was made. Walter East denied Stewart's charges of the fixing of earlier games (Akron baseball and Western University football) but he did not deny the Canton-Massillon fix—only the origin of it. He instead charged that Massillon coach Sherburne Wightman was behind the whole thing and that neither Blondy Wallace nor any "member of the Canton football team . . . so far as I know (was) connected with the deal in any matter whatever."[4] He further involved John Windsor, vice-president of the Akron baseball club, in saying that Windsor was to provide $4,000 to Wightman if the two teams split the series. Wightman, in turn, denied any wrongdoing and tried to shift the blame once again. He said that "everything (he) did in conjunction with East and Windsor was done in accordance with instruction from Manager Stewart and the backers of the Massillon team."[5]

The confusing accusations were flying from all sides and although nothing was ever proven for certain, it was clear that some underhanded deals had been made and the results were devastating for the Canton and Massillon football programs in particular and for professional football in general. In response to the scandal and the dwindling financial prospects of the team (the team was so far in the hole it could not pay its players which was one of the reasons for the vulnerability of the players to gamblers), the Canton Athletic Club issued a statement that said, in part, "In the future, (the management of the athletic club) will be confined to baseball and basketball only, but no games (will be played) with Massillon with the present crowd at the head of affairs."[6] Massillon had also experienced financial difficulty and ceased operations after the 1906 season. The effect of the scandal was dramatic on the immediate future of professional football. The first game of the Massillon-Canton championship series was historic in that it was the first game that attracted national attention. The best-known sportswriter in the country Grantland Rice had written about the series favorably, and reporters gave play-by-play reports of the game to newspapers all across the country. Only three days before the second game, there was serious talk of establishing a professional football league that would spread beyond the boundaries of Ohio and have more of a national representation. Less than a week later when Stewart's accusation hit the press, all of that talk evaporated. The Cleveland *Plain Dealer*, which had earlier been a proponent of a local pro team, now wrote that the scandal was "only what could be expected of the professional game." It added that professional football will never become popular throughout the country and the proposed league ". . . will probably never be formed."[7] The newspaper was wrong about that prediction, of course, but the scandal did have a negative effect and was partially to blame for the delay of any serious national professional football league for over a decade.

The "Black Sox"

About the time the current National Football League was forming, a gambling scandal rocked the national pastime to its foundations. The 1919 Chicago White Sox seemed unstoppable going into the World Series after winning the American League pennant that season. They were the heavy favorite even though their opponent, the Cincinnati Reds, had won more games that season (96–88). Just days before the series was to start, those odds began to drop as rumors of a "fix" began to circulate. The rumors were that a number of the Chicago players had been paid by gamblers to deliberately lose the series. For those in the know, the allegations were believable due to the notoriously stingy owner of the White Sox **Charles Comiskey**. White Sox players would often complain they were not getting paid what they were worth, but due to the reserve clause they were left with little choice: play for what Comiskey pays you or do not play at all. History looks back at this period and refers to the players who took part in it as the **Black Sox** but there is evidence that the entire team was known by that nickname well before any scandal. At one point Comiskey refused to pay for the laundering of the team's uniforms, so as a protest the players refused to wash their jerseys until they got increasingly dirtier and darker. It got so bad that Comiskey relented and had the uniforms washed (and then deducted the cost from the players' pay). It was this kind of atmosphere that lent itself to players seeking to earn money in other ways and also to exact their revenge on Comiskey. The rumors of the fix turned out to be true, and the plan was the idea of first baseman **Arnold "Chick" Gandil**. He had some ties to

Charles Comiskey.
Image courtesy of Library of Congress

Chick Gandil. Image courtesy of Library of Congress

Eddie Cicotte. Image courtesy of Library of Congress

small-time gamblers in Chicago, and he let it be known to them that it might be possible to throw the World Series. Those small-time gamblers got in touch with one of the biggest gamblers in the country at the time, **Arnold Rothstein** from New York, who supplied the payoff money (reported to be $50,000). Gandil knew which players he would bring into the scheme—there were a group of White Sox who not only resented Comiskey but even other members of the team. The Sox were split into two factions, and they rarely spoke to each other on or off the field. The one player Gandil knew he had to recruit was starting pitcher **Eddie Cicotte**.

Cicotte was the best pitcher the White Sox had and one of the best in the American League. Gandil knew he would be starting the most games in the series and that Cicotte had his own reasons for getting back at Comiskey. The owner had promised Cicotte a $10,000 bonus if he won 30 games in 1919 and, with two weeks to go in the season, he had won 29 games and was "rested" for the remainder of the season. He had done the same thing to him when he reached 28 wins back in 1917. Cicotte agreed to the fix and so did pitcher Claude "Lefty" Williams, outfielder Oscar "Happy" Felsch, shortstop Charles "Swede" Risborg, and utility infielder Fred McMullin (who would not have been included because of his limited role in the series but who found out about the plan and threatened to blow the whistle unless he was included). Two other players' involvement has been a source of controversy over the years—third baseman George "Buck" Weaver and one of the best hitters in baseball, outfielder **"Shoeless" Joe Jackson**. The controversy stems from their denials and the fact they performed outstandingly during the series; it was difficult to point to plays that they were involved in that looked suspect. While most of America had no idea what was happening in the Series, there was at least one observer who was hired by a New York paper to watch for suspicious play. The observer was extremely credible as he was one of the greatest pitchers of all time and a person known for his unimpeachable honesty—former New York Giant pitcher Christy Mathewson. Looking back with the advantage of hindsight, one of the most suspicious parts of the Series was its structure—instead of the normal best-of-seven games, it was increased to best-of-nine. This had only happened once before—way back in 1905, after which it was agreed to be a best-of-seven from that point on. Could it have been extended to allow gamblers to have more games on which to wager? What was not known by Mathewson (or anyone else, save a select few involved in the conspiracy) was that the second pitch of the series delivered by Cicotte that hit Reds leadoff hitter Morrie Rath squarely in the back was a signal to Rothstein that the fix was indeed on.

The 1919 World Series

Each game of the series was a drama unto itself with various players involved in the fix trying to get the job done without making it look too obvious. Probably the most evident performance of the series was Cicotte's in Game One in which he gave up an uncharacteristic five runs in the fourth inning and the Reds won 9–1. In Game Two, "Lefty" Williams, also involved in the fix, took the mound and wanted to make it look better than Cicotte had and pitched well until the fourth inning when he walked three and gave up three runs. Lack of clutch hitting the rest of the way—particularly by Gandil—left the Sox in a 0–2 hole in the series losing 4–2. By Game Three the White Sox had a starting pitcher who was not involved in the fix (Dickie Kerr), but he was from a different faction than the conspirators so they planned on throwing this game too; however, the money promised to the players by the gamblers had not been paid so the plan was falling into disarray. Many of the players decided to play full out and the White Sox won their first game behind an exceptional shutout by Kerr 3–0. Game Four starter was again Cicotte and he vowed to not make this one as obvious. It was actually a fielding play that probably decided this one—in the fourth inning Gandil called on Cicotte to cut off (intercept) a throw to the plate that would have surely been in time to get a Cincinnati runner, but the runner scored along with one more, and it was enough to win the game 2–0. In Game Five Williams again had one bad inning, and it was enough as Cincinnati shutout the Sox 5–0 and was one game away from winning their first-ever championship. Kerr pitched well again in Game Six and won, and in Game Seven even Cicotte got into the win column 4–1. Now with the series close at four games to three, Rothstein was getting nervous. Game Eight starter Lefty Williams claimed he was visited the night before the game by someone who made it known to him that if Williams did not blow the game in the first inning that not only was he in serious danger but so was Williams' wife. Williams gave up three runs in the first, throwing mediocre fastballs, and was replaced but the damage was done as the Reds went on to win the game 10–5 and the series five games to three.

The Fallout

As the rumors swirled before the series, they continued after and one of the biggest critics was **Hugh Fullerton**, a reporter for the *Chicago Herald and Examiner*, who sat in the press box with Christy Mathewson and compared notes during the series. Fullerton was reported to have been so disgusted at what he saw that he thought the World Series should be discontinued. As for Mathewson, he was careful in his evaluation and while he could have come up with more, highlighted seven plays throughout the eight games that he believed were evidence of a fix. Rumors and innuendo was one thing but outright accusations in print was another and no one was prepared to make those accusations except for Fullerton. His own paper, however, refused to allow him to make those accusations for fear of libel charges so, instead, Fullerton published a series of articles in the *New York Evening World* beginning on December 15, 1919, two months after the World Series ended in which he stated, "Baseball has reached a crisis. The major leagues, both owners and players, are on trial." He then got specific: "In the last world's series, the charge was made that seven members of the White Sox entered into a conspiracy with certain gamblers to throw the series."[8] He also called for a full investigation led by someone outside of baseball to decide whether the players who are rumored to be involved can either be found innocent or guilty. If found guilty, Fullerton said, "they should be expelled" from baseball.[9] Interestingly, Fullerton thought the impartial person to decide the matter should be Federal District Court Judge Kenesaw Mountain Landis whose district encompassed Chicago. Fullerton believed the investigation needed to be led by someone outside the sport as opposed to investigations by those inside, including Comiskey himself who offered $10,000 to anyone who offered proof that any of his players had been a part of a fix. Despite Fullerton's claims and others joining in his call for cleaning up the sport, including the *Sporting News* which called gambling a "cancer" to the sport, baseball made no moves in 1920 to launch any formal investigations. The sport seemed to be content with Comiskey's offer and the denials of White Sox players like catcher Ray Schalk (who was not in on the conspiracy) who told the *Sporting News*, "I feel that every man on our club (played to the best of his ability), and there was not a single moment of all the games in which we all did not try."[10]

The 1920 season started as usual and by the summer the White Sox were once again involved in the American League pennant chase with the Yankees and Indians. All of the alleged "Black Sox" were playing with the exception of Gandil who had held out for a higher salary and eventually announced his retirement. During the last month of the season, a story broke about another case of a gambling fix—this time in the National League between the Cubs and Phillies. Cubs president William Veeck announced immediately that he wanted to get to the bottom of the accusations and even supported a criminal investigation. As a result, on September 7 Cook County Judge Charles A. McDonald opened a grand jury investigation into the incident. Publicly, McDonald did it to help save "our national sport" and to bring back "wholesome recreation and entertainment to the public."[11] Privately, he may have had ulterior motives as some were mentioning his name as a possible new commissioner of baseball. Less than two weeks later, the grand jury widened its scope to cover all gambling in the game including the 1919 World Series. On September 22, official charges were brought against the White Sox by the state's attorney's office: "The last world's series between the Chicago White Sox and the Cincinnati Reds was not on the square. From five to seven players on the White Sox are involved."[12] Players, coaches, reporters, and even owners (Comiskey himself) were subpoenaed and, on September 28, a bombshell dropped when Gandil and Jackson confessed to their involvement in the fix. When they confessed they also named the other six players, and Comiskey immediately suspended all eight players. When the suspensions were made, the White Sox had one remaining series (three games) and were in a virtual tie with the Indians. By taking this action, Comiskey all but guaranteed his team would lose the pennant which they did by losing two of three to the Browns. There were even rumors that before the grand jury indictment, the 1920 White Sox threw some games down the stretch to avoid being exposed by gamblers but those rumors were never proven.

After the White Sox were edged out by Cleveland for the American League pennant, the Indians defeated Brooklyn in the World Series and, in the first meeting of major league owners following the series, they voted to restructure the governing body of the game. Since 1903 there had been a commission (essentially committee) that was the decision-making body of the game. Now the owners decided it was time to put all the power into one man—a commissioner. Much to the dismay of Charles McDonald, the owners decided the first commissioner would be another Chicago judge—**Kenesaw Mountain Landis**. He was given unprecedented powers over the game as the *Sporting News* described as "the power of baseball life or death over any person, high or low, connected with the game."[13] Initially, the trial of the "Black Sox" was supposed to take place before the 1921 season began, but, when it was delayed, Landis wielded his power by putting the eight White Sox players on his "Ineligible to Play" list. Comiskey went a step farther by giving all the players their unconditional release. The trial finally began in the summer and somehow, suspiciously, much of the evidence from the grand jury including the confessions of both Gandil and Jackson were lost. They had both since recanted their confession and without any further evidence the players were all acquitted on August 2, 1921. Their victory was short-

Judge Landis. Image courtesy of Library of Congress

lived, however, as the next day Landis issued the following statement: "Regardless of the verdict of juries, no player that throws a ball game . . . will ever play professional baseball."[14] He then banned all eight players for life.

The two players whose complicity in the fix remained controversial were Buck Weaver and Joe Jackson. The controversy stems from their stellar play in the series. Jackson batted .375 with 12 hits, six RBIs, and Weaver batted .324 with 11 hits including four doubles and a triple. Their play in the field was also spectacular. While Jackson was accused of being out of position at various times, he made no official errors and neither did Weaver. Jackson was illiterate and some say he was not sure what he was getting into. Gandil later said they basically used Jackson's name with the gamblers to lend some credence to their plan as Jackson was one of the best players in the game. There is no doubt that both Jackson and Weaver knew of the plot and that is why Landis

Buck Weaver. Image courtesy of Library of Congress

included them in the lifetime ban because, in his August 3 statement, he also said: "No player that sits in on a conference of crooked players and gamblers where the ways and means of throwing games are planned and discussed and does not promptly tell his club about it, will ever play professional baseball."[15] Jackson and Weaver's crime had been more of omission rather than commission—they knew about it and did not tell anyone and no matter how many times the players (Weaver especially) appealed the decision, Landis' answer was always no. Even after Landis' death in 1944, Weaver appealed to have his name removed from the permanent banned list but he was turned down again. None of the eight players ever played professional baseball again, and their departure had an immediate effect on the White Sox as the team sunk to seventh place, 30 games below .500. Charles Comiskey never again saw his team compete for a pennant before his death in 1931; and, for the next eight decades, the team endured what became known as the "**Curse of the Black Sox**," which supposedly kept the team from a World Series title until 2005.

Ty Cobb and Joe Jackson. Image courtesy of Library of Congress

Ty Cobb and Tris Speaker

The Black Sox episode and Landis's tough reaction to it also had an effect on the game itself. Knowing that they would be dealt with harshly seemed to deter players from gambling, and at least in the immediate future the game seemed to be wiped clean of scandal. In 1926, however, a new scandal emerged involving two of the game's greatest names. At the end of the season, Ty Cobb of the Detroit Tigers and Tris Speaker of the Cleveland Indians both announced their retirement from the game. Both had become player-managers of their respective clubs and although Cobb had not been particularly successful in that role, Speaker's Indians finished a strong second to a powerful Yankee team in 1926 so his resignation took many people by surprise. Then even more shockingly, it was announced that both Cobb and Speaker had been forced out due to a game-fixing scandal. The charge went back to that fateful 1919 season and was made by retired pitcher Hubert "Dutch" Leonard who had been a teammate of Cobb's. In 1918 baseball decided to award second and third place teams a share of the pennant-winner's World Series money. It was the last week of the season, and the White Sox had already wrapped up the pennant; the Indians were guaranteed second, but the Tigers were battling with the Yankees for the third

Tris Speaker. Image courtesy of Library of Congress

position in the American League. According to Leonard, the agreement was for the Indians to lose to the Tigers on purpose to allow Detroit to finish in third and thereby get a share of the money. Speaker and Cobb both denied the charges, and Cobb accused Leonard of making up the story because of animosity between the two. Cobb and Leonard hated each other and Cobb had once said there were only two players he had intentionally spiked over the years and Leonard was one of them: "Leonard played dirty," Cobb said. "He deserved getting hurt."[16]

Leonard was reported to have said the charges were his revenge against Cobb. Initially American League President Ban Johnson got the two men to retire and hoped the incident would fade away but, once Commissioner Landis heard about it, the players wanted it to be made public to prove their innocence. Landis eventually saw the charges for what they were, Leonard's revenge and having no evidence ruled that "These players have not been, nor are they now, found guilty of fixing a ball game. By no decent system of justice could such a finding be made. Therefore, they were not placed on the ineligible list."[17] Both Speaker and Cobb would play two more seasons including teaming up in 1928 for Connie Mack's Philadelphia Athletics before retiring at the ages of 40 and 41, respectively. John Sheridan, a columnist for the *Sporting News*, made an interesting point when writing about this "scandal." He was sympathetic to Cobb as he wrote that even if "Cobb had tried to bet, he tried to bet on his own team to win." Although technically against the rules (and illegal), betting on one's own team was something fairly acceptable in the history of the sport. He also pointed out the importance of the timing of this episode: "the alleged Cobb/Speaker affair also occurred in the old days, prior to the time that the White Sox scandal of 1919 made betting an anathema in baseball."[18] The Black Sox scandal had truly transformed how gambling was viewed by the players and the powers-that-be in the game. There would not be another major gambling scandal in the game for over half a century, and that would also involve a player who wagered on his own team—ironically, the man would break Ty Cobb's major league record for the most hits ever, Pete Rose.

Point-Shaving Scandal in College Basketball

The gambling scandal that rocked college basketball in the early 1950s that was mentioned in Chapter 10 was a long time in coming for those who had an inside knowledge of the sport. College basketball was first introduced to New York City in a major way during the Great Depression when Madison Square Garden played host first to the Relief Games and later the Garden Games. New York sportswriter John D. McCallum said that he first heard about college basketball games being fixed from an old boxing manager and degenerate gambler "Dumb" Dan Morgan who told him that he knew a guy who played for a New York college "in the Garden in the year 1934, which is when I first heard of games being dumped." He continued by adding how fixing games was different then: "There were no point spreads in those days, either. If you took a contract it meant you went out there and blew the game. The kids went all the way."[19] Having to outright lose a game was a difficult task for a team to agree to—especially the bigger the significance of the game. Legendary Kansas Coach Phog Allen told *TIME Magazine* that Utah coach Vadal Peterson "knocked down a gambler who came to his room in the spring asking how much it would cost to have Utah lose to Dartmouth in the 1944 NCAA final." Allen went on to say that big time basketball is becoming a "dirty" business and predicted an imminent "scandal that will stink to high heaven."[20] That scandal became even more possible shortly after Allen's prediction when a mathematics teacher named **Charles McNeil** invented a way to bet on sporting events based not on who wins or loses but the difference in the score—it became known as the **point spread**.

McNeil received his Master's degree in mathematics and then taught in schools in Connecticut and New York—his most famous pupil was future president John F. Kennedy. On the side he liked to gamble and he created a way that gamblers did not have to pick actual winners of the games but only how much they won by—if a point spread was 10 and you picked the favorite they would have to win by 11 for you to collect. If you picked the underdog, the favorite would have to win by nine points or less for you to win your bet. McNeil also (probably unwittingly) created an easier way to "fix" games because now favorites did not have to lose games but just not win by as much. This became known as "**point-shaving**." The increased presence of gamblers at Madison Square Garden in the late 1940s was also an indicator of their growing

Point spreads at a sports book. Image © Brian P Gleiczyk, 2013. Used under license from Shutterstock, Inc.

influence on the game. Reporters became suspicious during a game between NYU and Rochester when NYU led by 15 with seven seconds to play and Rochester made one of two foul shots to give NYU a 14-point victory and the crowd erupted as if a player had hit a game-winning shot. It turned out it was the bookies cheering because they had been able to take bets on NYU with a spread of 15 and on Rochester with a spread of 13 so they "hit the middle" which meant they collected from both sides. It was only a matter of time before this atmosphere led to the scandal that Allen predicted.

The scandal broke in 1951 when Manhattan District Attorney Frank Hogan brought charges of point shaving against 33 players from seven schools. Four of the schools were in the New York City area (City College of New York, Long Island University, Manhattan, and New York University) but three others were not (Kentucky, Bradley, and Toledo). Although the press focused on CCNY because they had won both the NCAA Tournament as well as the National Invitation Tournament (NIT) in 1950 to claim the national championship, eventually the investigation stretched back to 1947 and covered over 100 games in 20 cities and 17 states. Kentucky coach Adolph Rupp, who had originally challenged investigators saying that "They couldn't touch our boys with a 10-foot pole,"[21] later had to eat those words when his championship teams of 1948 and 1949 were shown to be some of the worst offenders. The Kentucky program was hit with suspensions from both the NCAA and Southeastern Conference and suffered for years as a result of the scandal. Although Kentucky was eventually able to rebound to national prominence, other schools were not. New York was the hardest hit as area schools received sanctions from which many of them were never able to recover. CCNY's excellent coach Nat Holman, who had been named *Sport Magazine's* man of the year only a week before Hogan's investigation was made public, never recovered. He claimed he had not known his players were taking money (critics found that hard to believe) but he ended up resigning as a result of the scandal. LIU's coach Claire Bee did not do himself any favors when, in defending his players, he said: "The public doesn't understand that the players were not throwing games. They were throwing points. They were not selling out to the extent the public believed, and somehow the players did not feel that what they did was wrong."[22] CCNY began to de-emphasize sports in general and moved down to Division III. LIU dropped its entire athletic program from 1951–57 and did not return to Division I sports for 30 years. The LIU basketball team began to return to prominence when it made the NCAA tournament in 1981, 1984, and 1997. As of the 2013 tournament, the school has made the field three years in a row. New York City also was affected by the scandal as schools refused to come play in the city and tournaments like the Garden Games ceased to exist. It would be almost a decade before even New York area teams would play in Madison Square Garden when NYU played St. John's in 1960.

Frank Hogan. Image courtesy of Library of Congress

Gambling and the NFL

Pete Rozelle took over as commissioner of the National Football League before the 1960 season, and he was determined to not let what happened in college basketball during the previous decade happen in football under his watch. **Paul Hornung** had won the Heisman Trophy in 1956 and had been the first pick of the 1957 NFL draft by the lowly Green Bay Packers. With the arrival of Vince Lombardi in 1959, and with the outstanding play of Hornung who was seemingly always on the field (playing running back on offense, safety on defense, and even serving as the placekicker for the team), the Packers were not lowly for long and won their first NFL championship in 17 years in

Paul Hornung, Vince Lombardi and
Bart Starr. © Bettmann/CORBIS.

1961. Hornung was the undisputed star of the team and the league (winning the MVP that season), but he was also known for his behavior off the field just as much as on. He was single and took advantage of the nightclubs, casinos, and racetracks—usually with a beautiful woman on his arm. In his autobiography, *Golden Boy,* he said that he had grown up around gambling from an early age in Louisville. He quoted a friend who said, "There are three things you do in Louisville—you either bet, book bets or do both." Hornung said he "could remember guys shooting craps on the street corners of my neighborhood . . . and, of course, I had begun sneaking into the racetrack at an early age."[23] Now that he was a high profile player in the NFL, his boss worried about some of his acquaintances that he was associated with not reflecting well on the league. Before the 1962 season, Rozelle visited the Packers and warned against gambling. Hornung said this was not unusual as the commissioner did that every year, but then he took Hornung aside and told him, "You're going to have to watch your associations. You have to be careful, Paul, because you're a bachelor and some people are always anxious to shoot down someone of prominence."[24] What Hornung did not know was the commissioner's office was already watching him very closely and was even tapping his phone, Hornung said later.

After another successful season in 1962 when the Packers repeated as NFL champions, Rozelle summoned Hornung to New York in January 1963 and informed him that he had evidence on his gambling and Hornung confessed that he had bet on football games. Hornung said that he did not think it was that big of a deal because he had "never bet against the Packers."[25] He said that the Packers were so good they almost always covered the point spread and sports books got so tired of paying out that they often took the Packers off the board to avoid losing. Hornung thought this might have raised red flags and been one of the reasons he and other members of the Packers might have been targeted. Upon his confession, Rozelle asked Hornung to take a lie-detector test with the FBI. Hornung refused knowing that he would be asked about other players. "Pete," Hornung told the commissioner, "we both know that other guys are betting. I know who they are and I'm not answering questions about anyone else." At that very time a senate subcommittee was investigating gambling and Hornung knew it. He continued with a veiled threat to Rozelle, "If I go to Washington and raise my right hand, this whole league is in trouble."[26] Rozelle told him he would inform him of his decision and the two parted. Three months later Rozelle called Hornung and told him he was going to suspend him and another player (defensive tackle **Alex Karras** of Detroit) from the league indefinitely. Rozelle hoped the suspension of two high-profile players might set an example to other players in the league—if they can do that to the big names, they certainly would have no compunction about doing it to lesser-known players.

Hornung and Karras both accepted their punishment without complaint or appeal, but they both knew that they were the scapegoats for the rampant gambling going on in the NFL. Hornung said he knew of players who would bet against their own teams, but even betting on one's own team could have negative ramifications. He cited Detroit quarterback **Bobby Layne**, whom he called a "legendary gambler"[27] and a game between the Packers and the Lions in 1958 when the Lions were favored by 3½ points. With the score tied and the ball at the Packer seven yard line late in the fourth quarter, Layne (who called all the plays) decided against a field goal that would have won the game but not covered the spread he had bet against. He overthrew a receiver in the end zone, and the certain victory turned into a tie because he risked the team's victory for his own personal wager. Hornung said there was even a rumor that gambling may have affected the famous championship game in 1958 between the Giants and Colts. The spread was also 3½ in favor of the Colts and, Hornung said, the Colts owner was a known gambler. Instead of kicking a field goal on third down, the Colts Johnny Unitas handed the ball to Alan Ameche, and he crashed into the end zone for a six-point victory and to cover the spread. Hornung said he did not believe the rumors because in those days no one ever kicked on third down as they sometimes do in today's game and, because of the angle of the kick, the field goal would have been no gimme. Hornung also knew his suspension had a lot to do with the people he hung out with (gamblers and members of the underworld) but he said he associated with them because they "were always where the action was, and I loved the action. The concept of guilt-by-association never entered my mind."[28] Eventually, Hornung realized to get back into the good graces he would have to cut his ties (at least while suspended) with these people. It was also at the urging of his coach, Vince Lombardi, who told him, "I want you to keep your nose clean. Don't go to Churchill Downs, do not go to the Derby, do not go to Las Vegas."[29] He followed his coach's advice and one year later he and Karras were both reinstated. The suspension probably cost the Packers a third consecutive championship, but it also seemed to have the desired effect on the league as gambling was viewed much differently by players after the suspensions. Hornung stayed away from gamblers for the remainder of his career and apparently so did other players. In terms of results, this episode was the "Black Sox Scandal" for professional football.

Pete Rose

Paul Hornung once signed a baseball that was auctioned off for charity on which he wrote, "I'm sorry I bet on football" and on the reverse side it was signed by **Pete Rose** who wrote, "I'm sorry I bet on baseball." While Hornung admitted his gambling immediately, it took Rose much longer to make that admission. Rose's incredible professional baseball career began in 1963 when he was rookie of the year for his hometown Cincinnati Reds. By the time it ended nearly a quarter of a century later, he would hold the record for most career hits in baseball history (4,256), most career games played (3,562), and most at-bats (14,053) among many other records. During mid-1970s he was a key ingredient to the "Big Red Machine" which won back-to-back World Series titles in 1975 and 1976. In 1978 Rose got his 3,000th hit and made a run at Joe DiMaggio's 56-game hit streak when he tied the National League record at 44 games. The following season he was traded to the Phillies who made him the highest paid athlete in team sports at the time (over $3 million per season) and he helped them to the World

Pete Rose. Image © Helga Esteb, 2013. Used under license from Shutterstock, Inc.

Series title in 1980. In 1984, the 42-year-old Rose returned to the Reds as a player-manager where he broke Ty Cobb's record for most hits in major league history in 1985 before finally retiring in 1986. He continued to manage the Reds until 1989.

In early 1989, outgoing Commissioner Peter Ueberroth first questioned Rose about his possible gambling on baseball. Rose denied it and Ueberroth dropped the matter. Immediately upon becoming commissioner in April, **Bart Giamatti** hired attorney John M. Dowd to investigate Rose's alleged gambling. The charges against Rose were first made public by the *Sporting News* just as the 1989 baseball season was getting underway and, by the summer, the **Dowd Report** came out that detailed his betting history during the 1985, '86, and '87 seasons. Dowd had spoken to associates of Rose's including bookies and bet runners. Faced with this information, Giamatti requested that Rose step down as Reds manager and voluntarily put himself on baseball's permanently ineligible list. Rose agreed and, on August 24, he stepped down and he was told that he could appeal for reinstatement after one year. It turned out to be one of the last things Giamatti did as he died of a massive heart attack one week later. Rose applied for reinstatement with Giamatti's replacement Fay Vincent but Vincent never acted on the application. In 1999 he reapplied with Bud Selig, but Selig also failed to approve his return to the game. One of the reasons given for Rose not being taken off the list is that he refused not only to apologize for his actions but even to admit that he had bet on baseball. For 15 years he maintained his innocence but then he decided to publish an autobiography and come "clean."

In his book, *My Prison Without Bars*, published in 2004, he admitted he bet on baseball and on the Reds but always maintained he never bet against his own team. The Dowd Report was quite thorough and it never found an instance when Rose bet against the Reds. In a 2002 interview, Dowd said he thought Rose probably bet against the Reds while managing them but he had no proof. Like Hornung, Rose had been around gambling from an early age when he would go to the racetrack with his father when he was six. He said, "Outside of baseball and my family, nothing has ever given me the pleasure, relaxation or excitement that I got from gambling. Gambling provided an escape from the day-to-day pressures of life."[30] He said that he now recognizes that there was a period when his gambling "got outta control." When he lost one of the main outlets in his life—playing baseball. After he retired as a player in 1986 he admitted that "I needed more thrills in my life. The more I gambled, the more I needed to gamble . . . ask any real gambler and he'll tell you: 'It's not about the money—it's about the action.'"[31] It may not have been about the money but Rose was betting a lot of it—anywhere from $2,000 to $10,000 a day in 1987. That was the year that the Dowd Report documented the best and it was also the year following his retirement as a player. He was, however, still managing the Reds and, as a manager, he had a large part in what happened on the field. He claims he bet on the Reds every night but Dowd disputes that. There is the argument that not betting on the game is the same as not betting on your team—but, in the grand scheme of things, it does not matter to baseball because a bet on a game by any individual who is taking part in that game automatically puts them on the ineligible list. The big embarrassment to baseball is that the player with the most hits in the sport's history is not in its Hall of Fame. Although it had always been an unwritten rule, in 1991 (undoubtedly due to the Rose situation) the Hall of Fame officially voted to exclude any members on the permanently ineligible list from induction into the Hall. Clearly, Rose wants into the Hall and that is the reason for the admission and the book. The first two sentences of his book make that very clear and phrase it as only Pete Rose could: "Of the 17 baseball players who have been banned for life, none have ever been reinstated. But since I have seven major league and 12 National League records, you'll understand why I would like to add just one more 'first' to my tally before I settle in for the big dirt-nap."[32] Although there have been some rumbling from the commissioner's office that it might be ready to revisit the Rose saga—there has been no official change in position in the nearly decade since he wrote those words. What are the odds Rose gets reinstated before, as he says, his dirt-nap? Don't bet on it.

NBA Officials Scandal

Most gambling scandals in sports revolve around players, coaches, and owners, but what about those who officiate the games? Who is better equipped to change the outcomes of games better than those who make the decisions on the field or court? The American sporting public was reminded of this during the first decade of the 21st century when an NBA official was charged with betting on games in which he had officiated. **Tim Donaghy** was targeted by the FBI between 2005 and 2007 and eventually pled guilty to two federal conspiracy charges and was sentenced to 15 months in prison. Basketball is arguably the sport in which the official could most effect the outcome of a game—especially in regard to the point spread. Fouls can be called or not called depending on who the official wants to win or, if he wants the total points to go up, he could call more fouls in general to get both teams to the foul line. The **over-under** number in betting gives a number that represents the total points scored by both teams, and if the bettor bets the "overs" and the actual total is greater than the over-under number than he wins. R.J. Bell, a sports gambling expert and president of the website Pregame.com, tracked every game Donaghy officiated for the four seasons between 2003 and 2007. He said during the two seasons he was investigated by the FBI, total points exceeded the over-under number 57 percent of the time. In the two years prior that only happened 44 percent of the time. He said there was no way this could have happened without some outside influence. There was also the fact that for 10 consecutive games that Donaghy worked in 2007 the point spread moved at least 1.5 just before tipoff—meaning a large shift in the money wagered on a particular team and in *every* case the team that the big money bet on won. One of the charges Donaghy admitted to was passing his influence on to gamblers in return for money. He pointed to two particular occasions in which he was paid a total of $30,000.

NBA Commissioner David Stern knew this was something that could hurt the league at a time that it was already reeling from declining attendance and television ratings. He tried to somewhat downplay it by referring to Donaghy as a rogue official. Donaghy retaliated by charging that other officials had improperly officiated games at the urging of the NBA. He cited playoff games that were called a certain way to guarantee the series be extended so as to add more money to the league's coffers. Although specific series were not mentioned by Donaghy, it was believed one of the series was Game 6 of the Western Conference finals in 2002 when the Lakers shot 27 free throws in the fourth quarter. Stern, of course, denied these accusations. Due to the skyrocketing salaries of athletes in all sports it would seem that the days of players "fixing" games for gamblers is over. Any player who would have a major impact on the outcome of a game is being paid more than most gamblers could afford to entice them with illegal compensation. Sports officials would seem to be the way to go if a gambler was looking to influence the outcome of a contest. Sports franchises and leagues would be wise to remember that when its officials are negotiating their contracts. Pay them what they want or risk another Tim Donaghy-type being tempted. At the very least fans may have to endure another season with replacement referees—ask the NFL how that went in 2012.

Conclusion

American history has seen varying views on sports in general and sports gambling in particular. It would be hard to argue that there has been any time in the last four centuries in which gambling has been more accepted by American society than in the last four decades. In 1964 New Hampshire became the first state to legalize a **state lottery**. In the half century since then 42 states, the District of Columbia, Puerto Rico, and the Virgin Islands have all established a state government-run lottery system. The proceeds usually go to building up the state's infrastructure (roads, bridges, etc.) or education but it is gambling nonetheless. The tickets are sold at nearly every gas station you can find and they are purchased almost as an afterthought by women as well as men of all ages. In 1976 Nevada legalized sports wagering in casinos. By 1990 bettors were wagering just under $2 billion annually in the state's 74 **sports books**. No one knows for sure how much is bet illegally per year, but conservative estimates put the number at four times that. By the end of the century, an even easier way to bet emerged with **online gambling** where an individual could play blackjack or place a bet on a team with the click of a computer mouse. A different way to watch (and gamble) on sports emerged in the 1980s with **fantasy teams**. "Owners" would draft their "teams" and compete against each other using the statistics achieved by the actual players. There is usually an entrance fee that is awarded to the ultimate winner at the end. The most common fantasy leagues tend to be football but basketball, baseball, and even individual sports like golf have entered the fantasy world. Fantasy sports have altered the way many watch sports—not always for the outcome of the game but often for how the individual players perform. With the ever-expanding popularity of the NCAA basketball tournament every March it is difficult to find anyone in the country who has not entered a bracket in the local **office pool**.

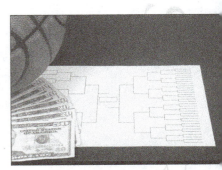

March Madness pool sheet.
Image © SAJE, 2013. Used under license from Shutterstock, Inc.

While all the powers-that-be in athletics uniformly rail against the evils of gambling, the dirty little secret remains that gambling has increased interest in sports across the board. The gray-haired grandmother who might not know a pick and roll from a full-court press is now suddenly interested in college basketball because she entered her grandson's March Madness bracket pool. Television ratings for an NFL game between two sub-.500 teams now increases because fantasy owners have players playing for these teams and want to watch. Why has this happened? Has American society suddenly become more tolerant of gambling? Are Americans becoming hooked on, in Pete Rose's term, the "action" of gambling? Perhaps, but more likely it has to do with Americans enjoying a shared experience. No one wants to feel left out, so to be part of the conversation, you join the fantasy league or you enter into a pool so you have something to talk about around the water cooler. It is a way to prove that you're right about something just like we did when we were kids and said, "Wanna bet?"

Notes

1. Foster Dulles, *America Learns to Play; A History of Popular Recreation, 1607–1940* (Gloucester, MA: Appleton-Century-Crofts, 1963), 65.
2. Marc Maltby, *The Origins and Development of Professional Football* (New York: Garland Publishing, 1997), 96.
3. Ibid., 98.
4. Ibid.
5. Ibid.
6. Ibid., 99.
7. Ibid., 100.
8. Robert C. Cottrell, *Blackball, the Black Sox and the Babe* (Jefferson, NC and London: McFarland and Co. Publishing, 2002), 117.
9. Ibid.
10. Ibid., 201–202.
11. Ibid., 212.
12. Ibid., 216.
13. Ibid., 251.
14. Ibid., 260.
15. Ibid.
16. Daniel Ginsburg, *The Fix is In, A History of Baseball Gambling and Game Fixing Scandals* (Jefferson, NC, and London: McFarland and Co. Publishing, 1995), 200.
17. Ibid., 207.
18. Ibid., 206.
19. John D. McCallum, *College Basketball, U.S.A., Since 1892* (New York: Stein and Day, 1978), 93–94.
20. Ibid.
21. Ibid., 96.
22. Ibid.
23. Paul Hornung, *Golden Boy* (Lincoln: University of Nebraska Press, 2004), 152.
24. Ibid., 138.
25. Ibid., 148.
26. Ibid., 152.
27. Ibid., 150.
28. Ibid., 155.
29. Ibid., 156.
30. Pete Rose with Rick Hill, *My Prison Without Bars* (New York: St. Martin's Press, 2004), x.
31. Ibid., xi.
32. Ibid., 1.

Glossary

Chapter 1

Backcountry: Considered the frontier to the west of the original colonies settled primarily by Scots-Irish from the borderlands of Britain. It was the last area of North American colonization. (p. 14)

Blue Laws: Pennsylvania laws that determined what activities were allowed on the Sabbath and what were not. The term "blue" referred to what citizens were supposed to look and act like on the Sabbath. (p. 13)

Book of Sports: King James' 1618 declaration of what sports were and were not allowed to be played on the Sabbath. The declaration came in response to the growing influence of the Puritans. (p. 7)

Festive Culture: Games played in conjunction with the gathering of large groups of people in British society celebrating religious or pagan holidays or simply celebrating life. (p. 3)

Foolstide: Derisive term used for Christmas by the Puritans. (p. 10)

Football: The most popular of the violent folk games—especially among the lower classes. (p. 4)

Ganderpulling: A popular blood sport in the Southern colonies usually staged on the Monday following Easter in which a goose was hung by its feet from a rope tied between two trees. The bird's neck was greased and the participants attempted to pull its head off from horseback. (p. 12)

Joust and Tilt Yard: The joust was a popular competition among the royals and the tilt-yard was where the joust took place—a field divided by a fence that helped prevent the participants from crashing into one another. (p. 5)

Kolven: A game introduced to the New York colony by the Dutch. It most closely resembles the modern game of golf. (p. 13)

Landed Gentry: A relatively small group of landowners in Virginia who owned most of the land and became the cultural elite of the colony. (p. 10)

Lawful Recreation or Sport: Activities allowed by Puritan society which were designed to refresh the mind and body of the participant while being completely disassociated from Britain's Festive Culture. (p. 8)

May Day: Annual rite of spring for British society and rite of passage for British youth. The most popular holiday of the British Festive Culture. (p. 4)

Middle Colonies: The colonies of New York, New Jersey and Pennsylvania. The area was settled for varying reasons. (p. 13)

Needful Recreation: Activities deemed to be appropriate in Pennsylvania. Similar to Puritan Lawful sport, needful recreation was allowed if it benefited the individual through exercise or providing food. (p. 14)

Oliver Cromwell: Leader of the Parliamentary forces during the British Civil War. Was the titular ruler of Great Britain after the Civil War when there was no monarch. (p. 7)

Primogeniture: British cultural tradition of the first-born son inheriting the family fortune. (p. 10)

Quarter Horses: A new breed of horse in the colonies that was much smaller than the British thoroughbreds with larger hindquarters bred to race shorter distances of a quarter mile or less. (p. 11)

Rough and Tumble: Popular violent sport with no rules in the Backcountry usually contested when there was a real or perceived slight to one's manhood. The ultimate goal of the sport was to gouge out the eyes of your opponent. (p. 14)

Sabbatarian Laws: Laws passed in the colonies to restrict recreation on the Sabbath. (p. 8)

Shrovetide: The two days before Ash Wednesday that marks the end of Carnival and the beginning of Lent. (p. 3)

Tennis: Also a popular royal sport imported to Britain from France during the Middle Ages. (p. 6)

Chapter 2

The Colonies Develop Their Own Culture and Break from Britain

Arminianism: The belief that God offered universal redemption to anyone who believed in him as opposed to predestination which only offered salvation to a select few. (p. 22)

Benjamin Franklin: Philadelphia printer, scientist and inventor. In his publication, *Poor Richard's Almanac*, he brought much of Enlightenment thought to the colonies. (p. 22)

Enlightenment: Movement away from religion and superstition and an embrace of science and reason. It began in Europe. (p. 22)

George Whitefield: Charismatic English preacher who started in the Anglican Church but eventually came to the colonies and led the Great Awakening. Those who followed him became known as the "New Lights." (p. 23)

Great Awakening: A revivalist (back to the bible) movement that began in the 1730s that emphasized a closer relationship with God. (p. 23)

Republicanism: The belief during the American Revolution that everything done by the colonists should be separate from Europe. The people in this new republic would have to be virtuous and idle recreation had no part in this society. (p. 25)

Tavern: Place where men gathered to seek shelter, enjoy each other's company and drink. The tavern could be found in every region of the colonies. (p. 20)

Toli: Game of stickball played by Native Americans most closely resembling lacrosse. (p. 18)

Sports in the Early Republic and the Victorian 19th Century

America's Cup: Award named for John Cox Stevens' yacht (the *America*) that was first awarded to the New York Yacht Club and eventually it would be the prize awarded to the winner of an international competition between American and foreign competitors. (p. 33)

Elysian Fields: Portion of John Cox Stevens' property in Hoboken, New Jersey, that was donated for use as cricket fields and the New York Yacht Club. (p. 32)

John Cox Stevens: Heir to a steamboat fortune, Stevens used his wealth to stage and promote sporting events (particularly races) involving horses, yachts and people. (p. 32)

Middle Class Victorianism: Named for the longest-serving monarch in British history (Victoria) it was a time period in which there was a belief that there was commonality between the middle class of the western industrialized world. The common themes included evangelical Protestantism, self-restraint and hard work. (p. 37)

Muscular Christianity: Second half of the 19th Century movement that stressed a balance of physical and spiritual exercise. Writer Thomas Wentworth Higgenson was a leading proponent of the movement. (p. 36)

Oppositional or **Counterculture:** Made up mainly of working-class men from the new industrial economy of the 19th Century who were no longer taking pride in their work. Immigrants also made up a large part of this group along with members of the upper class. They were rebelling against the restraint of the Victorian middle class in many ways including competitive sports. (p. 38)

Pedestrianism: A phenomenon of human foot-racing that was popular throughout America before and after the Civil War. (p. 33)

Positive Sports Ideology: The idea that sports and athletics is a positive alternative to the more negative aspects of city life. (p. 32)

Race of the Century: Considered by many the first major sporting event that received national attention and promotion in newspapers—it pitted a northern horse Eclipse vs. southern horse Sir Henry in a sectional battle at Union race track on Long Island. (p. 32)

Rational Recreation: Recreation that was deemed appropriate by the Victorian middle class including reading newspapers, books and playing musical instruments. Some sports were allowed but always under the umbrella of non-competitiveness. (p. 37)

Second Great Awakening: Religious revival movement of the 18th Century that was more widespread and longer-lasting than the movement of the previous century. (p. 35)

Separate Spheres: As part of the Victorian middle class, there was a separation of sexes. The public sphere (business, politics) was the domain of men and the private sphere (the home, family) was the domain of women. Rarely did the two mix. (p. 37)

Sporting Fraternities: Subcultures created by the counterculture for those who were interested in specific sports. It was also a place where men can find a surrogate brotherhood. (p. 39)

Sporting Spectacles: Games set up by fraternities to showcase their sports and their best competitors. Victorians were against them because of the competitiveness and the gambling and money paid to the participants went against their basic beliefs. (p. 39)

Triple Crown: Trio of stakes races that were developed in the 1870s (Belmont Stakes, Preakness and the Kentucky Derby). (p. 34)

Volunteer Fire Departments: A prime place for the Victorian counterculture to meet as every town had a volunteer fire department. It was a place that allowed working-class men to experience excitement and camaraderie. (p. 38)

Walking City: First of three stages of development of urban areas in which the edge of town was no more than two miles from the center of the city. (p. 31)

Chapter 3

Abraham Mills: Former National League president who served as chairman of the Mills Commission which was assigned to prove the origins of baseball. (p. 42)

Adrian C. "Cap" Anson: One of the earliest superstar players in baseball. He played first base for the White Sox for 22 seasons finishing with a career average of .333 and 3,418 hits. (p. 52)

Albert G. Spaulding: Former star pitcher for the Chicago White Stockings who would go on to become a sporting goods magnate. He wanted to prove baseball was a uniquely American sport. (p. 42)

Alexander Cartwright: Bank Clerk and volunteer firefighter who helped form the Knickerbocker base ball club and devised the games' first rules. (p. 45)

Barn ball: An early incarnation of baseball that included bouncing a ball off the side of a barn and allowing another participant to hit it with a stick. (p. 43)

Batting Average: Also devised by Chadwick to compare the batting success of various players not only in one's own time but throughout history. The average is reached by dividing a player's hits by the number of his at-bats. (p. 49)

Beer and Whiskey League: Officially called the American Association, it was an early rival to the National League. It received its nickname by serving alcohol at games (something the National League did not do). (p. 52)

Box Score: Way of showing how teams scored first used in cricket but altered by Henry Chadwick to be used for baseball. (p. 49)

Brotherhood of Professional Base Ball Players: First ever sports labor union formed by John Montgomery Ward designed to protect the rights of the players. (p. 53)

Cincinnati Red Stockings: First recognized all-salary team in baseball. In their inaugural season of 1869 they won 57 while losing none and tying one. (p. 50)

Gentlemen's Agreement: Owners agreed (though never in writing) to not allow African-Americans to play on their teams. (p. 53)

Harry Wright: Former cricket player who switched to baseball and was one of the best of the early players. He was the player-manager of the Cincinnati Red Stockings. (p. 50)

Henry Chadwick: Former British cricket player who embraced the game of baseball and became a sportswriter for the *New York Clipper* writing about the game. He was credited with inventing the batting average and box score and eventually became known as "Father Baseball." (p. 42)

Knickerbocker Base Ball Club: Recognized by many as the earliest organized baseball club. The club was reserved for gentlemen and was more interested in the social aspect of the club than the competitiveness of the games. They played the first organized games in Hoboken, NJ, at the Elysian Fields in 1845. (p. 45)

Michael "King" Kelly: Colorful player who started his career in Chicago but was famously sold to Boston for $10,000 in 1887. (p. 52)

Mills Commission: Committee that decided Abner Doubleday was the inventor of baseball based on the testimony of one man. (p. 42)

Moses Fleetwood Walker: Known as the last black player to compete in the major leagues before the color barrier set in during the late 1880s. (p. 53)

National Association of Base Ball Players: Formed just before the Civil War in 1858. It was the first organization that bound players together and codified rules that would be played by all. (p. 47)

National Association of Professional Base Ball Players: The first ever professional league formed in 1871. It signified the death of the old fraternity. (p. 51)

Glossary

National League of Professional Base Ball Clubs: Eight teams made up the original league and made sure none of the teams involved were owned by players. Cities in the league would have to have populations of at least 75,000 and have the approval of existing clubs to join. (p. 51)

New York Clipper: Newspaper that covered all sports in the New York area but it especially is credited with promoting baseball in its formative years. (p. 48)

One-Old-Cat: Next incarnation of the game that replaced the barn with a base. (p. 44)

Reserve Clause: Allowed clubs to reserve the rights of players for their careers. It left players with very little power when negotiating contracts and controlling their futures. (p. 53)

Shinny: Game played by native Americans that resembled the game of baseball. (p. 44)

Town Ball: Once three more bases were added the game was first called Four Old Cat and eventually town ball. Town ball most closely resembles the modern game of baseball and the name derived from towns fielding teams to play the game. (p. 44)

William Hulbert: President of the Chicago White Stockings who formed the National League in 1876. (p. 51)

Chapter 4

American College Base Ball Association: Organization formed by American colleges to govern the rules and eligibility of players. (p. 63)

Caledonian Clubs: Caledonia was the Roman name for Scotland and these clubs revolved around racing and track and field. They sprang up in America in the 1850s by Scottish immigrants and were responsible for setting up races all over the country. (p. 61)

Collegiate Way: It was the belief that students would learn better in supervised environments far away from the city and evil temptations. (p. 58)

Cross-Country: Eventually the torn paper of the paper chases were replaced with pre-marked course that would become known simply as cross country races. (p. 61)

First-ever international collegiate sporting event: Rowing match between Oxford and Harvard held on the Thames River in London in 1869. (p. 59)

Intercollegiate Association of Amateur Athletes of America (IC4A): Stepped in to oversee the running of track and field events for American colleges. (p. 62)

James Gordon Bennett: First generation Scottish immigrant who inherited the *New York Herald* newspaper. (p. 61)

Luther Halsey Gulick: Was an instructor at the YMCA's headquarters in Springfield, MA, and believed in the importance of balancing physical and mental conditioning. (p. 64)

Paper Chases: Called "hare and hound" races in England they were essentially cross-country races in which torn up paper would mark the courses. (p. 61)

Playground Movement: Also designed to keep children out of trouble it began in Chicago in 1903 and was responsible for the jump of cities with supervised playgrounds from 41 to 504 in a little more than a decade. (p. 65)

Public Schools Athletic League (PSAL): Organized in New York City by Luther Gulick in the early 20th Century to put on competitions between schools and also to keep youth (especially immigrant youth) out of trouble after school. (p. 64)

The Strenuous Life: Phrase coined by Theodore Roosevelt who believed the absence of a recent war had led to a feminization of the late-19th Century male. The Strenuous Life was designed to toughen up the American male through vigorous exercise and sports. (p. 64)

Tom Brown's Schooldays: Book by Thomas Hughes that helped increase the popularity of cross-country and track and field with young adults. (p. 60)

Young Men's Christian Association (YMCA): This was one place the Strenuous Life could be practiced was at the YMCA. Initially when it was founded in England in 1851 it focused more on the Christian part of its name but by the end of the 19th Century it had become synonymous with exercise and sports. (p. 64)

Chapter 5

Carnegie Report: Report in the late 1920s that said colleges were putting too much emphasis on money and winning in college football than on academics. (p. 81)

Charles "Cash and Carry" Pyle: Former theatre promoter who would gain fame as a sports promoter—most notably as Red Grange's agent. (p. 78)

First-Ever Intercollegiate Football Game: Princeton vs. Rutgers in New Brunswick, NJ, on November 6, 1869. What was played was known as "**Association Football**" which more closely resembled soccer than modern-day football. (p. 68)

Flying Wedge: Also known as the mass-momentum play first used by Harvard. The five heaviest players would form a v-shaped wedge around the ball carrier and run over opponents. These plays caused the most injuries in the early days of football. (p. 71)

Grantland Rice: Most famous sportswriter in the country during the 1920s most notable for his sayings and nicknames. (p. 78)

Heisman Trophy: Beginning in 1936 it was an award given to the nation's outstanding college football player by the Downtown Athletic Club in New York. (p. 82)

ICAA: Intercollegiate Athletic Association formed by 62 schools in 1905 not including West Coast schools and the "Big Three." Its primary duty was to establish rules for play by its member schools. (p. 74)

Knute Rockne: Norwegian immigrant who played and then coached for the Notre Dame football team. It was his innovations as both a player and coach that put Notre Dame football on the map by the second decade of the 20th Century. (p. 79)

National Collegiate Athletic Association (NCAA): Combination of the ICAA and the old rules committee into the National Collegiate Athletic Association in 1911. The combination of its founding and the new rules changes brought college football in the modern age in 1912. (p. 76)

New Middle Class: With Victorianism officially dead by the 1920s a new middle class emerged that searched for more excitement and were much more tolerant and even embracing of sports. (p. 77)

Progressive Era: Time period roughly spanning the first two decades of the 20th Century in which nearly every area of American Society was subject to reform measures. (p. 74)

Red Grange: First modern football hero who fit perfectly into the new middle class. He was an explosive player who played at Illinois and then in the brand-new National Football League. His ability to slip through tackler's hands earned him the nickname the "**Galloping Ghost.**" (p. 77–78)

Rose Bowl: The earliest of all the bowl games—established in 1902 in conjunction with the New Year's Day Tournament of Roses parade. It was designed to give two football teams a reward of an extra game for a fine season. (p. 82)

Scientific Management: Idea of Frederick Taylor to treat workers in the new industrialized economy as cogs in a machine to increase productivity. Walter Camp transferred the idea over to football and the idea of organized plays and emphasis on the team as opposed to the individual was born. (p. 71)

Social Darwinism: Belief that only the strongest cultures and nations will survive. (p. 71)

University of Notre Dame: Catholic school founded in South Bend, Indiana, in 1844. By the early 20th Century it was known for its academics and baseball team. (p. 79)

Walter Chauncey Camp: Captain for the Yale football team and advisor to the team after his graduation. Creator of many innovations in the game including separating the two teams with a line of scrimmage. Eventually would be known as the "Father of American Football" because of his contributions to the game. (p. 70)

Western Conference (Big 10): The first conference in college football history made up of seven Midwestern schools. When three more schools joined by 1912 it officially changed its name to the Big 10. (p. 72)

Chapter 6

Branch Rickey: General Manager of the St. Louis Cardinals who can be credited with the birth of the **Farm System** when he began purchasing minor league clubs. By the 1930s the Cardinals' system included 32 clubs and 700 players. (p. 101–102)

Byron Bancroft Johnson: "Ban" Johnson was a former sportswriter and editor in Cincinnati who would go on to take over the struggling minor Western Baseball League. After improving the status of the league immensely he decided to make it a major league to compete with the National League in 1899—he renamed it the **American League.** (p. 86–87)

Christy Mathewson: The heart of the Giants pitching staff from 1900–1917. Considered one of the greatest pitchers of all time and his win total (373) is third behind Young and Johnson. (p. 93)

Connie Mack: Full name was Cornelius McGillicuddy and he was the manager and part-owner of the Philadelphia Athletics. He was Ban Johnson's idea of the perfect manager for the American League—he was sober, well dressed, and never argued with the umpires. His teams would embody the first dynasty of the American League. (p. 92)

Dead Ball Era: Also known as the "National Commission" era because prior to 1920 major league baseball was governed by a commission (committee) rather than a single commissioner. It got its name because the ball used during the time was less tightly wound and seemed softer than later years. (p. 93)

George Herman Ruth: Began his professional career as a pitcher for the Boston Red Sox and later would transform the game of baseball when he was sold to the Yankees in 1920 and started hitting home runs. Others are often thrown into the mix with Ruth when the "greatest player of all time" discussions happen, but no one else changed the game like Ruth did in the 1920s. (p. 97)

Inside Game: The type of baseball employed by managers during the dead-ball era. The strategy was predicated on the fact very few runs were going to be scored so every run was important. Managers would do whatever it took to score those runs (bunting, stealing, hit and runs). The manager who seemed to most embody this game was John McGraw. (p. 94)

Joe DiMaggio: Took over as the star player for the Yankee dynasty after Ruth retired. The center-fielder set the major league record 56-game hitting streak in 1941. (p. 102)

Johannes Peter (Honus) Wagner: Pittsburgh Pirates shortstop who is considered the first star player of the 20th Century. He was a great hitter but also an excellent fielder and could play any position. (p. 91)

John T. McGraw: Hard-nosed former player for the Baltimore Orioles who took over as manager of the New York Giants in 1902 where he remained for 30 years. (p. 89)

Merkle Boner: Error made by New York Giant Fred Merkle against the Chicago Cubs in a late season game in 1908 that ultimately cost the Giants the pennant. (p. 90)

New York Yankees: Originally called the "Highlanders" the team name was officially changed to the "Yankees" in 1913. The original Yankee dynasty of the 1920s can be credited to the team being purchased by Jacob Rupert and Tillinghast Huston in 1915 and Red Sox owner Harry Frazee selling off most of his team to the Yankees (including Babe Ruth). (p. 100)

Ted Williams: During the same season that DiMaggio was hitting in 56 consecutive games (1941), the Red Sox outfielder batted .406. No player since has batted over .400. Many consider Williams the greatest pure hitter of all time. (p. 103)

Tyrus Raymond Cobb: Georgia native who played for the Detroit Tigers for 24 seasons and established the highest batting average of all time (.367). Although not well liked due to his abrasive personality, his abilities were always well-respected and he is often referred to as the greatest player ever. (p. 90)

Walter Johnson: Dominating pitcher for a not-so dominating team (Washington Senators). Considering the bad teams he played on his career win total (417—second only behind Cy Young) is even more amazing. Career spanned both the dead-ball era as well as the home run era. (p. 93)

World Series: The name of the championship series held at the end of the season between the pennant winners of the American and National Leagues. The first of these series occurred in 1903. (p. 89)

Chapter 7

1961 Sports Broadcasting Act: Included in Rozelle's "think league" ideology was the ability for the league to negotiate it own broadcasting rights. He was instrumental in advocating that this act be passed by congress to give the NFL and other sports leagues that power. (p. 121)

Alvin Ray "Pete" Rozelle: NFL Commissioner who served for nearly 30 years and led the league into its "Golden Age" by encouraging owners to "think league" first. (p. 121)

American Football League (AFL): Rival professional football league to the NFL founded by Bud Adams and Lamar Hunt in 1960 after their attempt to add expansion teams (Houston Oilers and Dallas Texans, respectively) to the NFL were rebuffed.

American Professional Football Association (APFA): Professional league that began in Canton, Ohio, which would eventually change its name to the National Football League (NFL). (p. 111)

Art Rooney: Former football player and coach from Pittsburgh who bought the Pirates football team and renamed it "Steelers" to honor the steel industry of the city. (p. 114)

Bert Bell: First owner of the Philadelphia Eagles and would also serve as NFL Commissioner. (p. 114)

Don Hutson: Green Bay Packers receiver who used the rules changes to become the best receiver in the game during the 1930s. (p. 115)

Earl L. (Curly) Lambeau: Football player who was expelled from Notre Dame after it was discovered he played professionally. He then founded a professional team in his hometown of Green Bay, Wisconsin, known as the **Packers** on which he played for ten years and coached for 30 years. (p. 112)

Howard Cosell: Controversial announcer on Monday Night Football who fans "loved to hate" and Roone Arledge just loved because of the ratings boost that not only MNF received but also ABC programming in general. (p. 124)

Joe Namath: The number one pick of the 1965 draft he was the highly-touted quarterback from Alabama. The New York Jets paid him $400,000, the highest contract ever signed by a professional football player. He would guarantee a Jets victory in Super Bowl III in 1969 and then back up that guarantee with a win. (p. 122)

Johnny Unitas: Baltimore Colts quarterback who was back-to-back NFL most valuable player in 1957 and 1958 and led the Colts to their first winning season in 1957 and to their first NFL championship in 1958. (p. 119)

Merger: The NFL and the AFL announced in 1966 that the two leagues would merge and there would be a common draft, a common commissioner (Pete Rozelle), and a championship game between the two leagues at the end of the season (Super Bowl). (p. 122)

National Football League (NFL): The NFL was founded in 1902 when the owners of major league baseball got together to form a football league. The league only lasted one season but the second NFL that emerged in the 1920s is still in existence today. (p. 109)

Paul Brown: Football coach who achieved success on three levels: High School (Massillon, OH), College (Ohio State), and professional (Cleveland Browns). His Browns team was one of three that the NFL absorbed in 1949. Innovative coach who was the first to call plays from the sideline and put assistant coaches in the press box for a better view of the game. (p. 116)

Pudge Heffelfinger: Believed to be the first professional football player in American history. (p. 108)

Roone Arledge: Director of sports programming for ABC who thought sports could improve overall ratings for the network if they were packaged correctly. He believed the drama was the key and with that in mind he created *Wide World of Sports* and **Monday Night Football**. (p. 124)

Rules Changes of 1933: Changes that occurred mainly as a result of the 1932 championship game: they included allowing the ball to be thrown from anywhere behind the line of scrimmage and moving the goalposts up to the goal line. (p. 114)

Vince Lombardi: Took over as the Green Bay Packers head coach in 1959 and led the team to five NFL titles in the 1960s and victories in the first two Super Bowls (1967 and 1968). (p. 120)

Chapter 8

Golf

Allan Robertson: Widely considered to be the first professional golfer and was the head pro at St. Andrews Golf Club. (p. 131)

Arnold Palmer: Brought golf into the television age with his go-for-broke style and everyman persona. He was crowned the "King" by the golf fans and remains one of the most beloved figures in the sport. (p. 141)

Ben Hogan: Great rival of Snead's who was very different from him—much smaller and more serious. He was almost killed in a car accident in 1949 but came back to win the U.S. Open in 1950 and winning six of his nine major championships after the accident. (p. 139)

Byron Nelson: Credited with creating the "modern swing" which involved more leg turn and power from the lower half of the body. In 1945 he won 18 tournaments including a PGA-record 11 in a row. He retired shortly after at the age of 34 to buy a ranch. (p. 140)

Francis Ouimet: 20-year-old former caddy at Brookline Country Club in Boston who won the 1913 U.S. Open at his home course in a playoff over great British champions **Harry Vardon** (winner of the British Open Championship a record six times) and Ted Ray. (p. 134)

Gary Player: Great rival of both Palmer and Nicklaus—the three were known beginning in the 1960s as the "Big 3." The South African won nine major championships in his own right and in 2012 joined Nicklaus and Palmer as an honorary starter to the Masters Tournament. (p. 146)

Gene Sarazen: Professional who was the first to win the four majors of the modern Grand Slam (U.S., British, PGA and Masters). He also is credited with inventing the sand wedge. (p. 138)

Gouf: The term used by the Scots to describe the game that would come to be called golf. It's believed to be a derivative of the Dutch term colf, meaning club. (p. 130)

Greg Norman: Charismatic Australian golfer known as the "Great White Shark" who held the number one position in the world for 331 weeks in the late 1980s and 90s. While he won two British Opens, he became more known for the tournaments he did not win. (p. 143)

Gutta or **Gutty Ball:** One of the first alterations to the game it changed the ball from a leather-covered, feather-filled ball to a ball made from the sap of a Gutta-Percha tree and it was a more durable ball that travelled a greater distance. (p. 131)

Jack Nicklaus: Came along in the 1960s as a rival for Palmer. He was never embraced by the public the way Palmer was. He would go on to win more major championships than anyone (18) and is often considered the greatest player of all time. (p. 141)

John Reid: Scottish immigrant who is credited with being the father of American golf who designed the first country club in the U.S. in Yonkers, NY and called St. Andrews. (p. 133)

Lee Trevino: Emerged as a rival to Nicklaus in the late 60s and 70s. He won six major championships in his career. (p. 142)

Nick Faldo: Won six majors during the 1990s including three Masters Tournaments. (p. 143)

"Old" Tom Morris: Club maker who was an apprentice to Allan Robertson at St. Andrews and would team up with him to win challenge matches until they went their separate ways in 1851. He finished runner-up to Willie Park Sr. in the first Open Championship. (p. 131)

Phil Mickelson: Emerged as one of the few rivals of Tiger in the first decade of the 21st Century. He won four majors between 2004 and 2010. (p. 145)

Robert Tyre Jones: Amateur who was the first dominant force in American golf. Between 1923 and 1930 he won five U.S. Amateur Championships, four U.S. Opens, three British Opens and one British Amateur championship. In 1930 he captured all four of the championships in the same season which was known as the **Grand Slam**. He retired after that season and designed Augusta National which would play host the **Masters Tournament**. (p. 137–138)

Royal and Ancient: St. Andrews Golf Club was named "Royal and Ancient" by King William IV in 1834. It came to be the governing body of golf throughout the 19th Century. (p. 130)

Sam Snead: Enjoyed one of the longest careers in golf history with 46 years separating his first victories from his last. He still holds the records for most total wins in his career (165) and most on the PGA Tour (82). (p. 139)

"Tiger" Woods: Would become world number one in 1999 and hold that position for most of the next decade. He won his first major (The Masters) in 1997 becoming the youngest to win that tournament at 21. He would win 13 more majors by 2008 trailing only his idol Jack Nicklaus by four. Arguably his best year was 2000, winning three majors in a row starting with the U.S. Open. When he won the 2001 Masters he held all four majors at once and although it was not officially the Grand Slam it became known as the "**Tiger Slam**." Tiger's fall from grace began in 2009 when it was discovered he had had multiple extramarital affairs. He lost most of his sponsorships, fell as low as 58th in the world rankings and has not won a major tournament since. (p. 143–144)

Tom Watson: Also a rival for Nicklaus and would equal Harry Vardon's mark of six British Open Titles. (p. 143)

United States Golf Association (USGA): Representatives from the first five country clubs in the country met in 1894 to form the USGA which would create uniform rules for the game and govern its operation. It would also be in charge of the U.S. Amateur and U.S. Open tournaments which began in 1895. (p. 133)

Walter Charles Hagen: Professional who was known for his style—he would help open up the clubhouses to the professional players. He was also quite skilled as he was the first American to win the British Open Championship in 1922 and win it three more times in the decade. He also won two U.S. Open titles. (p. 136)

Willie Park Sr.: Winner of the first-ever Open Championship in 1860. He and "Old" Tom Morris would dominate the Championship in the 1860s. (p. 132)

Tennis

Andre Agassi: Great rival for Sampras and great player in his own right. He is one of only five players in history to win all four grand slam events. He retired in 2006 with eight grand slam titles. (p. 154)

Bill Tilden: First great American champion who won six consecutive U.S. championships between 1920 and 1926. He was the number one player in the world for most of the 1920s. He would also win two Wimbledon titles before turning professional in 1930. (p. 149)

Davis Cup: Challenge cup competed for by Britain and the United States beginning in 1899. It was named for Harvard tennis player Dwight Davis who set up the rules and donated the cup. In 1905 the competition was opened up to other European nations and Australia. It has since been opened to any country in the world that wishes to compete. (p. 148)

Jimmy Connors: First great American champion of the "Open Era." He won eight grand slam events in the 1970s and 80s and played competitive tennis well into his forties becoming somewhat of an elder-statesman in the game in the 1990s. (p. 152)

John Albert "Jack" Kramer: Protégé of Tilden who looked up to him and wanted to play like him. He emerged as a great champion in the immediate post-war years but was forced to retire because of an arthritic back in 1954. After that he made his mission opening up the major (grand slam) championships to both professionals and amateurs. (p. 151)

John P. Mahaffy: Amateur Irish historian who invented the myth of the Greek amateur athlete. (p. 149)

John Patrick McEnroe: Combustible "Bad Boy" of tennis who came on the scene in the late 70s as a rival for Connors. He would also have a tremendous rivalry with the Swede **Bjorn Borg** including denying Borg a sixth consecutive championship at Wimbledon in 1981. McEnroe would end his career with seven grand slam titles. (p. 153)

Michael Chang: Became the youngest grand slam winner in 1989 when he won the French Open at 17. He would never win another grand slam event but he joined other Americans like Jim Courier, Andre Agassi and Pete Sampras in an American resurgence in Tennis in the 1990s. (p. 154)

Pete Sampras: Emerged as the greatest of these American players of the decade. He held the number one ranking in the world for most of the decade and retired in 2003 with 14 grand slam titles—most of all time. (p. 154)

Rafael Nadal: Spaniard who was primarily a clay court player (he won six French Open titles) but adapted his game enough to the other surfaces that he joined Agassi as a select few to win at least one of each of the grand slam tournaments. He and Roger Federer would emerge as great rivals. (p. 155)

Richard Sears: Won the first seven U.S. men's singles championships. (p. 148)

Rod Laver: Jack Kramer convinced Australian Rod Laver to go pro in 1962 and when many of the other great players did likewise it forced the grand slam tournaments to open up. Laver would win 200 titles including 11 grand slam victories and was ranked number one for seven consecutive seasons (1964–1970). (p. 151)

Roger Federer: Swiss player who would pass Sampras as the record-holder for most grand slam titles ever with 16. He is often mentioned as the greatest player of all time. (p. 155)

United States National Lawn Tennis Association (USNLTA): Established in 1881 and began hosting the United States championships at **James Gordon Bennett**'s Casino Club in Newport, RI for 34 years until the tournament was moved to Forest Hills, NY, in 1915. (p. 148)

William Larned: Tied Sears' record by winning seven U.S. singles championships during the first decade of the 20th Century. (p. 148)

William Renshaw: Great British champion who won seven Wimbledon championships in the 1880s. (p. 148)

Wimbledon Championship: First major tennis championship established at the All England Croquet Club near the Wimbledon train station in 1877. (p. 147)

Chapter 9

1972 Olympic Games: Games held in Munich that were marred by a terrorist hostage-taking of Israeli athletes. All the athletes were killed but the games were allowed to go on. (p. 171)

Adolf Hitler: Leader of Germany who wanted the 1936 Olympics in Berlin to show off German superiority both on the field of play and off. (p. 165)

Apartheid: The South African policy of racial segregation that would cause their Olympic teams to be banned from competition beginning in the 1960s. (p. 170)

Avery Brundage: American Olympic team member in 1912 who would later serve as president of the American Olympic Committee and IOC. (p. 161)

Babe Didrikson: Winner of three medals in track and field at the 1932 Los Angeles Olympics. (p. 164)

Baron Pierre de Coubertin: French nobleman who made it his mission to revive the Olympic Games and formed and served as the president of the **International Olympic Committee (IOC)**, which governed the games, for thirty years. (p. 158)

Carl Lewis: Equaled Jesse Owens' record of four gold medals in the same track and field events (100 and 200 meter, 4 x 100 relay and the long jump). (p. 173)

Cold War: Rivalry between the United States and the Soviet Union following World War II which permeated every part of society—even athletics. (p. 167)

Dream Team: American basketball team during the 1992 Olympics that consisted of professional players for the first time. It is widely believed to be the greatest basketball team ever assembled and easily won the gold medal. (p. 174)

First Modern Olympics: The revived games were first held in Athens, Greece, in 1896 as a tribute to the ancient Greeks who had originally held the games. (p. 159)

Iron Curtain: Countries that were under Soviet domination after World War II. (p. 168)

Jesse Owens: Track and field athlete who was the star of the Berlin Olympics in 1936 winning four gold medals and setting both Olympic and world records much to the dismay of Hitler. (p. 166)

Jim Thorpe: American Indian who won the pentathlon event in 1912 and was considered the greatest athlete in the world. (p. 161)

Johnny Weismuller: American swimmer who set Olympic and world records in 100 and 400 meter events in 1924 and 1928 and would later become famous portraying Tarzan in many Hollywood movies. (p. 163)

Mark Spitz: During the 1972 games he set a swimming record with seven gold medals that stood until Michael Phelps received eight in 2008. (p. 171)

Mary Lou Retton: First American gymnast to win the all-around competition during the 1984 games in Los Angeles. (p. 173)

Sporting Ideology: The idea that emerged post-WWII that sports are an integral part of what makes you an American. It was also an "us vs. them" ideology with the "them" primarily being the Soviets.

Tommie Smith and **John Carlos:** African-American track athletes who raised their fists in a "Black Power" salute during the medal ceremony in the 1968 Mexico City Olympics. They were both kicked off the team and given 48 hours to leave Mexico City. (p. 171)

Chapter 10

Adolph Rupp: Player on Allen's 1922 and 1923 "National Champion" teams he went on to make the University of Kentucky a national power as coach there for 42 years. He passed Allen achieving the most wins in college basketball history (876) and won four national championships when he retired in 1972. (p. 180)

American Basketball Association (ABA): Rival league to the NBA that formed in 1967. It forced the NBA into a merger in 1976. (p. 191)

Basketball Association of America (BAA): A rival league to the NBL that emerged following World War II. Unlike the NBL the league was formed by the owners of the arenas in which the teams would play. (p. 188)

Bill Russell: A contemporary of Chamberlain's who played center for the San Francisco Dons. They never met in college but would later develop an intense rivalry in the NBA. (p. 184)

Bill Walton: Was Wooden's next superstar center after Alcindor's graduation and contributed to championships in 1972 and 1973. (p. 184)

Bob Knight: Long time coach of Army, Indiana and later Texas Tech who retired in 2008 becoming the first coach to ever win 900 games. (p. 185)

David Stern: NBA Commissioner who came into the league the same year as Jordan (1984) and with the help of Jordan, Bird and Magic and an innovative marketing plan, brought the NBA into its "golden age." (p. 192)

Dean Smith: Played on Allen's final national championship team (1952) and took over as North Carolina's head coach in 1961. When he retired in 1997 he had won two national titles and passed both Rupp and Allen to become the winningest coach in history (879). (p. 181)

Dr. James Naismith: Canadian native who invented the game of basketball while an instructor at the YMCA Training School in Springfield, Massachusetts. (p. 178)

Edward S. "Ned" Irish: Sportswriter who organized college basketball tournaments in Madison Square Garden in the 1930s to showcase the best teams in the country. The tournaments became known as the **Garden Games**. (p. 181)

Ervin "Magic" Johnson: Great player for the Los Angeles Lakers who helped bring the exciting style known as "show time" to LA and also five championships during the 1980s. (p. 191)

Forrest Clare "Phog" Allen: Player and protégé of Naismith who took over for him as coach in 1907. After leaving for a decade he returned in 1909 and coached until 1956 guiding the school to 746 victories. (p. 180)

George Mikan: Another big man (6'10") who preceded Chamberlain and played for DePaul in the mid-1940s. When his team defeated Rhode Island in 1945 to win the NIT Tournament he scored 53 points which was more than the entire opposing team. (p. 184)

Hank Luisetti: First superstar college basketball player from Stanford who pioneered a new style of shooting—the jump shot. (p. 181)

Harold "Red" Auerbach: Took over the struggling Boston Celtics in 1950 and built them into a dynasty during the late 1950s and 1960s. His acquisition of great players like guard **Bob Cousy** and center Bill Russell propelled the Celtics to nine NBA championships including eight in a row (1959–1966). (p. 189)

Julius Erving: Most exciting player in the ABA and credited with bringing the slam dunk to the NBA because the ABA allowed it and NBA did not. The NBA changed its rule to allow the dunk in 1975 and after the merger "Dr. J" as he was known brought his exciting style to the Philadelphia 76ers. (p. 191)

Larry Bird: Played for the Celtics during the same period as Magic in LA and their rivalry helped bring the NBA into its golden age. He would win three championships with the Celtics between 1981 and 1986. (p. 191)

Lew Alcindor: Wooden's first superstar center who helped the Bruins win three consecutive championships (1967–69). He would later convert to the Muslim faith and change his name to **Kareem Abdul-Jabbar**. (p. 184)

March Madness: During the 1980s the NCAA basketball tournament expanded to 64 teams and became a three week miniseries culminating with the final weekend in which the semi-finals and finals were played in which became known as the **Final 4**. (p. 185)

Michael Jordan: Emerged as arguably the greatest player of all time and helped create the Chicago Bulls dynasty of the 1990s. (p. 192)

Mike Krzyzewski: Duke coach who once played and coached for Bobby Knight at Army. He has won four national championships and passed his mentor for the most wins in 2012. (p. 185)

Nat Holman: Legendary coach of New York's City College who was not impressed with the jump shot. The point-shaving scandal of the 1950s would involve his team and would eventually drive him out of the game. (p. 181)

National Basketball Association (NBA): In 1949 the NBL and BAA merged to create the National Basketball Association. (p. 188)

National Basketball League (NBL): Professional league made up of company-sponsored teams from the Midwest formed in 1935. (p. 188)

National Invitational Tournament (NIT): Began in 1938, it was the first college basketball tournament held at the end of the season that would crown the national champion on the court as opposed to sportswriters' votes. The NCAA Tournament would first be held the following year. (p. 181)

Original Celtics: Early professional barnstorming team in the 1920s based out of New York. (p. 186)

"Point-Shaving": The recent invention of the point-spread allowed gamblers to wager not whether a team would win or lose but whether it would "cover" (win by more points than the point-spread). It also allowed players to "shave" points (not win by as much as the spread) for the benefit of gamblers. (p. 182)

The Harlem Globetrotters: Also began as an all-black barnstorming team in the 1920s begun by Abraham Saperstein. Despite its name the Globetrotters started in Chicago and never left the country. (p. 187)

UCLA Bruins: College basketball's first major dynasty in the 1960s and 70s. They were coached by **John Wooden** who won an incredible ten national championships (including seven in a row) and a record 88-game win streak. (p. 184)

University of Kansas: An early power in Naismith's game who actually hired Naismith to be a PE instructor and first coach of the basketball team. (p. 186)

Wilt Chamberlain: 7'1" Center for the University of Kansas. Although recruited by Phog Allen he did not play for the legendary coach because of his retirement. Chamberlain was so dominant that many rules were changed as a result of him. (p. 183)

Chapter 11

Attendance Decline. As a result of the 1994 strike there was a noticeable decline in attendance from which major league baseball has not completely recovered. (p. 205)

Baby Boom: The greatest population spurt in American history which occurred in the years following World War II. (p. 196)

Barry Bonds: San Francisco Giants outfielder who beat McQwire's record by three (73) in 2001. When he retired he had passed both Babe Ruth and Henry Aaron on the all-time home run list but is also tainted with the steroid scandal. (p. 208)

Bob Gibson: Another dominant pitcher during the 1960s for the St. Louis Cardinals. His pitching helped the Cardinals to two World Championships (1964 and 1967). (p. 200)

Brooklyn Dodgers: Often would win the National League pennant only to lose to the Yankees in the World Series (known as "subway series"). They finally broke through for their first (and only) title in 1955. They were also the first team (along with the Giants) to relocate their organization in 1957. (p. 199)

Casey Stengel: Manager of the New York Yankees during the 1950s when attendance and television money allowed the team to sign the best players. The Yankees roster was so stacked that Stengel was able to implement the "platoon" system which allowed him bat left-handed hitters against right-handed pitchers and vice-versa. (p. 198)

Curt Flood: Unsuccessfully challenged the Reserve Clause but his case led to a hardening of the line against the Clause and led to future players like **Jim "Catfish" Hunter** to become free agents. (p. 202)

Darin Erstad: Number one pick of the 1995 draft who played most of his 14-year major league career with the Angels. He helped the Angels win a world championship in 2002. (p. 208)

De facto Strike Zone: Umpires were instructed at the end of the 1960s to lower (essentially shrink) the strike zone to try and balance things between the pitcher and the batter and bring back more offense to the game. (p. 201)

Derek Jeter: New York Yankee shortstop who helped the Yankees renew the dynasty in the 1990s and help them win four championships between 1996 and 2000 and another in 2009. Only Yankee to amass 3,000 hits and by the end of 2012 was 11th on the all-time major league hit list. (p. 205)

Designated Hitter: In the early 1970s the American League instituted the designated hitter which substituted a hitter for the pitcher in the batting order but allowed the pitcher to stay in the game. (p. 201)

George Steinbrenner: Bought the New York Yankees in 1973 and signed Hunter to a free-agent contract for the incredible sum of $3.75 million. (p. 202)

Interleague Play: Beginning in 1997 National League and American League teams were scheduled to play each other in the regular season for the first time. (p. 206)

Lou Brock: In 1974 the St. Louis Cardinal stole 118 bases to set the new record. (p. 203)

Maury Wills: Shortstop for the Dodgers who broke Ty Cobb's single season stolen base record of 96 in 1962 (104 stolen bases). (p. 203)

Mickey Mantle: Switch-hitting centerfielder for the Yankees who took over for Joe DiMaggio when he retired in 1951. Helped the Yankees win 12 American League pennants and 7 World Series titles between 1951 and 1964. (p. 198)

Pitch Count: A phenomenon that began in the 1990s in which coaches would count the number of pitches a pitcher has thrown and when the number gets to 100 his performance is usually thought to decline. (p. 204)

Rickey Henderson: In 1982 he set the new and current record of 130 stolen bases. When he retired in 2003 he had broken Brock's career mark of 938 by stealing 1,406. (p. 203)

Roger Clemens: One of the greatest pitchers of all time. He is ninth on the all-time win list with 354 and an unprecedented seven-time winner of the Cy Young award. His name has also been linked with performance-enhancing drugs. (p. 210)

Sammy Sosa: Chicago Cubs outfielder who battled during the summer of 1998 with St. Louis Cardinal **Mark McGwire** to break the single season home run title. Both beat Roger Maris' record of 61 (Sosa hit 66 and McGwire hit 70). They were both later linked to the steroid scandal. (p. 208)

Sandy Koufax: Part of the one-two pitching punch of the Los Angeles Dodgers (along with **Don Drysdale)** in the early 1960s which propelled the team to three pennants and two World Series titles (p. 200)

Suburbs: There was a major move from the inner cities to the outskirts of the cities where a housing boom occurred in the post-war years. (p. 197)

Walter O'Malley: Majority owner of the Brooklyn Dodgers who first removed Branch Rickey as general manager and then moved the Dodgers to Los Angeles after the 1957 season. (p. 199)

Chapter 12

Cassius Clay: Fighter out of Louisville who first came on the scene in the 1960 Olympics when he won the gold medal in the light-heavyweight division. (p. 226)

Gene Tunney: Defeated Jack Dempsey in 1926 and the rematch in 1927. The second match was held in Soldier field and became known as the **Long Count** fight. Dempsey knocked Tunney down in the 7th and the referee did not start the count until after Dempsey retired to his corner. (p. 222)

George Foreman: Defeated by Ali in October of 1974 in a fight in Zaire known as the "Rumble in the Jungle." Ali used the tactic of staying on the ropes while Foreman wore himself out that became known as the **Rope-a-dope**. Foreman would eventually make a comeback after his retirement to become the oldest recognized heavyweight champion in history at age of 45 in 1994. (p. 228)

Georges Carpentier: French fighter billed as the best fighter in Europe and also a war hero from World War I. His 1921 fight with Dempsey was billed as the hero (Carpentier) vs. the **Slacker** (Dempsey). The term "slacker" referred to someone who did not serve. The "slacker" won the fight. (p. 221)

Harry Wills: The best challenger of the 1920s who never got a shot at the title because he was black. (p. 222)

Howard Cosell: Announcer who was one of Ali's greatest defenders. He stood up for Ali when he refused military service when few others did. Both Cosell and Ali recognized the importance of the other in their respective careers. (p. 227)

Jack Broughton: British boxing champion of the 18th Century who helped devise the first rules of the sport known as the **London Prize Ring Rules**. (p. 213)

Jack Johnson: Defeated champion Tommy Burns in 1908 to become the first Black heavyweight champion. There was a constant search for white champion (**Great White Hope**) to defeat him. (p. 217–218)

Jack Kearns: Jack Dempsey's manager until they had a falling out in 1924. (p. 220)

James J. Braddock: In a major upset he defeated Max Baer in 1935 to take the title. Braddock was a representative of the difficult economic times as he worked his way up from working the docks to become what sportswriter Damon Runyun termed as the "Cinderella Man." (p. 223)

James Jeffries: Champion from 1899 to 1905 who was brought out of retirement in 1910 to be one of the "Great White Hopes" to defeat Johnson. The fight was promoted by newcomer **George L. "Tex" Rickard** who would become the greatest boxing promoter of the 1920s. Johnson knocked out Jeffries in the 15th round. (p. 218)

Jess Willard: Defeated Jack Johnson in 1915 in Havana, Cuba, to become the heavyweight champion. (p. 219)

Joe Frazier: Heavyweight champion while Ali was suspended. They fought in what was billed as the "fight of the century" in 1971 and it was Ali's first defeat as a professional fighter. Ali got his revenge when he defeated Frazier in January of 1974. (p. 228)

John C. Heenan: Although he was defeated by Morrissey twice, he nonetheless became the champion after Morrissey retired in 1860. (p. 214)

John L. Sullivan: Became the champion when he defeated **Paddy Ryan** in 1882. In 1889 he defeated **Jake Kilrain** to retain the title but in 1892 he lost the title to **James J. Corbett**. (p. 215–216)

John Morrissey: Irish immigrant who became the first official American heavyweight champion in 1853. (p. 214)

Larry Holmes: Was the first to ever knock Ali out (which he did in 1980 when Ali was clearly past his prime and showing the early signs of Parkinson's disease). (p. 229)

Luis Firpo: Argentinian who fought Dempsey and lost to him in one of Tex Rickard's million dollar gates in 1923. (p. 221)

Mann Act: White slave traffic act which prohibited taking women across state lines "for the purpose of prostitution or debauchery, or for any other immoral purpose." (p. 218)

Marquess of Queensberry: British nobility title that would eventually become synonymous with boxing. (p. 212)

Max Schmeling: German champion who held the title in the early thirties after defeating Jack Sharkey. Sharkey then got his revenge by first defeating Italian **Primo Carnera** and then Schmeling. Carnera got his revenge defeating Sharkey for the title. Schmeling would later fight **Joe Louis** in major fights that took on international implications as Schmeling was seen as representing the Nazi party of Germany. Louis would go on to hold the heavyweight title longer and defend it more times than anyone in history. (p. 223)

Glossary

Mike Tyson: Became the youngest heavyweight champion in 1986 at the age of 20. One of the most famous fights in history came in 1997 when he fought former champion **Evander Holyfield** and bit part of his ear off. Holyfield won the fight on points. (p. 229)

Muhammad Ali: Cassius Clay converted to Islam shortly after winning the heavyweight title in 1964 and rejected his "slave name" and changed it to Muhammad Ali. Ali would go on to become arguably the greatest fighter of all time and the most recognizable sports figure in the world. (p. 227)

Old "Q": The fourth Marquess of Queensberry who reportedly would wager on anything—even his own death. (p. 212)

Pugilism: Greek historian Plutarch named the sport of boxing pugilism for the Latin word pugnus meaning fist. (p. 213)

Queensberry Rules for the Sport of Boxing: Devised by the 8th Marquess of Queensbury in the 1860s. The main difference in the new rules was the addition of gloves. (p. 213)

Richard Kyle Fox: Owner/publisher of the *National Police Gazette* and he often promoted boxing in its pages. He is considered the father of the modern tabloid. (p. 215)

Roberto "Hands of Stone" Duran: One of Leonard's rivals during the 1980s who had a great nickname along with **Thomas "Hitman" Hearns** and **"Marvelous" Marvin Hagler**. (p. 230)

Rocky Marciano: Heavyeweight champ during the 1950s who is the only champ to ever retire undefeated (49–0). (p. 225)

Six Weight Classes: By the 1890s boxing clubs had become popular and they had initiated the idea of the different weight classes. Richard Fox helped by promoting the different weight classes in his magazine. (p. 217)

Sonny Liston: Fighter who won the heavyweight championship in the early sixties who had a long list of crimes to his name and had spent time in prison. Liston was an example used by those arguing boxing was being taken over by criminals and underworld figures. (p. 226)

"Sugar" Ray Leonard: Namesake of Robinson who won the gold medal in the welterweight division in the 1976 Olympics. He became the welterweight champion in the world in 1979. Retired temporarily in 1991 due to an eye injury but came back one last time to fight in 1997 at the age of 40. (p. 230)

"Sugar" Ray Robinson: First superstar boxer who was not a heavyweight. He fought as a welter and middleweight and held and lost titles numerous times in the two decades following World War II. He is often referred to as the best fighter "pound-for-pound" in history. (p. 230)

Tom Cribb: First superstar British fighter of the 19th Century who gained the title after he defeated former American slave **Tom Molineaux** in 1810. (p. 213)

William Harrison "Jack" Dempsey: Defeated Willard to take the title in 1919 and held it until 1926. (p. 219)

Chapter 13

Bob Devaney: Coach who came from Wyoming to Nebraska in 1962 and brought Nebraska football back from the wilderness and to even new heights including the school's first national championships (1970 and 1971). (p. 238)

Cornhuskers: The University of Nebraska decided in 1900 to change the school mascot name from the "Bugeaters" to the "Cornhuskers." (p. 237)

Democratized: College football was spreading out across the nation and being played and watched by a wider range of people—different classes, ethnicities, and regions than the Northeastern upper class of the Ivy League who started it. (p. 237)

Ewald O. "Jumbo" Stiehm: In his five seasons as Nebraska coach (1911–15) he only lost two games and had three undefeated seasons to finish with an even better percentage than Booth (.915). (p. 237)

Fiesta Bowl: Relatively new bowl (first played in 1971) which quickly gained in reputation and by the 1980s was considered a major bowl and even hosted the national championship game after the 1986 season. When the **Bowl Championship Series (BCS)** started in 1998 the Fiesta Bowl would be among the four sites that would rotate hosting the national championship every year. (p. 240–241)

Four-Team Playoff: In the summer of 2012 the NCAA decided to allow a playoff consisting of four teams that will commence after the 2014 season. (p. 242)

Joe Paterno: Penn State coach from 1966–2011 who is the winningest coach in college football history. In 2011 a scandal broke at Penn State involving one of Paterno's former assistants and molestation of underage boys on the Penn State campus. Paterno was fired and died two months later. Eventually the assistant was found guilty and the school was hit hard with NCAA sanctions. (p. 243)

"Sanity Code": The NCAA began to allow colleges to pay the tuition for athletes as long as they meet two conditions: first, the student would have to meet the same academic requirements and second, the student would have to show financial need. (p. 234)

Superconference: The combining of former conferences into a major conference of usually more than 20 teams. (p. 242)

Tom Osborne: Hand-picked successor of Bob Devaney who took over the Cornhuskers after Devaney's retirement in 1973 and coached for 25 seasons. He won three national titles in the 1990s including the 1995 team which was voted by an ESPN poll as the greatest college team of all time. (p. 238)

Walter Byers: Took over as the NCAA's executive director in 1952 and it was under him that schools were given permission to grant scholarships not based on academic need and they could cover tuition room and board, books and living expenses. Those receiving the scholarships would from then on be referred to as **Student-Athletes**. (p. 235)

Walter C. "Bummy" Booth: Early Nebraska football coach who put together back-to-back undefeated seasons in 1902 and 1903 and finished with an impressive winning percentage of .845. (p. 237)

Chapter 14

Alta Weiss: Female pitcher who played baseball for male teams in the early 20th century.

Association for Intercollegiate Athletics for Women (AIAW): National women's organization to coordinate women's sports. The female answer to the NCAA.

Babe Didrikson: One of the greatest athletes of the 20th century (male or female) and one of the founders of the LPGA Tour.

Battle of the Sexes: A series of three matches between male and female tennis players beginning with Bobby Riggs vs. Margaret Court and Billie Jean King and ending with Jimmy Connors vs. Martina Navratilova.

Billie Jean King: One of the greatest tennis players of all time who also did more for gender equity in her sport than anyone else.

Chris Evert: Developed a great rivalry with Navratilova but was always viewed as more "feminine" than Navratilova.

Flapper: The new ideal for the liberated woman that emerged in the 1920s. She wore her hair short, danced, and drank alcohol.

Gertrude Ederle: First woman to swim the English Channel and the embodiment of the flapper.

Gibson Girl: Artist Charles Dana Gibson's idea of the "new woman" being tall, slim, and athletic and was the new ideal beginning in the 1890s.

Helen Wills: First American female sports superstar (tennis player) who was never loved like Lenglen because of her colder demeanor.

Liberty Basketball Association (LBA): A female basketball league that was most known for their spandex "unitard" uniforms that never got off the ground because of financial difficulties.

Martina Navratilova: Tennis great who took over the mantle of greatest player in the world from Billie Jean King in the 1980s. Because of her weight-training regimen she was often viewed as "too masculine."

Nancy Lieberman: First female basketball superstar in America known as "Lady Magic."

National Women's Basketball League (NWBL): Initially formed for amateur basketball but also developed a professional league that lasted from 2001 to 2007.

New Woman: The new idea that women were emerging from the private sphere and taking advantage of new opportunities available to her.

Oberlin College: Ohio College which opened its doors in 1833. It was the first college to allow both women and blacks to enroll.

Philip K. Wrigley: Chewing gum magnate and owner of the Chicago Cubs who founded a professional women's softball league which would develop into a baseball league during and following World War II.

Rebecca Lobo, Sheryl Swoopes, and Lisa Leslie: Members of the gold medal-winning U.S. basketball team of 1996 who all were part of the inaugural season of the WNBA and part of the initial advertising campaign "We Got Next."

Softball: First developed as a sport to be played indoors in gymnasiums. It was modeled on baseball with smaller dimensions and seen as a good sport for women.

Steffi Graf: German tennis player who took over the mantle from Evert and Navratilova and is often viewed as the greatest female player of all time.

Suzanne Lenglen: French tennis player who became the first international female sports superstar in the 1920s.

Title IX: 1972 law designed to end gender discrimination in educational institutions. Eventually became more known for providing more gender equity in collegiate athletics.

True Womanhood: The 19th century view that women were the weaker sex and should be protected and confined to the home.

Venus and Serena Williams: African-American sisters who came from lower-class Los Angeles and brought women's tennis to new levels in the early 21st century.

Women's Basketball League (WBL): First women's professional basketball league founded in 1978.

Women's National Basketball Association (WNBA): Associated with the male NBA and is the longest-lasting professional female basketball league.

Chapter 15

Arnold "Chick" Gandil: White Sox first baseman who hatched the idea of throwing the 1919 World Series and got in touch with local small-time gamblers who got in touch with one of the biggest gamblers in the country, **Arnold Rothstein**, who supplied the money for the payoff—a reported $50,000. (p. 251–252)

Bart Giamatti: Named commissioner in 1989 and commissioned attorney John M. Dowd to investigate Pete Rose's gambling activities. When the **Dowd Report** came out that summer it detailed that Rose had gambled on baseball in 1985, 1986, and 1987 while a player and manager for the Cincinnati Reds. (p. 259)

Black Sox: Nickname given to the White Sox both due to the scandal but even before when the players refused to have their uniforms washed because Comiskey made the players pay for it. (p. 251)

Bobby Layne: Detroit Lions quarterback who, according to Paul Hornung, was a "legendary gambler" and often let the point spread influence his decisions in games. (p. 258)

Canton Bulldogs and **Massillon Tigers:** The two teams who dominated early Ohio professional football and were involved in a scandal in which there were accusations that the championship game in 1905 was "fixed."(p. 250)

Charles Comiskey: Owner of the Chicago White Sox who was reported to have been extremely stingy with his players. This was one of the reasons given for eight of his players to throw the 1919 World Series for money. (p. 251)

Charles McNeil: Mathematics teacher who invented the **Point Spread** to be used for gambling purposes. Instead of betting on whether a team will win or not a gambler could bet on whether the team would win by a certain number of points. (p. 256)

Curse of the Black Sox: No White Sox team would win a World Series for over 85 years until the 2005 team won the title. (p. 255)

Ed Stewart: Manager of the Massillon Tigers football team who first denied the rumors of a fix but then made the charges that Canton coach **Blondy Wallace** had talked to player **Walter East** about recruiting other players to lose the first game of the three-game championship series with the backing of $50,000 from gamblers. (p. 250)

Eddie Cicotte: Starting pitcher who was seen as key to being part of the fix because he would start more games than any other pitcher in the series. (p. 252)

Fantasy Teams: "Owners" can draft "their" players and the "teams" play each other throughout the season and eventually the winning team receives money out of a pot that all the owners contributed. (p. 261)

Hugh Fullerton: Reporter for the *Chicago Herald and Examiner* who made the first public accusation of the possible fix of the series. (p. 253)

Kenesaw Mountain Landis: Former Chicago judge who became commissioner of baseball in 1920 and immediately banned the eight accused White Sox players for life. (p. 254)

Office Pools: Different sporting events can be wagered on in the office with everyone contributing an entry fee and the winner receiving the money at the end of the event. The March Madness brackets have really brought office pools to another level. (p. 261)

Online Gambling: Gambling is now possible in one's home on their personal computer whether it's playing poker or betting on games. Most of the companies are offshore so as to avoid anti-gambling laws in the United States. (p. 261)

Over-Under: Number that is set for gamblers to bet on the total number of points scored in a game between the two teams. (p. 260)

Paul Hornung: Star player for the Green Bay Packers who was suspended by NFL Commissioner Pete Rozelle for the 1963 season after it was discovered he had gambled on football. Rozelle also suspended Detroit Lions player **Alex Karras** at the same time for the same reason. (p. 257–258)

Pete Rose: Played in the major leagues for 23 years and eventually broke Ty Cobb's all-time hits record and retired with 4,256. He was also banned from baseball for life due to his gambling on baseball. (p. 259)

Point-Shaving: The invention of the point spread made it easier for players to make money from gamblers because they no longer needed to lose games but just not win by as many points. (p. 256)

"Shoeless" Joe Jackson: Best hitter on the White Sox team and one of the best hitters in baseball. He knew about the fix and possibly accepted money but there is no evidence that his play was to blame for any of the losses—in fact, he played very well. (p. 252)

Sports Books: Nevada legalized sports gambling in 1976 and almost every casino in the state created a sports book which is where a gambler can legally wager on sporting events. (p. 261)

State Lottery: Forty-three states currently have them and they are essentially a gambling game in which citizens buy tickets and the winning number is drawn weekly and a cash prize is given to that winner. (p. 261)

Thrown: To deliberately lose a game for the benefit of gamblers. (p. 249)

Tim Donoghy: NBA official who was targeted by the FBI for betting on games in which he officiated between 2005 and 2007. He eventually pled guilty to conspiracy charges and was sentenced to 15 months in prison. (p. 260)

CPSIA information can be obtained
at www.ICGtesting.com
Printed in the USA
LVHW06s1104200818
587361LV00005B/42/P